This above all: to thine own self be true.

Hamlet I, 3

STUDIES IN PRACTICAL THEOLOGY

Series Editors

Don S. Browning

James W. Fowler

Friedrich Schweitzer

Johannes A. van der Ven

Formation of
the Moral Self

Johannes A. van der Ven

WILLIAM B. EERDMANS PUBLISHING COMPANY
GRAND RAPIDS, MICHIGAN / CAMBRIDGE, U.K.

© 1998 Wm. B. Eerdmans Publishing Co.
255 Jefferson Ave. S.E., Grand Rapids, Michigan 49503 /
P.O. Box 163, Cambridge CB3 9PU U.K.

Printed in the United States of America

03 02 01 00 99 98   7 6 5 4 3 2 1

ISBN 0-8028-4439-1

Contents

Contents

Series Foreword

In many countries around the world practical theology is gaining a new shape. It is stepping out of the shadow of being viewed only as the application of findings and guidelines developed by the so-called foundational theological disciplines of exegetical, historical, and systematic theology. Rather, the new practical theology is reminding all of theology of its practical nature, just as many of the great theologians of the past, from Augustine to Martin Luther and beyond, were in fact practical theologians.

In addition to the claim that all theology is practical, this movement is also asserting that practical theology is an academic discipline of its own and that its nature does not consist in merely being applied exegesis, dogmatics, or theological ethics, although it fully realizes the importance of its relation to these disciplines. This new identity of practical theology is not limited to a particular school of theology or to a particular country. Rather, practical theology has become the focus of an emerging international discussion that can be understood only by taking into account the various contributions from many countries and continents — North America, Europe, South America, Africa, and Asia.

Practical theology is a theoretical undertaking that builds on a practical basis. Although this discipline has much to learn from reflective practitioners — and in some of its forms actually begins with questions, problems, and descriptions from the field of religious practice — it is not an academic discipline to be identified solely with the processes going on in the field of religious practice nor with strategies and methods of stimulating these processes. The academic discipline of practical theology is a theory of the epistemological foundations, ethical norms, and general strategies of religious praxis in its various contexts. As a discipline, it should not be confused with the praxis itself, although it is highly relevant to all actual religious practice.

Practical theology should be understood as an empirically descriptive and critically constructive theory of religious practice. The empirical and descriptive dimension, which is pursued in close cooperation with other disciplines in the field of cultural studies, prevents practical theology from wishful speculative thinking and contributes to empirical theory building. The critical and constructive dimension, which is aimed at evaluating and improving the existing forms of religious practice, prevents practical theology from empiricism or positivism and contributes to a theology of transformation in the name of true religion.

Within the empirically descriptive and critically constructive framework of practical theology, religious practice may be studied on three different levels: with reference to society and culture, with reference to the church, and with reference to the individual. Christianity is not limited to the church, and practical theology should not be limited to a clerical paradigm. Its threefold focus is on ecclesial practices, on religious aspects of culture and society, and on the religious dimensions of individual life, including the interrelatedness of all three.

Consequently, this series includes major pieces of work in all fields of practical theology, with an emphasis on the emerging international discussion. The traditional subdisciplines of practical theology — from homiletics to catechetics and liturgical studies — are to play an important role in this series, but one should not consider them exhaustive of the entire discipline of practical theology. Rather, in addition to these subdisciplines we will sponsor more general practical theological studies on major topics within society and culture as well as investigations into the disciplinary nature and shape of practical theology itself. Furthermore, the series includes research that is based on various types of methodology — hermeneutical and historical, empirical and critical, quantitative and qualitative.

The books to be published within this series are addressed to a wide readership of all those with an interest in practical theology. Pastors will profit from them as well as students of theology and researchers or practitioners in the allied fields of sociology, psychology, cultural studies, social work, and medicine.

Don S. Browning, *Chicago*
James W. Fowler, *Atlanta*
Friedrich Schweitzer, *Tübingen*
Johannes A. van der Ven, *Nijmegen*

Preface

This study starts from the conception of practical theology as being a theory of religious practice, more specifically as an empirically descriptive and critically constructive theory of religious practice. This religious practice may be studied on three different levels: the macrolevel of society and culture, the mesolevel of the church, and the microlevel of the individual. By this distinction, the exclusive identification of "religion" with "church" disappears, while principally as much attention is given to religion's presence in society and culture and in the individual's life as to the intensity by which it permeates ecclesiastical processes and structures.

This study deals with only one aspect of today's religious practice, the moral aspect, and it does so from an intergenerational perspective. It considers morality as a subtext of religion, whereby religion as a text is localized in its own context, from which all kinds of other worldviews inspire and influence religion, including its morality. The intergenerational perspective implies that this study develops a theory of moral education in a broad sense, so that all kinds of moral agencies and agents as well are taken into account and studied from their interrelatedness: from the three levels of the religion-related practice of moral education on the macrolevel of society and culture (educational institutions, the media), the mesolevel of the church (denomination, congregation), and the microlevel of the individual (parents, siblings, peers, teachers, other adults). This study aims at contributing to a practical-theological theory of moral education by striving to integrate empirically descriptive insights on the one side and critically constructive insights from philosophical and theological ethics on the other.

It strives not only for advancing empirically oriented theory building regarding moral education, but also for evaluating the factual structures and processes found in this field from a transformative perspective, which may lead to true moral education.

This is my second book on moral education; I wrote my first book more than ten years ago in Dutch with the title *Vorming in waarden en normen* (Education in values and norms). Although it is now out of print, I decided not to approve a reprint or even a new edition, because it would have needed a fundamental restructuring and revision. In that book I distinguished four modes of moral education: value transmission, clarification, development, and communication, of which I chose the last to serve as the framework of my thought. Whereas I owed many of the ideas to Habermas's *Theorie des kommunikativen Handelns* and *Moralbewusstsein und kommunikatives Handeln,* I stressed both the argumentative and procedural character of this moral communication. Both of these aspects came to bother me more and more. I became aware that communication goes beyond argumentative (i.e., cognitive and logical) operations in that it intensely touches on and stimulates emotional and attitudinal processes, especially in the moral domain. I also became more and more aware that moral education must do more than just teach students to develop and apply procedural rules and criteria; this procedural dimension should at least be complemented by a substantive approach in moral thought and education. For those reasons I decided to write an entirely new book.

This plan drew nearer its realization when the dean of the Divinity School of the University of Chicago invited me to stand in for my colleague and friend Professor Don S. Browning in teaching a course on moral education in the fall of 1994. In that course, I developed the structure and content of this new book in that I distinguished between two modes of informal moral education (discipline and socialization) and five modes of formal education (transmission, development, clarification, emotional formation, and character formation). I considered moral communication, which can be defined as the ongoing process of moral exchange and understanding in the search of truth, to be the common denominator of those seven modes. I also decided to develop these modes in the direction of the "formation of the moral self." Discussion with students in the course and the questions and objections they raised stimulated my thinking and sharpened my thought.

Back home at the Divinity School of Nijmegen University in the Netherlands I further developed the text of this book by rewriting earlier drafts and discussing them with my colleagues and assistants in the Department of Empirical Theology. I am very grateful for the deepening and enriching communication we had, especially because it prevented me from making some false starts and from falling into certain conceptual and empirical mistakes.

Johannes A. van der Ven
Nijmegen

1

Introduction:
Modes in Moral Education

O ne hears that Western society is in a moral vacuum or even a moral crisis, marked by moral confusion, relativism, laxity, and deterioration. The factors that are believed to be responsible for this state of affairs are situated at different levels of individual and social life. Some blame the decline of the individual's moral will and convictions. Others see the main cause in the supposed erosion of primary group life within the extended and nuclear family. Still others blame the societal institutions with their oppressive bureaucracies, engendering deep feelings of social alienation and loneliness. Finally, some hold responsible processes on the scale of Western society as such. These processes comprise a cultural as well as a structural dimension. The cultural dimension refers to the epistemologically colonizing influence of scientism as a worldview that results in a secularization which permeates every part of personal and societal life, dissociating morality from religion and removing the ontological basis of life while pluralizing values and norms. The structural dimension relates to the growing power of the market as the core of Western society and its increasing colonization of other spheres of life. Moreover, the cultural and structural processes influence each other: scientism, secularization, and pluralism reinforce capitalism, and capitalism in turn advances scientism, secularization, and pluralism.

Closely related to these structural factors are some recent events of historic significance. The migration of millions of people to the West from countries of the Third World and the former Soviet Union has led to growing multiculturality and has disrupted what are sometimes held to

1

have been uniform patterns of values and norms in the past. The pulling down of the Berlin Wall, which symbolizes the end of the communist Soviet Empire, is generally interpreted as the victory of Western society's structure and culture, that is, of capitalism, liberalism, and scientism. This victory, however, merely results in the widening and deepening of the already existing moral vacuum of Western society, in that capitalism, liberalism, and scientism do not in themselves entail any connotation of moral beliefs, principles, values, or norms. Associated as it is with declining religious participation and church membership, this "victory" erodes all moral traces from Western history.

Moral concerns about contemporary Western society have been loudly and widely expressed, by experts and ordinary people alike, centering on questions like, What is good? What is right? What is wise? and What is purposive?

The aim of this study, however, is not to make a moral diagnosis per se of what ails Western society. Rather, I seek to translate the widespread moral concern throughout the West into the quest for moral education. I interpret the moral questions just mentioned from the point of view of developmental, learning, and teaching processes as they take place in the family, schools, associations, and congregations; and I describe, analyze, and evaluate these processes as carefully as possible. The questions that this study attempts to answer, then, are ones such as: What does it mean to educate for the good life, for justice, for wisdom in concrete situations?

This quest for moral education entails three groups of problems — moral, religious, and educational — that I deal with subsequently in this chapter. The first group, that of moral problems, deals with the moral criteria from which this kind of education should be developed, analyzed, and evaluated (section 1.1). Moral education must also grapple with religious problems, because morality and religion correlate not only historically and empirically but also systematically (section 1.2). Lastly, moral education evidently involves educational problems, which have to do with the aims, contents, and methods of this kind of education (section 1.3).

1.1 Morality

Central to the aforementioned problems is the question of the moral criteria from which moral education is to be developed, analyzed, and evaluated. Here I first wish to emphasize the general way in which I use the terms *moral* and *morality*. The explanation is necessary because of the many different definitions that exist for these terms, especially in relation to the concepts of *ethical* and *ethics.* Some scholars distinguish between ethics and morality, defining the former as what is good and the latter as what imposes itself as right and therefore obligatory. Ethics is understood as dealing with the aims of human life, and is therefore thought of as teleological, whereas morality is seen as dealing with the obligation to respect the norms, and is therefore viewed as deontological. Other scholars relate ethics and morality in a completely different way. To them, morality is the practice of moral sensibilities, of moral action, which includes experiences, beliefs, and actions, in daily life, while they understand ethics as the scientific reflection on this morality. Whereas morality is a dimension of concrete life in classes of concrete situations, ethics is "the science of morality," as the *Oxford English Dictionary* defines it.[1] In this study, I treat the terms *ethical/ethics* and *moral/morality* as synonyms, which means that the use of "moral" or "morality" does not imply any demarcation from "ethical" or "ethics." When I refer specifically to either the praxis of ethical or moral life or to its scientific reflection, the distinction will, I hope, be clear from the text and the context.

Purposive, Good, and Right

After this terminological clarification, let me start by examining the way Habermas looks at moral criteria and afterward reflect critically on his thought. He distinguishes among three groups of criteria: the purposive, the good, and the right (1992, 197-201; 1993, 1-18).[2] These are associated with three different pairs of adjectives: purposive/nonpurposive, good/bad, and right/wrong, and refer to what I do or should do in three different worlds: the objective, subjective, and social, respectively. They also relate to three different aspects of practical reason: calculating rationality *(Verstand)*, judgment *(Urteilskraft)*, and autonomous reason *(Vernunft)*. Finally, they imply three different aspects of the will: arbitrary will *(Willkür)*, resolute will *(Entschlusskraft)*, and free will *(freie Wille).*[3]

1. For the distinction between ethics and morality as referring to teleology and deontology, see, for instance, Ricoeur 1992, 170; Krämer 1992; Habermas 1992, 197-201; 1993, 1-18; and for the distinction between morality and ethics as referring to moral practice and the academic discipline that reflects on moral practice, see Frankena 1973; Meeks 1993, 4.

2. Here I leave aside Habermas's semantic distinction among the purposive, good, and just in terms of pragmatics, ethics, and moral philosophy. When I use the term *moral* in this study I take it as an overarching category.

3. The distinction between the purposive, the good, and the right is not the only possible one. Watson (1990) distinguishes between the good, the right, and the worthy

According to Habermas, the morality of the purposive has to do with which means lead to the aims I have in mind, the desire or value that dominates my strivings, or the state of affairs I prefer over others. The moral criterion resides in the relationship between the means and the end. The nature of the ends is predetermined and may be pleasure, enjoyment, health, individual welfare, or social welfare.[4] The means are variable. Through careful observation, investigation, comparison, and assessment the most effective and efficient means for reaching the preestablished purpose must be chosen. Morality lies in choosing and implementing the right programs, methods, and techniques by deliberating and weighing the various consequences of the various courses of action to be applied to the concrete, here-and-now situation. This is complicated by at least three factors. The first is that the here-and-now-situation must be understood in the light of the past events that have led to the existing situation, as well as in the perspective of events that may be expected to occur in the (near) future. The second factor is that the consequences must be distinguished into direct and indirect, foreseen and unforeseen, intended and unintended, desired and undesired. This distinction requires according priority to some consequences over others. The third factor is that as an agent one acts in a field in which other agents also act and intervene. The interventions of the one may have unforeseen and undesired consequences for those of the other. The moral criterion of the purposive thus contains the idea of developing tactics and strategies in which the possible actions, reactions, interactions, and transactions with regard to possibly competing social agents have to be taken into account. The kind of rationality that is at issue here is a calculating rationality: the agent calculates which means lead to the greatest profit, something that can be empirically established in the objective world from the viewpoint of the observer. There is no intrinsic relationship between means and end, because the substance and nature of the means are not important, only their effectiveness and efficiency. The will arbitrarily chooses the means, and the end justifies the means.

In Habermas's frame of reference, the criterion of the good transcends the restrictedness of focusing on the means and broadens one's scope to the

---

(or virtuous). Dewey (1994, 156-61) distinguishes among the good, which, to his mind, the Greeks stressed; the right or just, which the Romans emphasized; and the virtuous, which he personally considers especially important.

4. For the purpose of the discussion of the three moral criteria, especially the relation between the purposive and the good, it is worth mentioning Sunner's analysis (1992). He distinguishes between two theories of the good, i.e., as welfare and what is perfect. His conclusion is that the first theory, which emphasizes the good as welfare, is preferable because it takes the agent's purposes, interests, and needs into account.

whole of life. The ends that were fixed within the realm of the purposive, that is, pleasure, enjoyment, health, individual welfare, or social welfare, are called into question. Is pleasure a good to be strived for, as hedonistic utilitarianism would have it, or is it only an accompanying factor or unintended outcome of striving for other goods such as happiness, artistic fulfillment, or contemplation, as Aristotelian ethics holds? What should be the relation between individual and social welfare? Is social welfare to be understood as the aggregation of a number of individual welfares? Or is social welfare the common welfare, the common good? To what extent does my participating in this common good satisfy my striving for my own good, that is, my own welfare, my own good life? These questions are not calculating but existential in nature. They touch the core of life itself: who am I, where do I come from, what do I live for, what is my vocation, to what do I devote myself, to what do I commit myself? These questions, which concern the individual's own identity and way of life, are not empirical but hermeneutical, and demand hermeneutical self-understanding and self-clarification. The perspective of the observer therefore does not satisfy in this realm. Rather, the perspective of the participant is required to answer these questions. An outsider cannot answer them because only the individual himself/herself possesses the competence to deliberate and determine who he/she is and what is good for him/her. Developing an appropriate form of self-understanding and self-clarification implies the appropriation of the individual's own life history or autobiography, which is the task and challenge of the individual himself/herself only. It belongs to the subjective world of "me"; one "me" is not interchangeable with others. This also applies to the first person plural ("we"). It is up to "us" to decide who we are and what we stand for; "they" cannot do that. Only "we" can fulfill the task of expressing and articulating who we are, what we live for, and what values and virtues we deeply believe are appropriate for us. This task requires applying a specific form of practical rationality, which results in passing an appropriate judgment. It entails a form of will that expresses itself in a resolute decision.

Habermas's final criterion, that of the right, has to do with the fact that the decisions and actions that I/we perform with an eye to what is good for me/us may affect the life, interests, welfare, or good life of others who are not "us." In this case, there is a potential for conflict between our own concerns and interests and those of "others." According to the criterion of the right or just, this conflict must be resolved in an impartial way. Our own interests and those of others must be weighed from the unbiased perspective of the observer and our own and others' due fairly determined in such a way that personal prerogatives and subjective preferences are transcended. Impartiality gives the competitors an equal chance, which means that the others receive the same treatment as we. This approach accords a fundamentally different status to "the other" compared with the two preceding criteria, the purposive and the good. When the moral criterion of the purposive is applied, the other functions as the means of and/or the limit on my tactical and strategic actions; he/she may even be a pawn with whom I play my purposive game as effectively and efficiently as possible. The other functions essentially as an object for me. Using the moral criterion of the good, the other is seen as a member of the community to which I also belong. The other is one of "us." As one of "us" the other is treated in the same way as I am. He/she is a member of my family, group of friends, neighborhood, congregation, association, company, and so on. Insofar as we form one kind of group or another, we ourselves must determine who we are, what we stand for, and what is good for us. The other is cosubject of the process of self-understanding. Our lives are interrelated and interwoven, and for that reason and to that extent, what is good for me is good for him/her and the other way around, and what is of interest to me is of interest to him/her and vice versa.

The question that arises, however, is what I should do with the other who belongs not to my in-group but to my out-group, and whose interests conflict with mine. What do I do with the "alien" who confronts me or my group from outside? What about, for example, large numbers of "aliens," immigrants from other countries, whom we call "allochtones," the outsiders, in contrast to ourselves, the "autochtones" or natives? In this situation the criterion of the good, according to Habermas, is no longer adequate. Assuming that we do not wish to treat others as pawns for our own ends, we have no choice but to apply the criterion of the right and treat others' and our own interests in an impartial manner. This impartiality was demonstrated particularly well by President Nelson Mandela of South Africa, when he recognized that the white judges in the times of apartheid had been able to administer justice in a manner that transcended the beliefs about the common good held by the members of the white in-group at the time. This is an excellent example of the criterion of the just being applied in the social world, when the other is seen as being a subject deserving equal respect as I. The rationality required for an act of this nature is autonomous, that is, it is not dependent on anything except its own insight into what is equally good for me and for the other. Fundamental to the moral criterion of the just is the principle of universalizability: the term *other* in effect stands for "all." From this point of view, what is just is what is good for all, irrespective of their subjective beliefs, wishes, and positions. This means that, at least in principle, what is just can reasonably be freely accepted by all, and the moral criterion of the just is therefore associated with a particular kind of will — the free will.

As cogently as Habermas distinguishes among the three criteria — the purposive, the good, and the right — the relationship among them is nevertheless a matter of vigorous debate. To participate in this debate or even to sketch its main lines goes far beyond the scope of this study. All that is relevant or even useful here is to indicate two of the issues in this debate that will be pertinent to the discussion of moral education in the following chapters.

The first issue concerns the role of the purposive. The problem is whether it is on the same level as the good and the right. This problem leads us to two questions: What is the relation between the purposive and the good? and What is the relation between the purposive and the right?

Let us start with the relation between the purposive and the good. One of the main moral theories in which the purposive plays a key role is utilitarianism. Exactly this utilitarianism can be said to be a moral theory of the good, insofar as it aims at realizing the "greatest possible balance of good over evil or the least possible balance of evil over good in the world as a whole."[5] Utilitarianism tries to produce the greatest good for the largest number of people or "the greatest happiness of the greatest number," as Bentham puts it, and to do so in the most effective and efficient way. From this perspective, the purposive and the good are not coordinately on the same level, because the purposive is related and oriented instrumentally to the good (cf. Verschoor 1996, 137ff.).[6]

With regard to the relationship between the purposive and the right, one may again ask whether these two criteria are on the same level, because Habermas himself incorporates some aspects of purpose-oriented consequentialism into the universalization rule (U) of justice-directed communication. Rule U is: "Every valid norm must satisfy the condition that the consequences and side effects its *general* observance can be anticipated to have for the satisfaction of the interests of *each* could be freely accepted by *all* affected (and be preferred to those of known alternative possibilities for regulation)" (Habermas 1993, 32).[7] A fundamental reason for subsuming the purposive into the realm of the right is Habermas's concern to liberate

---

5. See Frankena 1973, 34; cf. Browning 1991, 100.

6. Some of today's scholars also subsume the purposive under the good. An example is Watson (1990), who distinguishes among the good, the right, and the worthy, where the worthy relates to virtue ethics and is distinct from the good.

7. This connection between the purposive and the right also applies to the revised universalization rule developed by Habermas's student Günther (Habermas 1993, 37).

the right from the danger of rigorism, and therefore he takes the consequences of action into account (ibid., 129).

Setting aside the relationship of the purposive to the good and the right, the second issue, which is also the most fundamental one, is the relationship between the good and the right. Does the good morally dominate the right, the good being more than the voluntaristic sum of personal preferences, because it has a status that is more than psychological (cf. Sandel 1992)? Or is it the other way around: has the right moral priority over the good? A complicating problem is that some scholars seem to subsume the just under the right or even identify only the just and the right (Rawls 1971). Other philosophers distinguish between two types of the just: the distributive just and the legal, procedural just, which refer respectively to the "sense of justice" and the "principles of justice," and subsume the first under the good and the second under the right (Ricoeur 1992, 227ff.).

The priority of the good over the right is advanced by the communitarians, whose ideas are advocated by thinkers such as Bellah (1985; 1991) and MacIntyre (1988). Whereas Taylor (1989) acknowledges the historical tension (p. 390) between the right of the Enlightenment and the good of Romanticism (p. 413), he evaluates the supremacy of the right over the good as a mistake of modernity (pp. 75-90). He counteracts this mistake by stressing that the emphasis on procedural justice by the liberal proceduralists implies a good, especially an extremely important shared good, namely, the good of liberal self-rule, as manifested in the nationwide rejection of President Nixon's abuse of executive power in the Watergate affair (Taylor 1989a). The good comes first, and the right is implied in it.

The priority of the right over the good is posited by many Kantian thinkers and other liberals and proceduralists, for example, Rawls (1971, 396). Considering today's pluralist and multicultural society, they argue that substantive claims for *the* good life are always claims for only *a* good life, because different communities and groups have different conceptions of what "good life" is. *The* good life does not exist — only different conceptions of what good life is. These thinkers restrict themselves to a proceduralist approach in which these different conceptions, along with their different values and interests, are evaluated according to the criterion of justice.

Is it possible to combine and integrate the criteria of the good and the right in a way that does justice to both? Taylor takes the middle ground in the debate between communitarianists and proceduralists, arguing for what he calls "holist individualism," in reference to Humboldt, who, as he says, "seems to have been forgotten by Mill's heirs in the English-speaking world" (Taylor 1989a, 163). Taylor nevertheless leans more toward communitarianism than toward proceduralism, as several publications show

(Taylor 1989; 1991; 1994). With Habermas it is the other way around. He interprets his own thinking as combining elements of communitarianism and procedural liberalism, because he develops procedural justice within the framework of communicative action (Habermas 1993, 91). Nevertheless he explicitly posits the priority of the right over the good (p. 69).

Good, Right, and Wise

The question remains whether it is possible or legitimate to interpret the relationship between the good and the right as a complementary one.[8] In my view, Ricoeur does precisely this by combining the good and the just in such a way that together they give birth, as it were, to a new, third criterion: the wise. In Ricoeur's three-phase model, first, the good has primacy over the right, because it is embedded in the community in which we live, the tradition from which we are fed, the context by which we are shaped. They form the original house we inhabit. Second, the values and norms that embody the good must be scrutinized, evaluated, and, if necessary, purified by putting them before the judge of justice and passing them through the "sieve of the right." They are tested according to the universal principles of justice, which transcend community- and context-bound values and norms. Third, the good, having been scrutinized and purified by the right, must be applied in the concrete situation by considering the specific circumstances that characterize this situation, including its singularity, fragility, and tragedy. For this to happen in an adequate way, we need a third criterion, the wise, which refers to practical-moral wisdom, moral wisdom in situation (Ricoeur 1992, 170, 203, 240).[9] In this study I take as my starting point Ricoeur's model of the complementarity of the good, the right, and the wise.

Moral Criteria and Moral Traditions

It would be a fundamental mistake to think that the foregoing criteria live a life of their own. They and above all their interpretations are linked with

---

8. From his analysis of friendship and duty, Stocker (1990) clarifies that the good and the right are not reducible to each other.

9. The three criteria recall the three phases that form essential steps in the study of human symbols and in research in the human sciences in general: participatory understanding, detached explanation, and again participatory understanding, but this time purified by the results of the second phase (Ricoeur 1987).

specific traditions, paradigms, and schools. Consequently, applying moral criteria in specific cases means using and applying certain paradigms, concepts, and ideas that stem from specific moral sources, systems, publications, and groups of authors. In short, the criteria are contextualized.

It would be an equally fundamental mistake to suggest that these traditions are clear-cut entities. On the contrary, they react and interact with, stimulate and influence, and penetrate and permeate one another, for they consist of — and are created by — various subtraditions, all using their own paradigms and establishing their own schools. The relationships of these traditions to one another depend on various people and institutions that embody and express these traditions meeting in various ways and at various times and places. Traditions do not exist independently any more than do criteria. They are, in short, contextualized.

Examples of the contextualization of criteria and traditions abound. The criterion of the purposive means something different in Bentham's utilitarianism, which stresses the "the greatest happiness of the greatest number," than in John Stuart Mill's social welfare utilitarianism, where social well-being is the moral end. What is good in terms of Aristotle's human excellence in the various forms of culture of the city-state differs greatly from what is good from a hedonist perspective. The criterion of the right in the context of social-economic and political human rights represents a correction of or at least a complement to the right in Kant's *Critique of Practical Reason*, which is based solely on individual human rationality. Clearly, the criteria cannot be applied separately from the moral traditions in which they are interpreted. As noted, however, these traditions themselves are intertwined. For example, MacIntyre's virtue ethics combines various and dissimilar threads from Aristotelian and Thomist sources (Miller 1994). Rawls's very influential theory of justice can be seen as a combination of both individualistic and social-welfare utilitarianism on the one hand and contractualism aiming at establishing certain common principles and rules on the other (Bell 1993, 2-8). Habermas's recent moral insights not only reveal their left-leaning neo-Kantian orientation but also incorporate some communitarian thought, especially inasmuch as they recognize the basic value of community ethics in the nation state (Habermas 1994).

1.2 Religion

Next to the group of moral problems discussed above, a second group also shapes the quest for moral education, that is, the group of religious problems. Why is it useful or even necessary to consider this group when reflecting on moral education? What has morality or moral education to do with religion? This is a modern question, one that mirrors the decline of traditional religiosity and church membership in the Western world.

Until a few centuries ago, morality and religion were inextricably and unquestionably linked. Morality was considered to be part of religion and to exist exclusively within religion, although within this framework a diversity of voices could be heard. For example, some religious philosophers and theologians held that morality can be taught without appeal to direct divine revelation, or at least should be based on human reason and experience, as advocated by the "natural law" tradition. By and large, though, religion functioned as the canopy that overarched all aspects of individual and social life, contributing to their integration and indicating the aims and goals, methods and means of that life: in short, it was the very source of its meaning, especially within the moral domain.

From the beginning of the Enlightenment, however, this marriage between morality and religion began to show cracks. The ideas of a few philosophers spread gradually to other intellectuals and the upper classes. A famous example is the French bourgeois morality of the seventeenth and eighteenth centuries. The secular system of values and norms distinguished the bourgeoisie both from the clergy with their official, church-bound moral doctrine and from the lower classes with their popular religion, devotions, and pious practices. The bourgeois "knows how to distinguish very well: secular morality and science for them, religion for the other" (Groethuysen 1979, 1:17). But gradually, year by year, decade by decade, century by century, this secular morality also reached the middle and lower classes. Ordinary people were thus increasingly influenced by the tendency to distinguish between morality and religion, and in the process they tended to forget the original religious roots of the moral practices by which they lived (Weber 1978, 536ff.; Habermas 1982, 1:205ff.).[10] The result is that it is not uncommon today to see the two domains, the moral and the religious, set in opposition to each other, to hear people protest against any influence religion might still exert in the moral domain and seek to eliminate all reminders of it, as conflicts over the very presence of Bibles, crucifixes, or other religious symbols in public

10. An example can be found in the moral tradition of human rights. Paradoxically, one of the most important human rights — the freedom of religion — and its implications, i.e., the separation of church and state, is not a so-called universal right at all, as comparative religious research shows, but is rooted in a particular religion: Christianity. Nowadays people interpret this right as an areligious or even antireligious right, but its root is religious (cf. Taylor 1994).

schools in Germany and the United States attest.[11] This is not a new phenomenon. At the beginning of this century, Durkheim was already arguing for religious education to be replaced by what he called secular moral education: "It is not enough to cut out; we must replace" (1973, 11). At the center of this secular moral education are rationality and personal autonomy: "to teach morality is neither to preach nor to indoctrinate; it is to explain" (ibid., 120).[12]

Today, the separation of morality and religion even occurs among groups of religious people and church members, as may be seen from the European Value Systems Study Group. Positive correlations may still be found between moral and religious convictions and between moral convictions and church membership, but they are moderate or weak. The conclusion is that many religious people and church members are dissociating themselves from religious morality and official church doctrine (Halman et al. 1987, 24-26; Ester et al. 1993, 62).

Is the connection between morality and religion, then, a thing of the past? This would be an overly hasty and overly generalized conclusion. Even in the Netherlands, one of the most secularized countries in the world, the so-called radical secularization hypothesis does not fit with empirical reality. Research shows that religion still influences people's attitudes with regard to (a) bio-ethical problems (abortion, suicide, euthanasia), (b) familial matters (marriage, divorce, family life), (c) political choices, and (d) economic values. Despite all the talk of radical secularization, religion still appears to play a moral role — not as visible and influential a one as in the past, but still a significant and relevant one. Nor does the so-called semi-secularization hypothesis, according to which secularization affects only the "private half" of life, fit the facts. Religion appears to influence not only private life but also public life (Felling et al. 1983; 1986; 1987; 1988; Spruit 1991; Spruit et al. 1992; Ter Voert 1994; Ter Voert et al. 1994; Schreuder 1994).

11. One of the reasons is the danger of religious intolerance, which is present in all religions to some degree, and especially in the Abrahamite religions: Judaism, Christianity, and Islam (cf. Philipse 1995, 20-21). For a discussion of the crucifix conflict in Bavaria, see *Der Spiegel* 33 (1995), and *Time,* August 28, 1995.

12. Durkheim (1973, 6-9) describes the weakening of the bond between religion and morality in three phases: the religion of so-called primitive people, which totally encompasses their culture; Christianity, especially Protestantism, in which love of God and love of other humans are considered to form a unity, but the latter becomes increasingly divorced from the former; modern times, in which there is no longer any need for a divine reality that functions as "the supreme guarantor of moral order."

Religion as Text

The conflicts inherent in the relations between morality and religion as well as the very empirical existence of that relation encourage us to reflect in a systematic way about this relationship. One way to examine the relation between morality and religion is to approach religion as a text. From this starting point, I will proceed through four steps, dealing with religion as an integrated text, the context of this text, the moral subtext, and lastly the grammar of this text.

In the first step, approaching religion as a text means viewing it as an integrated, structured whole. In other words, religion is understood as a system, the elements of which are related to each other in such a way that the whole is qualitatively more than the sum of those elements (cf. Lindbeck 1984). The emphasis on religion as an integrated text derives from the fact that religion is a web of meanings that can be discovered only through their interrelatedness. Hence it is in terms of this interconnectedness that one should study the various elements and their functions (Geertz 1973). In this sense I agree with biblical scholar Wayne A. Meeks, who sees religion as culture. Culture, too, is a network of meanings and itself can be seen as a text, "the text of culture." As Meeks points out, "we must be aware that the culture of any particular society or group, however complex, is so internally interconnected that if we pull out any one of its components — its ideas, its myths, its rules, its logical structures, its material supports — and disregard that element's embeddedness in the whole, we will fail to understand it" (Meeks 1993, 10-11).

Morality, then, insofar as it functions within religion-as-text, can be understood as its subtext. That is, morality functions as an integral part of religion; it cannot be separated from religion as if it were something independent, because its function is embedded in the whole of religious life. Separating this morality from religion would mutilate it, because it is interwoven with other subtexts (i.e., the experiential, ritual, cognitive, affective, social, and doctrinal subtexts) in a constitutive way (cf. Geertz 1969; Glock and Stark 1965). According to some scholars, morality is not simply one of the constitutive subtexts of religion, but its most distinctive, determining, and crucial subtext, serving as a criterion as to whether an individual, social group, or community is in fact religious at all. In this view, morality equals orthopraxis, which determines the very core of religion and has priority over all other subtexts (cf. Boff 1985; 1987a; 1987b).

In terms of the study of morality within religion, the conclusion is to reject an approach by which morality is isolated from religion as a whole or, more specifically, by which some moral elements are isolated from

13

religious morality as a whole. This is the case when one attempts to identify specific religious moral principles, religious moral values, and moral norms either in order to construct a system of religious moral thinking on them, or to deny that such construction is possible on the grounds that the specific religious moral principles, values, and norms being sought could not be found. It is true that many moral ideas, beliefs, and practices described in the Bible and in later religious texts stem from nonreligious sources. For example, within the New Testament, the lists of virtues in the Pauline letters originate in Stoic and Cynic ethics (Auer 1989). In patristic times, many church fathers borrowed moral ideas from their non-Christian environment. In his book *De officiis ministrorum,* Ambrose adopts the structure and reasoning of Cicero's thought and even borrows whole pages from his ethics (Von Campenhausen 1965, 104). In the Middle Ages, the great theologian Thomas Aquinas incorporates Aristotelian ethics in the "Secunda Secundae" of his *Summa Theologica* (Auer 1977b). To mention a controversial example, in the nineteenth century, the natural law concept, which is used by the teaching authority in the Catholic Church as a basis for condemning all kinds of "contra-natural" activities, especially in the sexual realm, was based on an almost purely biological type of anthropology (Vandermeersch 1992).[13] This short list of examples, which indicate Christian leaning on extra-Christian, nonreligious moral thought, could easily be lengthened. The question is, though, what is the meaning of such a list. Seriously considering religion as a text, a differentiated complex, in which morality and religion function within a part/whole relationship, implies seriously asking what then religion does with those moral elements it owes to nonreligious sources, like the various moral ideas, beliefs, values, norms, and practices referred to above. What does it mean to say that religion integrates nonreligious morality into its text as a subtext? Or, to use a musicological metaphor, what happens when that religion transposes nonreligious moral-

13. According to many Catholic moral theologians, the "modern" law of nature concept, as it has been used by the Catholic Church since the nineteenth century, contrasts sharply with the meaning given to it originally by Thomas Aquinas, whom the Catholic Church cites continuously (Jans 1994). The "modern" concept neglects the theological, social, and practical dimensions. The dimension of nature must be integrated into a well-balanced anthropology in which the spiritual, subjective, intersubjective, and social dimensions of human existence are taken into account (cf. Beemer 1983). Moreover, insofar as biological aspects are relevant, their description and analysis must correspond to the results of modern biological research (cf. Guindon 1986, 44-53). Vandermeersch (1992) is of the opinion that this concept functions as the legitimation of the church's need for power in the moral domain and for regaining moral power within a highly secularized society.

ity into the religious key? In what sense does this transposition change its very character? But questions like these go beyond the scope of the present discussion. Let us first dwell a little further on the nonreligious moral sources of religious morality.

This brings us to the second step, which has to do with the context of religion-as-text. Generally speaking, text and context are interrelated in the sense that the text must be understood from the context and vice versa. In other words, the text is influenced by the context, in which it functions; and the context is influenced by the text, because without this text the context would be different, since it would be determined by a different configuration. Text and context are dialectically related to each other. Looking at the way early Christianity weaves its religious text, including its moral subtext, from the dialectical relationship with its historical context, we see it being influenced by the Roman Empire, by Greco-Roman culture, and by urban life in this culture, while in turn influencing this culture and this society.

But Christianity was not the only worldview or religion in the Roman Empire. The web of meanings it weaves from the ideas of the Greco-Roman context into its religious text exists side by side with other texts like those of Judaism, Stoicism, Cynicism, and Epicureanism, with which it is connected through all kinds of intertextual links. Within this intertextuality, it is not easy to determine which is the genotext and which the phenotext. From the point of view of diachronic comparison, the genotext is the chronologically older text and the phenotext the later one. In this view, the genotext determines the phenotext. But from the perspective of intertextuality, as demonstrated in the synchronic approach in modern exegesis, it is the other way around, which is to say, the phenotext determines the genotext: "The genotext is not the pre-text or the text that already existed before the phenotext, but the genotext only becomes a text or only achieves significance through what the phenotext makes of it. The selection and form of the phenotext are therefore factors that help to determine the meaning of the genotext. Thus, the chronological or diachronic approach of comparative exegesis is replaced with the synchronic approach of the writer of a text" (Van Wolde 1989, 45-46). From this point of view, the religious texts of early Christianity as well as other religious and philosophical texts can be said to alternate continuously the functions of serving as genotext and phenotext to one another.

In this view, the author of a text is not a completely independent, autonomous authority who creates ex nihilo, but a rearranger of existing texts, because he/she is part of, and a participant in, an intertextual universe. Authors influence each other by belonging to the same contexts and are related through a complex of relationships that result in intertextuality, which is itself a process of mutual interaction.

The third step in the examination of the relation of religion to morality is the question of religious morality as a subtext of religion. In what sense does religion affect nonreligious moral ideas and beliefs by incorporating and integrating them? What kind of influence does it exert on those ideas and beliefs, so that they become its own subtext? I believe this question can be answered at two different levels, which I call the immanent and the transcendent levels.

At the immanent level, religion may be said to perform the three functions to which Auer refers in his theory of "autonomous morality in Christian context": an integrating, an orienting, and a critical function (Auer 1984).[14] First, it integrates external ideas, beliefs, values, and norms by relating them to the main Christian themes, that is, creation, alienation, liberation, and eschatological completion. In this way it establishes connections among moral elements such as freedom and responsibility, justice and love, or shame and guilt. Second, in the course of this integration process, it orients these moral elements in a particular direction: hope of the new heaven and the new earth, the kingdom of God, the new Jerusalem, the wholeness of the person, and the desired "Maranatha." It orients them toward the future, which is a future of surprise, a gift — not a *futurum* that is the product of extrapolations from the past and the present, but an *ad-ventus*, a new coming era (cf. Schillebeeckx 1989, 151-53). As a result of this orientation a specific kind of prioritizing takes place, for example, morals over rituals, or love over order (Kuitert 1988, 144); confidence, trust, and hope are stimulated. Third, within this orientation process, religion carries out a moral critique of historical developments, assessing them in terms of how well or how badly they fit into the intrinsic value of nature and humanity as aimed at in God's creation. It is from this perspective that Christian liberation ethics attacks the life-damaging and death-causing consequences of Western capitalism.[15] In short, the Christian

14. For the debate between "moral autonomy in the Christian context" and the "ethics of faith" *(Glaubensethik)* and "liberation ethics," see Lob-Hüdepohl 1993.

15. Based on his empirical-theological research on the motivational relation between religious and moral attitudes among church members and members of church peace movements, Jeurissen (1993, 249-52) calls Auer's model into question. The separation of the two groups of attitudes is a matter for debate. The ecclesiological dimension of these attitudes seems to be more important than Auer admits; not all religious attitudes appear to have a positively motivating function, and some even have a negatively motivating function. Although Jeurissen's research population is too select and small to allow generalizations to be made from the results, his research may be taken as a warning that Auer's concept must be viewed as a hypothesis only.

religion, in its integrating, orienting, and criticizing functions, is in permanent interaction with nonreligious moral texts, just as other religions or worldviews integrate, orient, and criticize texts that stem from sources other than their own.

At the transcendent level, religion takes the nonreligious moral ideas and beliefs and applies to them a qualitatively different perspective, thereby changing their very character. Earlier I used the musicological term *key*. When a composition's key (a text can be seen as a composition and a composition as a text) is changed, the composition itself — its whole character, nature, color, expression, affectivity, interpretation, and so on — changes.

Ricoeur explains this metaphorical language well in his discussion of the relation between morality and religion. The realm of morality, he argues, is characterized by a question-and-answer structure, in which "question" refers to asking what is true or false, good or bad, right or wrong, and "answer" is the response in terms of specific epistemic criteria. In the realm of religion, the question-and-answer structure also applies, but in a completely different way. Here "question" takes on the meaning of a call, while "answer" refers to the response to this call. Here, the question is: "Where are you?" and the answer: "It's me here, here I stand for you, I cannot do otherwise" (Ricoeur 1992, 22, 24, 352).

What then is the difference in level between morality and religion? In the seventies, Ricoeur was already of the opinion that the relation between the two should not be viewed additively, as if religion adds something to nonreligious morality (Ricoeur 1975, 333). He repeats this insight in the nineties: "it must be asserted that, even on the ethical and moral plane, biblical faith adds nothing to the predicates 'good' and 'obligatory' as these are applied to action" (Ricoeur 1992, 25). But this negative answer does not prevent Ricoeur from positively indicating the perspective he is looking for. Although he repeats his rejection of "such things as a Christian morality," he clearly points at the meaning of religion for morality in the following way: "Biblical *agapē* belongs to an economy of the gift, possessing a metaethical character, which makes me say that there is no such thing as a Christian morality, except perhaps on the level of the history of *mentalités*, but a common morality . . . that biblical faith places in a new perspective, in which love is tied to the 'naming of God'" (ibid., 25). In other words, by inserting religion into the moral discourse, morality is recapitulated through the names by which we indicate God.[16]

16. In this sentence I intentionally use two terms that Ricoeur uses himself: *inserting* (Ricoeur 1975, 333: *insertion*) and *recapitulated* (idem, 1992, 25), in order to

Premoral, Radical-Moral, and Metamoral Aspects of Religion

In this insertion of religion into morality and recapitulation of morality in religious terms at the transcendent level, I mention three aspects, which I owe to Ricoeur: premoral, radical-moral, and metamoral.[17] By naming them in these terms, I emphasize that the relation between morality and religion lies at a level that is not that of morality itself.

The first aspect is premoral in that it precedes all moral belief, values, norms, or action. It relates to the human being as a free individual, as a being who lives out of the conviction that his/her nature consists of being the author of action. The very essence of being a human person consists of this power-to-do. Or to put it dialectically: the human person essentially is the power to live and act; he/she has the power to live and act out who he/she is; he/she is the desire to realize himself/herself as he/she is. This identification of the human being with freedom as the power-to-do is implicit in the stories of creation; the release of this freedom is recounted in the stories of redemption and liberation and in the eschatological stories that hold out hope for the future.

The second aspect is radical-moral. Instead of offering a framework of moral ideas, lists of virtues, or systems of norms (which Christian texts have always done, still do, and should never cease to do), the specifically religious recapitulation of morality consists of something else, namely, turning the world of moral common sense, habits, and conventions — even that of so-called Christian virtues, values, and norms — upside down. By its very essence, religion breaks through all moral agreement and plausibility, strips away moral conventions we take for granted, revolts against all the common moral convictions and performances that characterize our daily lives. The parables are excellent examples in this respect: the shepherd who leaves the ninety-nine sheep in order to save the one lost sheep, the father who receives his lost son more graciously than he ever treated his eldest, or the host who sends away the guest because he is not wearing his wedding garment, or the workers of the eleventh hour who are paid the wages of the workers of the first, third, and sixth hours. The eschatological speeches in the Bible are of the same character, like Jesus' speech about

---

indicate the two ways from which one can approach the relation between morality and religion: religion can be inserted into morality, and religion recapitulates morality at a higher level.

17. As I said, I freely interpret Ricoeur's thought at this point (cf. Ricoeur 1975, 313-16, 333ff.; 1992, 16-25, 220, 317ff.). For a more elaborated and relatively different interpretation see Van Gerwen 1995.

"the least of mine," which leads the listener/reader into a crisis: does he/she belong to the sheep on the right hand or to the goats on the left hand? Texts like these disorient every person, Christian or not; they shock deeply and surprise absolutely. Hence they can be called, as Ricoeur says, radical-moral, because they question and discuss the moral discourse itself and prevent it from being developed, established, stabilized, and elaborated upon in a conventional way (Ricoeur 1975, 335).

The third aspect is metamoral, relating to facets of individual and social life that are paradoxical or even aporiacal, with which the moral discourse is confronted but which it cannot overcome.[18] They intrinsically deal with the tension between activity and passivity, because they emerge from the interrelationship between body and mind ("the body I have, the body I am"), the self and the other (the self as an other and the other as an other self), and calling and response ("conscience and attestation"). They reveal themselves in the tension within the permanence of time in the past (*idem*-identity) and the future (*ipse*-identity) as well as in the realm of evil, where I do (activity) the bad things I am confronted with (passivity).[19] Here the fragility, woundedness, and even tragedy of human existence emerge (Ricoeur 1992, 297ff.). From a religious point of view, chance is transformed into destiny, opportunity into gift, contingency into creation, release into redemption, and future into promise. But this religious interpretation does not occur in an atmosphere of absolute certainty. It occurs when a person makes his/her own uncertain choice without objective guarantees. The choice is its own guarantee, while practically knowing by attestation (Ricoeur 1992, 21-25).[20]

18. In his text about the foundation of morality, Ricoeur refers only to Weber's distinction between the ethics of conviction and the ethics of responsibility, while suggesting that both forms of ethics cannot and should not be reduced to each other, after which he calls ethics a wounded enterprise *(une enterprise "blessée")*. He goes on to say that "it is impossible to unite poetics of the will with politics, its utopia with its program, its imagination with the limited exercise of violence, which is implied in using power" (Ricoeur 1975, 336-37). This list of aporias points to some broader and deeper insights in this area, which can be found in Ricoeur 1992, especially the tenth study (pp. 297ff.).

19. Mongin (1994, 35) believes that Ricoeur's speaking of aporias culminates in the domain of time and evil.

20. A distinction should be made between "attestation" *(attestation)* and "testimony" *(témoignage)*, although they could be considered synonyms. "Attestation" means expressing one's conviction from the inside to the outside, which implies a kind of centrifugal movement, whereas "testimony" means listening and accepting a message from the outside, with the help of which we may be able to shape our life, and implies a centripetal movement (Van Gerwen 1995, 98-99).

In this way, I hope to have clarified what it means to integrate non-religious morality within religion and to consider it as a subtext of religion-as-text. At the immanent level, religion integrates, orients, and criticizes nonreligious morality. At the transcendent level, it recapitulates morality at a higher level, one that premorally, radically-morally, and metamorally transcends morality altogether.[21]

The fourth and last step refers to the grammar of religion as text, from which I wish to select only one element for special examination. Based on the foregoing, one might say that although there is no such thing as a specific Christian moral alphabet, the letters of the nonreligious moral alphabet are put together according to a special Christian grammar, with its own semantics, syntax, and pragmatics, in other words, the rules governing their meanings, relations to each other, and their use.[22] Now, one of the most fundamental assumptions of any grammar is that it is rule-governed, and the task of the science of grammar, or linguistics, is to describe and explain these rules, to present them for open and reasonable discussion. Continuing the metaphor of "Christian grammar" implies that the science of that grammar must describe and explain the rules of the grammar and present them for free and rational debate. Here the argumentability of morality within religion is at stake. Within Thomist thinking this argumentability is founded in the light of the human's natural rationality *(lumen naturale)* by which he/she participates in God's light *(lumen divinum)*. By turning upside down the perspective of the human's participation in God, by which one's thought goes from the human person to God, Thomas's thinking also goes from God to the human person, when he says that God's light is impressed in the light of human rationality *(STh* I-II 91.2c).[23] This means that citing religious codes, such as "God's calling" or "the will of God," does not absolve one from responsibility for giving a rational account

21. Van Tongeren (1992, 46) says: "It is not surprising that throughout the history of philosophy ethics has always assigned an important role to transcendence."

22. My suggestion to understand this framework as a grammar corresponds to the broader epistemological idea that there is no such thing as Christian experiences, cognitions, and affections, but only the Christian use of these experiences, cognitions, and affections (Bochenski 1965). According to the grammar metaphor, Christian traditions can be seen as collections of scripts, spontaneously used by "native speakers," resulting in narrative texts; and scientifically studied by scholars from inside and outside, resulting in discursive texts, all depending on specific contexts of time and space (cf. Lindbeck 1984).

23. Here Thomas cites Ps 4:6: "There are many who say, 'O that we might see some good! Let the light of your face shine on us, O Lord!" In his exegetical study on the *proprium* of Jesus' ethics, Dillmann (1984) supports the idea of the rationality and argumentability of Christian ethics.

of the morality under consideration. An authoritative argument — if it is an argument — can be and should be the object of rational debate — it does not replace it. Any morality within religion can be and should be brought to the forum of human rationality (Pfürtner 1979).

1.3 Education

Along with moral and religious problems, moral education also involves educational problems. The demand and the cry for moral education, emanating from all corners of the Western world, beg the question of what kind of education moral education is and how it is to be accomplished. Should we instill moral habits in the child through discipline, improve the socialization processes by which the child is shaped, focus on the transmission of morality in the school, stimulate the child's cognitive moral development, encourage moral self-clarification, create learning opportunities in the domain of moral emotions, or establish educational conditions conducive to shaping moral character? Which of these seven modes — discipline, socialization, transmission, cognitive development, clarification, emotional formation, or character formation — best corresponds to our ideas of what moral education in general should be? Can we combine them while giving priority to one or several of them? Or perhaps it would be possible to select elements of each and integrate them in a way designed to achieve our educational objectives most effectively.

In order to answer this complex question, we must seriously look at, first, the educational paradigm out of which moral education is to be developed; second, the common denominator among the modes of moral education mentioned above; and, third, the main differences between these modes.

Interactionism as an Educational Paradigm

Before we can choose the educational paradigm that can adequately serve as a frame of reference for the development of moral education, a brief survey of the main paradigms in this domain is in order. Much depends on whether it is the individual person, the community, the larger society and its institutions, the pluralist society, or the multicultural society that is taken as the starting point.

The first paradigm is individualism, which is to say that moral emotions, motives, attitudes, virtues, or decisions of the individual function as the springboard for reflections on moral education. Emotions such as sympathy, kindness, or love, attitudes such as loyalty or commitment, virtues like temperance, fortitude, or prudence may serve as the foundations. Next to these affective and conative aspects, the individual's cognitive functioning may provide the basis to elaborate on. The way in which the individual person's reason guides his/her moral actions may be the foundation for establishing principles of moral education.

Taking the individual as the point of departure can mean two different things. It is possible to start with the individual's own participatory perspective, the perspective from which he/she experiences himself/herself, including moral feeling, striving, thinking, decision making, acting, and so on. From this "I" perspective, the individual reflects, analyzes, and evaluates his/her own moral functioning. It is also possible to start from an observer perspective, the perspective from which an individual is perceived, and his/her functioning described, analyzed, and evaluated, from the outside. For example, Kant analyzes processes of moral reasoning in a personally detached manner in order to derive moral principles from which educational conclusions may be drawn. It is also possible to combine the two perspectives; in other words, the experiencing of one's own cognitive, affective, and conative processes in the realm of morality may be broadened, abstracted, and objectified by perceptions, ideas, and insights that stem from the "he"/"she" perspective of an outsider, for example, an observer or researcher. This results in more neutral diagnoses and analyses for educational directives to build on.

Next to this functional approach of taking the individual's cognitive, affective, and conative operating as the point of departure for reflections in the area of moral education, one can choose or even prefer a more substantial approach, in which one focuses on the individual's material or spiritual needs and interests. Material needs and interests refer to property, capital, profit, and power, whereas spiritual needs and interests relate to social position and self-esteem, respect, dignity, lust, pleasure, happiness, well-being, or "higher-order life plans." From this viewpoint, a group, community, or society is seen as a collection of individuals who, for instance, by contract, work for their own material and spiritual needs and interests. Individualism can be found in classic happiness-oriented forms of utilitarianism with Bentham ("the greatest happiness of the greatest number"), preference-oriented forms with Hare, or left neo-Kantian contract liberalism with Rawls.

The second paradigm is communitarianism, in which the individual's belonging to a community is taken as the point of departure. The community may be the nuclear family, extended family, primary life group, neighborhood, school, association, congregation, village, town, county, and so on.

By community, I mean the collection of networks of individuals in groups, insofar as they participate in each other's lives and hold in common, at least to some extent, beliefs, values, and norms. The individual is not considered the main focus, but rather the bonds, ties, and relations this person maintains with others. Within these groups, the individual lives his/her daily life, learns convictions about what is good and bad, right and wrong; communicates moral principles, values, and norms; and assesses events in the larger society from a moral point of view. This cognitive processing in the moral domain goes hand in hand with developing emotional and social connections among the group members. Stories are told, retold, and transmitted from generation to generation, from parents to children, teachers to students, pastors to church members. These narrations contain metaphors, symbols, and ideas by which the moral side of the group's life is impregnated, reinforced, and strengthened. Moral education is then the extension of these ongoing moral processes.

Two forms of communitarianism must be distinguished. The first consists of people who belong to the Responsive Communitarian Platform, which published a document, first drafted by Amitai Etzioni in 1991, that begins as follows: "American men, women, and children are members of many communities — families; neighborhoods; innumerable social, religious, ethnic, workplace, and professional associations; and the body politic itself. Neither human existence nor individual liberty can be sustained for long outside the interdependent and overlapping communities to which all of us belong" (Etzioni 1994, 251ff.). A few paragraphs further, it states: "America's diverse communities of memory and mutual aid are rich resources of moral voices — voices that ought to be heeded in a society that increasingly threatens to become normless, self-centered, and driven by greed, special interest, and an unabashed quest for power" (ibid., 254).

The second form of communitarianism consists of communitarian critics of liberal political theory who do not (yet) identify with the communitarian movement in the sense of the Communitarian Platform. Its representatives, like MacIntyre, Sandel, Taylor, and Walzer, hold themselves more or less separate from the communitarian movement (Bell 1993, 4), and indeed Taylor, Sandel, and MacIntyre do not consider themselves communitarians, at least not without qualification. For example, Taylor (1989, 159) does not think he belongs to the group of communitarians, to which he counts Sandel, MacIntyre, and Walzer. Walzer criticizes the communitarian critique of liberalism by taking a less forceful stand himself. MacIntyre declares openly: "I am not and never have been a communitarian" on the grounds that he thinks rebuilding community life in modern industrialized society is "ineffective and disastrous" (Bell 1993, 17).

23

The third paradigm I call institutionalism, meaning that the larger society and its social institutions are taken as the determining principle for the development of moral education. The point of departure is neither the inner processes of the individual person nor the community life he/she belongs to, but rather the functions he/she performs and the roles he/she plays within the core institutions of Western society. So the question arises: Is it not of utmost importance that the individual learn to behave adequately in profit-based organizations, commercial companies, economic unions, political systems, social associations, or cultural committees? This kind of learning process is essential in order to discover the moral margins of bargaining, making compromises, and concluding transactions, or, conversely and more cynically, to adjust oneself morally to the iron cage that forms their institutional structure, as Weber puts it. Either way, moral questions arise, such as "What is my moral duty?" "What is fair interaction?" "In what sense are self-interest and 'enlightened' self-interest morally justified?" and "How far may I morally go?" From this perspective, it would be wrong to restrict moral education to the microcosmos of the individual's private life or the mesocosmos of community life, because the "real" world does not take place only in this microcosmos and mesocosmos, but also and especially in the macrocosmos of societal duties and responsibilities, commandments and prohibitions, rights and obligations.

The most important examples of institutionalism are found among socialization theories, which start from the existing society as a system and its institutions as subsystems. The child needs to learn the roles it must play to function in these institutions. These roles can be understood as prescriptions for ways of dealing with classes of situations the individual will face. These prescriptions, including their underlying values and norms, have to be internalized by the child and acted on step by step (cf. Schulze and Künzler 1991, 128-31).

The fourth paradigm that can serve as a starting point for moral education is what I call pluralism. This can be seen as a kind of critique on the paradigm of institutionalism, which is assumed to be based on a common set of principles, values, and norms, although these may differ somewhat from one institution to another. It is questionable, however, whether such moral uniformity, even if it is institutionally differentiated, really exists. People who fall into different categories, classes, or groups do not appear to think, feel, and behave along common moral lines. For example, German society has been described as consisting of five different cultural style groups, characterized by various combinations of age and education. The criterion for age groups is forty (the younger group being less and the older group more than forty years old), while education levels are characterized as lower, middle, and higher. The five style groups are: older people with high education (high culture), older people with low education (trivial culture), older people with middle education (mixed high and trivial culture), younger people with high education (mixed high and tension culture), and younger people with low education (tension culture). These groups differ empirically with regard to lifestyles, values, and norms (Schulze 1992).

According to many researchers, modern Western pluralist society promotes individualism in the area of values and norms. People no longer accept values and norms because of convention or social plausibility; instead, they pick and choose their own principles, values, and norms. The moral person, in the pluralist society, is a moral preferentialist. He/she composes his/her own personalized moral package at the marketplace of convictions, virtues, rules, and habits. The so-called modern individual is what Lévy-Strauss calls "un bricoleur," a do-it-yourselfer. What was once the prerogative of the royal elite is now democratized. Henry V's claim in Shakespeare's play of the same name, "Dear Kate, you and I cannot be confined within the weak list of [the] country's fashion: we are the makers of manners," is everybody's entitlement now.[24] However, the individual's process of composition is not devoid of patterns, styles, or fashions. It is, in fact, based on collective moral structures, schemes, and repetitive action structures, and is largely a social construction. Neglecting this leads to what Schulze (1992, 415) calls the individualization error *(Individualisierungsirr-tum)*. In other words, it is important to distinguish between the surface level, at which people experience and like their individualism, and the deep level, at which this individualism is conditioned by social factors, mechanisms, and constraints.

The fifth and last paradigm, which I call multiculturalism, is an important one because today's Western society is characterized not only by moral pluralism within Western culture — whatever that may be — but by a moral pluralism that is the product of Western as well as non-Western cultures. Western pluralism can be understood as the diversity within Western culture, made up of its various cultural style groups and various stylistic combinations of convictions, values, rules, and habits. However, the migration to the West of millions and millions of people has imported into the culture of Western society beliefs, conceptions, norms, and customs that (apparently) contrast with or even contradict the traditional Western ones. This situation raises a number of fundamental questions. Should the im-

---

24. In this way Janssen (1994, 48) describes the individualization process in the history of Western society.

migrant groups be obliged to adapt to what are held to be Western core values, democratic norms, human rights, and so on? Or should they have the right to integrate into Western society while at the same time preserving and developing their own cultural identity? Is it society's task to protect this multiculturality? If the answer to these last two questions is yes, then moral education must accord equal importance to these cultural groups and treat Western culture simply as the culture of the white European group, alongside Indian, African-American, Hispanic, Islamic, or Asian culture. According to Habermas (1994, 138), an essential difference exists between communitarianists and multiculturalists in that communitarianism does not take into account the complex composition of today's multicultural society.

Some critical remarks are in order with regard to the five paradigms presented so far, because of certain difficulties, questions, and objections that they raise. Before being able to make a reasonable and legitimate paradigm choice, we need to reflect critically on these questions, explore the points of discussion, and clarify the paradoxes, contrasts, or even dilemmas that may exist between and within them.

The paradigm of individualism, if it is to be used as a basis for a theory of moral education, runs the risk of isolating the individual from the ties and bonds that he/she develops and maintains with the surrounding community. Being an isolated monad prevents the human individual from experiencing the relationships by which he/she is linked with communities like the family, neighborhood, school, church, and so on. Whether and to what extent one is isolated from or connected with other people is of utmost relevance both morally and educationally. It is important morally because morality, classically, always also refers to the other. It always also relates to concern for the other, whether the other be a person, group, or community. This does not necessarily negate the plausibility of self-interest, which plays a part in several moral theories. Whether self-interest is considered a morally relevant category or not, concern for the other is at the very core of moral principles, values, norms, and virtues. What would moral education be as a form of education if it were developed in the direction of moral and educational solipsism or even egoism? Similarly, pure individualism would separate the individual from the tasks to be accomplished and the roles to be played within the social institutions. These tasks and roles entail moral performances that presuppose knowledge of moral principles and procedures, especially with regard to justice, and the ability to apply them in the technical, professional, and scientific situations that are basic to these institutions.

The paradigm of communitarianism as a basis for moral education raises another difficulty. However emotionally warm the bonds between the individual person and the groups to which he/she belongs, the risk of taking these as the exclusive point of departure for moral education is that the subjects of such education will become socially adjusted exclusively to the worldview, values, and norms of just these groups. This would prevent the subject from actualizing his/her freedom, establishing his/her own life, and realizing his/her own goals and life plan. To what extent, one must ask, is moral education that is directed at socialization actually moral education? Although I would not necessarily argue that it is not, the question nevertheless must be asked. It leads to two subquestions: to what extent is socialization a legitimate aim from a moral point of view? from an educational point of view? Freedom is at the very core of morality, inasmuch as it is its necessary condition: without freedom, moral cognitions, emotions, decisions, and actions are correlates of determinism and lose their moral nature. Freedom is also at the core of education: it is its very aim. Education strives to develop and advance the child's and student's autonomy, self-determination, and emancipation. Moral education must break through tradition — social habits, customs, rites — insofar as they hinder this freedom. This is not to say that moral education should not ultimately appropriate such traditions, but not solely on the grounds that they are traditions. Only insofar as they can be freely deliberated and chosen by the individual for the reason that they fit into his/her goals and life plan should they form part of moral education.

Taking institutionalism as the paradigm for moral education would lead to still other problems. It would reduce the richness of life to that of economic, political, social, and cultural institutions. It would entail the risk that the mechanisms by which the processes in these institutions are determined would take priority over moral principles, values, and norms. At the beginning of this century Weber asked skeptically and even cynically how the iron laws of institutional life could fit with the ideals of brotherhood and sisterhood among people. What is likely to be the result of moral education, if children and students are predominantly confronted with the mechanisms of money, which determine profit organizations; those of power, which condition the political systems; or those of convention, which structure social and cultural associations? Where is the source of refreshment, renewal, reformation, or transformation? Is it in the give-and-take of industrial and commercial negotiations? Is it in the interplay of power that takes place in democratic institutions? Is it in the deliberations about rights and obligations, the shaping of civic, political, and socioeconomic human rights in the courts? Is it in the creation and discovery taking place in scientific and artistic organizations? Or should new moral life be explored outside these institutional systems altogether? Is it to be found in the life of the individual person or in his/her communities?

Despite the reality of today's Western pluralist society, the problem implicit in the paradigm of pluralism is too fundamental to be overlooked: does taking moral pluralism as the basis for developing moral education mean founding moral education on an ideology? As we know, the term *ideology* can have various meanings, from a set of convictions as such, to a set of convictions connected with a specific social group, to a set of convictions maintained by those in power to suppress lower-placed social groups.[25] The question I ask here is: if the ideology of pluralism is widespread in modern Western society, whose interests, or the interests of which group in power, does it serve? The question arises because empirical research does not provide an unambiguous answer as to whether contemporary societal life is ruled by moral uniformism or moral pluralism. To what extent is moral pluralism an ideology developed in order to hide the uniformity of bourgeois interests? Or, to put the question the other way round, to what extent does moral pluralism really exist? What is the true degree of moral disintegration in modern society? What evidence do we have that moral individualization and fragmentation are on the rise? The answers to these questions must be left open because of the ambiguity that characterizes the results of the empirical research at this point (cf. Ester et al. 1993; Ester and Halman 1994; Schreuder 1994).

If one takes multiculturalism as the paradigm from which to develop moral education, other problems arise. What multiculturalism is and how it is to be approached depend fundamentally on how it is conceived: as a danger to the dominant culture or an opportunity for society's culture to be enriched. If it is seen as a danger, minority groups are challenged to assimilate and adapt to the core convictions and values from a communitarian or institutionalist perspective, although marginal moral differences may be tolerated as an expression of the individual's authenticity in keeping with principles of human dignity. If multiculturalism is understood as an opportunity for enrichment, the cultures of minorities are approached in an affirmative way, not only at the level of their individual members but also and especially at the level of social groups. The reason, as Habermas (1994) rightly points out, is that the dignity of the individual person cannot be advanced without preserving the social group structures and contexts in which this individual lives his/her life.

It is in consideration of all these problems that I propose adopting the paradigm known as interactionism as the basis on which to elaborate a plan of moral education. Interactionism has been developed within the social

---

25. I systematically clarified these three meanings of ideology in earlier publications (cf. van der Ven 1982; 1993).

sciences in the last twenty-five years in an attempt to combine the two poles of human existence: the pole of the individual and the pole of community and society. More generally, it describes, analyzes, and explains human functioning by looking at the interaction between the individual and his/her environment. It rejects both personal and environmental determinism. Personal determinism is the theory that all processes in (moral) life stem from the individual's cognitions, emotions, motives, intentions, choices, and actions, while neglecting the influences of environmental factors. Environmental determinism is the proposition that all (moral) thinking, feeling, striving, and behaving are controlled by external stimuli operating in the environment, while the individual is limited to countercontrol and counteraction. From an interactionist perspective, the individual is not only counteractive but also proactive, and not only does the environment orchestrate the individual, the individual also orchestrates, conducts, and even creates the environment, albeit not from nothing (Bandura 1986).

This is not to say that interactionism is a recent invention. In the thirties social psychologists like Mead (1934) and Lewin (1936) argued for an approach within the social sciences in which "the whole situation" is studied, on the grounds that the individual's functioning appears to depend on his/her interaction with the environment, as Lewin formulated it in his field theory. The principles of interactionism may be summarized in four points.[26] (1) Studying the interaction between individual and environment exposes patterns of human functioning that reveal the variability of this functioning in a variety of situations. (2) The individual acts freely and intentionally in this interaction, and this freedom manifests itself to some extent in the determining of, selecting, and giving meaning to situations. (3) Social-cognitive factors such as cognitive competencies, strategies, expectancies, valuations, and self-regulation influence this acting and interacting. (4) Together with the objectively real situation, which exerts indirect influences, the perceived or experienced situation directly determines the interaction between person and environment.

Interactionism has both a structural and a process aspect. The structural aspect is characterized by the interdependence of personal and environmental factors. This is not to say that the influences exerted by the two sets of factors are symmetrical. Their intensity varies for different individuals, situations, areas, and actions. Sometimes they are strong, sometimes weak. But they never lose their character of interdependence. The process side of interactionism is revealed when this structure is studied in

---

26. See the summary of these four points in V. Peters 1985, 26-27, and his discussion of the fourth point (pp. 60-62).

the time dimension, and it becomes evident that the result of interaction, as manifested in actual human functioning, itself influences interaction in the future. The output of interaction changes the input by feedback and feed-forward processes. In other words, actual human functioning can be considered as both a dependent variable, which is determined by individual-environment interactions, and an independent variable, which in turn influences individual and environmental factors and their interaction. This gives interactionism a dynamic aspect over time. A simple example would be watching television. The programs to be offered are conditioned by environmental factors such as costs, talent, and broadcasting companies. The programs to be watched are chosen according to the individual's preferences and motives. The watching itself determines future offering, preference, and watching. Temporal dynamics in interactionism do not imply any simultaneity of output and input operations. The time lag may vary for different persons, environments, areas, and actions (Bandura 1986, 25; Lazarus 1991, 203-11).

In this study, the interaction that takes place between the individual and his/her communal and societal environment and influences both of them is considered the basic paradigm for the development of moral education. It synthesizes the paradigms of individualism, communitarianism, and institutionalism by emphasizing the reciprocal, though not simultaneous, interactions among the individual, community, and society. It continues the line of thought about education and moral education initiated by Dewey, in which the anthropological "innate ideas/blank slate" dilemma, which is based on the paradigm of individualism, as well as the educational "nature/nurture" dilemma, which is implicit in communitarianism and institutionalism, are transcended in the direction of mutual influences (Dewey 1994, 23-55). Moreover, the interactionism paradigm offers the possibility of dealing adequately with the problems associated with the two other paradigms, pluralism and multiculturalism. That is, within the framework of moral education, the interaction between the individual and his/her community and society must be critically studied in terms of the aforementioned suspicion that pluralism may in fact be an ideology used to advance the interests of particular groups, as well as in terms of the tension between social integration and cultural identity within multiculturalism.

Moral Communication as the Common Denominator

Having selected the paradigm that, in my opinion, can serve as the framework for the development of a plan of moral education, I now wish to look for a common denominator among the seven modes of moral education that were described briefly at the start of this chapter: discipline, socialization, transmission, cognitive development, clarification, emotional formation, and education for character. A common denominator is important because it might clarify why and to what extent these models appear, at least partly, to overlap.

This common denominator, I propose, is moral communication, because all seven modes are based in it, elaborate on it, and aim at it. Here I define moral communication as the ongoing process of moral exchange and understanding in the search for truth. Moral exchange means mutually expressing moral beliefs, principles, values, and norms, while also seeking to clarify, explain, and justify them. Moral understanding is the adopting of another's perspective and heeding another's clarifications, explanations, and justifications. It involves adopting, at least temporarily, and taking into account the individual and social history out of which these premises emerge. This moral exchange and understanding is part of the search for truth, the search for what is good and just so that one may act with wisdom in all of life's situations.[27]

This definition of moral communication is cognitively based, which in neurological terms means that it refers to the interconnections between the person's environment, body, brain, and mind. Two mistakes are sometimes made in this regard. The first is to assume that cognitively based communication is not affective or conative in character. Neurologically, the brain and the mind control not only the rational aspects of human behavior but also the affective and conative aspects, as I will explain later on (cf. Damasio 1994). The second mistake is the belief that cognitively based communication is essentially mental, conscious, or verbal. On the contrary, for communication to take place, the development of mental images is not required. When a musician plays one of Chopin's nocturnes, a musical message is being communicated, but without necessarily eliciting any mental picture in the musician's or the audience's mind. The relation between

---

27. Here I take the terms *exchange* and *understanding* from my *Practical Theology: An Empirical Approach* (1993), 49-51. The "search for agreement" (ibid., 50-51), which I owed to Habermas's communicative action theory (1982; 1983), is replaced by the "search for truth," because ultimately the only criterion for truth is not to be found in truth conceptions like agreement, correspondence, coherence, or practice, which I referred to in my *Ecclesiology in Context* (1996), but only intrinsically in truth itself. In particular, Zwart's dissertation, in which he critically analyzes the pressure toward consensus in today's moral theory instead of the search for truth, influenced me in this direction (Zwart 1993). I further refer to the three moral criteria discussed earlier in this chapter, the good, the just, and the wise, which I owe to Ricoeur (1992).

communication and consciousness is similar, in that communication can take place on different levels of consciousness, from the unconscious via the preconscious to the conscious to the hyperconscious. In the same way, communication can occur on different levels of verbalization, from the nonverbal via the preverbal to the verbal to the hyperverbal. In this sense, communication in the area of morality and moral education comprises rational and nonrational, mental and nonmental, conscious and nonconscious, verbal and nonverbal aspects to varying degrees. Sometimes moral communication is more nonrational, nonmental, nonconscious, and nonverbal; at other times it is highly rational, mental, conscious, and verbal indeed. If there is a breakdown in communication and people fail to understand each other, however, then greater, though not exclusive, emphasis must be placed on the more rational, mental, conscious, and verbal forms of communication (cf. James 1981, 123).

Moral communication as the common denominator among the seven modes of moral education can be analyzed at two different levels: first-order and second-order communication. In some modes the first level predominates and in other modes the second.

First-order moral communication is characterized by plausibility. The perceptions, experiences, images, metaphors, symbols, stories, convictions, principles, values, and norms that are dealt with and exchanged in this communication are taken as self-evident, reasonable, understandable. They do not need to be discussed or proved. They are part of people's life-world, their everyday lives. Plausibility means not only that these metaphors and ideas are self-evident but also that people act on them in a self-evident way, taking from them direction, inspiration, and guidance. This is not to say that they are never discussed. People may ask questions about them, think about them, have doubts about them. But fundamental to the discussion is the assumption that these experiences, symbols, norms are something valuable, held in common by all, and given by tradition. The discussion does not go beyond requests for information, explorations of the broader network of connected ideas, or searches for deeper understanding. It does not really call into question the collective context, or make it a subject of rigorous debate. Young people may ask why this or that rule or norm is worthy of being accepted. People caught in existential suffering may ask whether this or that moral idea is still valid. In special circumstances, there may be a question of how specific values should be applied because of potential conflict between them. To answer these questions some reasoning and argumentation are needed. Young people must be given reasons why using drugs, for example, represents a risk to their bodily and mental health. For people who are suffering acutely, the moral ideas being questioned need to be explained within a web of convictions about life and death, into which their life is also woven, so that this suffering becomes understandable and meaningful for them. In a situation where there is a potential conflict between values, rational criteria must be applied and prudently weighed. Thus first-order moral communication is characterized not only by narrative but also by argumentative thinking. This argumentation, however, takes place within the boundaries of the common life-world.

Second-order moral communication also is characterized by narration and argument, but the stories that are told and the arguments that are used are intended to evoke discussion, to break through the boundaries, the walls, of the common life-world. Questions are not meant to elicit further clarification and enrichment or deeper understanding, but to call into question the traditional rules, values, and norms. Stories and narratives contrast sharply with the common fabric of values, stem from different life-worlds in unfamiliar communities, and indicate how other people's habits and convictions are acted upon. Reason and logical persuasion are used in support of these alien norms and values. This reasoning, these debates, are not directed at socialization, as in the case of the young people who seek further clarification about their common life-world. They are not designed to provide support to people in severe existential suffering who desire to be nourished by the richness of their common tradition. They are not intended to solve conflicts between values held in common within the common life-world. These discussions are meant to pull down and dismantle these common principles, rules, and norms. They confront traditional convictions and values with new arguments in order to reveal the contingency or even worthlessness of the former and the importance and relevance of the latter. Words such as *traditional* and *new* take on a relative meaning only, because what is traditional for the one group may be new for the other. Gay rights may be shocking to rural, fundamentalist Protestant communities but commonly accepted among people living in certain metropolitan areas, who may even speak of the old tradition of gay rights within the Catholic Church's "Dignity" movement. In this kind of moral communication, narrative and argument arise from moral plurality and moral conflicts.

Thus narrative is not exclusively or even especially characteristic of first-order moral communication, as is sometimes assumed. It is equally typical of the second order. Acts and events within the "traditional" pro-life movement in conservative Christian circles may be recounted in a village pub with great relish. Yet stories are also told at gatherings of pro-choice activists in inner-city offices and convention halls, where events are narratively interpreted as signs of victory for their side. Nor is argument necessarily restricted to second-order moral communication, as is sometimes thought. It also takes place at the first order, which is characterized by a commonly held worldview in a collective life-world. Solving value conflicts in this life-world and applying values in circumstances where two or more different values seem to be equally appropriate can be done only by reasoning, taking on alternative perspectives, weighing choices, and making decisions. Practical rationality is as much part of the world of moral uniformity within first-order communication as it is part of the plurality of second-order moral communication. In short, both "modes of thought," narrative and argument, are involved in both levels (cf. Brunner 1986; 1990).

First-order moral communication can be called intracommunal communication, because it occurs within groups, networks, communities, without going beyond their frontiers. In second-order moral communication, relations between groups, networks, and communities give rise to moral conflicts. These can take place between families, neighborhoods, schools, congregations, and so on. On a larger scale they happen between different social strata — the lower, middle, and upper classes — and even more deeply and sharply between the "established" and the "marginalized," for example, drug addicts and homeless people. On a still larger scale, these conflicts occur between racial groups (e.g., whites and blacks), language groups (e.g., English-speaking and Spanish-speaking), and religious groups (e.g., Protestants and Catholics, Christians and Muslims). In this sense, second-order moral communication is intercommunal communication.

These intergroup conflicts, however, do not remain only between these groups; they also enter into the groups, networks, and communities through the back door. People do not belong to only one community, but to many. They are members of a nuclear and extended family, take part in the life-world or life-worlds in their neighborhood, are members of school associations, go to church, watch a variety of television programs, work in various companies or institutions located in many different parts of the city or the country, and so on. Depending on the various groups and communities in which people participate, and the differing degrees to which they identify with them, they introduce a variety of convictions, values, and norms into their various communities. These convictions may be complementary to those of the community, but they may also contrast and conflict, thereby giving rise to interpersonal conflicts within the communities. The repercussions are also felt internally by individuals, with the result that these interpersonal conflicts may develop into intrapersonal conflicts as well. From this point of view, moral communication is both interpersonal and intrapersonal communication.

In short, one can see moral communication as the common denominator of all seven modes in moral education, provided that several aspects are taken into account. Moral communication, as I have defined it, is the process of moral exchange and understanding in the search for truth. It may be either first-order or second-order communication, both of which involve narrative and argument. Beyond these two levels, moral communication can also be broken down into intracommunal and intercommunal communication. Because intercommunal conflicts are reiterated at the personal level when individuals move from one community to another, they may engender interpersonal and intrapersonal conflicts, which require first-order communication to be complemented by second-order communication within the community.

Seven Modes in Moral Education

If moral communication is accepted as the common denominator of all modes of moral education, the question arises: communication to what end, or more precisely, moral communication to what moral-educational end? Moral communication certainly does not exhaustively define what moral education is all about. It can be said to be the communicative infrastructure on which the different modes in moral education build their different sets of educational aims, contents, and methods. It provides the communicative conditions out of which the different modes develop their different sets of educational goals, materials, means, and techniques. But the purpose, the aim, of the moral-educational process remains undefined.

In the following chapters, the seven modes outlined at the beginning — discipline, socialization, transmission, cognitive development, clarification, emotional formation, and education for character — will be dealt with in a systematic and critical way. In the process I will try to answer two questions — the first descriptive, the second evaluative. The descriptive question is: What are the characteristic features of each of these modes? The evaluative question is: To what extent is each of these modes morally and educationally appropriate?

At this point, I would like to give a brief explanation and rationale for each of the seven modes of moral education. Why have I selected these particular concepts to form the subject of the present study? The observation that each of these modes can be found in research, development, and practice does not satisfy, the more so in that different authors — myself included — offer different lists.[28]

28. Some authors emphasize only one mode, for example, socialization (cf. Kay 1975) or emotional formation (Spiecker 1991). Others think the mode that they focus

It is important first to distinguish between informal and formal moral education. By informal moral education I mean the educational processes in the moral domain that go on in the informal setting of the relationship between the child and its parents, siblings, and anyone else who participates in the life of the primary groups, particularly the family. Informal moral education also refers to the educational processes in the moral area that occur in the informal setting of the broader community, and in which the primary group — neighborhood, association, church, and so on — participate. The adjective *informal* means that educational processes take place in groups and networks that are not primarily set up, organized, and formalized for that purpose. They transcend the aim of education in the sense that education does not exhaustively define their nature. By formal moral education I mean the educational processes that take place within an organization set up primarily for the purpose of systematically and methodically coordinating educational activities, formalizing educational tasks and responsibilities, exercising professional leadership in the field of education, and explicitly legitimizing its educational structures, procedures, and processes.[29] Today this formal education may take place at primary, sec-

---

on contains some or even all of the others. Cognitive development is thought of as overarching (cf. Kohlberg 1981; 1984) in the same way as character formation is interpreted as all-encompassing (cf. McLean et al. 1986; Steutel 1992). Other authors treat two modes, as Hirst (1993) does; he starts with initiation, followed by critical reflection. Still others establish three modes, like Durkheim (1973), who distinguishes among discipline, socialization, and cognitive self-determination. Ellrod (1986) describes four modes: transmission, cognitive development, clarification, and cognitive-analytic formation. The last one is designed by John Wilson based on Hare's principles of universality, prescriptivity, and overridingness. It combines aspects of cognitive development and clarification. From a psychological perspective, Clouse (1993) lists four modes: psychoanalytic, learning, cognitive, and humanist. In previous publications, I mentioned four modes: transmission, cognitive development, clarification, and communication. I wrongly neglected discipline, socialization, emotional formation, and character formation as relatively independent modes. This is not to say that I did not acknowledge certain conditions or aspects that are implied in these modes, such as modeling (socialization), motivational learning (emotional formation), and valuing (character formation). But I did not consider these modes to be at least mutually irreducible in moral education. In this study I do. Moreover, here I do not see moral communication as a relatively independent mode next to other modes, but, as I said, as the common denominator of all modes (cf. van der Ven 1980; 1982; 1985; 1987a; 1987b; 1992).

29. From the perspective of comparative organization theory, coordinating, formalizing, executing professional leadership, and legitimizing can be said to belong to the core characteristics of any organization, especially the organization within formal education, i.e., the educational organization (cf. Lammers 1984; Braam 1986).

ondary, tertiary, and adult-education levels. These levels include not only the formal educational processes of schools, public or private, but also those educational processes that are organized within associations, congregations, and other institutions.

If formal education is defined as taking place within the setting of a bureaucratic, professional organization, two qualifications must be added.[30] First, the presence of such a bureaucratic, professional structure does not mean that there is no organizational variation within the various settings of formal education. For example, at the primary and adult-education levels, the degree of organization is less and the structure looser and more flexible than at the secondary and especially tertiary levels. Second, perhaps paradoxically, this organizational structure is called on to perform four basic functions: determining and categorizing the child's, student's, or adult's learning needs and interests, selecting the standard procedures and programs to use so that the desired teaching and learning processes can take place, applying these procedures or implementing these programs in an appropriate way, and testing and evaluating their teaching/learning effects.[31] I add "perhaps paradoxically" because in summarizing these four functions, I refer not to the oppressive and alienating aspects of bureaucracy, but use the term in a purely formal, neutral way, referring to organized, standardized student-centeredness.

This is not meant to say that informal and formal moral education are two entirely separate phenomena because in fact this is not the case. Their relation is a dialectical one: the educational processes taking place in informal education may be seen as the conditions for those that make up formal education, while the formal processes explicate, differentiate, and integrate at a higher developmental level the subject matter covered in the informal processes.[32]

In chapters two and three I deal with two modes in moral education

30. Mintzberg (1979, 299) distinguishes between five different types of organizations: entrepreneurial organization (or simple structure), machine bureaucracy, professional bureaucracy, divisionalized organization, and "ad-hocary." According to this classification, formal education can be said to take place in the setting of a professional bureaucratic organization.

31. According to Mintzberg (1979, 352), the professional bureaucratic structure has to perform two basic tasks: "(1) to categorize the client's need in terms of a contingency, which indicates which standard programs to use, a task known as diagnosis, and (2) to apply, or execute, that program." Here I break down both tasks into four functions in applying them to the formal education organization.

32. Educational psychologists like Piaget (1975) and social theorists like Habermas (1982; 1983) formulate the aim of educational development in terms of differentiation and integration at increasingly higher levels.

that are the substance primarily of informal education: discipline and so-cialization. Taking place in the setting of the primary group, especially the family, discipline aims at habituation and self-regulation, in such a way that the spirit of discipline, which I will discuss in greater detail later, is inter-nalized by the child in an atmosphere of open, reciprocal communication. This process is known in educational parlance as "induction." Socialization takes place in the broader community of which the family is part — the neighborhood, school, church, and so on — and aims at the internalization of the values and norms that determine this community. It is more accurate of course to speak of communities, because each person participates in more than one, and the various communities tend to socialize different value and norm systems, which may well conflict. The conflicting processes that result require the development of what I call the dialogical self, with the ability to communicate with people from other communities within a pluralist and multicultural society, with other people (interpersonal), and with him/herself (intrapersonal) in order to make choices, make decisions, and reach compromises.

In chapters four through seven, in looking at formal education at the primary, secondary, tertiary, and adult-education levels, I grapple with the core problem: What are/should be the goals of moral education, and how can we attain them most effectively? This problem has at times given rise to lively discussions and even heated debate about whether formal moral education should be cognitively, experientially, or emotionally based. In order to delineate this problem as sharply as possible, I pose the following four statements:

1. Because the aim of formal moral education is to produce a cognitive understanding of moral issues, the educational process should have as its priority to introduce the child or student more consciously and deeply to the moral and religious traditions of his/her community or communities.
2. Because, again, the aim of formal moral education is a cognitive one, it would be preferable to place less emphasis on the "extrinsic" con-tent, drawn from the moral and religious traditions of the communi-ty/communities, and to emphasize the "intrinsic" structure of the child's or student's developing moral judgment.
3. We must shift from these cognitive approaches to an experiential approach, because what really matters in the realm of morality is how one experiences good and bad in one's own life, chooses between right and wrong in one's own decision processes, and puts into practice values and norms in one's own activities. In other words, the aim of

moral education should consist in helping the child or student clarify his/her own values.

4. We should go a fundamental step further, leave behind the cognitive and experiential approaches, and focus on the emotional formation of the child or student. Moral psychology, which deals with emotions like love, justice, guilt, and shame — to name just a few — is the field where morality is nourished from emotional sources.

In chapter four, which deals with moral transmission, I look at the first of the two aforementioned cognitive approaches, which emphasizes the "extrinsic" traditional content drawn from the more or less classic moral and religious traditions in the distant as well as the more recent past. Here agreement will have to be reached on what these traditions are and how to present them in a coherent fashion, given their various and often mutually conflicting backgrounds and histories. How is it possible to introduce children and students to these traditions without resorting to indoctrination and taking away their rights of freedom of conscience and of religion? In this discussion I borrow heavily from Ricoeur's three-stage model of the good, the right, and the wise.

In chapter five, which is titled "Cognitive Development," I treat the alternative cognitive approach that focuses on the "intrinsic" developmental structure. I explain Kohlberg's developmental theory of moral judgment at the preconventional, conventional, and postconventional levels, and show how it can be legitimately applied if the so-called hard stages of moral development are transformed into "soft stages" and reconceptualized in premoral, conventional, and convention-critical stages.

In chapter six, about clarification, I describe the experiential approach that forms the heart of what is known as the value clarification movement, which aims essentially at educationally assisted self-clarification. I analyze the strong and weak points of this approach and evaluate it from a hermeneutical perspective. I also examine the implications of multiculturalism for this approach, something that the value clarification approach totally ignores.

In chapter seven, which deals with emotional formation in the moral domain, I look at how moral education should relate to emotions, the special function of emotions and their meanings — not only generally but also specifically — as I examine particular emotions like trust, empathy and sympathy, sense of justice, shame and guilt, sex and love. I argue for different types of emotional learning, such as emotional learning by observation, by experience, and by concept.

Here it is appropriate to repeat what I said before about the dialectical relationship between informal and formal moral education. From the perspective of moral education as a whole, they presuppose and complement one another. The four formal modes I mentioned (transmission, cognitive development, clarification, emotional formation) do not begin only when formal education begins. They are already present in the discipline and socialization modes, where they — fortunately — occur for the most part in a nonsystematic, nonmethodical, and unorganized way. At the formal education stage they then become explicit objectives. At this point the teaching/learning processes are intentionally structured in such a way that these modes can be explicated, differentiated, and integrated at increasingly higher levels of performance.

After having dealt with two basic modes in informal moral education (discipline, socialization) and four modes in formal moral education (transmission, cognitive development, clarification, emotional formation) in chapters two to seven, this study culminates in chapter eight with what I call education for character. I use the word *culminate* because education for character, in my view, is the highest objective of moral education. I am aware that the term *character* may be the object of misunderstandings, because it may recall the old-fashioned, ascetic, will-driven, rigid form of education that not only suppresses all competence to think and experience freely, but also and especially suppresses all potential to feel freely. Here, however, I take the term *character* in the sense of modern virtue and character ethics, which interpret the concept of character, taken from the ancient masters, in interactive and especially narrative terms. According to this narrative conception, *character* is used in the sense of the classic tragedy. Among the many examples, I see Sophocles' Antigone and Mark's struggle of Jesus in Gethsemane as the most relevant to education for character.

It is in this sense that the title of this study, *Formation of the Moral Self,* should be understood. *Formation,* which encompasses both informal and formal moral education, has both transitive and intransitive aspects. That is, formation is a dialectical process: I am not only formed, I also form myself. *Moral* refers to the three moral criteria that I owe to Ricoeur's work: the good, the just, and the wise, in a nonreligious as well as a religious way. Lastly, the term *self* is meant to be understood in an interactive as well as a communicative sense. The formation of the moral self takes place within the parameters of the developing self, which is intrinsically in interaction with its environment, especially its human environment: family, other primary groups, neighborhood, congregations, as well as the broader pluralist and multicultural society. As part of this interaction, the self is in communication with all the people it directly or indirectly contacts; and in this process of interpersonal communication, it develops its intrapersonal communication. By actively and passively, narratively and argumentatively participating in this multidimensional communication, the self tells and is told its own moral story, spins and is spun its own web of meanings, from which character emerges.

For this narrative meaning of the self, music plays an important part, not only in the strict sense of patterns of tunes and rhythms, whether with accompanying words or not, but also in the broader sense of the Greek *mousike techne*, which includes theater, dance, sculpture, and painting. Music not only brings relaxation and pleasure; it also imparts joy, nobility, and character, as Aristotle says (*Pol.* 8.5). By participating in music in this broad sense, one forms one's own self, especially one's moral self.

2

Discipline

After another child killed Ruben Bell, the forty-eighth child under the age of 15 to die violently in Chicago in 1994, a self-described "USA citizen" wrote a short letter to a local newspaper that was printed under the title "Parents' Dilemma." It read: "Children are turning into killers because no one cares enough to discipline them. Yet . . . parents, discipline your children, and we'll put you in jail and take away your kids! Pretzel logic!"

This letter is a cynical comment on the topic of this chapter. Cynicism is generally the product of two conflicting emotional processes. The first is a strongly held conviction, as in this letter, where the writer equates caring for children with disciplining them. The second process is a sense of disappointment and futility at the inability to put this conviction into practice, which leads ultimately to deep frustration. The writer implies that in today's society disciplining children is equated with cruelty, and may even be considered a criminal act. Children need discipline, says the writer, yet discipline is frowned on, and the writer closes with the cynical words: "Pretzel logic."

Despite the complaint of the "USA citizen," discipline seems to be popular not only among parents but even among children. The Roman Catholic high school in Chicago known as Providence St. Mel, located in one of the city's toughest neighborhoods, where crime abounds, poverty is everywhere, and the school dropout and teen pregnancy rates staggering, the students are proud of attending this "hard work school" and growing up with discipline. No crap shooting, no cutting class, no gum chewing, no sagging pants, no sunglasses, no biker pants or tank tops, no earrings for boys, no designs carved in the hair, no overly tight or revealing clothing. No gangs, no guns, and no drugs. The principal's bottom line is: "You, students, shape up or ship out." In an interview the students say: "He is strict on us. It's not just to be hard on us, it's to better us."

When the letter by the concerned citizen and the views of students at St. Mel are compared, discipline appears to be an ambiguous topic, welcomed on the one hand and surrounded by doubt, irritation, and frustration on the other. Why is this? The reason may be found in the essence of education in general and moral education more specifically, which lies in the tension between authority and freedom. Education is meant to develop the child's emancipation and autonomy, but it does so by means appropriate to the child's condition, means that, especially in early childhood, are carried out by persons in positions of authority and include guidance, direction, training, assignment, orders, and prohibitions. But the tension between freedom and authority, as essential as it is, is not purely ontological; it is conditioned by changing circumstances of space and time, in other words, by the societal context. This societal context can be divided into a structural and a cultural dimension. The first refers to varying economic conditions over time and their influences on political and social systems and processes. The second concerns convictions, values, and norms that people hold and live by and that also vary over time. Changes at the structural level influence changes at the cultural level and vice versa.[1] Ideas and practices in the field of education, especially those having to do with discipline, change with society's changing structural and cultural conditions.

This insight may be illustrated by historical examples of rigorism, permissiveness, and neglect. August Hermann Francke (1663-1727), spiritual director of Friedrich Wilhelm I of Prussia, was known for his extreme strictness. His thought must be placed in the context of early capitalism, which demanded virtues and behaviors such as diligence, cleanliness, reliability, punctuality, of attitudes that advance the domestication of the child (Elias 1977). Francke argued for what he called the breaking of the child's wicked will as the core of the parents' disciplining practice. This

---

1. According to Weber the relation between structural and cultural processes is a dialectical one. That is, structure determines culture, while culture functions as a switch that allows structural processes to occur: "Interessen (materielle und ideelle), nicht: Ideen, beherrschen unmittelbar das handeln der Menschen. Aber: die 'Weltbilder,' welche durch 'Ideen' geschaffen wurden, haben sehr oft als Weichensteller die Bahnen bestimmt, in denen die Dynamik der Interessen das handeln fortbewegte" (Weber 1978, 252).

will, he maintained, had to be limited and constrained, and prevented from unfolding by continuous and all-encompassing control. Every moment must be devoted to work and to keeping a diary in order to restrain and curb the child's evil inclinations. This rigorist approach must be seen in the societal context of the time, where the structural processes were characterized by early capitalistic and especially mercantilist developments within the framework of state absolutism. These structural/economic tendencies required a legitimizing ideology, and the eighteenth-century Lutheran Pietism, of which Francke was the founding father, fulfilled this need. On the one hand, this religious ideology legitimizes the educational breaking of the will by interpreting it in terms of a pious praxis — *praxis pietatis,* as Francke calls it (Blankertz 1972, 21-23; Gamm 1979, 146). At the same time, this pietism also influenced rigorist practice by relativizing and softening it. It was impressed on parents that they must practice piety themselves, especially in relation to their children. To treat their children with uncontrolled brutishness or cruelty would be sinful. Rather, they must break the child's "wicked will" with prudence, patience, and tenderness (Francke 1957).[2]

Whereas educational rigorism may be understood as an answer to economic scarcity, educational permissiveness can be interpreted as a response to economic affluence. Educational permissiveness characterizes the process of educational reform that originated in the social movements of the sixties, when student protests in Berkeley, Paris, Frankfurt, and Amsterdam expressed the general cultural atmosphere and influenced liberal educational thinking. Antiauthoritarianism became fashionable as an educational method and philosophy. Economic growth and affluence like that which characterized Western society in the sixties and seventies not only tolerate antiauthoritarian relationships between parents and children in families, and between teachers and students in schools, it actually requires them. For economic growth to remain strong, firm control has to be replaced by lax control in order to generate consumerist attitudes, or what is known as "commodity fetishism." These attitudes are formed by economic companies and delivery systems in order to broaden and deepen the markets of consumption by creating needs and demands. They are wrapped in experiences and emotions by which the intrinsic value of goods is replaced by the way they look and the image of the consumer they create by their extrinsic, "esthetic" worth. The acquisition of material goods is legitimized by the ideology of self-realization, in which satisfying one's material needs

2. This relativizing and moderating aspect of German Lutheran Pietism is often overlooked (van der Ven 1982, 76-79).

is seen as a necessary condition for spiritual growth.[3] The period we now live in, and especially the youth, have been described as narcissistic (cf. Ziehe 1975; Lasch 1979; Schulze 1992). However, it is important to understand the economic conditions underlying this narcissism, lest one run the risk of collective moralization (Bowles and Gintis 1977, 201ff.).

The third example of the relationships between economic processes and discipline illustrates the principle of neglect. The child-centeredness of modern education would seem to suggest that neglect is a thing of the past, but in fact it is not. In its sharp and massive contours it emerges in the nineteenth century, during the period of large-scale industrialization. Because of the economic pressures on families — parents as well as children — to participate in dirty, badly paid, and alienating slave labor, and the erosion of traditional communities along with their values and norms, young children in particular were neglected and suffered from financial, social, and cultural rootlessness. Between 1750 and 1850, in some places in Germany the majority of children between the ages of six and fourteen sometimes begged on the street (Voigt 1973, 66). In our own time, we see the reappearance of neglect because of new economic pressures, this time from decreasing wages, diminishing social security benefits, rising unemployment, and the reality of the family with two wage earners. Where the father or mother and most often both are extremely busy earning a living for their family, children are often left alone from morning to evening. Much of their education comes from television. Time with parents is confined to telephone contact and a few hours of quality time a week, for example, to arrange a family meeting. These parents and children meet like ships passing in the night. A well-known bumper sticker reminds adults, "Have you hugged you child today?" The "children's revolt" expresses itself in depression, anorexia, bulimia, alcohol and drug abuse, staggering rates of teen pregnancy, criminality, gangs, and violence. Between 1985 and 1992, for example, the number of murders committed by white boys between the ages of 14 and 17 in the United States doubled, and the number committed by black boys in the same age group tripled. Discipline, if it is present at all, simply does not work, because parents are not sufficiently present in their children's lives to look after them, care for them, direct them, and guide them. The result is a situation of educational neglect characterized in the words of one author as "gliding down from a normative frame of reference because of insufficient societal sup-

3. From decreasing scarcity Inglehart (1977; 1990) predicts a lifestyle increasingly oriented toward self-realization. Whether economic recession and unemployment have a negative effect on this lifestyle is a matter of debate (Clarke 1991).

port and poor help with regard to identity development" (Gamm 1979, 63).

The examples of rigorism, permissiveness, and neglect are presented here as historical varieties of valuing educational discipline. They illustrate the influences of economic structures and processes on cultural and educational beliefs. This is not to say that these convictions are only the reproduction of changes within the economic infrastructure, as if the influence is only one way. The relationship between infrastructure and superstructure is generally a dialectical one.

Along with diachronic variety, or changes over time, synchronic diversity, that is, plurality of educational practices in our own time, can also be observed. Social stratification, referring to social inequalities among groups in society, provides a good example of this plurality. These groups differ not only in their social standing but also with regard to values and norms (Turner 1984). Let us look again at examples of educational rigorism, permissiveness, and neglect.

The educational processes that take place in lower-class families, which are aiming at (their children's) vertical mobilization toward a higher class, may tend to be characterized by rigorism, as the interview with the students of Providence St. Mel shows. Few of the six hundred students come from affluent families. For most, the tuition of three thousand dollars a year is a sacrifice well worth the promise of education and a dream of hope for their children.

Children who grow up in higher-class families do not feel the same parental pressure to move upward because they are already near or at the top of the social scale. They will tend to be confronted with ideals of freedom, self-exploration, and self-realization, and their education will be far more permissive. The statistical correlation between the parents' socioeconomic status on the one hand and educational values and practices on the other must be seen in this light: the higher their socioeconomic status is, the more the parents prefer the child's autonomy, and approve, stimulate, and support his/her self-actualization (cf. Gerris et al. 1991, 216).

In marginalized families, which are influenced, for instance, by drug abuse, interactions between parents and children tend to be determined to a much larger extent by neglect. In his address on child-welfare issues in 1994, President Clinton referred to the so-called Keystone case as an example of apparent neglect. In Keystone police conducting a drug raid found nineteen children and six mothers living in appalling conditions in a West Side apartment. Most of the children were heaped on two soiled mattresses, sharing a single blanket among them. Another child gnawed at a bone dropped from the mouth of a dog. One of the children, a five-year-old boy with cerebral palsy, lay in the middle of the living room, curled up in a fetal position caused by a lack of attention to his medical condition. He had scars and cigarette burns on his torso and limbs, healing burns on his hands and legs, and whip or belt marks over his chest and abdomen. Five of the women were admitted cocaine or heroin users. A more horrifying example of neglect, educational or otherwise, would be hard to find.

If actual disciplinary practice can vary as widely as these diachronic and synchronic examples of rigorism, permissiveness, and neglect show, the question then arises: What is discipline, what is its purpose, and in what spirit should it be developed? The examination of the nature of discipline is restricted here to the period of early childhood (section 2.1). The purpose of discipline is approached from the standpoint of self-regulation (section 2.2). The question of the spirit in which discipline is to be developed is approached from the perspective of critical reflection on the three moral criteria that I owe to Ricoeur: the good, the right, and the wise (section 2.3).

2.1 Discipline in Early Childhood

In this section we look more closely at three concepts: discipline, habituation, and self-regulation. We examine what discipline is and what it means to discipline children from their second year onward. Second, we look at the goal of discipline at this stage of life, which is primarily the formation of appropriate habits that will help children learn to perform desired actions in a routine way. This is known as habituation. The goal of habituation, in turn, is self-regulation. The relationship of discipline, habituation, and self-regulation is instrumental-final in nature, an insight that I owe to Durkheim (1973).[4]

---

4. Here I am interested only in the instrumental-final character of the relationship of discipline, habituation, and self-regulation as proposed by Durkheim, not in the content of these concepts themselves. Durkheim (1973) distinguishes among three "elements of morality," of which discipline is the first. He understands discipline in terms of its spirit ("the spirit of discipline," as he calls it), which means that the child has to learn to respect the authority which is embodied in discipline. In a way typical of him (it may also be observed in his treatises on religion [1965] and suicide [1951]), Durkheim refers to the social group to which the child belongs and its values and norms. Here I leave this content of the discipline concept aside and concentrate only on the formal relation of discipline, habituation, and self-regulation.

Discipline

The relation between rigorism, permissiveness, and neglect can be visualized in terms of two dimensions: control and support. The control dimension refers to the parents' demands on the child, while the support dimension has to do with how the parents respond to the child's demands on them. Cross-tabulation of these two variables produces four cells representing four distinct disciplinary patterns. These are authoritative (high control, high support), authoritarian (high control, low support), indulgent (low control, high support), and indifferent (low control, low support), as illustrated in the table below (cf. Maccoby and Martin 1983, 39-51).[5]

The first cell, labeled authoritative, represents both high control and high support by the parents. The parents set clear standards for the child and firmly reinforce these standards by using commands and sanctions when necessary. At the same time, however, they encourage the child's growing independence and individuality. This authoritative pattern is characterized by open communication, in which the parents carefully listen to the child and also express their own views. Problems are openly discussed, rules agreed upon, and compromises aimed at. There is a give-and-take between the needs and desires of the child and those of the parents.

The second cell, the authoritarian, is marked by the parents' high control and low support. Their interaction with the child is rejecting and punitive. Whereas authoritative discipline is characterized by a balance

---

5. From a conceptual-analytical point of view Siebenheller (1990, 9), Dekovic (1991, 24-27), and Ten Haaf (1993, 4-21) are right in raising some objections against the way in which Maccoby and Martin develop four cells from these two dimensions. Here I use the scheme for heuristic-conceptual reasons only and describe the four cells from insights mentioned by its critics.

		SUPPORT	
		strong	weak
C O N T R O L	s t r o n g	authoritative	authoritarian
	w e a k	indulgent	indifferent

between the demands by the parents and the child, authoritarian discipline is determined by the absence of this balance. The demands of the parents rule over those of the children.

The third pattern of discipline can be described as indulgent. It is characterized by low control and high support on the part of the parents. The child's impulses are tolerated and even wholeheartedly accepted. There is very little or no punishment. Asserting parental authority and imposing restrictions are avoided whenever possible. The child regulates his/her own behavior and makes his/her own decisions. There is almost no discussion about discipline.

The fourth cell is labeled neglecting or indifferent. It is characterized by low control and low support. The child receives no behavioral standards and guidelines, and the parents display little interest in the child's needs, wishes, activities, or person. There is no confrontation or even contact, because the parents want to avoid inconvenience. They do not want to be involved in their child's life.

Empirical research on parent-child interaction from the second year onward reveals that, generally speaking, the authoritative discipline pattern is associated with positive aspects of child development such as activeness, independence, taking initiative and responsibility, spontaneity, social competence in interaction with peers, and lesser levels of impulsiveness, aggression, or inclination to withdraw. The other three discipline patterns lack associations with some or many of these characteristics. The conclusion that suggests itself is that neither rigorism, which corresponds to the authoritarian pattern, nor permissiveness, which correlates with the indulgent pattern, nor neglect, which equates with indifference, is desirable as a style of discipline. Instead, the optimum approach consists of an appropriate involvement in the child's person and life, that is, an appropriate combination of high control and high support. What appropriate involvement is will depend on the child's level of development. Typically, it must be high when the child is immature, and diminish as the child is increasingly able to conduct his/her life independently.

The dimensions of high control and high support that together make up the authoritative pattern merit a closer look. I distinguish two aspects associated with high control and two others associated with high support (cf. Ten Haaf 1993, 22).

High control within the authoritative pattern implies first and foremost encouraging the child toward maturity, meaning that the child increasingly initiates independent social contacts and increasingly becomes responsible for his/her own person and life. The aim of the control is the child's autonomy and independence. For that reason appropriate information, with the help of which the child is able to manage his/her life, is delivered and its processing facilitated. The child's ideas, wants, and initiatives are considered seriously; they are taken into account when agreements have to be reached and decisions made. As a result, the child's developmental tasks are accomplished in the perspective of freedom. In comparison with the authoritarian pattern, which is marked by restrictive control, the parents' high control, or demandingness, in the authoritative pattern is characterized by what is called authoritative control. In restrictive control the parents use rigid, arbitrary, and incomprehensible norms, rules, and limits. The child's compliance is obtained by force and coercion. Rules are not discussed, consensus is not strived for. The parents' authority is maintained by inhibiting the child's questions, challenges, or objections. In authoritative control the parent-child interaction is not parent-centered, but child-centered. Parents exercise their authority with the aim of the child's becoming a free, independent, autonomous person. This may be understood by going back to the Latin roots of the word *authority*. The Latin *auctoritas* and *augere* mean "to increase" and are also the source of the Latin *augmentare*, "to augment." Authoritative parental control, then, is used to help the child "increase" his/her abilities and skills, to grow in independence.

The second aspect of high control associated with the authoritative pattern is induction. Induction means that when the child is encouraged, requested, or ordered to do or to refrain from doing something, reasons are given, standards, rules, and norms are explained. Norms are not bluntly imposed on the child, but clarified so that they can be understood and agreed upon. The reasons can refer either to the child's own self-concern or to concern for other people, including peers. The first is self-oriented induction, the second other-oriented induction. In the child, this other-oriented induction may evoke empathy for harm and distress that the child has caused or contributed to in others. Research indicates that the mother's use of reasons within the authoritative pattern is positively associated with the child's empathy and prosocial behavior. But it is not enough that the parents perform induction. It is essential that the child recognize and interpret this induction for what it is. Not only the actual performance of induction by the parents, but especially the perception of induction by the child clearly contribute to open interaction between parents and child and advance reciprocity and equality in their communication (Gerris et al. 1988).

Next to the two aspects of high control in the authoritative pattern (i.e., authoritative control and induction), two aspects particular to high support within this pattern should also be pointed out. High support implies empathy, warmth, affection, intimacy, love, or, more specifically, being enthusiastic about the child's activities and experiences, expressing interest in his/her desires and feelings, stimulating the child and showing affection and interest. Empathy, warmth, and love form a necessary condition for high control or demandingness within the authoritative pattern. Without them, high parental demandingness will not challenge and stimulate the child, but instead result in specific internalized responses, such as anxiety and inauthentic shame and guilt. It is for this reason that the withdrawal of love as a technique of discipline is counterproductive, as empirical research shows. It may lead to immediate compliance but fails to produce the free internalization of norms and standards, and therefore does not result in the child becoming an independent, autonomous, free person.

The second aspect of high support that is essential to the success of the authoritative disciplinary pattern is the parents' sensitive, contingent responsiveness to the child and the signals he/she gives off. This responsiveness manifests itself in understanding questions, reassurance, encouragement in performing difficult tasks, comforting, and consoling. Although both warmth and responsiveness are part of support, warmth is expressed as a direct result of the parents' initiative, whereas responsiveness is a reaction to the child's behavior. The first involves child-oriented conversation on the initiative of the parents; the second is child-oriented conversation in response to the child's signals (Ten Haaf 1993, 55).

Habituation

The combination of high control and high support within the authoritative discipline pattern, including authoritative control, induction, warmth, and responsiveness, appears generally to be associated with positive aspects of child development (cf. Hoffman 1993). But here the question arises what specific relevance this authoritative pattern has in moral education. The answer that I elaborate on in the following is that discipline is directed toward habituation and habituation toward self-regulation. This is not to say that habituation and self-regulation are the goals of moral education in general, but simply that they are the perspective from which one of the seven modes in moral education, that is, discipline, may be interpreted.

What, first of all, is habituation? Leaving aside all historical connotations, here I am interested in its conceptual content. Habituation is the formation of behavioral habits, actions that are marked by their repetitive, routine character. Intellectual habits, competencies, dispositions, and skills are not behavioral habits. Moreover, habituation does not refer to the formation of all behavioral habits but only to certain ones. For example, nervous habits such as nail biting, snuffling, and running one's hand over one's hair, or addictive habits such as cigarette, alcohol, or other drug abuse, are evidently not behaviors that are considered worthy of being consciously taught and formed. These nervous or addictive habits can be explained by or traced back to certain causes, but they cannot be attributed to particular reasons — they are by definition irrational. This distinction between causes and reasons is fundamental. All kinds of neurotic traumas may cause nervous or addictive habits, which even may be said to serve certain purposes or goals of the individual, but they do not serve a human goal, from which reasons could be derived.[6] In other words, the term *habit* in habituation as an educational process refers to habits governed by a rule, for which reasons can be given. This reasoning or rational aspect is relevant not only to the difference between nervous or addictive habits and educational habits, but also between habits and nonhabitual automatic behavior. Certain basic physiological needs are automatically taken care of without any human intervention. The needs for oxygen, temperature regulation, sleep, and elimination are met by adequately functioning physiological reflex processes. But to relieve hunger and thirst depends on someone's repetitive action, at least from the second year onward. It is here that habituation comes in. The child must be taught the habits of eating and drinking — that is, eating and drinking in a proper way at a proper time in a proper social context. The reasons to be given are self-maintenance, welfare, and well-being (Passmore 1980, 120-45).

The word *proper* in the phrase "doing something in a proper way at a proper time in a proper social context" has both a negative and a positive aspect. The negative aspect consists in that habit formation regulates the child's wants, desires, and expected positive sensations. Here regulation has a negative meaning in the sense of refraining from action; in other words, it inhibits and corrects the child's inclination to realize his/her wants, desires, and expectations beyond certain limits. These limits are set in accordance with specific ideas and ideals with regard to education and human existence. If the child enjoys taking away somebody else's property to use or consume it against the other's will, the parent will prevent him/her from doing so or correct the behavior. If the child enjoys beating another child, the parent must prohibit that. If the child puts a ball from the street into his/her mouth, again the parent will forbid such action. These prohi-

6. Here the difference between "a goal of a man" or "goal of an individual" and "a human goal" is important, as is the difference between "an act of a man" *(actus hominis)* and "a human act" *(actus humanus)*. Only a human goal and a human act affect a human being's selfhood.

bitions may be divided into three categories, each of which has two parts. Two of them concern the child himself/herself (actions that are dangerous to self, quasi dangerous, unsavory), two concern other people (harmful to others, inconsiderate of others), and two concern situations (destruction of property, making a mess). Almost all negative actions are covered by these six categories (Lamb 1993).[7]

The positive aspect of habituation relates to situations that the child must undergo and endure, or activities that he/she must perform, even though he/she feels and shows aversion to them. If the child does not enjoy eating or going to bed, the moment will come when he/she must nevertheless do so, against his/her inclination. If the child has been refusing to do chores or homework, he/she will be forced by the situation itself or by some person to do what is required.

In short, habituation as a process implies the formation of habits by which specific positive and negative acts are repetitiously performed with a view to following justifiable self-oriented and other-oriented rules, for which reasons can be given.

Let us look now at the two control aspects, authoritative control and induction, and the two support aspects, warmth and responsiveness, in order to see how they are related to this process of habituation.

Authoritative control, which encourages the child's initiative and aims at his/her autonomy and freedom, prevents the habituation process from resulting in strict, inflexible, and rigid habits. Habits must have a certain plasticity if they are to fulfill their proper function, which is to simplify the individual's actions to achieve given ends, make them more accurate, and diminish fatigue in constantly varying situations (James 1981, 109-31).

Induction provides the reasons for the standards and rules that the child is expected to follow within the habituation process. The parents should set out these reasons as clearly and intelligibly as possible (cf. Rawls 1971, 465-66).

However, there is something paradoxical in this induction. The habits

---

7. Lamb investigated the relation between mothers' emotional intensity and numerical frequency while performing these negative actions. The intensity with which mothers prohibit their children appears to be inversely proportional to the frequency with which they take prohibitive actions. That is, their emotional involvement with regard to harm to others and the child's safety was higher than in the case of unsavory situations, whereas the number of times that they prohibit their children from doing harm to others or running a risk of danger for the children themselves was lower than in these unsavory situations, with regard to which mothers more frequently take disciplinary actions. To these six categories, Lamb added a seventh category as a kind of rest category (Lamb 1993, 24).

to be formed are explained by presenting reasons to a child that the child, because of his/her developmental stage, is not fully able to understand. This paradox can be resolved only if the reasons that are given and the way in which they are given do not interfere with the child's intellectual and emotional development. Or, to put it in a more positive way, the intellectual and emotional framework within which the habits are explained must be open-ended and quest-oriented (R. S. Peters 1974, 254-80).

The warmth in which this authoritative pattern of discipline is embedded permeates the process of habit formation and lends it a decent, dignified, and human character. From this perspective habituation and the withdrawal of love are opposites, as I noted above. In order to achieve its true aim, habituation must be surrounded by interest, affection, and love.

Responsiveness means taking the child's signals into consideration and reacting to the child as quickly and appropriately as possible. This is essential to the habituation process, as the formation of desirable habits requires the presence of another person to define standards and to provide guidance, comfort, reassurance, and appropriate feedback.

In short, taken together, authoritative control and induction prevent habituation from being guided by dysfunctional actions such as power assertion, coercion, punishment, and direct commands. When it occurs in a setting of warmth and responsiveness, habituation facilitates the growth of the child toward a state of true humanity.

Self-Regulation

The process of growing toward a truly human self sounds like an ideal that lies in the far future. An intermediate step is needed. This step can be called self-regulation.

According to Durkheim, discipline and its outcome, habituation, lead to two results that are worth mentioning here. The first is regularity in behavior. This regularity is important because the whole of social life that the child will be introduced and initiated into rests on the continuity, rules, and patterns of social cooperation. Human life is not the life of isolated monads; it does not take place in a social vacuum. It depends on living and working together, as familial, professional, and civic life reveals. This is especially evident in industrial societies. The more they are characterized by the division of labor, the more they require cooperation and hence regularity. The second outcome of discipline and habituation is the moderation of the child's needs and desires. This moderation is important, because the child by his/her very nature has no awareness or notion of limits. The child is driven by needs and wants that tend to exceed what is necessary or even safe for his/her own welfare or that of others. If allowed to satisfy all of his/her impulses and urges, the child could well damage his/her own well-being, that of his/her peers, or that of other people. Little children are not able to distinguish between the desirable and the possible. They live in an oceanic, narcissistic world, in which dreams are taken for reality. "There is one emotion," Durkheim explains, "that shows with particular force the character of the child's temperament. This is anger." Quoting Darwin, Durkheim goes on: "'When young children become infuriated,' Darwin says, 'they roll on the ground, on their backs, on their stomachs, crying, flailing with their feet, scratching and striking out an anything within range.'" Durkheim concludes: "Now, there is no mental state more clearly opposed to the self-mastery implied in discipline" (1973, 133).

In sum, both aspects, regularity and moderation, which are the outcome of discipline and habituation, shape the conditions from which the child is able to master his/her life both individually and socially. Moderation refers to the inner, individual aspects of the child's life, the drives, passions, needs, wants, and desires, which need to be kept within certain limits, not only for the sake of the child's individual well-being but also for his/her healthy social functioning in family, professional, and civic life. Here the importance of regularity comes in. It prevents the child's social life from being chaotic, unpredictable, and unreliable, and helps the child grow into a cooperative, productive, and trustworthy adult. In short, moderation and regularity prevent the child from being at the mercy of all kinds of internal and external forces that he/she does not understand and cannot control.

2.2 Discipline and Self-Regulation

Up to this point I have emphasized the progression from discipline to habituation to self-regulation. Now I will reverse the order and look back from self-regulation to discipline. I wish to examine whether the concept of self-regulation, which is the desired outcome of discipline, has something to say about discipline itself. In other words, to what extent can self-regulation serve as a perspective from which to understand the concept of discipline? The answer to this question will provide further evidence that discipline should not be exclusively associated with external, restrictive, authoritarian control and obedience. It advances a humane understanding of discipline, along the lines already inchoatively implied in the pattern of authoritative discipline, as described above.

Three Functions of Self-Regulation

In literature about self-regulation, the individual is localized in the inter-action with his/her environment, and his/her actions are explained as a function of this interaction. The individual's behavior is not the fruit of internal processes only, as it would be if it stemmed solely from rationality, affection, or will. Nor is it purely the product of external influences, as would be the case if human life would fit into the stimulus/response scheme, as described in Chapter 1.

From this interactionist framework, three functions may be distin-guished within self-regulation. These are self-observation, self-judgment, and self-reaction. They apply to all kinds of domains, including the moral domain. Together they describe what human self-regulation is and how self-regulatory human action, or self-directed change, takes place (Bandura 1986, 335-89).[8]

Self-observation means that the individual perceives and monitors the situation he/she is in and the actions he/she performs. This perception is not purely passive registration. The individual always pays special attention to specific aspects. What he/she perceives always depends on preconcep-tions, convictions, ideas, values, and interests. There is no perception that could ever take place outside the individual's cognitive map, which already contains convictions, ideals, and expectations. But emotional moods also influence what we observe. When I scan the situation I am in, whether I am feeling emotions of joy or sadness, gratitude or aggression, trust or paranoia will make a great deal of difference. Self-observation is influenced not only by individual processes but also by social ones. The person senses specific people present or acting in particular ways, attentively watches what they do or refrain from doing, and attends to how he himself or she herself acts, reacts, and interacts. The person monitors the quantity, quality, or originality of the social character of his/her own and other people's behavior and the moral nature of his/her own and these people's convic-tions, attitudes, intentions, and actions. This self-observation for the most part functions quietly and unconsciously, especially when what is being observed consists of regular procedures, habitual patterns of behavior, or routines. This changes when unexpected situations arise, undesired actions are performed, or new insights make the conventional processes problem-atic. Then the individual is warned to pay special attention to what is happening. Although perception of the self within its situation is the central

---

8. Bandura (1986) also labels the second function "judgmental process" (p. 337) and the third "self-reactive influences" (p. 350).

focus, this perception never takes place outside the social context. Self-observation always implies social observation, especially in the moral domain.

Without self-observation, self-regulation cannot take place, for self-observation provides the requisite data about the situation in which the individual finds himself/herself and which he/she wishes to change. If the dominant factors in this situation are not readily identified because of the complexity or confusion of factors, some personal experimentation may help to sort out what factors merit special attention. This varying of the individual's own functioning is also an opportunity to vary the situation itself, by which one may detect the key factors, especially when this experimentation brings rapid and relevant information. The more highly valued the domain in question, the more important this information. In any case, self-directed, corrective change starts with self-observation.

Self-observation leads to the second function, self-judgment, which contributes to setting standards. The word *contributes* is essential here, because observation itself does not establish standards, and standards cannot be established without the information provided by self-observation. In other words, the relation between self-observation and self-judgment is dialectical: without the data collected through self-observation, setting standards would take place in a vacuum, and without the standards in mind provided by self-judgment, collecting data would lack any goal or direction.

The standards determined by self-judgment stem from learning processes that take places from early childhood on. Modeling is a very influential part of these processes, especially when the standards are not only acted on by the persons who appear to function as models but also verbally expressed, clarified, explained, and justified by them. However, discrepancy between the verbally transmitted standards and those that are practiced reduces the modeling effect. This applies to hypocritical models, who preach high standards for others but do not live up to them, as well as to magnanimous models, who set high standards for themselves but are indulgent toward others. Nevertheless, hypocrisy is more disadvantageous than magnanimity, because it arouses opposition and resentment. Moreover, modeling produces the strongest effect when different models offer similar standards. If the standards of various models are inconsistent, uncertainty may result. When this discrepancy applies only to values that are not of vital interest, it is not a matter of serious concern or worry.

Parents are obviously important models, but so are peers. When parents and peers differ greatly with regard to standards, those of the peers are preferred to those of the parents because of the peers' generational and social proximity as well as their similarity in competence. Nevertheless, parental modeling appears to be an important factor in the child's selection of peers. Next to parents and peers, societal institutions, like schools, associations, congregations, and political institutions, greatly influence people's standards. The antidiscrimination movements and their promotion of values, norms, and human rights that have since been confirmed by the Supreme Court appear to have had a significant effect on the American public.

Self-judgment has two aspects. The first relates to the future, the second to the past. The first aspect concerns the goals of action to be performed. These goals indicate what dimension of morality should be achieved — for example, love, justice, temperance, honesty, or authenticity — in which context, and to what extent. Because of the dialectical relation between self-judgment and self-observation, the peculiar aspects of the situation in which these standards are to be implemented are taken into account, because being good, just, or honest in one situation differs from being so in another. This judgment according to context is applied not only to the extent to which love, justice, and authenticity are achievable, but also to the manner in which they can be achieved. The second aspect relates to valuing activities that have actually been performed. People frequently judge their past performance in areas that are important to them. For example, they compare their friendliness or unfriendliness in specific situations with their behavior in other situations (self-comparison), or compare their patience or impatience with other people's behavior in similar kinds of situations (social comparison). Causal attributions for success or failure play an important role in this regard. Both success and failure can be explained by factors that are inside or outside the person's capacity to influence them. A right action can be said to be internally caused by the person's own moral achievement or externally by what is called moral luck. A wrong action can be judged to be internally caused by the person's bad intention or externally by a combination of circumstances. Most people prefer to attribute their successes to their own performances (internal attribution) and their failures to contingencies in random situations (external attribution).

The third function is self-reaction. Self-reaction starts to operate when the standards that are established by self-judgment begin to work as incentives for action. These standards function not only as goals for actions to be performed or as criteria for actions to be evaluated, but also as incentives for concrete actions to be carried out in concrete situations.

Two aspects of this mechanism explain why the standards work as incentives. The first is that they function as values that represent people's aspirations, and are therefore considered important, relevant, and salient. The second aspect has to do with the dialectical relation between self-judgment and self-observation. Thanks to this relationship, the individual estimates the extent to which the standards are achievable in the situation under consideration. Here the expectation of attainability is paramount. Whereas the first aspect of self-reaction is perceiving the standards as values, the second has to do with the expectation of attaining those values. It is this product of value times expectation that makes the mechanism work and transforms standards into incentives (Nuttin 1981; Heckhausen 1980; Van der Ven and Van Gerwen 1990; Miles 1994).

Through this mechanism, the standards established in the self-judgment process mobilize the individual's energy and trigger his/her motivational forces. These are not so much external factors (financial reward, career advancement, and the like), but the individual's own anticipated satisfaction of desired outcomes. The individual is able to appreciate these outcomes because of the intrinsic value they represent for him/her. Performing virtuous acts falls into this category of self-incentive. Acting on the virtue of fortitude or strength is prized for no other reason than acting on this virtue. Its reward lies in acting virtuously, not in anything beyond or outside this. The same is true of the other virtues. Justice, benevolence, magnanimity, and prudence are sought for their own sake. These internal rewards are long-term ones, which may be challenged and overruled by the appeal of short-term external rewards, as when addictive overeating, drinking, or smoking leads to immediate external effects.

In short, the three functions — self-observation, self-judgment, and self-reaction — are all part of self-regulation. This threefold model shows that self-regulation should not be understood as wishful thinking that calls on people to act on unrealistic convictions and values. It shows that, on the contrary, self-regulation can be developed and improved, especially with the help of an understanding of how it functions.

Self-Regulation and Discipline

How does the paradigm of self-regulation contribute to the humanization of discipline? Or, more specifically, how is the authoritative discipline pattern, which represents an optimum approach to discipline, advanced by emphasizing self-regulation?

To answer this question I go back to the two dimensions of the authoritative pattern, that is, control and support, the former including the aspects of authoritative control and induction, the latter consisting of warmth as well as responsiveness. Self-regulation as the goal of discipline can now be considered as the direction in which this twofold control and twofold support are brought to bear. First, both control and support must be directed toward stimulating the child's capacity for experiencing and perceiving himself/herself in his/her situation, cognitively, emotionally, and socially (self-observation). Second, they must be oriented toward facilitating the child's competence in establishing standards for actions to be performed or evaluation criteria for actions already performed (self-judgment). Lastly, they must be aimed at transforming standards into incentives by balancing the values that these standards represent and the expectations of achieving them (self-reaction).

An example of how this is done in practice is health education programs in which the child is motivated to take responsibility for his/her own health. These programs focus on three groups of factors that are have been found to greatly influence the child's health behavior (cf. Kok 1985; 1987).

These three groups of factors are the child's social environment, his/her attitudes, and his/her behavioral repertoire. By reinforcing or changing some of these factors, one can shape or change the child's behavior. First, the social environment, such as family and peers with their values, norms, and habits, greatly influences the child's behavior with regard to health. The configuration of the family setting and the peer group can be varied or even changed, if desirable or necessary, thereby changing the child's action patterns. The second factor, the child's attitudes, includes such things as the preconceptions and ideas through which the child perceives his/her situation, the emotions that play a role in conceiving and processing these ideas, and the social processes that take place between the child and his/her parents, siblings, and peers (self-observation). The way in which the child judges the situation and his/her actions in the situation are highly relevant. The standards by which this judging occurs have been and continue to be learned by modeling processes in the family, among peers, and in social institutions such as the school, and it is from these that the child develops self-comparison and social comparison. They determine the goals for future actions and the criteria for evaluation of these actions (self-judgment). To the extent that these standards are seen as relevant and also achievable, they work as incentives for self-regulatory action. The rewards of this action are not primarily external but internal. Meeting the standards is experienced as something valuable in itself, to which the child is very sensitive (self-reaction). Changing elements of the child's self-observation, self-judgment, or self-reaction leads to reinforcing or changing his/her behavior. An important attitude that I have not dealt with yet is self-efficacy. This is the child's belief in his/her capacity to achieve whatever he/she wishes to achieve. Self-efficacy is perceived self-regulation, which includes perceived self-observation, perceived self-judgment, and perceived self-reaction. It can be improved by changing observation and thought patterns about oneself and the emotional reactions which these patterns evoke (Bandura 1986, 390-453). Lastly, the child's behavioral repertoire can be broadened by providing relevant information about different behavior patterns and lifestyles and by exploring them and experimenting with them.

The example illustrates how discipline is developed in the direction of self-regulation. Self-regulation is not an unrealistic objective. By learning self-observation, self-judgment, and self-reaction, the child effectively broadens his/her capacity for self-mastery. If these three functions are taken into account, discipline can assist children to develop their self-regulation in a concrete way.[9]

2.3 The Spirit of Discipline

The line of reasoning up to here started from discipline, passed through habituation, and ended in self-regulation, including self-observation, self-judgment, and self-reaction. The question we have to deal with now is, From what spirit do we develop this discipline as self-regulation? By connecting this question with the three moral criteria I owe to Ricoeur, as I indicated in Chapter 1, one can see that the moral character of this spirit is at stake here. In other words, is discipline as self-regulation to be developed from the spirit of the good, the right, or the wise? In order to answer this question appropriately, first I will deal with the spirit of the good from the perspective of communitarianism and then with the spirit of the right from the human rights movement within multiculturalism. I will conclude with some reflections regarding the spirit of the wise from the concrete situation, in which discipline takes place. But before I do this, I think it is appropriate to spend some words on "the spirit of discipline" from the perspective of the author who coined the expression, Émile Durkheim.

Durkheim's Spirit of Discipline

In order to understand "the spirit of discipline," which Durkheim (1973, 17-55) explicitly deals with in three chapters of his *Moral Education*, we need

---

9. In later years developing self-regulation remains relevant, for example, with regard to alcohol consumption by adolescents (cf. Cox 1994; Hester and Miller 1989). Self-regulation programs that include a moral perspective may have an effect of reducing alcohol consumption (Roemer 1994).

to take into account the scientific context in which he developed this idea. That context was greatly formed by utilitarian individualism, which views society as a collection of individuals who seek to maximize their individual profit at the market of exchange by advantageously balancing the benefits and costs of their future actions. Hobbes's problem, which arose out of the same context, can be formulated as: How is it possible for humans to live peacefully together in this "Wild West" market of exchange? Why do not they kill each other? Hobbes's answer is that people establish a social contract in which the exercise of power is reserved exclusively for the state. This answer does not satisfy, at least not in the eyes of some social thinkers, who do not like to restrict the problem of living together to a problem of social order — meaning the negative notion of the absence of violence — but cast it in terms of social cohesion, which has to do with the bonds that draw and hold individuals together in a positive sense. Marx opposes Hobbes's idea by saying that the market does not bring about equal exchange, but rather forced, unequal, and unjust exchange, and hence sooner or later will fall to pieces. Durkheim questions the notion of society as a collection of individuals,[10] and argues that society's maintenance depends on people being members of intermediary groups and holding values and norms in common in these groups. Whereas Marx's answer to utilitarianism is economic, Durkheim's is sociocultural. Durkheim rejects the individualistic point of view from which utilitarianism approaches society, and advocates looking at society and the groups within it. He also rejects the one-sided consequentialist approach of utilitarianism. People's social behavior does not depend only on calculating the profitable and costly consequences of their actions. Individuals also consider the values and norms of the social groups to which they belong as representing an authority worthy of absolute obedience, irrespective of the consequences (cf. Ultee et al. 1992, 77-78, 195-201).

Durkheim's emphasis on educational discipline, especially the "spirit of discipline," is part of his belief in the importance of shared values in providing social cohesion. The spirit of discipline refers to the child learning to respect the groups to which the child belongs as well as the values and norms that inhabit these groups. This interpretation of discipline and its

10. Durkheim especially emphasizes the irreducible social nature of society and of social groups in society. Hence his interest can be understood in terms of the difference between psychology and sociology, or between psychic and social facts. He defines a social fact as "any way of acting, whether fixed or not, capable of exerting over the individual an external constraint," or "which is general over the whole of a given society whilst having an existence of its own, independent of its individual manifestations" (Durkheim 1982, 59).

relevance in moral education contrasts sharply with the utilitarian approach. According to Durkheim moral education has nothing to do with learning to weigh and calculate the costs and benefits of acts to be performed: "But it is a certain and incontestable fact that an act is not moral, even when it is in substantial agreement with moral rules, if the consideration of adverse consequences has determined it. Here, for the act to be everything it should be, for the rule to be obeyed as it ought to be, it is necessary for us to yield, not in order to avoid disagreeable results or some moral or material punishment, but very simply because we ought to, regardless of the consequences our conduct may have for us. One must obey a moral precept out of respect for it and for this reason alone" (1973, 30).

In his views on punishment, Durkheim again rejects utilitarian thinking, as his evaluation of Herbert Spencer's idea of punishment reveals. Spencer follows in the footsteps of Rousseau, who is of the opinion that children should not be punished except by the natural consequences of their own actions, at least up to the age of twelve: "Émile breaks the windows in his room; we shall then restrain ourselves from repairing the damage he has done and the cold of the night will give him a cold which will be completely his own punishment." Spencer extends Rousseau's idea to the whole period of education, including the age from twelve years onward, and places it in a utilitarian framework, which is based on the balance between happiness and sorrow, or rather between benefits and costs. According to Spencer, punishment should be understood in terms of what can be called intrinsic retaliation: a good act is rewarding in itself, because it contributes to happiness, and a bad act is punishing, because it contributes to sorrow. Therefore no additional punishment is needed. By contrast, Durkheim favors external punishment. In his view punishment aims at reaffirming the values and norms at the moment they are violated by the child. It is practiced "in order to strengthen the sense of duty, both for the guilty party and for those witnessing the offense" (Durkheim 1973, 182). In other words, the authority of the values and norms violated "must assert itself in the face of the violation and react in such a way as to demonstrate a strength proportionate to that of the attack against it. Punishment is nothing but this meaningful demonstration" (ibid., 166). Durkheim absolutely rejects corporal punishment, however, because he does not see the goal of punishment as being to make the child suffer or intimidating and terrorizing him/her (ibid., 168-73).[11] This point is worth mentioning, espe-

11. Aristotle favors corporal punishment for those who are insensitive to reason (*Nicomachean Ethics* 10.9), but he is against it for children, because the child's reason is not corrupt but underdeveloped (cf. Sherman 1989, 164-65).

cially against the background that the Supreme Court of the United States has upheld a lower court that ruled that the Constitution does not prohibit corporal punishment for children. In the United States a number of states consider corporal punishment as an effective measn of discipline (Etzioni 1994, 94).

The Spirit of Communitarianism

Durkheim's ideas about discipline and punishment will be evaluated differently depending on whether one looks at them from the point of view of communitarianism or of multiculturalism, two approaches that are influential in the contemporary moral debate.

Communitarianism tends to view discipline in a positive light. In his book *The Spirit of Community,* Etzioni (1994) calls it a master key for reinventing society and for shoring up morality. Discipline is not understood as something negative, like punishment, but as concentration, impulse control, self-motivation, and the ability to face and overcome stress, as a commitment to what is good and right. Communitarianism sees the lack of discipline as one of the most important causes of the unfortunate situation of education in general and of the schools in particular. It is the lack of discipline, say communitarians, that is at the root of teen pregnancy, drug and alcohol abuse, and violence. Yet communitarianism is not blind to the risks attendant on this emphasis on discipline. Etzioni seriously takes into account the results of social-scientific research with regard to a healthy balancing of overcontrol and undercontrol (1994, 91-95). Overcontrol relates to excessive containment of impulse and delay of gratification, whereas undercontrol refers to insufficient modulation of impulse and inability to delay gratification. An overcontroller is constrained, does not reveal emotions, and tends to think rigidly. He/she is other-directed in an extremely conformist way and is not able to enjoy pleasurable events. An undercontroller is quite the opposite. He/she is impulsive and disregards habits and customs. He/she is always longing for immediate gratification of his/her needs and is generally unreliable because of the lack of consistence and coherence. Overcontrol, especially among men, is found in families with a restrictive, authoritarian discipline pattern, whereas undercontrol, among both men and women, appears to be caused by neglect of the child in families with egocentric parents. A balance of overcontrol and undercontrol, which leads to appropriate control, is found in families that use the authoritative discipline pattern described earlier (cf. Block 1971, 258-66). From the communitarian viewpoint, balanced or appropriate self-regulation is a kind of psychic infrastructure for living a moral life and acting from moral virtues, values, and norms. It may be considered as a necessary condition for morality. Balanced self-regulation is positively interpreted and evaluated by communitarianism as purposive, in the sense in which that term was used in Chapter 1, in other words, as a means to an end, a communitarian end. In short, "the spirit of discipline" corresponds to "the spirit of community."[12]

However, the problem is that the end is not reflected upon. It is already fixed and thus beyond discussion. In evaluating balanced self-regulation as purposive from the perspective of communitarianism, as I suggest, one considers community life and living in the community as an unquestionable end. This is not to say that communitarianism takes the maintenance of existing communities as the unquestioned end. On the contrary, it strives for community reform, consisting of rebuilding old and establishing new communities, in which people share common responsibilities, values, and norms, for example, in families, schools, or neighborhoods. Discipline is conceived of as the master key for reforming society into webs of communities of this kind. The habits that will be formed through this discipline are to be the habits that fit into these communities. The self-regulating self to be shaped through this habituation process is to be a communitarian self. In other words, the discipline is communitarian discipline, the habits communitarian habits, and the self a communitarian self.

The image of communitarianism that I present here is in fact incomplete, because the focus of communitarianism is not restricted to the local community, but expands in the direction of intercommunity relationships and of society as a community of communities. When specific communities cannot ensure their own survival and maintenance, they need to be able to call on communities with richer resources at their disposal for help and support. The task of the society as a whole is to stop cannibalizing communities, as Etzioni (1994, 134) puts it, and instead protect and preserve them.

---

12. Considering discipline and self-regulation as purposive does not necessarily imply a communitarian end, because it depends on one's view regarding what individual and social life are all about. The European Value Systems Study interprets self-regulation in different ways: as an attitude of innovation, which contrasts with tradition (Stoetzel 1983, 29); of imagination, which contrasts with obedience and hard work (De Moor 1983, 143, 147); of individualism, which contrasts with both social conformism and achievement (Halman 1987, 151); or of self-centered achievement, which contrasts with conformity (Ester 1993, 118). It can be an instrument in the life of a moral saint but also in that of a destroyer, whether military, political, or criminal, or all three together (cf. Steutel 1991, 59).

What is the reaction of communitarianism with regard to multiculturalism, which refers to the growing demographic, social, and cultural influence of minorities and immigrants within the existing society? The phenomenon of multiculturalism typically elicits two opposing responses by two hard-line groups. The one group, which consists of "ethnic separatists," wants young people to be initiated exclusively into the values, habits, and customs of origin of the subcultural group concerned. The other group, consisting of Eurocentric whites and their affiliates, holds that young people must be inculcated exclusively with the "canon" of Western habits, values, and norms. Communitarianism rejects the first solution as one that leads to a balkanized society, divided into a multiplicity of warring tribes. But it also rejects the second, Eurocentric, solution, because it is blind to the richness of the cultural traditions that can be brought into the society by other ethnic groups and would prevent the larger community from potentially benefiting from them. The communitarian approach is to reject or-or solutions in favor of and-and solutions — in other words, respecting the convictions, values, and norms of origin of the different groups and their subcultures and what are called the core values of democracy and human rights. Young people need to be educated from the spirit of the community of communities, which is characterized by "pluralism-within-unity" (Etzioni 1994, 155).

The Spirit of Multiculturalism

Perhaps, though, this solution is too harmonious. The exact nature of the "canon" of democratic values and human rights is far from clear. Durkheim emphasizes that "the spirit of discipline" refers to the values and norms of the groups to which the child belongs, values and norms that are, or at least are believed to be, more or less uniform. The "spirit of discipline" is a "uniform spirit of discipline." The habits are "uniform habits" and the self is a "uniform self." In today's Western society values and norms are pluriform. These values and norms cannot be considered as a system of concentric circles, of which the innermost circles constitute an unchangeable, uniform hard core, while the outer circles are variable, changeable, and pluriform. This, however, is the notion with which communitarianism appears to operate when it speaks of the varying subcultures on the one hand and the "core values" of democratic society and human rights on the other. The fact is that multiculturalism is not restricted to the "surface" of today's culture. It touches on and indeed permeates the core values as well. This is especially true of the area of human rights. Although they do belong to the "core" of today's democratic society and culture, at least in the Western hemisphere, and their roots stem from official, seemingly un-changeable declarations, which apply across different cultures from the seventeenth century onward,[13] they do not altogether escape the influence of multiculturalism. Paradoxically, the essence of human rights supports and promotes multiculturalism. Anyone who emphasizes human rights as a starting point for discipline of children intrinsically argues for respecting multicultural habits, advancing multicultural interaction, and regulating a multicultural self. Let me examine this in more detail from two different aspects, the first purely conceptual and the second moral.

To begin with the conceptual aspect, the communitarian movement, despite its strong support for human rights, advocates a so-called rights moratorium, meaning postponing for the next decade the acceptance of new rights. This is necessary, say the communitarians, because the incessant granting of new rights disturbs the equilibrium between the rights of citizens and the responsibilities they have toward their fellow citizens and society as a whole. Along with "no new rights," communitarianism also claims that several existing rights deserve reexamination. People forget, so the com-munitarians say, that rights presume responsibilities; they seek what they can take and fail to consider what they have to give in return. There are "too many rights, too few responsibilities" (Etzioni 1994, 161), and "those most concerned about rights ought to be the first ones to argue for the resumption of responsibilities" (ibid., 10).

Communitarianism therefore emphasizes a conception of discipline in which responsibilities are superior to rights, habits are responsible habits, and the self is a responsible self exercising responsible self-regulation. Who would deny that responsibility is a major concern in education in general and in the field of discipline more specifically?

The underlying idea of the communitarian attitude is what is called the principle of correlativity, which holds that one person's claim or rights correspond to another's obligational responsibilities, and that a sound equi-librium must be maintained between them. At present, according to the communitarian view, the scale is tipped toward rights and must be counter-balanced with responsibilities.

13. The historical basis of some human rights may be found in the Magna Carta (1215); the Charter of Maryland (1632); the Bill of Rights (1689) on the occasion of the Glorious Revolution, which brought William of Orange and his wife Mary to the throne of England; Virginia's Declaration of Rights (1776); the Bill of Rights (1791) that was attached to the U.S. Constitution; the French Déclaration des droits de l'homme et du citoyen (1789); and the Universal Declaration of Human Rights (1948).

The principle of correlativity is not universally accepted, however. According to the so-called will or choice theories of rights, the relation between rights and obligations is asymmetrical. That is, one person's right takes precedence over another person's duty. The reason is that the first person is not able to act in only one way, but in two different ways. Sometimes the first person uses his/her competence to make a firm claim against the second person to act or refrain from acting. But sometimes the person uses that competence to waive or relinquish the right and release the other from his/her duty. By this act the first person transforms the right into a supererogatory act, which he/she performs without being obligated to do so. This makes him/her a "small-scale sovereign," as the philosopher Hart puts it (cf. Cronin 1992, 50-61). In other words, at least some rights are prior to duties.[14]

The reason that rights and responsibilities are seen as opposites stems from a peculiar conception of what human rights are. Here the second, the moral aspect, comes in. Many voices have said in the past and continue to say that the emphasis on human rights grows out of and contributes to egocentric or even egoistic attitudes. Claims for rights are assumed to be made in the pursuit of the individual's own interests and to be preoccupied with the individual's own desires, wants, and needs. The complaint is made that people treat rights the same way they use property: from a possessive attitude, without taking into consideration the welfare and well-being of others and of the community as a whole (Etzioni 1994, 9). This charge that the pursuit of rights is egocentric or egoistic is closely connected with the charge of individualism. From the perspective of individualism, society is only a collection of individuals who all seek the maximization of their own profit. Historical analysis of the human rights movements in the seventeenth and eighteenth centuries shows that rights were invoked not only to claim freedom from feudal despotism and oppression, but also for protection of property, legitimation of acquisition, and maintenance of the existing state of welfare. The communitarians complain that this human rights individualism ruins real community life and erodes moral habits, values, and norms.

The historical connection between human rights and individualism cannot be denied. But this is not a reason to decry human rights from a moral point of view. It is necessary to distinguish between the historical origin of human rights on the one hand and today's human rights culture on the other. In today's human rights culture we are bombarded with stories, articles, and television images about people who suffer from inequality and

14. In some situations some rights are not a matter of free choice, both in one's own life and in the lives of others (Cronin 1992, 51).

discrimination, whose human rights are not respected. These people —
women, children, gays, strangers, homeless, and poor — are at the margins
of Western society, where they occupy a position similar to that of the Jews
in the eyes of the Nazis, the heathens in the eyes of the Christians, the
Protestants in the eyes of the Catholics. The human rights culture breaks
open the biased parochialism of our communities and confronts us with the
suffering of these marginalized people. It opens us to the claims for rights
that these people carry with them and challenges us to undertake advocacy
for them (cf. Rorty 1993).[15]

Whereas from an historical-individualistic interpretation human
rights and responsibilities are opposites, in today's human rights culture this
is not the case, because a shift has taken place from the "I" perspective of
self-concern to the "you" perspective of other-concern, especially toward
the oppressed, alienated, and marginalized. Respecting human rights intrinsically requires taking seriously one's responsibilities toward other
groups. This change of focus can be elucidated with the help of two systematic concepts in moral philosophy and theology, having to do with what
Toulmin calls the "ethics of strangers" (cf. Cronin 1992, 71).

Moral philosophy asks: "Why should I care about a stranger, a person
who is no kin to me, a person whose habits I find disgusting?" (Rorty 1993,
133). The answer is that this person is a human being as I am, that his/her
dignity as a human person is to be respected as mine is, and that his/her
human rights are to be taken seriously just as mine are. Why is that? The
moral claim that I apply to myself is justified if and only if it satisfies the
criterion of universality. This criterion implies that moral obligations
should not only transcend the individual's wishes, preferences, or needs but
also the convictions, wants, and desires of specific groups, communities, or
societies. They go beyond the interests of "me" and "us." They have to
"pass through the sieve of the right" (Ricoeur 1992, 170) or "the royal gate
of universality" (ibid., 206). They transcend the differences between in-
group and out-group because they apply to all people, without exception.
Therefore claims are morally just if and only if they can be accepted by
everyone whom they affect. This criterion of universality is so important
that when the universality aspect of a specific rule is in doubt, the rule
itself is in doubt (Hare 1973). In case of doubt, there are two tests. First,
apply the rule to yourself and see how you react, especially with regard to
its consequences. Second, apply the rule to other people to whom you think

15. Here I rely on Rorty's idea of the human rights culture without adopting his
rejection of philosophical foundationalism with regard to questions such as "What is
'human' in human rights?" "What is human nature?" and "Why be moral?"

it should apply and consider again its consequences (Schüller 1980). The criterion of universality as formulated by Habermas is that "Every valid norm must satisfy the condition that the consequences and side effects its *general* observance can be anticipated to have for the satisfaction of the interests of *each* could be freely accepted by *all* affected (and be preferred to those of known alternative possibilities for regulation)" (Habermas 1993, 32). Following in the footsteps of his pupil Günther, Habermas adds a special "time and knowledge index": "A norm is valid if the consequences and side effects of its general observance for the interests of each individual *under unaltered circumstances* can be accepted by all" (Habermas 1993, 37). In other words, the criterion of universality implies impartiality. However, impartiality does not mean taking the observational perspective of "he," "she," or "it," as this would make "he," "she," or "it" operate as an isolated subject. Impartiality is not a result of isolation, but of communication. It is the result of a process in which the conflicting interests of all participants involved are given their due (Habermas 1993, 40, 48-49, 180n.39).[16] By interpreting human rights from the criterion of communicative universality and communicative impartiality, a strong antidote is given to the historical interpretation of human rights in terms of egoism and individualism (Cronin 1992, 90).

Moral theology also has some fruitful thoughts to offer in this area. Human rights are based on the principle of the dignity of the human person. This is stated both in the United Nations Universal Declaration of Human Rights of 1948 and, for example, the Vatican II Constitution *Gaudium et Spes* of 1965 (no. 29). The secular and religious declarations concur in emphasizing human dignity on philosophical grounds.

Some theologians are of the opinion that recognizing and respecting human rights does not require a religious legitimation, because purely moral reasons already satisfy (Cronin 1992, 250). But as noted in Chapter 1, religious traditions, especially those of the prophetic religions, that is, Judaism, Christianity, and Islam, contain elements that recapitulate purely moral ideas from three different aspects: premoral, radical-moral, and metamoral. These are worth elaborating on (cf. Ricoeur 1975).

Let me begin with the premoral aspect, which refers, as I said in Chapter 1, to the human being as a free person, a being who lives out of

16. Here Habermas diverges from the social cognition theory of the developmental psychologist Selman, who pays a great deal of attention to the development from the participant "I" perspective to the participant "you" perspective to the observational "he" perspective, "she" perspective, or "it" perspective, as Habermas himself did in his magum opus on communicative action (1982).

the conviction that his/her constitution consists of being the author of his/her life and action and having the power-to-do. This identification of the human being with freedom as the power-to-do precedes all moral belief, value, norm, or action, and is implicit in the stories of creation, especially those in which the human being is said to be created in God's image and according to God's likeness (Gen 1:26). The dignity of the human being lies in God's relation to him/her and thus has transcendent roots that no secular or religious institution is entitled to damage. It also means that the connectedness of humans to one another is essentially rooted in God. Their being one another's brothers and sisters stems from God as a gratuitous gift to them. This is a unique idea compared with other religions in which only the ruler, the emperor, or the king is worshiped as image of God or son of God. In Abrahamic faith, ordinary man and woman are created in the image of God (Moltmann 1990). The human person has an absolute worth, is an intrinsic end in himself/herself, never simply a means to another end only, as Kant puts it in his second formulation of the categorical imperative. The stories of creation offer a religious deepening of this Kantian universal principle. That is, whoever touches the human person and this person's human rights enters sacred ground.

The radical-moral aspect relates, as I said previously, to the recapitulation of morality by religion in the sense of turning the world of moral sense, habits, and conventions upside down. Some of the most splendid examples of this revolutionary insight can be found in the stories about the covenant. It may sound paradoxical to call these stories radical-moral, because they are intrinsically connected with the Decalogue, which is seen as the coordinate system from which all morality must be developed, not overthrown. Hence it is necessary to pay special attention to the all-encompassing framework of the covenant in order to see its critical-moral meaning.

One of the most important stories of the covenant is that of Noah's ark. The radical-critical meaning of this story is that the ark metaphorically contains all people from everywhere, from all races and religions. This story can be read as the basis on which Israel establishes and should develop its relationship to the non-Jews. Jews and non-Jews, citizens and aliens, belong together.

The most important complex of covenant stories are those of Moses, especially insofar as they refer to the moral code governing the treatment of strangers. In connection with the liberation of the Jews out of Egypt, God orders: "You shall not oppress a resident alien; you know the heart of an alien, for you were aliens in the land of Egypt" (Exod 23:9). Or: "When an alien resides with you in your land, you shall not oppress the alien. The alien who resides with you shall be to you as the citizen among you; you shall love the alien as yourself, for you were aliens in the land of Egypt: I am the LORD your God" (Lev 19:33-34). God even tells his people that they themselves are aliens in their own land: "The land shall not be sold in perpetuity, for the land is mine; with me you are but aliens and tenants" (Lev 25:23). Here a fundamental-radical insight turns all property rights upside down. In modern language, not only immigrants and minorities are aliens; the members of the dominant group are aliens as well.

The metamoral aspect has to do, as I said in the previous chapter, with the paradoxes or aporias that result when purely moral ideas, values, and actions confront the tension between activity and passivity that is experienced in the dialectical relationship between body and mind, self and other, call and response. This paradox fundamentally relativizes the notion of freedom as absolute self-determination. This happens especially when I am confronted with the face of the other, who suffers, from whom the voice and the call arise: "you shall not violate me." Moral-contrast experiences do not consist of direct observation of violent processes and structures, but of being open and sensitive to the other self, on whose face these violent processes and structures have left their traces. These traces evoke a no against violence: the no of morality. This no is expressed in the prohibitions implied by the Golden Rule of religious traditions: you shall not lie, you shall not steal, you shall not torture, you shall not kill. Following in Lévinas's footsteps, Ricoeur says: "Each face is a Sinai that prohibits murder" (Ricoeur 1992, 336). This call, which reaches me through the "epiphany of the face," constitutes my responsible self, which means that not I myself but the other self takes the initiative, to which I respond. The other self initiates my moral thought and action. As a subject, the other precedes my own being a subject. As an author, the other precedes the authorship of my own moral thought and action. In short, immigrants, aliens, and minority groups constitute my subjectivity and authorship.

In order to summarize what these premoral, radical-moral, and metamoral aspects of religion mean for human rights, let me turn briefly to liberation theology. Human rights are at the core of liberation ethics. The struggle for the poor is, concretely, the struggle for their rights to housing, nutrition, health, work, and education (Galilea 1979). For that cause, Paulo Arns (later Cardinal Arns), who received an honorary doctorate from Nijmegen University in 1993, together with the Presbyterian minister Jaime Wright established the famous human rights organization Clamor. This organization can be regarded as an instrument for realizing the kingdom of God for the poor (Van Nieuwenhove and Klein Goldewijk 1994). Where people claim these rights and stand up and die as martyrs for claiming rights that the ruling powers refuse to recognize, they witness that

God's ultimate concern is the dignified life of human beings: "This ultimate concern, precisely because it is ultimate, renders plausible the ultimacy called for in the witness of martyrdom" (Sobrino 1989, 183). In the light of this ultimate concern all people will be judged on the basis of what they have done for the rights of those at the margins of society, the widows, orphans, strangers, homeless, pariahs with whom God identifies himself. The symbol of the Last Judgment places us before the challenging, essentially unanswerable question: "'When was it that we saw you hungry and gave you food, or thirsty and gave you something to drink? And when was it that we saw you a stranger and welcomed you, or naked and gave you clothing? And when was it that we saw you sick or in prison and visited you?' And the king will answer them, 'Truly I tell you, just as you did it to one of the least of these who are members of my family, you did it to me'" (Matt 25:37-40).

What does all this mean for the moral perspective from which we look at discipline as a mode in moral education? How do human rights relate to "the spirit of discipline"? One answer refers to the criterion of the good or the good life in the realm of community. When Durkheim speaks of "the spirit of discipline," he means respecting the groups to which the child belongs and the values that are held as sacred by these groups. From the perspective of communitarianism "the spirit of discipline" also corresponds to "the spirit of community," but the focus is somewhat wider. In considering society as the community of communities, communitarianism does recognize a certain degree of "pluralism-within-unity," as I said. It is open to the original cultural thought, values, norms, habits, and practices of the many different minority groups in society, the only condition being, however, that these groups in turn respect the core values and human rights of democratic societies. One might say that communitarian discipline is a kind of "community of communities" discipline, a "pluralism-within-unity" discipline. This means that children within their own communities are disciplined on the basis of the characteristic cultural traditions of those communities, and at the same time are inculcated with the democratic core values and human rights. One might say that children are disciplined into what communitarianism considers the good life.

At the same time it is important to keep in mind Ricoeur's saying that the ideas and practices of the good life have "to pass through the sieve of the right" (Ricoeur 1992, 170) or "the royal gate of universality" (ibid., 206). This is because the "good life" may imply aspects of what Piaget (1975) refers to as egocentrism and sociocentrism. Egocentrism and sociocentrism are the result of failed decentering, because one sees oneself or one's own group as the center of life and holds one's own perspective ("I" perspective) or that of one's group ("we" perspective) to be the only valid one. Decentering is the process of transcending this egocentrism and sociocentrism by taking the perspective of the other or others ("you") as a relevant or even corrective one. What Kant calls the categorical imperative of universality is the philosophical translation, purification, and perfection of the Golden Rule: "Do not do unto your neighbor what you would hate him to do to you. This is the entire law; the rest is commentary" (Babylonian Talmud, *Shabbat* 31a); "Do to others as you would have them do to you" (Luke 6:31); "You shall love your neighbor as yourself" (Matt 22:39). The Golden Rule starts from the "I" perspective, as evinced in the phrase "as you would have them do unto you." Kant's categorical imperative can be understood as a purification and perfection in that it starts from the perspective of the other, the "you" perspective, which is apparent in Kant's aforementioned second formulation: "Act in such a way that you always treat humanity, whether in your own person or in the person of any other, never simply as a means, but always at the same time as an end" (Kant 1964, 96). Here the perspective of the other is fundamental, applying both to me as an other for myself and to the external other. In other words, I must treat myself in accordance with my own dignity as a human being, and the other in accordance with his/her own dignity as a human being as well. This applies not only to relationships between "you" and "me" as individuals, but also to those between "you" and "us" as groups and communities. Here the perspective of the personal good and the community-bound good is transcended by the perspective of the impartial, universal right (Ricoeur 1992, 218ff.).

Therefore "the spirit of discipline" cannot be restricted to "the spirit of the good life in the community." It must be broadened to include "the spirit of the right," especially "the spirit of human rights," which embodies the fundamental idea of human equality without power over, dominance, or violence.

These human rights apply not only to adults but also and even more so to children, especially children from poor and marginalized social groups. According to the United Nations Declaration of the Rights of the Child of 1959, the child shall be given opportunities and facilities to enable his/her physical, mental, moral, spiritual, and social development. He or she shall enjoy the benefits of social security, and the opportunity of receiving understanding, care, and love. He or she also has the right to education. He or she shall be protected against all forms of neglect, cruelty, and exploitation. These rights contrast with the fate of children who are subjected to corporal punishment, an act that is sometimes even defended by reference to Proverbs 13:24: "Those who spare the rod hate their children, but those who love them are diligent to discipline them," as the United Nations discovered in certain situations in Britain in 1995.[17] This statement of rights also contrasts with the results of hundreds of inquiries that indicate that, on a large scale, children are neglected, unloved, and exploited by their parents, or growing up in an atmosphere of aversion and indifference (Suchodolski 1979). The right to education is officially declared by the Catholic Church in the Vatican II Constitution *Gaudium et Spes* and the Declaration on Christian Education, both dating from 1965. *Gaudium et Spes* is concerned with the dignity of the human person and the rights that must be respected for this dignity to be developed. One of these is the right to education. The Declaration says: "All men of every race, condition and age, since they enjoy the dignity of a human being, have an inalienable right to an education that is in keeping with their ultimate goal, their ability, their sex and the culture and tradition of their country, and also in harmony with their fraternal association with other peoples in the fostering of true unity and peace on earth." This is the first time the Catholic Church transcends its traditional concern for the right to Christian education and stresses the right to education in general for all children based on their own culture and tradition. It unselfishly and disinterestedly does so in the very first sentence of the very first chapter of the Declaration (Hurley 1966, 66).

From this perspective, interpreting discipline in terms of the child's rights is clearly different from viewing discipline, habituation, and self-regulation predominantly in terms of the child's responsibilities, as is the case with the communitarian approach. Instead, discipline is based on a recognition of the child's freedom and dignity as a human person, as well as on equality as the cornerstone of human rights in general (Lukes 1993).

The emphasis on freedom and equality fits in with the authoritative discipline pattern described in the previous sections of this chapter. This pattern is characterized, as I said, by two dimensions, control and support, made up, respectively, of the dual aspects of authoritative control and of induction, warmth, and responsiveness. These aspects are necessary, albeit not sufficient, conditions for children to grow up as free and equal human beings.

The Spirit of Wisdom

Do "the spirit of the good" and "the spirit of the right" give enough moral direction to enable us to determine the spirit in which discipline, habituation, and self-regulation should be actualized? From the concrete good life

17. *Nieuwe Rotterdamse Courant Handelsblad*, Feb. 11, 1995.

in concrete communities we have moved to the abstract, impartial, universal question of the right, especially in the context of human rights, and now we double back to concrete life as it occurs in the concrete situation of the here and now. According to Ricoeur, this turning back to the concrete situation must take place from the perspective of wisdom. It means applying the idea of the good life within the concrete situation, after this idea has been put to the court of justice and purified by the principles of the right. Applying the idea of the good life in the concrete situation is thus intrinsically a critical act, and this critical application requires taking the perspective of wisdom.

To Ricoeur, wisdom is wisdom-in-situation, which implies considering all relevant aspects that determine the two main and interrelated features of every concrete situation: singularity and contingency. Let me explain these two features and show how they are relevant to the spirit of discipline from the perspective of wisdom.

Singularity refers to the uniqueness of the situation, and it means that general ideas or principles cannot be applied without qualification, because to do so would damage exactly those characteristics by which one situation is distinguished from another. To give an example, let me return to the categories of prohibitions that play an important role in the child's discipline. Harming others appears to be the activity of the child that mothers are most concerned with and prohibit most intensively (Lamb 1993, 25). From a communitarian point of view, harming other people, especially peers, does damage to the idea of the good life of mutual support and connectedness in the community, and must be prohibited for that reason. From a multicultural and human rights perspective, it is harmful activities directed at people, especially peers, belonging to (other) subcultural or minority groups that must be most severely prohibited. These are general principles. In applying those principles, it makes a difference whether the child whose harmful activities are to be prohibited belongs to the dominant societal group or to a minority group, and whether the child the activity is directed toward is a member of the higher classes or of the marginalized pariahs. Much also depends on the individual and social biography of both children, by what kind of emotional processes they are formed or deformed within their family, and what sort of relationship exists between them. Lastly, the positive or negative moral influences the children are exposed to from the various social environments they inhabit, the positive or negative moral models they confront, and the positive or negative disciplinary patterns they grow up with, that is, authoritative, authoritarian, indulgent, or indifferent, will also contribute to the singularity of the situation. This is not to say that harmful activities by some children in some situations should be tolerated, but that the moment at which, the manner in which, and the extent to which prohibitions, sanctions, and punishments are imposed will be determined by taking into account and weighing all relevant factors that contribute to the singularity of the concrete here-and-now situation.

Contingency refers to the fact that the concrete situation is not as it is out of necessity but is only an occasionally realized possibility. A concrete situation is a situation that comes into being by chance and ends by chance as well. It is not a human creation, construction, or production, which is not to say, however, that people do not have a hand in forming the situation into what it stands for. Contingency is based on a dialectical process, which means that the actor forms the situation in which he finds himself. Here passivity and activity come together. What does this mean for the spirit of discipline? An example can be found in the process of stimulating the child's prosocial behavior in order to routinize it into habitual patterns, so that he/she learns to conduct self-regulatory prosocial activity. From a communitarian perspective, the empathy and sympathy that a two-year-old is inchoatively capable of need to be developed toward members of the child's community, especially toward peers. From a multicultural perspective, this empathy and sympathy need to be developed also toward members of other communities who may be different in class, race, skin color, or religion, especially when they are in need. In both cases, certain limits must be considered, both with respect to the child who develops prosocial behavior and the child who receives it. The giving child may suffer from some deficiency in his/her capacity to respect the freedom and equality of an other child, because, for example, he/she has grown up in a center care arrangement, where the child's social competence is less developed than in a home care environment (Clarke-Steward 1991). It is not impossible that this may result in social retardation, which may lead to a sedimentation of a lack of social habituation and character. By this sedimentation, the growth of selfhood may be endangered, which means that one cannot socially interact and communicate the way one really likes, because a gap exists between ability and desirability.[18]

Certain limits may exist on the side of the receiving child as well, however. Perhaps the child suffers from an incapacity to accept sympathy and support, so that in a sense receiving may be more difficult than giving. This applies all the more if the two children are from different social and cultural backgrounds, and intercultural communication habituation is required. Without this kind of intercultural habituation, the child who is

18. In case of such sedimentation, Ricoeur (1992, 121) would speak here of the overlaying of *ipse*-identity by *idem*-identity.

supposed to be on the receiving end may develop resistance and rejection toward the sympathy and support shown by the giving child, because the recipient unconsciously feels inferior or that he/she is being treated as inferior (cf. Pedersen 1988). All of these factors, which together constitute the contingency of the situation, mean that acting with wisdom in the concrete situation can be a complex challenge. That challenge is always met only to some degree, because it is fundamentally impossible to control all factors that determine its operation.

More generally speaking, the processes of discipline and habituation in the specific situation in the here and now affect the extent to which self-regulation can be developed. In other words, self-regulation is a limit concept, the operation of which is determined by the dialectics between activity and passivity, self-determination and suffering. If this dialectical relationship is not taken into consideration, self-regulation deteriorates in the direction of its opposite, fanatical self-mastery, which in the end leads to self-slavery. Here the spirit of wisdom is important because it provides an awareness and respect for the relationship between ability and desirability. It takes all relevant factors into consideration by weighing them in terms of the practical question of what action is both desirable and achievable in this specific situation. The spirit of practical wisdom-in-situation consists of a practical judgment about what to do in the concrete situation in the light of the singularity and contingency of that situation.

3

Socialization

In the fall of 1994 in Chicago, two boys, age 10 and 11, with long police records, threw five-year-old Eric Morris from a 14th-floor window because he would not steal candy for them. The older boys, apparently angry that Eric would not shoplift for them, had lured Eric and his half-brother Derrick, 8, into a vacant apartment. They grabbed Eric, police say, pushed him over the 14th-floor window ledge, and hung him by the wrists. As Eric swung against the side of the building, Derrick tried desperately to save his brother. But when one of the boys hit him hard on the hand, he lost his grip on Eric's arm. Neighbors heard a scream. "He hit the ground and he was all broken up," said a girl, 13, who saw Eric fall. "His face and everything was all bloody and he did not have no teeth. He was spitting up blood." Eric died of massive internal injuries. Police reported that the boys, both of whom have a father in prison, admitted to the crime. A professor of law commented: "Kids who have been as minimally socialized as these kids pose a threat." In his speech during the annual meeting of the International Association of Chiefs of Police in Albuquerque, President Clinton referred to this case: "Kids are going to look up to somebody, and it is up to the adults in this country to decide who they are going to look up to. The 5-year-old looked up to parents who had taught him the difference between right and wrong, but who did the other two kids look up to? Who did they come in contact with? Who could have taught them right from wrong and did not? . . . But what we must worried about is wave upon wave upon wave of these little children, who do not have somebody both good and strong to look up to, who are so vulnerable that their hearts can be turned to stone

81

by the time they are 10 or 11 years old. And when there is a good one —
a 5 or 10-year-old kid in different circumstances, blooming like a flower in
the desert, knowing that it is wrong to steal candy, he actually has his life
at risk."[1] During the funeral in the Holy Angels Catholic Church in Chicago,
which was packed, Father Dennis Riley said: "In the body of Eric, there
lived the spirit and the soul of a saint." "Our newest saint," he concludes,
"St. Eric Morris." The service lasted two hours. Through everything that
was said — "no to violence, yes to discipline" — the atmosphere was heavy
with one hope: that Eric did not die in vain. At the end of the service,
Father Riley promised: "We can stop the violence, if each of us has the
courage that he had, the courage to say 'no,' the courage not to make
excuses." In the middle of the gospel songs, the prayers, the tears, 11-year-
old Joe stepped onto a stool behind the lectern. He read a poem, which he
had hand-printed on lined paper, recalling the park called Sunshine where
he and Eric used to play. It was titled "Eric": "I would bet my last dime/you
and the angels in heaven are having a great time/Just like we did in
Sunshine."[2]

The Eric Morris case, a case of children murdering children, raises
many questions about socialization. First, some people commented on Eric
Morris's cruel death in terms of discipline, as the liturgy report — "yes to
discipline" — indicates, while others, like President Clinton, responded
with thoughts about socialization. What is the relationship between discipline and socialization? As noted in Chapter 1 in the discussion of the
different modes in moral education in general, there is some overlap between the modes of discipline and socialization, but their cores are mutually
irreducible. The overlap is attributable to the fact that discipline aims not
only at the formation of individual habits, such as eating, drinking, and
sleeping, but also at the development of social habits, such as cooperation,
empathy, and sympathy. This habituation is directed toward the development of self-regulation, which is not restricted to moderating the child's
inner drives, passions, and needs, but also governs regulated, that is, predictable and reliable, social functioning in groups, such as the family, peer
group, or day care center. Habituation-based self-regulation can be considered the infrastructure of socialization inasmuch as the latter builds on
and continues along the lines of the former. If the relation between discipline and socialization is visualized as a Venn diagram, however, the two
sets may overlap while their centers do not coincide. They cannot be
reduced to each other. In the case of discipline the emphasis is on the

1. *New York Times,* Oct. 18, 1994.
2. *Chicago Tribune,* Oct. 21, 1994.

individual child who enters into progressively larger and more complex groups, whereas socialization refers directly to the social processes that take place in those groups and in which the child must learn to participate. From the perspective of interaction between the individual and his/her context, which was examined in Chapter 1, discipline refers primarily to the pole of the individual child in his/her relation to groups, while socialization relates to the pole of the social life of those groups, the processes of which the child must learn to engage in.

Then, President Clinton refers to the "adults in this country whom the kids have to look up to." Do they really exist, the "adults in this country," and who are they, aside from being particular socialization agents within particular socialization settings? What is the relationship between the various socialization agents, such as parents, siblings, peers, teachers, club leaders, pastors, or television heroes, and between the different socialization agencies, such as the family, neighborhood, school, association, church, or television? The words "adults in this country" suggest a uniformity, whereas speaking of agents and agencies points to pluriformity or even plurality. Pluriformity refers to differences in form but not content, whereas plurality, when explicitly used in contrast to pluriformity, also relates to differences in content, in this case differences in the content of convictions, values, and norms.

To speak of "adults in this country" obscures not only the pluriformity and pluralism that exist among and within families and schools as such, but also and more seriously that which exists among and within families and schools from different social strata and different cultural communities. It glosses over the influences of social stratification and multiculturalism. Socialization does not occur in a free cultural zone. It takes place in the struggle between the dominant stratum of the middle class and the lower social strata, as well as in the struggle between the society's dominant culture and its subcultures or countercultures. Nor do these struggles always take the form of a dispassionate dialogue between different social strata and cultural groups. Often the exchange is complicated or even prevented by harsh criticism, protest, demonstration, provocation, aggression, and crim- inality, any or all of which may actually be internalized by the younger generation through socialization, and may be an expression of a particular group's lack of social prospects as manifested in lack of adequate housing, schooling, work, social welfare, and security. The concept of moral social- ization therefore must take into account the aspects of social stratification and multiculturalism and their societal implications of alienation and op- pression.

President Clinton spoke of children "looking up to adults." This "looking up to," in the president's mind, probably referred to some popularized Freudian conception of identification: the child looks up to a person with whom he/she identifies. Two different forms may be distinguished: dependent and defensive identification. Yet speaking of only one "somebody" does not correspond to reality, because a (multicultural) plurality of "somebodies" socialize the child. Not only the father but both parents, school teachers, leaders of clubs or sports organizations, church members and pastors, and especially peers influence the child. The psychoanalytic definition of identification, in which identification may be dependent (the child identifies with his/her parents and imitates their values and behavior because by doing so he/she ensures the parents' continued love) or defensive (the child, usually the boy, identifies with the father because he/she fears punishment, e.g., castration, for expressing his/her incestuous wishes toward the mother and murderous drives toward the father), is not conceptually satisfying because he/she assumes that the child only or mainly develops dependent or defensive identification with the parent(s), whereas in fact a plurality of socialization agents in a plurality of socialization agencies influence the child. A different conceptualization of socialization is needed, one that takes plurality and multiculturalism into account.

Finally, what are the purposes and the effects of socialization? Is the aim to "say no to violence," as those who spoke at Eric Morris's funeral put it? As understandable as this negative formulation may be, is this the only aim of socialization? Is violence only one form of social evil, or is it the fundamental principle, because it contravenes the Kantian categorical imperative: "Never treat the other person simply as a means, but always at the same time as an end"? Is saying no to the evil of violence the only possible response because, in the final analysis, morality cannot do otherwise than take the form of a prohibition: the no of morality (Ricoeur 1992, 221)? President Clinton mentioned a positive aim: teaching and learning "the difference between right and wrong." What is this difference and who establishes it? But even more fundamentally, is learning "the difference between right and wrong" the alpha and omega of moral education, especially socialization? Why should socialization be restricted to the right and not include the good, or even set the good above the right? Eleven-year-old Joe, referring to the shared playtimes in Sunshine Park, felt the good life important enough to read a poem about it at Eric's funeral.

These questions and problems form the background of the present chapter. I begin by examining the nature of socialization, especially as it applies to moral convictions, values, and norms, within the frame of reference of the theories about socialization and internalization developed by Berger and Luckmann (section 3.1). The next step is to look at the problems associated with this socialization theory, by critically analyzing the three different levels covered by Berger and Luckmann: the levels of society, interaction, and the individual. Then I present some thoughts with regard to the socialization of the self, in other words the dialogical self (section 3.2). Finally, I examine the moral implications of this socialization of the dialogical self — that is, the moral self (section 3.3).

3.1 Socialization and Internalization

It is remarkable that the socialization of morality does not count as a special subdiscipline or dimension within socialization in general. There is no such thing as a theory of moral socialization. This is surprising, considering the many different paradigms — for example behavioral, psychoanalytic, structural-genetic, functionalistic, system-theoretical, role-oriented, interaction-oriented, society-oriented, or biographical — that exist in the field of socialization theory and research. The neglect of moral socialization is even more surprising in view of the dimensions that are dealt with in the literature about socialization, which range from gender and health to linguistic, cognitive, emotional, political, or religious socialization.[3] One of the few exceptions is psychoanalytical studies, which do deal with moral socialization. But the importance that these studies accord to the oedipal phase, in which the moral apparatus, including the conscience, is established, is too restrictive to function as a basis for understanding the multifaceted phenomenon of moral socialization. For example, in psychoanalytic theory the thrusting of autonomy on the child by the mother is labeled as the "mother's paternalistic anal culture." This interpretation is too narrow to provide an authentic understanding of the plurality of aspects that together constitute the problem of developing autonomy in today's society and culture (cf. Mertens 1991, 93).

Because there exists no theory or theories of moral socialization, I draw here on a theory that is closely related to the topic of this chapter. This is Berger and Luckmann's theory of the socialization of knowledge. The subject of socialization takes up about one-third of their *Social Construction of Reality: A Treatise in the Sociology of Knowledge* (Berger and Luckmann 1967; cf. Berger and Berger 1972). In this study "knowledge" does

---

3. Hurrelmann and Ulich (1991) distinguish the paradigms and dimensions mentioned, although they do not look at religious socialization, which is perhaps somewhat less underdeveloped than moral socialization is (cf. Van Bolhuis 1987; Henau and Schreiter 1995).

not primarily relate to theoretical thought, but rather to pretheoretical and even preconscious ideas and rules that are part of actual living in a particular society. Knowledge here is the whole of beliefs and principles that are taken for granted; it is plausible commonsense knowledge in a common life-world.[4] Because of its social character it precedes the individual; it is prior to his/her experience and imposes its order of meaning on him/her.[5] One of the central aims of the sociology of knowledge is to describe and explain how new generations are introduced into the order of meaning that the older generations inhabit. What processes take place, what mechanisms play a role in the intergenerational interaction by which the young are initiated into the existing life-world and its order of meaning? These questions, which Berger and Luckmann raise, have to do with what can be called the socialization of knowledge or meaning.[6]

From the perspective of this sociology of knowledge, moral convictions, values, and norms belong to the existing order of meaning. They form an essential part of the commonsense knowledge of the shared life-world. They determine what the good life is in a particular society, how to strive for it, and how to live and behave. They provide moral meaning. Moral socialization can be seen as the socialization of a particular domain of knowledge, in other words, the socialization of moral meaning. This is the process by which new generations are initiated into the moral order of the existing ones, by which the young recognize, accept, and lastly internalize

4. The history of the sociology of knowledge has its roots in various theories, such as those of Karl Marx (human consciousness determined by social class) and Wilhelm Dilthey *(Sitz im Leben)*. The term was coined by Max Scheler, who stresses the social location of knowledge. Karl Mannheim develops the sociology of knowledge further with his ideology concept. Instead of developing a radical conception of the sociology of knowledge, in which ideology refers to social corruption, he elaborates a moderate conception using the term *relationism* to indicate the relation between social context and social knowledge. Alfred Schütz especially influenced this moderate conception by stressing the social distribution of knowledge, which refers to the mutual relations between different forms of knowledge and different social groups in society. For Berger and Luckmann social distribution is not a central concept, although they refer occasionally to it (Berger and Luckmann 1967, 1-18).

5. The priority of knowledge as the common order of meaning over the individual is one of the tenets of the theory by Berger and Luckmann, which they refer to in terms of institutionalization. Institutionalization may be understood as the institutionalization of this knowledge (see further below).

6. This socialization of knowledge in the sense of Berger and Luckmann is quite different from what is called cognitive socialization. The first refers to the sociocultural context of the symbolic order of meaning, the latter to the sociocultural factors that influence the child's intelligence, thought patterns, cognitive styles, and memory strategies (Huber and Mandl 1991).

the moral convictions, principles, and rules passed down to them by the old. I should make clear here that Berger and Luckmann do not explicitly deal with moral socialization, but only with socialization in general. I believe it is appropriate, however, to apply their concept of socialization more specifically to the moral domain, because this domain is a dimension of the order of meaning, to which their entire study is dedicated.

Primary and Secondary Socialization

Berger and Luckmann distinguish between primary and secondary socialization, from which one may deduce the distinction between primary and secondary moral socialization. Primary moral socialization refers to the comprehensive and consistent induction of the individual, as Berger and Luckmann might say, into the world of moral meaning in general.[7] It enables the individual to take part in the common life-world and its moral meanings. Secondary moral socialization is the induction into the moral principles and rules that are part of the professional roles that individuals play in society. It is based on the division of labor, which creates various "subworlds" and thus various "suborders" of moral meaning.

Socialization as induction comprises cognitive and affective aspects. The cognitive aspects involve the pure knowledge, comprehension, and skills that are required in order to participate in the common symbolic order. The affective aspects are important in that they concern the emotional identification of the individual with significant others, from whom he/she takes over the moral meanings of convictions, attitudes, virtues, and actions. Through this identification the individual internalizes and personalizes these meanings. This identification gives him/her an identity, a self.

As the child grows older, the cognitive and affective aspects together engender a continuing abstraction process by which the child generalizes from his/her significant others to the generalized other, as Berger and Luckmann put it in Meadian terms.[8] They give the example that the child learns to generalize from "Mummy is angry with me *now*" to "Mummy is

7. Berger and Luckmann (1967, 130) define socialization as "the comprehensive and consistent induction of an individual into the objective world of a society or a sector of it." The word *objective* here refers to the universe of symbols, which overarches social reality, defines its meaning, and symbolizes it in such a way that it takes the shape of an external reality which imposes its structures and forms on individuals.

8. Berger and Luckmann (1967, 205) pay explicit tribute to George Herbert Mead's symbolic interactionism, as their notes 3, 6, 7, and 9 indicate.

angry with me *whenever* I spill the soup" to "All significant others are angry whenever I spill the soup" to "*everybody* is against soup-spilling," all the way to the abstract norm "*One* does not spill soup" (Berger and Luckmann 1967, 132-33).

This abstracting identification process is characteristic of primary rather than secondary socialization. When the time comes for secondary socialization, the individual has already developed and completed the process of intellectual abstraction. Moreover, professional role socialization, which is what secondary socialization consists of, does not always require a process of identification as strong as that which occurs in primary socialization. It ranges from low-profile identification in the case of jobs such as engineer or company manager, to high-profile identification with functions such as diplomat, musician, or priest, which are frequently referred to as "callings."[9] Because of their high profile, the latter professional socialization processes, including their moral dimensions, take longer, especially in the case of becoming a priest, because the plausibility structure of the religious context has fallen away in modern society.

Socialization, including moral socialization, is not a one-sided process, neither in its primary nor in its secondary form. The child or individual is not only the object of socialization but also the subject. This is because the child's/individual's significant others always make a selection from the symbolic universe, for they are not capable of transmitting it in all of its infinite dimensions and aspects. At the moment the individual becomes conscious of this selection, because he/she sees it as the particularization of the whole symbolic universe, he/she has the ability to complement and correct what he/she has already been socialized to. In other words, in light of the social distribution of knowledge, including moral knowledge, the individual who reflects on the knowledge that is passed on to him/her becomes aware of complementary or corrective knowledge that originates in social positions other than his/her own. Because this reflection is an ongoing process, the dialectical relation between the objectivity of the symbolic world and the subjectivity of personal identification is an ongoing process as well. It implies an "ongoing balancing act," as Berger and Luckmann put it (1967, 134).

Both primary and secondary socialization depend heavily on language and speech. The symbolic order of meaning, including its moral dimension, is transmitted to the individual child in linguistic structures. From his/her

---

9. Bernfeld (1973) holds the ironic opinion that to become a diplomat one needs only a short period of time in order to acquire the necessary cognitive skills, but a much longer period to internalize all kinds of social and moral abilities.

significant others, the child internalizes convictions, beliefs, values, and norms according to pragmatic patterns, which are based on various semantic and syntactic forms. Language itself must of course be socialized in order for linguistic competence to be developed. And this linguistic socialization is a necessary condition and means of internalizing the content of the symbolic world, including its moral conceptions, ideas, principles, procedures, and norms.

Berger and Luckmann's socialization concept consists of what can be called a multilevel approach. It comprises three levels to which every socialization concept must refer: the macrolevel of society, the microlevel of the individual, and the mesolevel of interaction. At the macrolevel of society, socialization initiates the child into the society's symbolic universe, including the moral dimension. At the microlevel of the individual, the child is not merely reduced to the object of socialization because, in the process of reflecting on the knowledge passed on to him/her in light of his/her social distribution, he/she dialectically combines selected parts of the symbolic universe and establishes his/her own moral package. At the mesolevel of interaction, the child internalizes the convictions, beliefs, values, and norms he/she adopts from the various significant others with whom he/she is in intense communication. Through this identification, the child develops his/her dynamic identity, his/her own dynamic self. All of this is realized in and through speech acts in multifaceted pragmatic-linguistic settings.

Socialization and Institutionalization

Berger and Luckman's socialization concept is located within the larger framework of their institutionalization theory. That is, they approach society from the viewpoint of institutionalization. Within that approach, socialization is conceived as the internalization of this institutionalization by the individual. They call institutionalized society "objective reality" and its internalized counterpart "subjective reality." Because socialization provides the intergenerational link between "objective reality" and "subjective reality," it is worthwhile to explain what is meant by "institutionalization."

Berger and Luckmann distinguish among three moments, as they call them, of institutionalization, which are dialectically related to each other. The first moment, externalization, has to do with the fact that people produce institutions by externalizing their social relations, the relations between and within groups. They express these relations and put them outside themselves by establishing particular social patterns. Thus relations with friends, fellows, or bosses would be externalized as "friendship," "fel-

lowship," or "employee-employer relationship." The second moment, ob-
jectification, relates to the fact that people objectify their institutional group
life, meaning that they consider this group life more or less as "objective
reality," because it is not only outside themselves but also and especially
independent of them. In other words, people adapt to the institutions that
impose themselves on them. They speak of "friendship," "fellowship," or
"job" as a thing, an objective social reality, which "acts back on" its pro-
ducers, as it were. The third moment, internalization, has to do with the
phenomenon that people develop a plausibility structure for justifying the
institutions they produce. They establish a "symbolic universe" in order to
give meaning to the existing institutions. They build a "canopy of legitimations, stretching over it a protective cover of both cognitive and normative interpretation" (Berger and Luckmann 1967, 62). From this "symbolic
universe" or "canopy of legitimations" Berger and Luckmann interpret all
kinds of systems and strategies of meaning, such as myths, stories, conversation, (auto)biography, therapy, worldview, religion, philosophy, and theology, that are developed and manipulated to guarantee the institutions'
survival and continuation. Moreover, this analysis enables Berger and Luckmann to offer a dynamic theory rather than a static one, because the three
moments, as I said, are dialectically related. Their mutual relationship may
be understood as a dynamic spiral.

   According to this theory, socialization functions as one of the most
important means for the survival of institutions. Whereas social control
guarantees the adult generation's attachment to the institutions, socialization binds the new generation to them. The members of the younger
generation are initiated into the "canopy of legitimations," learn their cognitive and normative meaning, and internalize them. Through this internalization, they create their personal identity from their identification with
the institutions and their legitimations. They come to embody and incorporate the institutions; they live in them and from them. In a sense, they
are these institutions. This relationship between institutionalization and
socialization is a strong point of Berger and Luckmann's theory. Their study
counts as one of the few attempts in sociology to bridge the gap between
macro-, micro-, and mesosociological levels of analysis, binding together
society, interaction, and the individual (Wallace and Wolf 1991, 313).

3.2 Socialization of the Dialogical Self

As impressive as the synthetic quality of Berger and Luckmann's socialization theory is, some critical remarks relating to the three levels I just

mentioned — the macrolevel of society, the mesolevel of interaction, and the microlevel of the individual — are nonetheless in order.[10]

The Macrolevel of Society

At the macrolevel of society, the first criticism relates to the assumption that a society's "symbolic universe" is one and uniform. This is one of the cornerstones of Berger and Luckmann's analysis. The essential function of the "canopy of legitimations" is that it justifies the various institutions precisely by relating them to each other, that is, by integrating them from and within an overarching framework. This symbolic universe regulates the whole of processes within institutional life, orders their history, and renders the various institutions plausible by applying to them one coherent vision. It even understands deviant versions of the symbolic universe and explains individual and collective heresies. It gives meaning to the "objective reality" of the institutions and the "subjective reality" of the individuals within them. It interprets their biography, their daily life, and especially the marginal situations in which they find themselves, such as guilt, illness, dying, death, and mourning. It "locates" these marginal experiences (Berger and Luckmann 1967, 101).

One may ask whether Berger and Luckmann are right in stating that the "symbolic universe" is one and uniform, or at least whether this qualification applies to today's society. The only pluriformity their theory accepts is the social distribution of knowledge, the social distribution of the "symbolic universe" along the various strata in society. In other words, the symbolic universe is one, uniform whole, but some parts of it are more represented in some groups and other parts in other groups. Berger and Luckmann acknowledge that they do not emphasize this social distribution of knowledge as strongly as does Alfred Schütz, although they borrow their main ideas from him (Berger and Luckmann 1967, 16). Today's socialization research does not speak of the social distribution of parts of the common

10. Berger and Luckmann's socialization concept might be considered as "the most repressive form of socialization" from Habermas's perspective, which refers to integration, identification, and conformism (Habermas 1973). However, Berger and Luckmann follow the paradigm of Mead's symbolic interactionism, from which they borrow their most important insights in order to relate socialization and internalization. The Meadian paradigm can be seen as a critique on the monological "most repressive form of socialization," because it takes into consideration the dialogical interaction between the child and his/her educators and the development of the child's self that results from this interaction (cf. Ziebertz 1990, 36ff., 48ff.).

belief and value system among different groups, but of a plurality of connections between different social strata and different moral styles and patterns. The idea of commonness is replaced by diversity. As an example, lower-status urban subcultures consider it normal and right for a boy to lie to the authorities, steal from public corporations, and be sexually promiscuous, whereas children from higher strata are prohibited from doing these things (Kay 1975, 53). At a more abstract level, some significant relations are found between social structure, especially occupation, experienced occupation, socialization styles (such as coercion and induction), and child development (Steinkamp 1991).

The concept of institutional differentiation makes problematic the oneness and uniformity of society and its "symbolic universe." Institutional differentiation refers to the phenomenon of the increasing distance between and autonomy of societal institutions with regard to each other and to the emergence within these institutions of subinstitutions, which in turn become more distant and more autonomous. This process is based on the growing division of labor, which is a characteristic of modern society. Whereas in the past the societal functions were embedded in the matrix of family and religion, we now have economic institutions with their own autonomy and laws in the realm of property, money, markets, labor, and productivity; political institutions with their own bureaucracies at the various levels of the city, county, state, and nation; legal institutions with their own territories, competencies, rules, and procedures; social institutions with their own codes, patterns, habits, and customs; and lastly a large number of cultural institutions, such as educational, recreational, artistic, moral, and religious institutions (cf. Parsons 1965, 239ff.). Each of these institutions is developing its own meaning system, values, norms, and legitimization procedures, while creating its own "symbolic universe." The melody of an overarching canopy is progressively disappearing and being replaced by a polyphonic, sometimes even chaotic, mixture of often discordant voices. Plurality is replacing oneness and pluriformity (cf. van der Ven 1996a).

Berger and Luckmann's theory does offer a way of handling this problem. As I said, they distinguish between primary and secondary socialization. Primary socialization covers the symbolic initiation process as a whole, in which the child is inducted into the symbolic universe of a given society as a whole, before secondary socialization introduces the individual to the particular symbolic system that is fundamental to playing particular professional roles in particular societal institutions. Secondary socialization as professional socialization for a plurality of institutions builds on the common base of primary socialization into the one and uniform symbolic universe that takes place primarily at home, where the parents function as the most significant others of the child.

It is questionable, however, whether the family indeed transmits unitary, conflict-free value and norm systems. From empirical research, we know that families transmit at least two different main value systems: familialism and economism. Familialism is expressed in a set of convictions such as "it is important to be married, to have children, and to live for one's family." Economism is reflected in a set of values such as "it is important to get on in life, to practice one's occupation, to be in a good financial situation, and to have social security." In the Netherlands, in 1979 about 62 percent and in 1990 about 55 percent of the population valued familialism as positive to very positive. In the same years economism was positively to very positively rated by 53 percent and 59 percent, respectively (Eisinga et al. 1992, 73).[11] Pluralism is revealed in the fact that people value both familialism and economism positively, even though the orientation of the two values systems is entirely different (Felling et al. 1983) and may even be contradictory, as evidenced by many working fathers and mothers who strive to be both a "good enough parent" and to get ahead in their career.

Empirical insights like these call into question the assumption that the family is a uniform and unitary social unit. Is the family a collective "we" or a collection of subunits and dyadic relations? Is there such a thing as an irreducible core of the family? A third way between the notions of the family as a unit or as the sum of its parts is suggested in the following definition: a family is "a collection of individuals who have a commitment to the general well-being of one another and who label themselves a 'family'" (Landesman et al. 1991, 66). This description includes three levels of analysis: the individual, the subunit, and the family group as a whole. At each level, that is, at the level of the individual, subunit, and family group, the goals, strategies, resources, and life experiences of well-being play an important role. This well-being includes six domains of development: physical, emotional, social, cognitive, moral-spiritual, and cultural-aesthetic (Landesman et al. 1991).

Such a description makes it possible to take into account the gender, role, and professional differences between father and mother, which touch on the moral domain and affect the moral socialization of the child. From empirical research we know that, especially in industrial society, pro-

---

11. In 1979 familialism appeared to be esteemed more highly by church members than nonchurch members, whereas no significant difference with regard to economism was found between the two groups (Felling et al. 1983, 145).

fessional work and the way this work is experienced influence and change father's and mother's beliefs, values, and norms during the course of their lives (Steinkamp 1991, 263-64). Moreover, the child is not only the "receiver" of convictions, principles, and rules from his/her parents but also influences each of them from his/her side, because their reacting to the child's reactions directly or indirectly changes each of them. In other words, the relation between each of the parents and the child is bidirectional (Landesman et al. 1991).

Siblings, with whom about 80 percent of children grow up, also bring a variety of influences into the home situation. First, they enter the family in a certain birth order, which affects not only the second child in relation to the firstborn but this firstborn also. They enter the family at different moments in its life history, which influences this history. They develop their individuality, which includes their gender and temperament, in their own unique way, which is dealt with differently by each of the parents and each of the siblings (Schaffer 1991). Siblings interact by imitating each other, playing, provoking, fighting, and exchanging emotions of affection and hostility. They also participate in different worlds outside the home (Dunn 1991). These worlds consist of different values and norms, which stem from different day care situations, different peer groups, and different school classes. These worlds give each member of the family his or her own "nonshared environment," which makes the family an ever-changing, dynamic social phenomenon with its own phases and life history (Kreppner 1991).

What about the school as a socialization agency? Let us assume that the family socializes the child in a climate of love and warmth, in which values such as empathy and sympathy are highly appreciated. The school, by contrast, is a meritocracy in which individual achievement and success, competition and rivalry are positively valued (Bowles and Gintis 1977). This meritocratic attitude is reinforced by continuously testing and evaluating the child's learning outcomes and comparing them with absolute and relative standards, a process that begins during primary education and continues throughout the child's school career.

The socialization effects of the peer group depend on many factors, such as whether the group is a conformist group or a gang in conflict with other gangs or with the law, whether the child is accepted and popular or rejected and marginalized, whether he/she has some special friends in the group or only "neutral," equal comembers of the same age, whether he/she exchanges confidence with them, and whether he/she develops some self-esteem in the group. In brief, it all depends on the child's position and experiences in this "children's society" (Krappmann 1991).

The mass media are another agent of socialization that influences the order of meaning, specifically moral meaning. At a very young age, the media already confront the child with convictions, principles, and models, which may sharply contrast with the beliefs, values, and norms the parents want for their child. This is especially true of violence and sex on the television screen. Although the idea that the mass media monologically and directly cause a deterioration in the morality of the individual, especially the child, is based on outdated, obsolete behavioral stimulus-response theories, some kind of impact cannot be denied. It is difficult to say, however, what form this influence takes and how it operates. This question can only be answered with the help of a multifactorial design that takes into account factors such as the cognitive and affective mind-set of the viewer before he/she starts to watch TV, the viewer's emotional dependence according to which he/she will use the program to understand himself/herself and actual situations, the social setting in which he/she watches TV, especially the opinion leaders in his/her group who direct his/her evaluation of the program, the active selection of the program by the viewer, the extent to which the program reinforces his/her moral mind-set or effects some "cognitive dissonance," and lastly the way in which the viewer cognitively and affectively structures the message of the program and evaluates it. Moreover, we should not forget that the working of the mass media takes place within the parameters of the broader society and culture, whose various beliefs, values, and norms they broadcast, interpret, and reinforce (Schorb et al. 1991; Tuchman 1988).

Thus the diversity of socialization agencies — the family, the school, peers, and the mass media — already becomes apparent in childhood. It would be too simplistic to suppose that all these agencies transmit the same "world" of convictions, virtues, principles, and rules. It would also be too simplistic to assume that each of these agencies works in the same way or in the same direction. Many differences, contrasts, and even contradictions may be observed between and within them.

What is an appropriate response to the fact that the child is confronted with different and often highly contradictory value systems from different socialization agents in different socialization agencies? Must the child develop a split personality, or at the least become adept at playing different roles to function in different systems — playing in different orchestras, singing with different voices, speaking with different tongues?

Some scholars say that in order to avoid confronting the child with such contradictions, education or socialization should take place in a uniform, "holistic" world, or should even build up such a world. Evil, they say, must be kept outside, because it damages the child's innocent mind and

95

soul (cf. Jaschke 1974). In the past, some advocates of this approach made a plea for the "pädagogische Provinz," the "educational island" (cf. Von den Driesch and Esterhues 1964, vol. 2, passim). In our time, some scholars argue that people should return to their own "polis," their own communities (MacIntyre 1981), where the child can be socialized into the virtues of this "polis" life. But this is an unrealistic, speculative, and illusory idea, because even in the ideal community or educational setting, value contradictions inevitably enter into the socialization process through the front door and the back, through the interactions between the adults and the child in the family, the day care settings, the school, the neighborhood, the parish, and so on.

Others see a different solution. Because the players of the different instruments in the orchestra are following different scores, resulting in a cacophony of sound, they need a conductor, a strong personality to lead them. In the realm of education or socialization, only the state, they argue, can fulfill this function (Weniger 1952; 1965). Opponents of this plea view the idea that the state could be the society's top musician or conductor as patently ridiculous, because it presupposes a matter of faith: faith in the state (Klafki 1968). State pedagogics, which brings to mind communist and Nazi historical experiments or, in our own time, religious fundamentalist teaching, would be downright deleterious, they say. To believe that the state could fulfill this role is, at the very least, wishful thinking (Schulenberg 1968). The state is only one of the players in the societal money and power game (Bekke and Kuypers 1990). It is even a weak player in the educational arena (Voigt 1973).

But if not the state, who or what will fulfill the role of conductor? Some say religion, specifically Christianity, that is, the church. In earlier times, the church coordinated and integrated the multiple players, instruments, and voices, imposed its social control on them, reinforced and sanctioned their behavior through sacred gratification and punishment. It dictated the socialization processes in the family and the school. For all these reasons, religion was a strong moral force for upholding societal unity and integration.[12] However, processes of modernization and secularization in the West have caused the churches to lose much of their integrative function. In northern Europe there is a distinct downward trend with regard to church membership and organized religion. Denmark and Sweden lead the

---

12. Some scholars hold that this is still the case, at least in the area of civil religion, especially in the United States (Bellah and Hammond 1980; Berger 1974; Bellah et al. 1985). They use the so-called functional religion conception, whereas I am interested in its substantial conception here.

way, followed by France, Belgium, Norway, the Netherlands, and Germany (Ester et al. 1993, 48). For example, in 1992 in the Netherlands (15 million inhabitants), 57 percent of the population were nonchurchgoers. It is predicted that by the year 2000 this figure will increase to 62 percent, in 2010 to 68 percent, and in 2020 to 73 percent. In the space of just one generation, research predicts, 15 percent of the Dutch population will belong to the Catholic Church, 6 percent to the Dutch Reformed Church (Nederlandse Hervormde Kerk), and 3 percent to the Reformed Churches in the Netherlands (Gereformeerde Kerken in Nederland). Only about one-fifth of Catholics — or 450,000 — will go to church one or more times a month. In concrete terms these statistics mean that based on the current number of Catholic parishes, about 275 Catholics per parish will go to church (Becker and Vink 1994, 69-76). A downward tendency is also observable in the United States, although the decline is not as sharp as in northern Europe. Still, authors like Gallup and Castelli speak of "mainline Protestants losing young adults" (1989, 26). Regardless of how the distinction is made between church and religion, the tendency is away from religious institutions, as public opinion polls reveal: "Spirituality yes, church no!" (cf. Roof and McKinney 1987). In any case, the churches' influence is decreasing, in the moral domain as well as in every other area. Even if maintaining the moral power of the church were seen as eminently desirable, it could not be done, because the role the church played from medieval times into this century is finished.

With neither church nor state in a position to play the leading moral role, must we agree with Durkheim that the only possible outcome is anomy (1984, 291ff.)? By "anomy" Durkheim meant normlessness, comprising three related aspects: the absence of values and norms, the absence of consensus about values and norms, and the absence of conditions necessary to realize them (Giddens 1978, 107-8). Anomy means that people have the feeling that there is "only empty space above them" (Durkheim 1951, 257). Is anomy our only prospect?[13]

The conclusion is that there is no longer any institution at the macrolevel of society that can act as the conductor who brings order to the various and sometimes clashing voices. It is possible, however, that some such agents of order may be found at the two other levels mentioned earlier,

---

13. Durkheim is not so pessimistic as some consider him to be. According to the interpretation by Giddens (1978), he evaluates the contract, which is at the very core of modern society, as the embodiment of moral values such as respect, solidarity, love, and compassion, as his *Division of Labor* (1984) and *Professional Ethics* (1957) reveal (cf. van der Ven 1993a).

the mesolevel of interaction and the microlevel of individual, which we will now look at more closely.

The Mesolevel of Interaction

In their discussion of socialization and internalization, Berger and Luckmann emphasize the importance of the interaction between the child and the "significant others" with whom he/she identifies. This interactive identification process is based on a strong emotional attachment to "significant others," especially the parents. The child takes over the parents' identity, roles, and attitudes in a variety of emotional ways and builds his/her own identity on them. Finally, "by this identification with significant others the child becomes capable of identifying himself, of acquiring a subjectively coherent and plausible identity" (Berger and Luckmann 1967, 132).

As suggested earlier, there is some doubt as to whether this Meadian view of identification adequately explains the entire process of socialization, and especially moral socialization, which involves not only identification with the parents but also with a variety of socialization agents in a variety of socialization agencies.

When the child identifies with "the parents," with whom exactly is he/she identifying? Parents are individuals who differ from one another and within themselves. Parents differ in their family backgrounds, histories, beliefs, attitudes, and professional activities, all of which determine, or at least codetermine, their identities. Each parent also plays a number of different roles in various institutions, such as the family, the neighborhood, cultural or recreational associations, and, not the least, the place of employment. Both kinds of differences may lead to various role conflicts. These role conflicts may take various forms: person/bearer conflicts, bearer/sender conflicts, and inter-sender conflicts. The person/bearer conflict concerns the discrepancy between the convictions the parent personally holds, for example, "sexual morality should be free," and the values and norms that he/she as a parent thinks should be transmitted to the child. The bearer/sender conflict refers to the tension between what a parent values in his/her parental relationship to the child and the pressure he/she feels from outside, for example, from the other parent, the day care, school, association, or company. The inter-sender conflict arises when the parent is confronted with divergent, antagonistic influences originating from different senders who try to influence him/her in opposite directions. To the extent that there is any such thing as an identification process, it is certainly not a simple, uniform process.

Taking now the perspective of the child vis-à-vis parents who may suffer from various person/bearer, bearer/sender, and inter-sender role conflicts, one may well ask: How is the child able to identify with his/her parents? with which of them, and with which aspect? to what extent? Moreover, as I said earlier, significant others include not only the child's parents but also siblings, caregivers, teachers at school, people in the neighborhood, other members of recreational associations, people in the congregation, and peers. Television programs, videos, and other media also play an influential role. I believe that the concept of identification, which Berger and Luckmann borrow from Mead, does not in fact adequately describe and explain what goes on in these many, multifaceted processes.

Instead of the concept of identification, which covers only some aspects of the relation between child and parents, I would like to introduce the theory of observational learning, which I believe provides a fuller and more accurate interpretation of what happens in socialization. Observational learning is learning that happens through observation of other people who function as models. The child observes convictions, values, and norms *in actu,* and is then able to enact them in a similar form. This learning by observation, or modeling, as it is called, enables us to understand why not only the parents but a wide range of other socialization agents as well transmit virtues, convictions, and principles to the child. Modeling is not limited to "significant others" with whom the child "identifies." Rather, we see that the child is constantly exposed to many different kinds of people who function as models to him/her, in all situations where he/she is together with others, be they siblings, peers, classmates, or adults such as neighbors, relatives, teachers, church members, and — of course — entertainers.

Observational learning consists of four groups of processes (Bandura 1977, 22-55; 1986, 51-80). The first group is that of attentional processes, by which the child perceives the relevant aspects of modeled convictions, values, and norms. These attentional processes involve the child's selective, focused attention, without which modeling does not take place. The child is surrounded by innumerable stimuli in the moral field, but he/she attends to only one or one set of them at the moment of modeling. The choice of stimuli that the child attends to depends on the special attributes the human model has for him/her, because this person — whether parent, teacher, peer, or other — attracts him/her in a special way. Another cause is implied in the special features the modeled convictions, values, and norms have for the child, such as being honest, acting prudently, or eating and drinking temperately. A last cause may be that the special characteristics of the interaction situation the child is in affect him/her while learning observationally.

The second group of processes that occur during modeling are known as retention processes. If he/she does not remember the modeled moral ideas, the child is not influenced by other people at all, because if he/she does not remember he/she cannot enact the model's behavior. The convictions, values, and norms must be represented in the child's memory in symbolic form to enable him/her to act in the same way as the model. These forms are based on symbolic, that is, conceptual, as well as narrative and imaginal codes. By using these codes, the perceptions made during observational process undergo symbolic transformations. No two convictions verbalized, values narrated, or norms acted on are identical. Each observer constructs his/her own general symbolic conception containing the essential aspects and basic pattern. Many times they construct their own moral prototype. One consequence of retention is the need for rehearsal. If moral ideas are not rehearsed after they are first perceived, they risk being lost from memory. In the moral field, this rehearsal is cognitive in nature: the child visualizes the interactions in which he/she observed the convictions, values, or norms in action. The rehearsal, in turn, stimulates the child's attention. The retention function also means that the model need not be continuously or permanently available for observation.

The third group of processes in observational learning are called production processes. In these the child converts the symbolic concepts into actions that match those of the model. That is, he/she formulates convictions, expresses values, tells stories about virtues and vices, and acts on norms in a manner in keeping with the models. By doing so, the child integrates in his/her own way into relatively new patterns all that he/she perceives in the moral field. After this he/she acts morally from these unique integrative patterns. Lastly the child observes his/her own actions and compares them with the model's. Insofar as the child's moral actions are not totally observable or comprehensible to him/her (and this especially applies to their intentions and effects), he/she infers what he/she is doing well or right from the apparent aspects of these actions. This gives the child so-called performance feedback in the moral field, which means that he/she perceives which convictions he/she states, what values he/she expresses, which virtues and vices he/she evidently prefers, or what norms he/she acts on. This self-observation develops the child's moral ideas and behavior. It leads to what is called experiential or enactive learning or learning by experiencing or doing (Bandura 1986, 106-41).

The last group of processes within modeling are the motivational processes. The child does not enact everything he/she learns, and it is motivation that determines whether and to what extent the convictions, values, and norms acquired through observation will actually be performed or acted on. The greater the positive value (reward), the more likely the child will be to act on what he/she has learned; the greater the negative value (risk of punishment), the less likely. High rewards motivate performance, while high risk of punishment restrains it. Rewards and punishments may be imposed externally, for example, by parents, teachers, or peers, or internally, by the child's inner standards. If a child behaves in a socially desirable manner, because he/she expects to avoid punishment by doing so, the absence of punishment and the ensuing praise from others strengthens this behavior and motivates the child to repeat it. If a child acts courageously because he/she feels that this is the right thing to do, the self-observation of having acted in keeping with his/her own moral values, in this case of having displayed courage, enhances the child's motivation to continue to act in this way in the future.

These four kinds of processes most frequently take place in a social context, within which the encounter between the model and the child occurs. In the course of the encounter, adjustments take place in relation to earlier social interactions, both on the side of the model and on the side of the child. This makes observational learning and modeling into a mutual and dynamic social event, in which especially social activities, skills, and attitudes are exchanged (Uzgiris 1991).

Does replacing the identification concept, which is key to Berger and Luckmann's theory of socialization, with the theory of observational learning solve the problem of how socialization can be accomplished by a plurality of socialization agents? Yes, it clearly does. Does observational learning provide the hypothetical agent of order, the conductor, whom, we concluded, was lacking at the macrolevel of society? The answer is no. The observational learning theory describes and explains plurality: that plurality exists, how it exists, and why it exists. In principle, there are as many socialization agents as there are models, and there are as many models as the child observes, remembers, imitates, and is motivated by. However, the theory of observational learning provides no evidence of a strong guiding hand, a single model that imposes order on these many observations and learnings. Observational learning is multiple.

One is tempted to ask, then, whether this multiple observational learning does not damage or preclude the development of the child's self, in the sense that the self presupposes some unity, oneness, wholeness. Will socialization turn the child into a "split personality"? Would the child have a part of his/her "self" in common with every adult with whom he/she comes into contact? Or is it possible to think, once again, in terms of a "third way," which dissolves the dilemma between the whole, one, undivided self and the split, fragmented self? This question leads us to look at how socialization takes place at the microlevel of the individual.

The Microlevel of the Individual

As noted earlier, Berger and Luckmann emphasize that the child is not only the object of socialization but also the subject, in that the child reflects on his/her own socialization results, that is, reflects on the social distribution of knowledge and selects from other social strata and groups for his/her own use. In Meadian terms, socialization creates the self of the individual, but this does not mean that the "I," which refers to individual spontaneous freedom, is submerged in the "me" that is the result of the influences of the institutions on the self. These institutions "make" the "me," because they expect the "me" to behave in the way they prescribe. Within the self, the relation between "I" and "me" is dialectical in nature: every time the "me" seems to be defined by the moral beliefs and principles that the family and other institutions inculcate into the child, the "I" breaks away in order to make a free selection from them and combine them with beliefs and principles from other sources.

What is the significance of this dialectical relation between "I" and "me"? Because Berger and Luckmann draw heavily on Mead, it is fruitful to deal with Mead's theory of the self at some length. I will describe its core concepts and then interpret them from a rather critical point of view.

Mead's point of departure is the symbolic interaction between people, from which he builds his theory of the development of the child as a self (Mead 1934). In his/her interactions with other people, the child learns to distinguish within the self between "I" and "me." "Me" is that dimension within the self into which the self incorporates the character, the attitudes, values, and norms of the person or persons with whom the child interacts. This "me" develops in two stages, which are evident in the child's play and games. In play, the child begins to dialogue with himself/herself, switching back and forth between the character of, say, a parent, friend, or authority figure on the one hand, and himself/herself on the other. In some deprived areas, on the occasion of somebody having been murdered, the child may even play funeral rituals and exchange the roles of the policeman, the preacher, the people in the pews, the mourning relative, and the deceased, who has been innocently murdered. In each case, the child takes turns, in which the policeman or the deceased addresses himself to the child and the child reacts to the policeman or the deceased. The child thus takes the perspective of the other and also responds to the other from his/her own perspective. From the perspective of the other, the child sees "me," and from his/her own perspective, the child understands himself/herself as "I." In the game, the child does not take the perspective of only one "significant other," but of several and in some cases of all of them. The child takes the

102

rules of the game and applies them to all the players, including himself/herself. In Meadian terms, the child is looking at "me," while taking the perspective of the "generalized other" looking at "me." To put it yet another way, the child is looking at "me" in an objective way that is determined by the rules of the game. The "rules of the game" of course vary with the "game." The game and its attendant rules may be those of the family, day care, neighborhood, peer group, school, or local community. Then, as one's perspective broadens, there are the rules of the wider community, the town, state, or country. As the child grows older, he/she develops the ability to take increasingly broader perspectives, and the "generalized other" is broadened at the same time. The child is increasingly able to look objectively at himself/herself and to handle himself/herself objectively.

As the child takes increasingly more universal perspectives, there is the risk that he/she becomes increasingly conformist. Here Mead's "me" resembles Freud's "superego," the means by which the child internalizes the values and norms that dominate the societal institutions and society in general. "Conscience" is a function of this internalization process. It issues "warnings" when the child does not take seriously enough the commands implicit in the institutions' values and norms. "Guilt" is another internalization function: it "speaks" internally when the child transgresses against his/her duties and obligations. But there is a difference between the Meadian and the Freudian view. "Conscience" and "guilt," as interpreted by Freud, are self-restrictive mechanisms originating with a small number of "significant others" with whom the child is intimately linked, whereas Mead sees them as self-transcending functions that are directed toward the objective "rules of the game" of the "generalized other," as reflected in the societal institutions.

The "I," however, is able to intervene in these internalization processes. Mead compares its interventions with the nonconventional approaches of an artist, an inventor, a scholar, and a self-assertive participant in daily communication, who do not abolish the rules received from established traditions but restructure and reconstruct them. Mead speaks of impulsions, which generate the actions of "I."

Here I would like to point out that to my mind, the impulsions that Mead speaks of need not be understood as intrinsically directed against the conventions of social life (cf. Hermans and Kempen 1993, 102-21). As Mead himself says: "There are certain recognized fields within which an individual can assert himself, certain rights which he has within these limits" (Mead 1934, 210). In light of these recognized fields — I would add: socially recognized fields — the interpretation that "me" is the product of socialization and internalization, and "I" is not, is inadequate. According to Selznick, the dialectical relationship between "I" and "me" is socially conditioned, and within this process of socially influencing factors, the "I" also is a product of social life: "If group life is restrictive, the 'me' dominates the 'I' and individuality is minimized, though never eliminated. Under more congenial conditions the 'I' influences and restructures social meanings, rules, roles, and relationships. Indeed, on some occasions the 'me' legitimates and encourages the free expression of the 'I'" (Selznick 1992, 161). From social research we know that the extent to which people experience themselves as a "self" depends heavily on the social structure they are in, especially their professional autonomy, status, and roles (Steinkamp 1991). Consequently, both the developing "I" and "me" depend on the social context in which the individual is situated. Both "I" and "me" are socially conditioned.

This insight calls for some clarification of the terminology we use in speaking about the self. "Me" is generally understood as being contextually conditioned, while "I" is not, but in fact it is just as much conditioned by its context as "me." To speak of "I" as something internal, in contrast to a socially conditioned "me," makes "I" into something mysterious, even though in principle, as far as its formal relation to the social environment is concerned, it is no different from "me." For the sake of conceptual clarity, "I" and "me" must therefore be understood as two different perspectives from which I relate to myself as well as to my human environment.

This brings us back to the question of plurality, this time in terms of the different perspectives of the self. How can this plurality of perspectives be combined with the concept of the one, unitary, whole self? This question is becoming rather pressing because we have already looked at the macro-level of society, where there appears to be no overriding conductor, either in society (the state) or in religion (the church), who coordinates and harmonizes the effects of the plurality of socialization agents, and at the mesolevel of the interaction between the socialization agents and the child the problem remained unsolved as well. According to the theory of observational learning, there are as many models as there are people with whom the child comes into contact. Two questions arise: First, does this lead the child to be socialized as a "split personality," a "split self"? In other words, is the child "split" by the divergent influences coming from a wide variety of models? Second, is there a "third way" that breaks down the dilemma between the unitary, undivided self and the split, divided self? Is there a third theory of the self that may be helpful for understanding how plural and even antagonistic moral beliefs, principles, and rules enter into the socialization process?

Indeed, two candidates do exist, two theories that give a plausible account of divergent and even contradictory convictions, values, and norms in socialization. The first is the open self theory, the second the theory of the dialogical self.[14]

The open self theory starts from the fact that people play a number of different roles in their communities and institutions. In order to function appropriately in these roles, their consciousness must be sufficiently "open" that, as they are playing a particular role in a particular situation, they remain aware that they will play another role in another situation and a third role in a third situation, possibly all within a short period of time. This requires some role distance, which means that the self never completely identifies with any one role. The individual is always conscious of the other roles and is able to reflect critically on the tensions, divergences, and contradictions among them. The phenomenon of the open self enables people to play all kinds of roles in an attitude of plasticity and flexibility (Selznick 1992, 219-22). At a deeper level, the open self provides a means of protecting one's own vulnerable identity, ensuring that it is not damaged by conflicts between roles and by the conflict of interpretations of these roles. Goffman gives the example of a subordinate who fears to utter criticism about things his superior orders him to do. He also wants to show that he has not totally capitulated, however, and does this by making joking, ironic, sarcastic remarks (Goffman 1961, 114).[15] Developing the open self and role distance, which may be seen as a measure of self-responsible self-care, has a horizontal and a vertical dimension (Mollenhauer 1972). The horizontal dimension concerns the range of roles played at any one period of time in various current institutional settings from a synchronic perspective, and determines to what extent I transcend the situations I am in, instead of being absorbed by them. The vertical dimension is the continuity or biography of the self over time (i.e., from a diachronic perspective), and relates whether and to what extent I continue to be the same person under the flux of changing events.

Nevertheless, the theory of the open self does not account for the fact that the roles each individual plays are not only plural but are often contradictory or in competition with each other. An example given by James

14. Both of them refuse the so-called consistence models in psychology, i.e., the congruity, balance, and cognitive dissonance models. These models are based on the idea that the self needs a uniform, overarching canopy of convictions, values, and norms, in order not to be drawn into psychologically unbearable or even pathological ambivalence (Billig 1982). They do not take into account the conflicts alluded to by Merton with reference to the tension between institutional differentiation and divergent social roles on the one hand and beliefs, principles, and rules on the other. Different roles imply different belief and value systems (Van der Lans 1991).

15. MacIntyre (1981, 116) evaluates Goffman's analysis positively because it fits in with his one-self-in-the-community concept.

encapsulates the contradictions between the roles played by the same individual: "As a man I pity you, but as an official I must show you no mercy; as a politician I regard him as an ally, but as a moralist I loathe him" (James 1890, 295). The theory of the dialogical self tries to account for this problem of conflicts and contradictions. Its starting point is the multivoiced self, where each voice is related to a different role or position and is engaged in a dialogical process with the others (Hermans and Kempen 1993; Hermans 1995; Hermans and Hermans-Jansen 1995; Van Loon 1996).

First, the dialogical self theory describes the way in which these voices speak to, talk with, criticize, and correct each other. To take James's example of the self that is both a politician and a moralist: the voice of the politician says to the moralist that values are nice things to preach, but politics requires that one take into consideration all possibly foreseeable, direct and indirect strategic and tactical effects of one's actions — in short, that one apply a Weberian ethics of responsibility *(Verantwortungsethik)*.[16] The moralist voice points out that this political maneuvering ignores the moral values that in the long run determine the human quality of society and that serve as indisputable orientations for political action in concrete situations — the ethics of conviction *(Gesinnungsethik)*, as Weber (1980) put it.[17] The two voices represent not only different but opposing opinions. They exchange these opinions to each other (cf. Larmore 1987, 144ff.).

The theory of the dialogical self then posits a second step. The exchange of opinions is followed by an exchange of perspectives. What does this mean? Let us assume that the voices of the moralist and the politician within the dialogical self are engaged in a dialogue. The moralist puts his case from his own "I" perspective, and the politician counters from his own "I" perspective. In each case, the "I" perspective of the one is the "you" perspective of the other. For the purpose of the dialogue, the moralist adopts the politician's "you" perspective and has an exchange between his "I" perspective and the other's "you" perspective. At the same time the politician takes on the moralist's "you" perspective and develops an exchange between his "I" and the moralist's "you" perspective.

The third step is the process of reaching agreement between the parts or, if no agreement can be reached, arriving at a provisional, partial agreement or compromise, as fragile as it may be. How is this done? The answer

16. Ricoeur (1968, 71) identifies Weber's *Verantwortungsethik* as "ethics of power," as Weber himself called it, whereas Van Gerwen (1995, 117) translates this consequentialist ethics as "ethics of calculation."

17. Van Gerwen (1995, 118) translates Weber's *Gesinnungsethik* as "ethics of absolute intentions."

is that reaching an agreement or a compromise is only possible with the help of a third perspective, known as the "he," "she," or "it" perspective. This third perspective is higher, more abstract, and from it the two lower perspectives can be recognized, acknowledged, understood, and even explained. It is a metaperspective. Whereas the "I" perspective and the "you" perspective are participatory, the third is observational. The first two perspectives are subjective, the third is objective. The compromise is the product of this objective, more abstract — one might even say impartial, scientific — perspective (cf. Selman 1980; Habermas 1982).

I wish to point out, however, that although this metaperspective develops at a higher level than the first two perspectives, it cannot accurately be described as an objective, impartial, scientific perspective.[18] If the metaperspective was indeed the equivalent of an impartial, scientific observer on a mountain, an Archimedean viewpoint completely detached from all the confusion and chaos of human life, it would objectify the dialogue between the voices. It would in fact objectify the voices, stripping them of their participative, subjective character. The metaperspective can, however, be described as a "higher" voice. Because it comes from a higher level it makes possible dialogical switches between the "lower" voices and allows them to speak with each other, take each other's perspective, and develop a compromise, but it does so without dissociating itself from the conversation. The "higher" voice engages in dialogue with both the other voices (Hermans and Kempen 91ff., 115ff.).[19] It dialogues in a "chronotope way," in Bakhtin's words, where "chronotope" refers to the various temporal and spatial relationships that the self maintains in time and space (Sampson 1993, 95ff.). The metaperspective does not function so much as the conductor that Weniger seeks, but — to use another metaphor — as the first violinist in a chamber orchestra. The first violinist guides not only the first violins but also the second violins, the cellos, contrabasses, flutes, oboes, bassoons, trumpets, and even the tympani. He/she guides the whole orchestra while — or more precisely by — participating in its performance.[20]

18. These remarks also apply to my previous work on moral education; cf. van der Ven 1985; 1987a; 1987b.
19. Cf. Hermans 1987a; 1987b; 1993.
20. It is remarkable that, in his study on discourse ethics, Habermas explicitly mentions that taking an impartial perspective "cannot abandon the performative attitude of participants in interaction" (1993, 25). He accuses Thomas Nagel of confusing "the standpoint of impartial judgment of moral questions with the 'external standpoint' of an observer" (ibid., 180n.39). The impartial judge is not "a neutral observer" (ibid., 48). Habermas thereby partially abandons Selman's theory on social perception, on which he draws in his work on communicative action (Habermas 1982).

An example from psychotherapy may illustrate the nature of this third perspective, which mediates between the voices of the "I" and the "you" perspective. Imagine a person suffering from some inner conflict, like narcissism, that quintessential disorder of the late twentieth century (Lasch 1979; Kohut 1988; Solomon 1989) that causes the subject to swing between self-absorption and self-doubt. In the therapeutic sessions, as the two voices are encouraged to engage in a continuous dialogue, each from its own perspective, they also increasingly exchange perspectives. Gradually a third voice arises, a metavoice, which intervenes in the dialogue, talks with the other voices separately and together, and attempts to coordinate their convictions and needs. This third, "higher" voice, which is brought out by the therapist, develops sensitivity for the pain and suffering that the other selves are going through; it tries to be compassionate for them, and even to accept them. This third voice is like a friend to the other two. It models to them, as it were, what it means to be a friend to yourself. From this new voice, this voice of self-care, the self is able truly to take care of others, because authentic self-care implies authentic care for others (Jacoby 1990) — because, if one sees oneself as another, one is able to see others as other than oneself (Ricoeur 1992).

The Importance of the Dialogical Self

What is the importance of the dialogical self for socialization in general and moral socialization more specifically? As I indicated, the dialogical self embodies the voices that represent the various roles an individual plays in different social institutions, roles that may be associated with divergent and even antagonistic convictions, values, and norms. This dialogical self is also present in each of the socialization agents with whom the child interacts in the family, neighborhood, school, or peer group, and the dialogue within the selves and between selves continues when the socialization agents interact with the child. It is impossible to shut down the dialogical self during socialization interactions and communication. This means that the dialogical self is modeled to the child, and the child therefore learns by observation what it means to be a dialogical self in his/her own way.

To return to Bandura's modeling theory, one can say that in the first processes of modeling, that is, the attentional processes, the child observes the moral values and so on expressed by the dialogical selves of the various socialization agents with whom he/she comes in contact, and the way in which they arrive at agreement or compromise. In the retention processes, the child stores into his/her memory the various moral values and principles he/she has observed, as well as the ways in which the socialization agents structure, relate, and combine them. In the production processes, the child constructs his/her own moral beliefs, convictions, and patterns of actions from memory by restructuring and recombining the moral beliefs transmitted by the socialization agents through their dialogical selves. In the fourth and last processes, the motivational ones, the child is inspired to maintain the moral commitment he/she has learned and constructed for himself/herself, and to act from the internal moral dialogue he/she engages in.

Is this dialogical self, which is the product of socialization by other dialogical selves, a danger to the self? Yes, if the ideal self is conceived of as a whole, united self, which holds its own substance, exists independently, and acts autonomously. No, if this substantialist conception of the self is replaced by what Bruner calls the "distributed self." This is a self that is distributed, as it were, over various situations, positions, and roles. It fashions many and varied stories about living and acting in these situations and roles and relates them to others and to itself. These stories tell of the plurality and diversity of human practices. The self, we might say, consists in the plurality and diversity of meaning in these practices, both cross-situational and longitudinal. In telling stories, this "distributed self" also narrates the tensions and conflicts evoked by the various situations, the dialogues it holds with others and with itself, and lastly the agreements it reaches with others as well as with itself. Socialization can be understood as the social-ization of the "dialogical self" or "distributed self," and moral socialization as the socialization of the "morally dialogical self" or "morally distributed self" (cf. Bruner 1990, 99-138).

3.3 Socialization of the Moral Self

In this section, I ask whether and to what extent the moral socialization of the dialogical self can be said to be morally legitimate. In other words, how does this moral socialization of the dialogical self contribute to the devel-opment of a moral self? This general question can be broken down into more specific questions, which I will deal with in this section. First, to what extent does the dialogical self contribute to the human self in a philosophi-cal-anthropological sense? Second, how do we know that the convictions, values, and norms that children observe, remember, and produce as a result of being in contact with socialization agents cum dialogical selves are morally appropriate? Third, what criteria can be used to determine whether the choice and compromises made by the socialization agents cum dialogical selves in response to value conflicts are morally adequate? This last question

109

requires some reflection on the moral meaning of these conflicts, choices, and compromises.

The Morality of the Dialogical Self

Contemporary psychology and philosophy offer a number of different concepts of the self. The list of these concepts, presented in the following, stems from the philosopher Wren (1993),[21] and places the concept of the dialogical self in a more systematic context. (1) The substantialness concept of the self refers to an entity that is internally conscious of itself from its place within the external (natural and/or transcendent) world and vice versa. (2) The bundle concept of the self looks at the self as a random being together of cognitions, affections, desires, and other psychological states and tendencies. (3) The eidetic concept of the self assumes that the self is a construction or projection, which enables a person to organize his or her multitudinous experiences. (4) The noumenal concept of the self understands the self as a purely formal unifying principle of subjectivity. (5) The dialectical concept of the self refers to the fact that the self is interwoven in a web of social relations. (6) The identity concept of the self relates to the self as a storytelling and self-interpreting agent within a specific tradition and context.

The concept of the dialogical self discussed in the preceding section is associated with some aspects of both the dialectical and identity conception of the self in Wren's list. The parallel with the dialectical conception lies in the fact that the dialogical self is understood as woven into a web of interpersonal relationships with significant others. The self is not a self-sufficient subject but a dialogical being, whose orientation is essentially relational. The

21. Within the general theory and research of the self, different aspects of the self are distinguished, such as the material self, which refers to the body and property, the social self, and the spiritual self (William James), the actual self (how one actually is), the ideal self (how one should ideally be), and the possible self (what one might become, hope to become, or is afraid of becoming), but the moral self is never mentioned (Marsh et al. 1992). Even in the experiential-developmental model of the self concept by L'Ecuyer (1992), the moral self is absent, which is remarkable because of the long list of aspects of the self it contains, i.e., the somatic and possessive self, the self-image, self-identity, self-esteem, and self-activities, the social self with its social attitudes and sexual connotations, and lastly the self/nonself, which concerns references to others and opinion of others. The study by Hermans and Kempen (1993) on the dialogical self does not mention the moral self either. In the field of moral psychology and philosophy the situation is different, as the study by Taylor (1989) and the reader by Noam and Wren (1993) show.

moral philosopher Taylor would say that the moral space of this self — "orientation" implies the concept of space — is the interchange of speakers in the community (Taylor 1989, 35). The parallel with the identity conception of the self consists in the fact that this relationship with significant others has not only an external but also an internal side. Communication with significant others constitutes the intrapersonal dialogue that the self as an "I" engages in with itself as a "me," and vice versa. About identity, Taylor says: "We define this always in dialogue with, sometimes in struggle against, the identities our significant others want to recognize in us. And even when we outgrow some of the latter — our parents, for instance — and they disappear from our lives, the conversation with them continues within us as long as we live" (Taylor 1991, 33). This inner dialogicality, as Taylor calls it, constitutes the "ethics of authenticity" (Taylor 1991, 127).[22]

This concept of the moral self is of utmost importance within moral socialization. It refers to both the interpersonal and intrapersonal dimension that must be developed in moral education. With regard to the interpersonal dimension, the child needs the feeling of being in a continuing relation with significant others. This creates the experience of social bonding from which basic trust emerges. The child needs to engage in an ongoing conversation about who he/she is, about his/her roles in life, his/her goals, the meaning of his/her existence. It is important that the socialization agents serve as positive models for the child in this area of identity, goals, and meaning, so that he/she can learn positive values from observing them. All this creates for the child the experience of being a self. But this only happens if the conversation in the interpersonal dimension alternates with that in the intrapersonal dimension. The stories that are told to the child by the significant others, and those that the child tells to them, must be lengthened, broadened, and deepened from the outer to the inner moral space — to use Taylor's phrase — in order the fertilize the child's inner life. In this way the child learns to develop his/her own story, compose his/her own melody, orchestrate his/her own part — in short, to write his/her own biography. This process also needs to be modeled by the child's significant others. They do this by expressing not only their positive feelings, ideals, convictions, and values, but also their negative feelings, ambivalences, and disappointments. They serve as models for the child by revealing their inner life, expressing their expectations and hopes for the future, and sharing their

22. With regard to this inner dialogicality, Taylor (1991, 127n.25) mentions the work of the Russian literary scholar Bakhtin, who strongly influenced the theory of the dialogical self by Hermans and Kempen (1993), which I referred to in the previous section.

own autobiographies, albeit within the mutual limits of emotional competence and tolerable intimacy. Writing one's autobiography is an intrinsically dialogical, socially learned activity.

Ricoeur's narrative conception of the self has two dimensions, spatial and temporal. The spatial dimension refers to the person's being in the world, acting in a variety of situations and playing a variety of roles. From this perspective one may speak of the spatialization of the self.[23] The temporal dimension refers to the continuity of the self over time, that is, from the present into the past and into the future. Continuity from past to present enables a person to say that "through all the events and vicissitudes I experienced, I remained the same *(idem)*." Continuity from present to future allows the person to say: "Here I am, I, myself *(ipse)*. This is what I stand for and I will continue to stand for it." This temporal dimension is expressed in stories told by me and to me, referring to actions performed in the past, actions in a state of performance in the present, and actions to be performed in the future. The spatial dimension is part of these stories, as the "characters" play various roles in a variety of situations. This storytelling is essentially a dialogical activity, insofar as the human self constitutes itself in the storytelling dialogue with other selves and with oneself as another (Ricoeur 1992, 113-68).

Values and Norms in a Moral Perspective

In moral socialization, parents, teachers, pastors, peers, and so on model their moral convictions, values, and norms, while children observe, remember, and produce these convictions, values, and norms and are motivated by them. But the content of these convictions, values, and norms is not morally indifferent or neutral. Convictions can be described as beliefs people are committed to, values as things or persons people attribute meaning to, and norms as rules people prefer to follow in situations of choice and decision; but these are formal definitions only. The content of "convictions" may range from "all people are brothers and sisters" to "people are wolves"; "values" include empathy as well as apathy, love and hate, honesty and dishonesty; and "norms" include rules ranging from "serve the country" to "take whatever you can get." It is reasonable to ask, therefore, which convictions, values, and norms are morally appropriate to be socialized to children, and by what criteria the selection can be made.

23. Hermans and Kempen (1993) especially focus on this spatialization of the self.

112

Returning once more to Ricoeur's model, discussed in Chapter 1, I would answer this question by applying Ricoeur's two main moral criteria, the good and the just, while keeping the third criterion, the wise, for the last part of this section. In short, the convictions, values, and norms that are modeled by socialization agents can be said to be morally appropriate to the extent that they contribute to the good life and the realization of the principles of justice. Let me elaborate briefly on this statement in anticipation of the next chapter, which deals with this aspect at greater length.

The good life has essentially three components: living one's own life, living with and for others, and living in just institutions. The main moral values associated with living one's own life can be summarized as acting in accordance with (socially defined) standards of excellence in all one's different functions — in other words, being a good husband or wife, a good parent, a good worker, a good citizen. Living up to these standards of excellence contributes to self-esteem and thus to the individual's view of himself/herself as the author of his/her own life. Living with and for others requires values of sharing, cooperation, friendship, solicitude, and love. Living in just institutions refers to a societal structure in which benefits and burdens are distributed in a proportional way (Ricoeur 1992, 169ff.). One can say, then, that inasmuch as the convictions, values, and norms that the socialization agents model to the child contribute to the good life — self-esteem, friendship, love, and lastly distributive justice — they are morally worthy of being transmitted.

The values and norms associated with the good life must also pass through the sieve of justice to determine whether they satisfy the criteria of reversibility and universality. The same three components of the good life must be considered. In living one's own life, the test for reversibility is to decide whether I would like the actions and principles associated with being a good husband or wife, a good parent, a good worker, or a good citizen to apply in reverse: from my husband or wife to myself, from my children to myself, from my coworkers to myself, from my fellow citizens to myself. Then it is necessary to ask whether the values and norms that I follow are morally applicable to everyone else (universality). The overriding value here is autonomy, because living one's own good life depends on the universality of reversibility that creates the free, rational, self-legislating will. In living with and for others, the values and norms again must pass the tests of reversibility and universality, with the ultimate moral value being absolute respect for the other person. Lastly, the values and norms associated with societal institutions need to be evaluated according to whether they contribute to the ability of the people to rule themselves in a true democracy that guarantees respect for human rights. In sum, the values and norms modeled by the agents of socialization can be said to be morally appropriate to the extent that they accord with the principles of justice: autonomy, respect for others, and democracy based on human rights (Ricoeur 1992, 169-239).

Moral Conflicts

Socialization is not only the modeling of convictions, values, and norms; it also includes learning about conflicts between different convictions, values, and norms, conflicts that involve the dialogical self. What is the moral status of such conflicts and what is their moral status in the context of socialization? Ironically, the history of morality can be described not only as a history of moral conflicts but also as a history of moral conflicts about the moral status attributed to such conflicts. This history itself appears to be a conflicted one, entailing two different approaches to handling moral conflicts.

The first approach is to ignore, deny, or eliminate the conflicts from the moral discourse. Since the Enlightenment, principle-oriented moral theories have tried to avoid moral conflicts by preventing them from arising in the first place.[24] The principle of utility, which is used by hedonistic, preference, and welfare utilitarians, is meant to overcome the antagonism between moral claims. Generally speaking, the more those claims advance the actualization of hedonistic experiences, the satisfaction of preferences, or the maximization of welfare, the more they deserve to be realized

---

24. Some hold that both Aristotle and Thomas Aquinas have no room for moral conflicts at all. They say that Aristotle considers conflicting moral convictions to be a result of ignorance, while never recognizing them as conflicting moral claims. For him, a tragic dilemma between two claims, which stand for two different, contrary, or even contradictory goods, is based on a misconception or misunderstanding only: "The apparent and tragic conflict of right with right arises from the inadequacies of reason, not from the character of moral reality" (MacIntyre 1988, 142). The same appreciation of rational harmony in morality emerges, some authors say, from Thomas Aquinas's analysis of the four cardinal virtues: prudence, justice, temperance, and courage. Following in the footsteps of Plato and Cicero rather than Aristotle, Thomas deals with the mutual relationships between these virtues. Each virtue requires the other three. The virtues build a unity (*STh* I-II 61.4). Therefore, conflicts between claims arising from different virtues cannot exist (cf. Lukes 1989, 127). But other scholars think differently. With regard to Aristotle, Stocker (1990a, 51-84) indicates that, for instance, his theory of mixed actions (actions for their own sake and for the sake of something else as well) allows for conflicts and dirty hands. Janssens (1994) points to Thomas Aquinas's theory of proportionality, which aims at coping with and resolving value conflicts.

(Goodin 1994). Another principle-based theory that strongly influences moral thinking is Kant's categorical imperative in both its first and its second formulation. In its first formulation, the principle "act only on that maxim through which you can at the same time will that it should become a universal law" generates a test of universalization, by which all conflicts at least principally can be banned (Kant 1964, 88; Ricoeur 1992, 208). The same applies to the second formulation, which I already referred to in Chapter 1: "Act in such a way that you always treat humanity, whether in your own person or in the person of any other, never simply as a means, but always at the same time as an end" (Kant 1964, 96; Ricoeur 1992, 222). Still another, very influential, principle-based moral theory is Rawls's theory of justice, which is in some respects a modern version of the Kantian categorical imperative. Instead of deducing this imperative from the very essence of human rationality, however, it derives its principles of justice from the "original position." This "original position" replaces the Kantian categorical imperative (Zwart 1993, 196). It refers to the fact that people who take part in moral conversation reach a moral consensus from behind a "veil of ignorance," that they are not conscious of their actual roles and interests in society. The first principle of justice reads as follows: "Each person is to have an equal right to the most extensive basic liberty compatible with a similar liberty for others," and the second: "Social and economic inequalities are to be arranged so that they are both (a) reasonably expected to be to everyone's advantage, and (b) attached to positions and offices open to all" (Rawls 1972, 60). A last example of principle-oriented moral thought is Kohlberg's six-stage theory, which is based on Rawls's study on justice. In order to solve moral conflicts or dilemmas, as Kohlberg calls them, the individual must develop in the direction of the sixth stage, at which he/she is able to resolve such dilemmas in accordance with the principle of justice, which in his theory is based on respect for the dignity of human beings and their equality in terms of human rights (Kohlberg 1981, 412). In short, "Modern moral philosophy, with its desire for explicit and univocal decision-procedures, has stubbornly assumed that moral conflicts must be only apparent, that there must be some single higher-order principle that captures our most basic intuitions. Indeed, when moral theories of this monistic sort have run up against recalcitrant moral intuitions that conflict with their favored higher-order principle, they have too often resorted to the tactic of denying those intuitions their very status as 'moral' ones" (Larmore 1987, 10).

Moral relativism and moral subjectivism also try to eliminate conflicts from moral discourse. In a sense, relativism explains away moral conflicts by saying that every moral claim must be exhaustively understood from its historical, social, and psychological context. Lukes notices correctly that this relativism does not explain why the claims appeared to conflict in the first place (cf. Lukes 1989, 128).[25] Moral subjectivism also deprives moral conflicts of their meaning, in that it rejects any possibility of developing a rational basis for moral claims or even of offering "good reasons" for them. It holds that moral judgments are not based on truth, but directly express our subjective reactions — thoughts, feelings, desires, and strivings — to facts, circumstances, or events. In emotivism, which is one of the branches of moral subjectivism, moral judgments are viewed as the expressions of moral sentiments that emerge when "you turn your reflexion into your own breast," as David Hume puts it. Reason alone, say the emotivists, can never tell us how to act; it only informs us about the nature and consequences of our actions; it is only emotion that helps us to decide what action to take: "morality is determined by sentiment" (cf. MacIntyre 1988, 300ff.).

In the Christian tradition, moral conflicts are either denied, as in the case of the manualists who declare such conflicts untrue or nonexistent, or depreciated in the sense that they are seen as arising from "sinful situations." If I must make a choice between killing a man or being killed by him, the necessary evil of killing is tolerated because it can be understood as a proportionally adequate means to achieving a good such as self-defense and self-preservation. Nevertheless, although it is not a sinful act, it relates to a "sinful situation." In this regard, Anthony Blasi, who wrote a dissertation on moral conflicts in the Christian tradition, observed that "it is more obscurantist than enlightening to speak of 'sinful situations.' Humans live in a sinful condition, and it is humans who sin; situations do not sin. . . . Sin is not occasioned by the situations per se but by inappropriate responses to the situations" (Blasi 1988, 11).

In the second approach, moral conflicts are not denied or eliminated from the moral debate, as they are in the first approach, but wholeheartedly recognized, acknowledged, and understood, regardless of how many difficulties they may bring with them. In this way the different types of conflicts — diversity, incompatibility, and incommensurability — are faced and dealt with (Lukes 1989, 133-39).

The first type of conflict arises out of the diversity of values and

25. Moral relativism and moral perspectivism should not be treated as identical, although several authors do so. Even MacIntyre's reflection on both approaches does not satisfy this criterion of nonidentification. According to him, moral perspectivism denies any rational debate on whether moral truth exists, whereas moral relativism goes even further by denying any rational debate on the existence of rational choice (MacIntyre 1988, 352).

norms within and between cultures. Whether this diversity really exists is an empirical question. Some moral authors speak of the prevailing or dominant ethos of Western society, by which they mean a bourgeois ethos, without empirically defining what a bourgeois ethos is and how it relates to social classes and groups. From empirical class-culture research, we know that one's values and norms depend greatly on the social milieu in which one grows up, the social class to which one belongs, the social position one holds, and the tradition in which one participates. Generally speaking, the diversity of culture (i.e., values and norms) is the effect of social distribution and composition (cf. Schreuder 1994). Along with this class-culture research, individualization research indicates that the diversity of values and value orientations is increasing in the Western world, concomitantly with the rise of individualization. This leads to moral fragmentation in the social, political, cultural, and religious spheres. The conclusion of the European Value Systems Study Group is: "No coherent patterns of either traditional or individualized values were found in the societies which were studied. Only the hypothesis that individual value systems in modern societies tend to be fragmented remained plausible" (Ester et al. 1993, 232). Another factor is also responsible for the increasing diversity of values and norms within society. This is migration, by which innumerable groups of people from other countries enter the Western world, bringing with them their own particular moral beliefs, values, and norms, which diversify the moral and religious domain even further (cf. Barot 1993).

The phenomenon of value diversity does not of itself lead to moral conflicts: "Even if . . . there can be value conflicts only where there are plural values, there seems no need for there to be conflicts wherever there are plural values" (Stocker 1990a, 165). Such conflicts occur when virtual confrontations become real. This happens when the person whose tradition is determined by one value or value system feels an inclination and tendency to choose a contrasting or even contradictory value or value system, usually because social mobility and new social contacts move him/her in that direction. Research regarding intercultural socialization problems shows that this may cause serious problems when it involves youth who develop a bicultural moral identity, or, in the worst case, some cultural moral identity that is neither that of the traditional society nor that of the modern country but somewhere in between, which severely marginalizes them (Liegle 1991, 229). On the side of the dominant Western population, confrontations with such foreigners may lead to ethnocentrism, which is an indication of the moral conflicts that this increasing diversity entails for the Western population (Eisinga and Scheepers 1989).

The second type of conflict is the phenomenon of incompatibility. A classic example is Sartre's pupil during the time of the Second World War who was torn between going to England to fight with the Free French Forces or staying with his mother, who was suffering from the death of both her elder son in 1940 during the German offensive and her collaborationist husband afterward. This pupil had to make a choice between two different kinds of action: the one concrete, direct, and individually oriented, the other related to something infinitely greater, a national collective, but with a highly uncertain outcome. Moreover, the pupil was also confronted by two different types of morality: on the one hand a morality of compassion and personal commitment, on the other a mix of duty (deontology) and risk calculation (consequentialism) (Sartre 1967, 25-28).[26]

Although the pupil's problem of incompatibility could be solved by suggesting that the closer a person is to one, the more he/she merits one's moral attention, in the case of the third type of conflict, that of incommensurability, one has no such scale to measure moral alternatives. None of the alternatives is superior to the other, because they are not comparable. A single currency is missing. I cannot offer any rational basis for my preference for Bach over Mozart or the other way around, because the two cannot be measured by the same standards. As Lukes bluntly puts it, the relationship is analogous to the relationship between "your belief in the fetus' right to life and mine in the mother's right to choose" (Lukes 1989, 135).

Which approach, one might ask, should be used in moral socialization: to deny conflicts or to recognize, acknowledge, and understand them? This question, of course, begs the answer, which I would like to make explicit by formulating a practical syllogism, the first premise of which is that education must meet the criteria of solid cognitive development, which means that the child is progressively introduced to the areas of life relating to the various sciences, especially the human sciences, but should not transmit ideas that will have to be corrected at a later stage of the child's development. The second premise is that recognizing, acknowledging, and understanding conflicts is the result of advancing (scientific) knowledge about conflicts. The conclusion, finally, is that from the point of view of education in general, moral socialization should prevent children from ignoring moral conflicts that are revealed by progressing (scientific) knowl-

26. The interpretation of the pupil's dilemma in terms of deontology and consequentialism is not Sartre's but mine. Philipse (1995, 89) objects to Sartre's analysis on the grounds that Sartre starts from the idea of the absolute freedom of the life project, which does not take into account the natural and social constraints on the human condition.

edge and should introduce them gradually to such conflicts, as children are directly or indirectly confronted with such conflicts in real life. In other words, as the child's significant others or other models undergo conflicts in their own personal and social lives, these should not be hidden from the child, but shared as far as the child's level of cognitive and emotional development allows.

Choices in a Moral Perspective

Moral conflicts require one to make choices, but this does not mean that all choices entail moral conflicts. Many of the moral choices we make do not involve any moral conflict at all. When I decide to take the train to travel to my friend who is in trouble, I make a series of choices, such as immediately leaving off working in the garden after she calls me, taking the train instead of driving by car, spending the whole day with her instead of visiting the theater in the evening, listening to her instead of giving direct advice. But these choices do not entail moral conflicts per se. They are means toward what I intend to do: support my friend.

But some choices we make do indeed entail moral conflicts. Such choices frequently center on plural values, which are determined by the three characteristics mentioned earlier: diversity, incompatibility, and incommensurability. According to the Aristotelian theory of the good, the good is not a single idea, the good is plural: "Things are called good in as many senses as they are said to exist" (*Nicomachean Ethics* 1.6). The good consists of a diversity of goods, which may be both incompatible and incommensurable. Wealth, honor, wisdom, friendship, and pleasure are all goods, but one cannot have them all at the same time. As Sartre's pupil came to realize, he could not be loyal both to his mother and to his country at the same time. However, loyalty to one's mother and one's country are not only incompatible but also incommensurable. Although both fall under the heading of loyalty, they are not on the same scale. They are not in fact instances of the same value. Loyalty to one's mother is not a greater virtue than to one's country or vice versa. Although they are designated by the same word, *loyalty,* they differ qualitatively. The first is the loyalty of love, the second group loyalty. One cannot really compare them (Fletcher 1993).

Can the choice we make in such a case ever be the result of deliberation and weighing? Yes, in a sense it can. But what manner of deliberating and weighing? In the case of moral conflicts arising from incompatible or incommensurable values, which are resolved by making moral choices, the values are not measurable on the same scale and thus cannot be weighed

119

or rated relative to one another. This is why certain ideas in the tradition of moral theology, such as the idea of the *ordo bonorum* or the lesser evil *(minus malum)* within the theory of double effects, are not effective in resolving moral conflicts and dilemmas, as Blasi (1988, 140-47) rightly points out. There is no metric solution, as he says. In this case, then, deliberating and weighing mean deciding which value to aim at and which actions to perform, given the particular circumstances and the person or persons involved. Applying this principle of appropriateness is not the same as applying a preestablished value or value scale to a concrete situation, which would be an example of theoretical reason, or deduction. Appropriateness is determined by the operation of practical reason. Practical reason summarizes what has been learned from past experiences, explores and scans the actual situation, and estimates the direct and indirect consequences of future actions for different persons or groups. From this synthetic insight, it judges what action should be taken.

The principle of appropriateness has a very old and respectable history, especially within the Catholic tradition of moral theology. It is implicit in the doctrine of teleology and proportionality. According to Thomas Aquinas, teleology means that the principal criterion and ultimate aim of moral action is the final end of human life, and that particular actions must be evaluated according to their orientation toward this end (*STh* I-II, 1, Introduction). Proportionality means that this orientation must be defined in terms of proximate and remote ends. An action has only one proximate end *(finis proximus)*, but may be oriented toward several remote ends *(fines remoti)*, as Thomas puts it (*STh* I-II, 1.3 ad 3). Proportionality means, therefore, that the circumstances must be taken into account: "But acts are made proportionate to that end by means of a certain commensurateness *(secundum commensurationem quandam)*, which results from the due circumstances" (*STh* I-II, 7.2). Killing aims at the other's death (proximate end), but if this killing is in self-defense and thus aims at my self-preservation (remote end), and the concrete situation does not provide other measures that can prevent me from being killed (circumstances), it is morally justified, albeit not morally good in itself (Janssens 1994).[27]

27. Janssens (1994) indicates that the encyclical *Veritatis Splendor* does not take into account the classical moral theory of teleology and proportionality of Thomas Aquinas. Moreover, the encyclical confuses teleology and consequentialism in nos. 71-83, especially 75. Vosman (1994, 49n.46) is right in saying that the encyclical's treatment of teleology, proportionalism, and consequentialism fails to present these theories in the way intended by the respective authors. For instance, killing in order not to be killed is morally justifiable. No serious moral theologian would say that this is morally good, as the encyclical suggests in no. 76.

Again, what is the moral significance of this deliberating and weighing, or determination of appropriateness, in the context of moral socialization? Should the concepts of teleology and proportionality be kept out of the socialization process? Should they be hidden? These questions are illusory because, in fact, deliberating and weighing cannot be eliminated or silenced. They are inherent in life itself. If that is the case, the only real choice is to model this deliberating and weighing as honestly and authentically and, especially, as carefully as possible. Nothing should be hidden, everything — at least as far as it contributes to the child's moral development — should be out in the open. Thinking aloud, externalizing one's inner speech, discussing reasons and options, performing what previously I have referred to as induction: that is what is good for the child. In this way moral conflicts and their resolution are modeled to the child, who in turn learns how to deal with such conflicts in his/her own life.

Compromises in a Moral Perspective

Just as in the preceding section I distinguished between choices and moral conflicts, now I separate what Stocker calls unexceptionable compromises from morally compromising compromises (Stocker 1990, 122). The first kind refers to, for example, agreements about the division of roles between husband and wife, siblings taking turns doing the dishes, or the choice of which movie to go to among friends. In themselves, such compromises do not entail any moral conflict at all.

The second kind of compromise, however, is morally compromising.[28] It demands painful decisions to be made, especially when a bad or wrong action has to be performed in order to reach a remote good or prevent a remote evil from coming into being. Aristotle gives some examples of such compromises. The most famous example is that of jettisoning cargo in bad weather. "In general no one willingly throws away his property; but if it is to save the lives of himself and everyone else, any reasonable person will do it" (*EN* 3.1). Another is the man whose parents and children are in the power of a tyrant; he is ordered to "do something dishonorable on condition that if he did it their lives would be spared, and if he did not they would be put to death" (*EN* 3.1). It is not difficult to find other situations of this

---

28. Morally compromising compromises may be divided into those between individuals and those within individuals. Those between individuals have interpersonal, societal, and political aspects (cf. Pennock and Chapman 1979). Here I restrict myself to intrapersonal compromises.

sort. For instance, is it justifiable to torture someone suspected of placing a time bomb in an overcrowded skyscraper in order to find out the location of the bomb and defuse it before it explodes?

The examples of the cargo, the tyrant, and the bomb are outside the scope of our day-to-day experiences. Nevertheless, morally compromising compromises happen in our everyday life in the same way. People desist from criticizing their boss in order to keep their job. They participate in family gatherings, even though they disapprove of the immoral actions of some members of the family. They vote for a political party although they loathe parts of its platform and policies. They participate in a religious community, even though they are unhappy with some of the institutional arrangements. As Edmund Burke puts it: "All government, indeed every human benefit and enjoyment, every virtue, and every prudent act, is founded on compromise and barter" (Golding 1979, 7).

This kind of compromise involves conflicting direct loyalties of the agent. I borrow the next example from Stocker: "Suppose that the marriage of relatives has been seriously troubled, but is now on the mend. Pleased for them, I offer to do whatever I can. Drawing me aside, my cousin says there is something I can do. As her husband suspects, she had been having an affair. Unless his suspicions are allayed, there will be no chance of a reconciliation. For both her sake and his, she asks me to help convince him that she had not been having the affair. She asks me to help her keep the truth from him, perhaps even to deceive or lie to him. This, I suggest, can involve dirty hands" (Stocker 1990a, 18-19).

According to Aristotle, generally speaking, "in some cases . . . the action, though not commended, is pardoned: viz. when a man acts wrongly because the alternative is too much for human nature, and nobody could endure it" (*EN* 3.1). There are limits, however, to this license, for Aristotle adds: "But presumably there are some things such that a man cannot be compelled to do them — that he must sooner die than do, though he suffer the most dreadful fate" (ibid.). Even Max Weber might support this view. As I already said in this chapter, he distinguishes between the deontological ethics of conviction *(Gesinnungsethik)*, which refers to what ought to be done, what is one's duty, irrespective of the circumstances, and the consequentialist ethics of responsibility *(Verantwortungsethik)*, which takes into account the circumstances, including the action's direct and indirect effects. The first is the ethics of the preacher, the second the ethics of the politician. Nonetheless, there is a point at which even a politician ought to say, as Luther did: "Here I stand, I can do no other," and switch from consequentialism to deontology (Weber 1982; cf. Lamore 1987, 144ff.). But Aristotle wisely concludes: "Yet it is sometimes difficult to decide what sort of advantage is to be chosen at what sort of price, or what fate endured for the sake of what advantage" (*EN* 3.1).

The aforementioned examples illustrate that choices may be dirty choices, and that the actions performed as a result of these choices leave the agents with dirty hands. Nonetheless, the actions must be performed, even though they are regrettable. Actions have costs. No one is totally free, because no one is able entirely to avoid doing what is evil, bad, or wrong. One is both in control and out of control, and there is a tragic element in this. "What is special about cases of dirty hands then is not that they are dirty, but that they are nonetheless justified or even obligatory" (Stocker 1990a, 26). These are cases of "moral immorality," or even "admirable immorality" (Stocker 1990a, 37). One may be justified in making or even obliged to make such morally compromising compromises, but the compromise does not lose its "dirty" character because of it. On the contrary: "Despite the dirty feature, the act is to be done. Nonetheless, because of the feature, the act is regrettable" (Stocker 1990a, 13).[29]

Again, the question arises of the moral significance of morally compromising compromises in the process of moral socialization. Let us be quite clear that the question is not whether these compromises are socialized by adults to the child, because they inevitably are. Generally speaking, there is no moral socialization in which no compromises of any sort are modeled to the young. Compromises are part of life, and because life is socialized, compromises are also socialized. The real question is not an empirical one but a moral one: what is the morally desirable way of dealing with compromises, especially morally compromising compromises? Since trying to conceal these compromises is doomed to fail in any case, the only moral alternative is to deal with them openly — talking about them, discussing the underlying reasons and circumstances, making explicit the principles of teleology and appropriateness, and showing the tragic aspects. In this way the child is prepared to respond to situations of moral compromise as responsibly and reasonably as possible.

The conclusion that it is educationally advisable to approach compromises, even morally compromising compromises, from the perspective of "moral immorality" can be further deepened by applying Ricoeur's

29. Here the distinction between "good" and "justifiable" is crucial. The act that is performed in accordance with the morally compromising compromise may be morally justifiable, but it is not in itself morally good. This distinction is overlooked in no. 76 of the encyclical *Veritatis Splendor* (1993), which condemns theories which state that actions which are against divine law or natural law may be justified as morally good. "Justifiable" and "good" are two different qualifications. Van Ouwerkerk (1965, 15) rightly sees compromises in terms of best possible actions, not of good actions.

criterion along with the good and the just: that of the wise, on which I elaborate in the next chapter. What is to be done in concrete situations, which are determined by their singularity, contingency, and tragedy, cannot be logically deduced from abstract, general values, rules, or norms, but must be decided by recourse to the virtue of wisdom. This wisdom is not wisdom about situations, which can be had by observing from the outside, but wisdom in situations, which is gained by participating on the inside. It is those who know the situation and are acquainted with it from the inside who have the authority to make the choices and decisions in the concrete situation. They are in a position to deliberate on the concrete aspects that must be taken into account and weigh their concrete meaning and saliency. They feel intuitively the tragic suffering implied in the choices, regardless of what these are. Moral socialization that prevented children from being confronted with the singularity, contingency, and tragedy of concrete moral situations would prevent them from gaining an understanding of what real life and real morality are all about (cf. Ricoeur 1992, 241-49).

4

Transmission

What might one see while walking around in some schools today? Education professor William Damon reports: "A counselor is calling a student's home about apparently excused absences, only to find out that the parent's letters have been forged. A young boy is in the principal's office for threatening his teacher with a knife. Three students are separated from their class after hurling racial epithets at a fourth. A girl is complaining that her locker has been broken into and all her belongings stolen. A small group of boys are huddling in a corner, shielding an exchange of money for drug packets. In the playground, two girls grab a third and punch her in the stomach for flirting with the wrong boy."[1]

This picture is surely not representative of what goes on in formal education in schools everywhere, the subject I deal with now, as I indicated in Chapter 1 while distinguishing between informal and formal education. Formal education, which most extensively takes place in the context of the school, be it a school of primary, secondary, tertiary, or adult education, is mainly characterized by the many good and right things that happen among students and between teachers and students. Nevertheless, Damon's report shows a picture of some trends that, to a lesser or greater extent, may regrettably be perceived in some situations in some schools in some contexts at some moments. At the same time, it makes us conscious of the discrepancy between the ideals we have about school and the reality of what school life is all about. Should not school be the place where the pure, innocent,

---

1. Quotation from Etzioni 1994, 100-101.

and noble character of the child is developed and formed? Should it not deliver opportunities for deepening and enriching the values the child already received within family and church? But one who consciously asks these sort of questions and relates them to what is really going on within the three institutions mentioned, that is, family, church, and school, immediately knows that he/she must moderate his/her demands and claims. Where the family fails in morally disciplining the child and morally socializing him/her in an appropriate way, the school cannot compensate. Where the church lacks the opportunity to support and reinforce the values that the family fails to initiate the child into, the school cannot stop that hole. The school is not able to replace family or church, because the school simply is neither family nor church.

What then, ideally, should be the school's aim in the realm of moral education? The traditional or even classic answer is the transmission of values and norms, to which the title of this chapter refers. This transmission can be defined in relation to the two modes dealt with in the previous chapters: discipline and socialization. Through discipline and socialization, the child is initiated into habits and values, in such a way that he/she is able to practice them, but without explicitly and consciously understanding their uses, the relations between them, and the principles underlying them. The child learns these habits randomly, not in a programmed and planned way (cf. Knoers 1973). The acquisition of moral habits and values through discipline and socialization, especially primary socialization, can be compared to the acquisition of language. The child learns language by participating in the language community. He/she develops, unconsciously, a knowledge of and ability to apply semantic, grammatical and pragmatic rules. The characteristic aim of transmission is to transform this know-how into know-that. In the case of language, the unconscious assumptions, rules, and patterns that underlie the concrete practice of speaking are explained and related to each other in an explicit, intentional manner in the teaching of grammar, literature, and so on. The same process of transmission takes place in the moral sphere: the unconscious assumptions, rules, and patterns that underlie the concrete practice of morality are intentionally taught by a teacher and intentionally learned by the child. This intentional teaching and learning is important, because a person who explicitly knows these rules and assumptions and how they work will be able to use them in all kinds of novel situations in the future, and to do so independently. He/she will be able to operate adequately even in complex situations, by interpreting the new situation in light of the known rules and patterns, combining elements, and reshaping, restructuring, and applying them in a creative way (cf. Snik 1990, 312-20). Thus "know-how" implies being able to unconsciously use regularities by convention, "know-that" means that one is able to use them consciously in new, complex situations by combining convention and invention (Eco 1979).

Of course, what happens in the school in the realm of moral education is not restricted to transmission. In the corridors, the classrooms, the cafeteria, all of the modes in moral education that I deal with in this study are in evidence. For instance, the discipline mode is first and foremost when the teacher introduces or enforces classroom regulations, such as "be kind to one another," "no fighting," or "no talking during fire drills." It is also in evidence when the teacher intervenes with a spontaneous moral commentary, for example praising or censuring a student. Rituals and ceremonies, for example, at the beginning or the end of the day, week, month, or year, are part of the mode of socialization, as are posters or other displays that include moral content, such as "Don't be a fool, stay in school" or "Life is a gift." Although not always easy to detect, the socialization mode may be present covertly in what is sometimes called the curricular substructure. Moral rules and principles play an important role in this substructure, because they are the shared understandings and assumptions that are supported by plausibility structures within a (supposedly) common life-world. Examples of these rules and principles are "teaching implies telling the truth," "education advances what is worthwhile," "the teacher should behave in an attitude of justice and fair play" (Jackson et al. 1993, 14-29). When students are introduced to the moral teachings of the Christian or humanistic traditions as a formal or as a regular part of the curriculum, the emphasis is on the transmission mode. As a formal part of the curriculum, this introduction to moral teachings occurs because it is prescribed officially, whereas in the regular part, it occurs as a secondary aspect of lessons in other subjects, especially language and social studies. The cognitive development or clarification mode also may be part of the formal or part of the regular curriculum. The emotional formation mode is emphasized when a teacher's facial or other bodily expressions support a student's moral experience of sympathy, care, sense of justice, or shame and guilt. The character formation mode is in evidence when a teacher shows preference for a virtue, such as strength and courage, temperance and modesty, prudence and wisdom, or fairness and justice (Jackson et al. 1993, 1-44).[2] Thus the trans-

---

2. Jackson et al. (1993, 1-44) distinguish between two groups of moral education processes at school: deliberate attempts to advance moral instruction and to develop moral behavior on the one hand, and moral practice that concretely embodies morality on the other. The first group consists of five forms: formal moral instruction, regular moral instruction, rituals and ceremonies, visual displays with moral content, and spon-

mission mode is not identical with moral education in the school setting, since the latter is much broader. Nor is it the defining mode of moral education in the school, since both the clarification mode and the cognitive development mode are frequently used as well. Nonetheless, it is a mode that is typically appropriate to the school, and no other institution, be it the family, neighborhood, peer group, or day care, places as much emphasis on the transmission mode as does the school. The church may be an exception, insofar as it offers formal programs in moral education, which are based on transmission.

The context in which the school and the church operate today is marked by a fundamental plurality of worldviews, convictions, values, and norms. In that context, the traditional transmission mode is no longer adequate or appropriate. In a society, a life-world characterized by plurality, which of the plural worldviews, beliefs, values, and so on should be transmitted?

In the following, I look at why traditional transmission is not able to solve the problems raised by moral plurality, but actually heightens them (section 4.1). I explore the extent to which an approach based on moral rationality may contribute to resolving this question (section 4.2). Because none of the forms of rationality discussed there, that is, substantive and procedural rationality, theoretical and practical rationality, is entirely satisfactory, I turn to Ricoeur's theory of moral complementarity, in which the main approaches in moral thought are transmitted in such a way that they critically correct and complete each other (section 4.3). This theory, however, does not take into account the developmental stages of the child or student, which I deal with in the next chapter.

4.1 Moral Plurality

Because moral tradition is increasingly beset by moral plurality, the traditional mode of transmission suffers from various shortcomings, which may be described in terms of two dimensions: content and aims.

---

taneous interjections of moral commentary. The second group takes three forms: classroom regulations, expressive morality (such as in facial expressions), and the morality of curricular substructure. I have distributed these eight forms over the different modes of moral education examined in this study.

The Content of Traditional Transmission

Traditional transmission has a clear content. That is, the know-that which distinguishes transmission from the know-how modes of discipline and socialization consists of a system of propositions, values, principles, rules, and norms that are expressed in a particular moral practice. This know-that is stated in an explicit, lucid, and at least tentatively convincing way. The propositions derive or are supposed to derive from documents that form part of the sources of the moral tradition concerned.

These sources can be divided into three phases or parts, as Weber (1980, 279-81) puts it. The first is the initial phase, during which the moral tradition comes into being and specific texts are accepted as genuine. These texts form a moral canon, which contains the principles and rules for the moral community or communities concerned. The best-known examples are in the world religions, especially the Abrahamite religions, Judaism, Christianity, and Islam. The canonization process takes varying periods of time, as may be seen from the difference between the gradualness with which the Jewish canon was established and the relative speed of New Testament canon formation. The rate of canon formation depends on whether there is an urgent need for fixing a list of texts that can be used to put an end to intra- and intercommunity conflicts about moral theory and practice. These conflicts always have their roots in divergent inter-pretations of a variety of moral influences that originate in social contexts and disturb the moral community's unity and cohesion.

The second source is documents that interpret the canonical texts to provide answers to questions that arise later in response to specific spatial and temporal circumstances. Again, these questions are the result of differ-ences between various groups within the moral community and between moral communities, in response to the pressure of the societal context. Although the canonization process is considered to establish conclusively the list of texts that are held to be foundational, invariable, and sacrosanct, this does not mean that they do not require subsidiary interpretation as individuals, groups, and communities change over time. Although this phase does not produce a fixed list of texts, it does establish as authoritative certain documents that every group or community is supposed to refer to when difficulties, tensions, and conflicts arise. In the Catholic tradition, the au-thority of the works of Thomas Aquinas, especially the "Secunda Secundae" of his *Summa Theologica,* which refers to the moral domain, is a prime example.

The third source is not texts, but rather an official organ, function, or office, from which the holder(s) can proclaim the sole correct interpretation of both canonical and traditional texts. Examples that come to mind are synods, councils, or moral and religious leaders to whom is attributed ultimate authority, power, or even infallibility.

In every religious or moral tradition, this Weberian triad determines the system of propositions that define and guide the traditional transmission process. The reason is simple. When adults agree on answers to questions or on solutions to conflicts in order to maintain the unity of their moral community, it is only logical that these adults initiate their children into exactly the same solutions. According to Weber, this is precisely the purpose of preaching and pastoring in the religious realm. Preaching consists of teaching religious and moral principles for use in daily life to a group of people. It concentrates on what Weber calls the practical way of life *(praktische Lebensführung)*, and provides concrete instructions for the art of moral life. Weber distinguishes preaching from pastoring *(Seelsorge)*, which aims at teaching individuals how to live religiously and morally, and may take the form of moral counseling, comforting and consoling, hearing confession,[3] or charismatic healing. Preaching is teaching religious morality on a collective basis; pastoring is doing the same on an individual basis. From this frame of reference, moral education in its traditional transmission mode can be seen as a variation of preaching morality (i.e., to a small group of people), or as a variation of pastoring (i.e., to a collection of individuals) (Weber 1980, 283-85).

3. The practice of hearing confession is not nearly as uniform throughout history as Weber would have it. In the early church, official public confession developed gradually into private confession, which was meant to take place once in a lifetime. The Council of Toledo in 589 actually rejected frequent confession. From monastery life, a nonofficial mode of confession, the so-called devotional confession, was adopted in some circles of pious laypeople as a technique for advancing their spiritual and moral life. In the Celtic church, where public confession probably never existed, a secret confession developed in the monasteries and was later introduced among laypeople for therapeutic reasons. In the Carolingian renaissance, the axiom was: secret confession for secret sins, public confession for public sins. Because of its public character, many people feared public confession and restricted themselves to personal confession without priestly intervention, i.e., a direct confession *coram Deo* (Van Eupen 1962). The rise of the secret confession is related to the development of the Handbooks of Penance, which indicated the kind of penance, such as fasting, praying, giving alms, pilgrimage, or flogging, that was to be given for various sins. These handbooks may be considered as "moral thermometers," but because of the divergence among them, they actually encouraged moral laxity (Van Eupen 1963).

The Aims of Traditional Transmission

The second dimension of traditional transmission is its aims, which can be distinguished as cognitive, affective, and volitive. Generally speaking, the cognitive aims of teaching/learning processes fall into two subcategories: developing knowledge and developing cognitive abilities. The very core of developing knowledge consists in the memorization of the propositions that have been transmitted. Developing cognitive abilities consists of four different activities: comprehending, applying, analyzing, and synthesizing units of knowledge. They require the student to engage actively and critically in the content, use it in relatively new situations, deconstruct and reconstruct it from different perspectives, and judge its relevance and value.[4] It is significant that, by and large, traditional transmission is restricted to the first subcategory, that is, developing memorizable knowledge, and fails to recognize the importance of critical thinking and autonomous problem solving, which are part of the second subcategory. It does not encourage the student to develop his/her own judgment, which may deviate from the traditional propositions and conclusions, does not stimulate his/her freedom of thought, and does not correspond to Kant's maxim: "Dare to use your own rationality."

The second category of educational aims is affective in nature. It may be divided into two subcategories: motivation and attitude development. Motivation refers first to activities such as receiving and attending, which require awareness, willingness to receive, and selective attention; and second to responding, which entails acquiescence in responding, willingness to respond, and satisfaction in response. Attitude development consists of three complex levels of interrelated activities: valuing (acceptance of a value, preference of a value, commitment), organizing a value system, and, finally, integrating the value system into one's life in such a way that one is characterized by it.[5] Traditional transmission covers the whole range of

---

4. Here I refer to the taxonomy of cognitive objectives in education by Bloom et al. (1956), which distinguishes among six levels: knowing, comprehending, applying, analyzing, synthesizing, and evaluating. According to De Corte (1973) and De Corte and Van Bouwel (1978), the sequence between synthesizing and evaluating should be reversed and the distinction between analyzing and evaluating eliminated (cf. van der Ven 1982, 524-29; 1985, 235-36).

5. Here I refer to the taxonomy of affective aims in education by Krathwohl et al. (1964). I distinguish between lower affective aims (receiving/attending and responding) and higher ones (valuing, organizing, and characterizing), because the first refer mainly to (separate) behavior or classes of behavior, whereas the second relate to the level of attitudes, which implies a deeper level of interiorization (cf. van der Ven 1982, 530-34; 1985, 236)

affective educational aims, from receiving and attending to characterization. Thus traditional transmission focuses on transmitting propositions in such a way that the student knows them by heart and integrates them into his/her personality. Any possibility that the student might come to his/her own evaluation of the educational content and deviate from traditional choices, however, is neglected. There is simply no place for it in the traditional scheme of things. The traditional convictions, values, and norms must take possession of the student's head and heart.

This objective is accentuated even further by the focus of traditional transmission on the third category of educational aims, the volitive. Traditional transmission strives to bring the student to the point where he/she uses his/her will to maintain firmly and persistently the convictions, values, and norms that have been transmitted, and stimulates him/her to systematically put them into practice, in personal as well as social life. The focus of traditional transmission on formation and exercise of the will and on developing self-discipline is not exclusively a thing of the past. More recent educational approaches also place considerable emphasis on the formation of the will, as I noted in Chapter 2 with reference to discipline and self-discipline. Many works of humanistic psychology also attach importance to making choices and following through on them, as for example Assagioli's (1973) work on psychosynthesis. The same is true of educational programs that emphasize the mode of value clarification in moral education (see Chap. 5 below). But the fundamental difference between traditional transmission with its strong volitive emphasis and these more recent developments is that the former trains the child's will within a rigidly established set of values and norms, which the child is not allowed to deviate from or transcend, whereas the humanistic-psychological approaches stimulate the child to make his/her own choices based on his/her own preferences, experiences, and emotions. In short, traditional transmission transfers traditional values and norms to the child with the intent that they be cognitively memorized, affectively internalized, and volitively programmed.

Does this memorization, internalization, and programming equate with indoctrination? That depends on how one defines indoctrination, and what part critical thinking plays in the transmission process. Does critical thinking in fact take place or is it left out, and if so does this leaving out happen incidentally or intentionally? If it is incidental, then the higher cognitive objectives (developing cognitive abilities as opposed to developing knowledge) are simply overlooked. This is different from the situation in which these objectives are intentionally left out. From this distinction between intentional and incidental omission of critical thinking, I deduce two poles that form the two extremes of a continuum. The continuum, which allows for all kinds of intermediate stages, is important because educational objectives, like the human mind itself, pass through a range of unconscious, subconscious, preconscious, and conscious mental stages. Insofar as critical thinking is intentionally rejected in order to protect and keep intact the doctrine being transmitted, I believe it is correct to speak of indoctrination. Thus inasmuch as traditional transmission intentionally suppresses critical questions, objections, and doubts, indoctrination is evidently taking place. When critical thinking is unintentionally neglected, however, this is not the case. In other words, indoctrination can be seen as a continuum with intentionality as its central aspect.

Some authors also relate indoctrination to the content of transmission. They define indoctrination as the transmission of doctrine, moral doctrine. But what then are doctrines? According to the sociology of knowledge by Berger and Luckmann, doctrines are part of a symbolic universe that consists of an established set of ideas about humanity, society, and cosmos as well as the actions these ideas imply. They may be distinguished into "naive" and "sophisticated" doctrines, and all kinds of intermediate ones. Doctrines anticipate questions from inside and outside, and try to provide answers. Questions about doctrines are asked by children who are being initiated into them, by deviant groups from within, by heretics from without, and by people from other societies and cultures. Such questions may elicit different types and patterns of answers. The keepers of doctrine may see these questions as a danger: "The appearance of an alternative symbolic universe poses a threat because its very existence demonstrates empirically that one's own universe is less than inevitable" (Berger and Luckmann 1967, 108). Or they may react in a relaxed way and feel themselves stimulated and challenged. Thus doctrines vary in their open- or closed-mindedness.[6] Each has its own code and coding system that determines the amount and type of influence it tolerates or even accepts from the environment (e.g., rival doctrines). Examples of open-minded doctrines are the liberal religious and moral traditions within Protestantism. Closed doctrines are typified by

6. Here I apply Rokeach's distinction between the open and closed mind (1960) with regard to religious and moral convictions, which he investigated within the tradition of Adorno's authoritarian personality. Thus I transfer Rokeach's ideas from the individual to the institutional level, because open- and closed-mindedness can be institutionalized. An example is the Index of Prohibited Books. Moreover, an institutionalized open- or closed-minded doctrine influences one's personal open- or closed-mindedness, as far as one adheres to this doctrine (Peters 1977, 52-53). Rokeach himself tried to establish a correlation between the degree of feeling threatened on the one hand and the degree of closed-mindedness, absolutism, and dogmatism that emerge from various canons of twelve Catholic councils on the other (Fortmann 1968, 225-28).

fundamentalist religious and moral traditions of all kinds. An example of a doctrine that varies in open- and closed-mindedness on different levels and over time is the moral doctrine of the Catholic Church. At the grassroots level this doctrine is more open than at the top, as is evident from the discussion about birth control, and generally it was more open in the sixties than it has been under the pontificate of John Paul II in the eighties and nineties (Haarsma 1981; 1991).[7] Taking the two dimensions—aims and content—together, we can say that indoctrination happens when critical thinking is intentionally rejected and when the doctrine to be transmitted is characterized by closed-mindedness.[8]

Moral Plurality and the Limits of Traditional Transmission

Traditional transmission is therefore ambivalent. On the one hand, insofar as it favors indoctrination, it prevents maturing human beings from becoming freely choosing, self-responsible individuals. Students are trained to obey moral authorities, such as parents, priests, and other educators, so that they can take their place in the tradition that is transmitted to them. Their moral responsibility consists in responding positively to the moral values and norms of this tradition. This leads to conventionalism and conformism, as exemplified by Adolf Eichmann's words at his Jerusalem trial: "I only did what was normal in my society." On the other hand, this approach produces harmonious and disciplined communities and a predictable, well-organized, and safe society. Immoral or at least abnormal behavior is banned because immoral or abnormal thought, emotions, and volitions are banned. Crime is prevented or at least its spread is controlled. These are the two sides of the same coin: by causing the individual to conform to traditionally established standards, this kind of transmission reduces the sense of personal responsibility on the one hand, and advances societal harmony on the other (Bauman 1995).

A first consideration is that traditional transmission indicates the way in which it can help us develop understanding of the good life and of

7. In their social psychology of organizations, Katz and Kahn (1978, 434) indicate that the position people occupy in an organization determines the extent to which they are open-minded or closed-minded. This explains the differences in attitude between those at the grassroots and those at the top.

8. I agree with authors who discuss indoctrination, such as Hare and R. S. Peters (cf. Spiecker 1991, 94-110). I disagree with them, however, insofar as they do not take into account the twofold continuum of aims and content that is implied in indoctrination.

ourselves. Everybody knows that one ought to work, love, learn, and worship. Traditions offer us their substantial insights into which work has to be done, how to love, what to learn, and to what end to worship. They tell me what is good for me. They tell me who I am (Fleischacker 1994, 72ff.).

In the Greek honor ethics, for example, which in some circles endures into the present time, the dominant paradigm is the warrior or citizen-soldier who returns victorious from battle. His honor is connected with virtues such as energy, strength, and courage. In Stoicism it is self-mastery, not honor, that is the overriding goal. The ideal is the unbiased, disinterested self, which perceives its natural and human surroundings as calmly and coolly as it does its own inclinations and emotions. The romantic tradition rebels against this self-mastery, which instead values authenticity as the apex of morality. It favors the expression of emotions from their natural sources in the depths of human existence. The Christian tradition is marked by a transformation of the will, in which the conception of self-mastery is directed toward self-dedication to God, Jesus, and fellow human beings in authentic, personal love (Taylor 1989; 1991). In each of these traditions, the content and aims of moral education differ.

It is precisely this phenomenon that poses a serious problem. With so many different traditions to choose from — the foregoing are but four examples of many — which one should serve as the basis for the trans-mission mode in moral education? Historical arguments are not convincing because all four of the above examples are rooted in history and yet are positively valued at present. Honor ethics still count, not only in societies that are known for their belligerent attitude but also in those that have converted weapons industries into peace-related ones. Honor and shame are of all times, strength and courage count in all times. Especially in a capitalist society, self-control is highly valued because it channels "ir-rational" drives and emotions so that economic life can be organized in an effective and efficient manner (Elias 1977). It advances self-mastery, which is indispensable for civilization to evolve to higher stages, as Freud showed in his *Civilization and Its Discontents*. The romantic ethic of authen-ticity is perhaps the closest to our current moral Zeitgeist — I mean the process by which materialism is being replaced by what is called post-materialism, which is characterized by the longing for existential self-realization (Inglehart 1990). Lastly, the Christian ethic of conversion and transformation to divine and human love still operates as a very strong moral factor in structuring and developing social and personal life. So: what tradition to choose?

A second consideration is that traditions always contain subtraditions and streams. This means not only that a plurality of convictions, values, and norms exists in every tradition, but also that these subtraditions and streams complement, criticize, and conflict with each other. Consequently, the moral guidelines offered by traditions also complement, criticize, and conflict with each other. This is because traditions are anything but context-free. They are formed by different communities, which are determined by all kinds of spatial and temporal factors. Traditions are continuously being reinterpreted and transformed. Their contingent and accidental nature cannot and should not be denied. From here, Lessing's statement that "accidental truths of history can never become the proof of necessary truth of reason" receives both its fundamental and actual meaning (Fleischacker 1994, 68). When the existence of different traditions is recognized, and when each of these traditions is known to consist of subtraditions and streams, wherein then lies their authority? The least we can say is that any authority derived from any tradition whatsoever does not emerge spontaneously and cannot be established in advance.

4.2 Moral Rationality

As already noted, the fundamental problem to be solved in relation to the transmission mode in moral education is: which moral content is to be transmitted? The traditional transmission mode does not appear to satisfy because of the challenge it faces from the plurality of moral traditions. Perhaps rationality, rather than traditionalism, could solve this problem. But then we must ask: which rationality?

The problem of plurality of traditions and thus of moral plurality might be approached through either a substantive or a procedural rationality, that is, by using substantive or procedural arguments in order to determine which of the various moral traditions to choose for the purpose of transmission. In the substantive approach, values from one tradition are compared with those from another and critically evaluated. But this generates further questions: By what criteria are these values evaluated? Perhaps a third moral system is needed from which to judge? Which tradition is to be chosen and for what reasons? Ought it to be Aristotle's, Thomas's, or MacIntyre's teleology? Why? The substantive approach, which is meant to cope adequately with moral plurality, generates its own questions and renders the problem of plurality even more pressing. Alternatively, the problem might be dealt with using procedural rationality. Here it is not the substance of the different moral traditions that is compared, but the extent to which they correspond to a specified procedural principle. This principle might be human rationality, or it might be human autonomy or respect, which in turn are linked with rationality. Then the question is to what extent the various moral traditions realize this rationality, or this autonomy or respect. But a cursory glance at this approach reveals a number of complications. To borrow from the title of MacIntyre's book: whose rationality? which rationality?[9] Should it be, for example, Kant's, Rawls's, Hare's, or Habermas's so-called deontological rationality? Or Bentham's, Mill's, or Moore's utilitarianist and consequentialist rationality? Each of these implies all kinds of substantive assumptions, presuppositions, and convictions. Thus procedural rationality seems necessarily to imply a substantive rationality.

Another set of approaches to the problem of moral plurality is theoretical versus practical rationality. In theoretical rationality, abstract and general moral principles are applied directly to concrete situations. This deductive approach guarantees that the general and abstract rules maintain their obligatory character when people are confronted with concrete problems of life and death, self-love and other-love, duty and sympathy, truth and untruth, and so on. The problems are solved by directly deriving conclusions from obligatory premises. Practical rationality entails taking the complexity of the concrete situation into account and looking for an appropriate moral answer. Such an approach requires practical judgment of the goods or values that are at stake and what actions or aims are most desirable in light of the good life.

In the following sections I examine in more detail the forms of rationality that have been briefly mentioned here: substantive and procedural rationality, and theoretical and practical rationality (cf. Taylor 1994a), always with an eye to whether and to what extent these forms of rationality provide solutions to the problem of moral plurality in the transmission mode of moral education.

Substantive and Procedural Rationality

As in Chapter 1, here, too, I take my starting point in Habermas's distinction between different types of moral thinking. Habermas distinguishes between two main types, substantive and procedural, and divides the procedural types into utilitarian subtypes on the one hand and deontological subtypes on the other. From this he establishes three moral criteria, the good, the purposive, and the just (Habermas 1992, 197-201; 1993, 1-18). Let me

9. The title of MacIntyre's book is: *Whose Justice? Which Rationality?* (Notre Dame, 1988).

elucidate this a bit further in terms of moral plurality and the problem of choice with regard to the transmission mode in moral education.

Habermas suggests that the substantive approaches within moral thinking may be understood as teleological ones. They contain a vision or a set of visions concerning the good life, which is to be strived for and acted on. These visions are embodied in all kinds of inclinations, feelings, attitudes, interests, habits, customs, lifestyles, decision patterns, and action chains, which are taken for granted. They have emerged from specific cultural and moral traditions that have taken shape in specific communities in specific contexts of space and time, and are transmitted by the older generations to the younger ones in a dialectical process of continuity and discontinuity, or transformation. Hence they are living visions within living traditions in living communities. They inform the members of the community of what life is all about, put questions like "Who am I?" and "Who are we?" into perspective, and establish ideals and goals for the individual and the community. This substantive approach implies the fundamental work of hermeneutics from three aspects. First, it helps to clarify descriptively the actual situation we are in, with the help of images, symbols, and concepts stemming from the moral tradition concerned. At the same time it enrichingly presents us with the possible situation we might arrive at, one that is within our reach. Lastly it gives us a picture of the desirable situation we have to strive for. The hermeneutical work within teleological self-clarification combines at once the actual, the possible, and the desirable world.

An excellent, or perhaps the preeminent, example of teleological moral thinking and moral education as well may be found in Aristotle's ethics. Aristotle sees the ultimate aim *(telos)* of human life as the happy life *(eudaimonia),* which is embedded in the social life of the community or polis *(politikon zoon).* The content of this happy life is excellence or virtuosity, which equals quality: the quality of good living *(euzoia)* and the quality of good acting *(eupraxia)* as well. Excellent or virtuous living and acting is the equivalent of the artist's excellent or virtuous pottery or painting, or the musician performing a piano concerto according to truly professional and esthetic standards. Happiness is not identical with pleasure, but pleasure accompanies and is the outcome of living virtuously and acting excellently. To achieve this happiness, one must practice the virtues. They are the means to *euzoia* and *eupraxia,* but also an intrinsic part of them. In other words, they are practiced for both extrinsic and intrinsic reasons. Virtues like courage, magnanimity, generosity, temperance, justice, liberality, or benevolence are good in themselves, representing the so-called Aristotelian mean. Virtue lies between two extremes. The extremes, or vices, are excess and deficiency, overdoing and underdoing, overacting and underacting, overexperiencing and underexperiencing. Thus each virtue lies between two vices: courage between rashness and timidity, liberality between prodigality and meanness, and justice between doing injustice and suffering injustice.[10] The Aristotelian mean is not an arithmetic one, as if the virtue lay exactly at the midpoint of the scale. It is a proportional mean: it is "my" mean, in that it applies to the concrete situation, setting, and context in which I find myself (Aristoteles *EN* 1.4-8; Barnes 1976).

Perhaps the most important virtue in Aristotle's ethics is friendship. It is the basis of the communitarian life of the polis. It represents a shared acknowledging, striving for, and enjoying the same good or goods. This friendship is not primarily founded in affection, and it is not limited to private life. It has its roots in a common project (cf. MacIntyre 1984, 156). Friendship is of three different kinds. It may be developed for reasons of mutual utility, as a way of reaching extrinsic goals. It may be based on mutual pleasure: friends spend time together having fun and enjoying hedonistic experiences. It may be rooted in personal respect for and interest in the other. In the last case, one wants what is truly good for the other as another self, as one also wants what is truly good for oneself. Such friendship is self detached engagement in the other's life, as one also self-detachedly engages in one's own life. In it, one approaches and meets the other as another self, in the same way as one is himself/herself approached and met as another self (*EN* 1; cf. Ricoeur 1992). It is this last kind of friendship, that is, the sharing of the good life for both oneself and the other, which has paradigmatic worth for living in the community of the polis.

Another insight from Aristotle's ethics that is important for moral education is his idea about the relation between virtues, emotions, and desires. Aristotle sees virtues as ordering emotions and desires, thereby helping the individual to decide which ones to cultivate and encourage, and which ones to moderate and restrict. "To act virtuously is not, as Kant was later to think, to act against inclination; it is to act from inclination formed by the cultivation of the virtues. Moral education is an 'éducation sentimentale'" (MacIntyre 1981, 140). In other words, moral education, in the Aristotelian sense, is educating the emotions by directing them to the virtues. Among these virtues, some traditionally are called the cardinal virtues: justice, prudence, temperance, and courage. But friendship may be seen as the culmination of moral education. More than any other virtue, it

---

10. Thomas does not accept the Aristotelian mean for justice, because for him the opposite of justice is injustice, which he sees as a single-minded vice (*STh* II-II, 59; cf. MacIntyre 1988, 204).

paves the way to the good life and embodies it. It may be seen as the cornerstone of moral education.[11]

As insightful, convincing, and even seductive as Aristotle's ethics may be, they raise a number of problems. They are based on a scientifically obsolete biological-teleological anthropology (Van den Beld 1985),[12] imply a set of virtues that are typically aristocratic and masculine in nature (Bulhof 1989), and embody a conception of the polis that belongs to the premodern context (Mieth 1987). This set of archaic views is evident in Aristotle's saying that a husband is to his wife as a statesman is to his citizens, a father is to his child as a king to his subjects, and a slave possesses less capacity for reason and virtue than his master (*Pol.* 1.12-13). Above all, they presuppose a society characterized by moral uniformity instead of the pluriformity that is typical of modern life. Especially this last problem concerns me here. The polis as a singular city-state no longer exists. Modern society consists of a huge number of poleis, each embodying divergent moral practices and thoughts, within a plurality of societal systems, institutions, sectors, and situations. There is not only one substantive approach, be it Aristotle's or any other: there are many, because there is a plurality of different conceptions of the good life and of the goods it implies. From the perspective of moral education, the question arises whether a substantive approach can be maintained at all. Is there another way to satisfy the different claims made by different substantive approaches? Is it, perhaps, the procedural "high way"?

As I already said, procedural approaches are of two kinds, utilitarian and deontological. According to MacIntyre's analysis of the fundamental difference between the two approaches, utilitarianism starts from the principle of utility, which serves the purposes of both interests and passions, whereby interests are understood as the collective expression of the passions of individuals, whereas deontology begins with the rational principle of

---

11. Ruprecht (1994, 139) asks whether the polis or friendship is the chief focus of Aristotle's ethics. As he points out (n. 39): "It is surely significant that the longest sustained discussion in the entire *Nicomachean Ethics* concerns *philia*, not the *polis*, in books VIII and IX (1155a-1172a)."

12. MacIntyre, who sees Aristotle's ethics as foundational for his own ethics of virtue, replaces Aristotle's teleology, which is rooted in his biology, with a teleological approach based on a cultural-anthropological conception of the good life on the one hand and a sociological analysis of existing practices on the other. He sees practices as "any coherent and complex form of socially established cooperative human activity through which goods internal to that form of activity are realized in the course of trying to achieve those standards of excellence which are appropriate to, and partially definitive of, that form of activity" (MacIntyre 1981, 175).

justice as having an authority independent of interest and passion, so that appeal against one's interests and passions can be justified (MacIntyre 1988, 213-14). Let me first give some examples of the utilitarian approach in order to see how far it brings us with regard to the transmission mode in moral education.

There are many varieties of utilitarianism.[13] But for my purpose, a few well-known examples will suffice. They all converge in seeking to balance the satisfaction of passions and interests against their dissatisfaction for both the individual and society.

A fundamental topic, which utilitarianism deals with, relates to the following question: useful to what passion and interest and for whom? One of the founders of classic libertarian utilitarianism is Locke. In *An Essay Concerning Human Understanding,* he elaborates on the hedonist idea that for humans good is pleasure, pain evil: Things then are good or evil only in reference to pleasure or pain. Humans desire pleasure and seek to avoid pain. They are impelled by nature to maximize pleasure. Morality consists of finding the rational instruments for this maximization.

Although this hedonist approach shocked many of Locke's Christian contemporaries, he was a believing Christian himself. His view of nature as pleasure-related is founded on the belief that God created this nature. To seek pleasure and to try to further it by rational means is to do God's will, which is embodied in the nature he created. This pleasure maximization applies not only to oneself but also to one's fellows, because they also are meant and made by God to be in his image. Here belief in God prevents humans from sinking into egoistic hedonism. It encourages them to attend to one another's pleasure, which is one another's good, the common good. God guarantees "the harmony of interests" (cf. Taylor 1989, 234-47).

Following in Locke's footsteps, Bentham elaborated on the pleasure/

---

13. Because of these varieties, sometimes utilitarianism is understood as a teleology, which implies a theory of the good, or more precisely a theory of producing the most good. Whereas Habermas interprets utilitarianism in terms of the right ("the right thing to do"), as I indicated, Rawls (1971, 22-27) does so in terms of the good. But this "producing the most good" implies that utilitarianism overlaps with consequentialism or at least may be seen as a subclass of consequentialism, because consequentialism does not merely honor the good to be valued, but promotes it by calculating alternative options and prognoses (cf. Pettit 1994). Because of this calculating process, which sometimes is derided as moralistic computer science, Habermas unbiasedly connects utilitarianism with pragmatism, which stresses the purposive. But this European use of "pragmatism" probably differs from American pragmatism in the sense of William James and John Dewey.

pain principle. From his anthropological perspective, in which usefulness rules his utilitarianism, he says that we have always to choose that action which will produce as its consequence the greatest pleasure, that is, the greatest quantity of pleasure with the smallest possible quantity of pain, for the greatest number of people (MacIntyre 1981, 63).[14] On this principle a utilitarian orientation of moral education can be based (Verschwur 1996).

This hedonistic approach was broadened and enriched by John Stuart Mill. As the first Benthamite philosopher, who nevertheless felt uneasy with the plainly hedonistic approach of his father, James Mill, and the latter's sympathizer Bentham, he differentiated between "higher" and "lower" pleasures. The first are those that advance other people's happiness, and the second one's own pleasure and interest. Here we already have not just one principle but at least a complex principle with several facets, so that we have to ask the questions: which pleasure and whose pleasure? which pain and whose pain? (MacIntyre 1981, 64, 70).

From this differentiated utilitarianism, John Stuart Mill elaborated on the "higher" pleasure in the direction of individual liberty as a societal aim. This liberty is ultimately what makes possible creative self-realization, which society must nurture by establishing conditions favorable to it. The individual should have the opportunities to enact his/her rich potentialities, thereby gaining self-fulfillment and real joy (Mill 1977).

Here Mill combines his libertarian utilitarianism with what could be called a mild form of socialism. In that sense he is one of the predecessors of the social liberals or utilitarians like Hobson and Hobhouse (Selznick 1992, 375-76). It is interesting that Richard Rorty, who calls himself a liberal ironist, considers John Stuart Mill's attempt to find a balance between liberty and solidarity as "pretty much the last word." He sees Mill's emphasis on taking care of people who suffer from pain as the very basis of the principle of solidarity that should rule societal life (Rorty 1991, 63).

While libertarian utilitarianism makes pleasure outweigh pain, later utilitarianism focuses on other passions and interests that are held to be an intrinsic part of human nature, like knowledge, understanding, autonomy, achievement, success, health, beauty, or more social ones like sympathy,

---

14. Of itself, Benthamite utilitarianism does not lead to either politically left or right-wing solutions to the question whether goods should be redistributed to achieve the balance for the greatest number of people. The reason is that it lacks a theory of justice (Rawls 1971, 26). The key consideration is which distribution brings the greatest satisfaction for the greatest number: when everybody receives a relatively equal share or some receive substantially more than others, because otherwise the general level would sink (cf. Goodin 1994).

friendship, or intimacy. The choice of which action to perform depends on the extent to which this action is useful in advancing the particular passion(s) or interest(s).

Still others are of the opinion that utility is not a criterion for what is intrinsically worthy, and that the distinction between what is intrinsically worthy and what is instrumentally worthy is far from evident (cf. Hare 1967, 137-40). Are values such as pleasure, knowledge, understanding, success, or friendship of intrinsic worth, or are they instrumental to something else, and if so, what? Happiness, self-realization, or self-fulfillment? The only clear criterion is individual preference. As Charles Stevenson says in *Ethics and Language* (1945), "'This is good' means roughly the same as 'I approve of this; do so as well'" (cf. MacIntyre 1984, 12). From the viewpoint of his preferential utilitarianism, Hare would add that this individual preference and its advice to "do so as well" must be made universalizable in order to be morally obligatory. This universalizability depends on what I myself would actually say and do if I were in the same situation as the other person (Hare 1973, 127). This Kantian universalizability approach in Hare's thought, which I will come back to presently, means that I must apply to my own situation the rule or norm that I commend to others in their situation, in order to determine whether it is valid (cf. Hare 1981, 222). This guarantees impartiality.

Within utilitarianism, the problem of moral plurality still exists because the plurality of passions and interests is not transcended by applying the procedure of utility. This procedure leaves open the question of how to define utility and which passions and interests are served by it. There are an infinite variety of passions and interests, and they are not mutually comparable, for lower and higher pleasures, success and self-realization, achievement and beauty, sympathy and intimacy are not points along an arithmetic scale (Heeger 1985, 22-29). Moreover, there is the dilemma of what to do when passion and interest contradict, for it is too simple to suggest that interests are the expression of passions: "When rational calculation shows someone that the expression of some passion presently felt in action will not be to their longer term interest, how is that passion to be inhibited?" (MacIntyre 1988, 213). Nor does the answer to the problem of moral plurality lie in preferential utilitarianism, because one must still ask: should all preferences of all people be satisfied, and if not, what is the criterion for selection? Do all present preferences with regard to the present have the same moral meaning? Do all present preferences with regard to the future have the same relevance? Do all future preferences with regard to the future (e.g., the good life for our children in a just society within an ecologically sustainable environment) have the same weight? And how do these three kinds of preferences relate to each other? Perhaps we could agree that nonprudential or antisocial preferences will be rejected automatically, and that only "true" preferences that people should have and not the "manifest" preferences they actually have will be considered. But this raises the question of how nonprudential and antisocial preferences are determined and by whom, and why they should be rejected (Heeger 1985, 31-35). If these questions cannot be answered using procedural rationality, at least not a utilitarian one, perhaps deontological procedural rationality offers a way out?

The founder of deontological moral theory is, of course, Kant. His starting point is the existence of the human being as a moral agent. Being a moral agent means that one has a free will, which implies that one is free to choose between acting and refraining from acting. For this will to be truly free, any action has to be free from any determination or even influence by any external phenomena such as religious rules and injunctions, social conventions and habits, or even emotional inclinations and experiences. The free moral agent does not take utilitarian passions and interests into account, because their commendations or obligations are heteronomous. The moral agent is autonomous, especially with regard to religious or political authority and his/her emotional inclinations. This premise is fundamental to Kant's thought, even though all kinds of phenomena apparently contradict it. For example, if a person steals something, this action may be explained by biographical, psychological, or sociological factors that, as social scientific research suggests, influence behavior. Nevertheless, the conscience, the voice of the free moral agent, can speak, holding the person responsible or accountable by suggesting that he/she could and should have done otherwise.

If religious ideas, social conventions, or emotional inclinations are to be bypassed, neglected, or even rejected, what then is this moral autonomy based on? Kant's answer is that only human rationality is able to provide direction for free moral action. Any other foundation — be it God, the good life, pleasure, happiness, self-realization, or preference — would deprive human morality of its autonomy.

For these moral directions to be derived from human rationality, only their formal nature counts, not their substantive content. This formal nature is implied in the principle of universalizability, dealt with earlier. It says that moral obligations are valid if and only if they are universalizable. Kant expresses this in the first formulation of the categorical imperative, which is known as the "Formula of Universal Law": "Act only on that maxim through which you can at the same time will that it should become a universal law" (Kant 1964, 88). For example, if I consider not to give back the money that someone lent to me, I have to think of the possibility that this not giving back would become a universal law that also applies if I lend money to somebody else. Or if I feel the inclination to steal something, I have to ask the question whether I would agree when other people would steal something that belongs to me. The point at stake here is that I am obligated to respect the other person as a free, rational, moral being in the same sense as I have to respect myself as a free, rational, moral being. The only thing that matters is human rationality, on which human morality is based. From this perspective, Kant offers a second formulation of his categorical imperative, which is known as the "Formula of the End in Itself": "Act in such a way that you always treat humanity, whether in your person or in the person of any other, never simply as a means, but always at the same time as an end" (ibid., 96).

Kant's theory appears to offer a way out of the moral problem of plurality. For him, nothing can be a moral obligation that cannot be an obligation for all. Adopting a maxim like "it is alright to make false promises" cannot stand the test of universalizability derived from the categorical imperative, because this principle would entirely destroy intrapersonal, interpersonal, and societal trust, and make living with others impossible. To be quite clear, failing to keep promises, according to Kant, is not wrong because of its negative effects, as utilitarianism would suggest, but because it cannot be willed as a universal maxim (Frankena 1978, 35-38). Practically speaking, deontology may come up with a list of mostly negatively formulated universal maxims, that is, prohibitions against actions that are held to be intrinsically wrong, like making false promises, lying, betraying, killing, torturing, coercing. They all correspond to the universal rule that it is wrong not to respect every human being as a free, rational human being.

Nevertheless, all this cannot hide the instrumental reasoning that underpins deontological thought. Why are the aforementioned actions wrong? The injunction against false promises has to do with the calculation of the multitude of advantages and especially — in this case — disadvantages that would ensue in the intrapersonal, interpersonal, and societal domain if this principle were to be adopted as a universal maxim. This calculation is not really different from calculative consequentialism, which is inherent in utilitarianism. Moreover, what has Kant to say of situations in which a conflict of so-called universal maxims occurs, a conflict of duties (Frankena 1978, 35-38)? Is it intrinsically wrong to lie in order to avoid harming another's well-being? Is it intrinsically wrong to kill one person to save a whole community? Problems of this sort, arising from conflicting obligations, again bring us to the problem of moral plurality.

Some refer to the principle of double effect as a kind of rescue.[15] It does not mitigate the wrong character of intrinsically wrong actions but places them in a more concrete context, that is, the plurality of their effects. This principle says that "to violate deontological constraints one must maltreat someone else intentionally. The maltreatment must be something that one does or chooses, either as an end or as a means, rather than something one's actions merely cause or fail to prevent but that one doesn't aim at" (Nagel 1986, 179). But this does not conceptually satisfy. As I said in Chapter 3, the two effects (e.g., killing a person and self-defense) are not comparable because they are not on the same scale, or in the same dimension (Blasi 1988, 140-47). Moreover, Ricoeur makes the point that in cases like this it is misleading to speak of two duties or obligations in conflict, because in fact only one rule or one principle applies here as a duty or obligation. He quotes Kant: "if it is a duty to act according to one of them, it is not only not a duty but contrary to duty to act according to the other. It follows, therefore, that a conflict of duties and obligations is inconceivable" (Ricoeur 1992, 279n.62). This reasoning, which appears conveniently to explain away conflicts of duties (cf. Taylor 1994a, 39), does not tell us which of the two obligations applies in the concrete situation. In my view, deontological thought does not provide an answer to the question of how to deal with moral pluralism in conflict situations.

The conclusion is that neither substantive nor procedural rationality is able to solve the problem of moral plurality or even adequately deal with it. Substantive rationality leads to the crucial question of which of the various, divergent, substantive approaches to choose. Procedural rationality does not solve the problem either. Utilitarian rationality confronts us with the same challenge as substantive rationality: which or whose pleasure, self-realization, friendship, or, more generally, preference to choose? Deontological rationality fails to provide guidance when we are confronted with conflicts of obligations in concrete situations. For moral education, which is education about how to respond to concrete moral problems in concrete situations, the problem of moral plurality remains.

---

15. The rule of double effect refers to four conditions: (1) the nature of the act, which must be good or at least neutral (independent of its consequences); (2) the agent's intention, which aims at the good effect, whereas the bad fact is not intended; (3) the distinction between means and effects, which prevents the bad effect from being a means to the good effect; (4) proportionality between the good effect and the bad effect (Beauchamp and Childress 1994, 207).

Theoretical and Practical Rationality

Two further forms of rationality could potentially be used to deal with the thorny problem of moral plurality. These I call theoretical and practical rationality.

For my purpose, theoretical rationality accords with what the cognitive psychologist Mark Johnson (1993) calls the "Moral Law Folk Theory." According to Johnson, this is a theory — or, more accurately, a hypothesis — about the set of statements that ordinary people generally use in thinking about moral themes and problems. Though I disagree with Johnson's interpretation of theological ethics in Christianity and with his view of the nonreligious moral theories of Kant, Hare, Rawls, and other proceduralists, what I find valuable in his analysis is the list of elements that operate in popular moral thinking (though not necessarily, as he claims, in academic thinking as well).

I divide these elements into two groups. The first group belongs to what Johnson calls the "Metaphorical Folk Theory of Faculty Psychology," which underlies the Moral Law Folk Theory. This theory holds that each human being has four faculties at his/her disposal: perception, passion, will, and reason. Perception is the receiving of sense impressions, which are passed to passion and reason. Passion emerges from bodily experiences, which influence both will and reason in a way that is difficult to control. Will refers to the capacity to choose. It may be negatively influenced by passion. Reason is the ruling principle that structures the perceptions, controls the passions, and guides the will. For reason to adequately direct the human being in concrete situations, it exerts force on will and channels the passions. According to Johnson, "This Folk Theory of Faculty Psychology is shared by virtually everyone in Western culture" (1993, 15).

The second group consists of elements that directly and strictly belong to the Moral Law Folk Theory itself. This theory states that morality depends on the existence of universal moral laws. They tell us which acts we must do (prescriptions), which acts we must refrain from (prohibitions), and which acts we may do if we like (permissions). These universal moral laws are commanded or revealed by God, belong to a long chain of honorable traditions reaching back to prehistoric times, and are knowable and recognizable by human reason. If understood within a nonreligious frame of reference, these laws take their universality from the universality of human reason, which everywhere and always is identical with itself. For decisions to be morally right, human reason must derive a set of principles from these universal laws and consequently derive conclusions from these principles in order to respond adequately to moral problems in concrete situations. For actions to be performed in a right way, these rational conclusions must be transposed into free deeds, which requires the deeds to be ruled by human rationality. Moral freedom means freedom to make moral decisions and perform moral deeds under the guidance of reason. This reason must not be hindered by passions, which distract human beings from right decisions and actions. Morality equals free will, free will equals rationality, and rationality equals emotional control. In a word, morality is the product of "pure reason."

In this description of theoretical rationality, some elements of the deductive-nomological approach in mathematics and science are recognizable. This approach is characterized by a two-way strategy. The first aspect consists of deducing lower nomological principles from higher ones and deriving conclusions from these principles; the second consists of subsuming concrete phenomena under the headings of principles and subsuming these principles under higher ones. In the same way, moral phenomena are explained, moral solutions justified, and moral questions answered. Morality consists of processing a chain of deductive reasoning from the top down or from the bottom up. This gives morality the character of necessity: it leads to conclusive, indisputable, and incontrovertible claims. All principles and claims stem ultimately from only one, overarching, self-evident moral truth. From there, all principles and claims correspond to at least two criteria. The first is that they are all-comprehensive, coextensive with the whole of reality. The second is that they are consistent, free from contradictions. This morality is *axiologia more geometrico*.

Some objections to this approach are that the more abstract the principles become, the emptier they are and the more they lose their motivating power. They are polyvalent and indeterminate, like for instance the utilitarians' principle of pleasure or happiness, Schweitzer's self-evident truth of life, or Kant's axiom of rationality. They can be used to legitimize or justify any decision or action. In order to provide real guidance for moral decision and action, they need to be complemented by insights, ideas, and information from other sources. Moreover, they reinforce the illusion that people, when confronted with moral problems, deduce their decisions from preceding premises. In fact, people do not have a coherent system of principles and rules at their disposal, but act from a combination of competing convictions, calculations, intuitions, and emotions (cf. Lazari-Pawlowska 1979). They decide and act in concrete situations, which they may experience as ambiguous, ambivalent, messy, or even aporetic, and yet have to take responsibility for, one way or the other, without possessing perfect certainty that they are doing good and acting rightly (Bauman 1994; 1995).

Can these objections against theoretical rationality be overcome by practical rationality? Two approaches to practical rationality must be distinguished. I call them the traditional and the modern approach.

The traditional approach to practical rationality is the classic one set out in Aristotle's and Thomas's moral theory. Thomas's moral thought is of course a synthesis of Aristotle's and Augustine's, but here I examine what they have in common with respect to their conceptions of practical moral reasoning.

Aristotle's idea of moral reasoning is based on the practical syllogism, which differs fundamentally from the theoretical syllogism. In the latter, both the premises and the conclusion are descriptive, the classic example being: all human beings are mortal; Socrates is a human being; therefore Socrates is mortal. In the practical syllogism only the second premise is descriptive, while the first premise and the conclusion are normative. The first premise refers to the ultimate good or the good derived from it, that is, the good as such for human beings as such. The second premise relates to the concrete situation (or class of situations) in which a concrete person finds himself/herself. The conclusion then makes an inference by combining the first and the second premise and stating that the good as such applies to the concrete person in his/her situation.

The structure of this practical syllogism may be given a teleological orientation. The first premise refers to the person-as-he/she-could-be-if-he/she-realized-his/her-essential-nature. The second premise relates to the person-as-he/she-happens-to-be. The conclusion enables the human person to understand how to make the transition from the person-as-he/she-happens-to-be (second premise) to the person-as-he/she-could-be-as-he/she-realized-his/her-essential-nature (first premise) — it points to how to realize one's essential nature in a particular situation (cf. MacIntyre 1984, 52). It should be pointed out that the practical syllogism offers only the structure of reasoning, not the sequence of reasoning. The sequence comprises various bottom-up and top-down processes — in other words, dialectical processes. What happens in fact is that one develops a prima facie idea about the concrete good to be achieved, and then reasons from this concrete good to the good as such. After that, one establishes what the good as such is, and then reasons from the good as such to the concrete good to be achieved in one's concrete situation (cf. Hare 1967; Brennenstuhl 1980; Van Ijzendoorn 1980; Verbiest 1984).

Although this structure of practical rationality sounds clear enough, it does not prevent ambiguity, ambivalence, and uncertainty from arising when one is confronted with concrete moral problems that demand concrete decisions and actions. According to Thomas, this is because concrete situations are subject to endless variation. Ethics and politics differ radically from mathematics, notes Aristotle. Every concrete moral problem contains aspects that fall under the principles under consideration, but also aspects that do not. Therefore the judgment within the conclusion (which in the individual case, to which the second premise refers, indicates what should be done from the perspective of the principles in the first premise) has to be left to a specific personal capacity or habitus, which transcends syllogistic reasoning altogether — in other words, to *phronesis* (wisdom or prudence), which the individual person has or should have at his/her disposal. This habitus or virtue — one of the four cardinal virtues according to Thomas — means that one must take into account the circumstances of the concrete situation to which the second premise refers, and from there identify which elements in these circumstances call for the principle in the first premise. In other words, with the help of wisdom or prudence one analyzes the situation, selects the aspects that are relevant, and connects them with a principle, which may or may not be chosen in advance. The prudential emphasis, then, is on the concrete situations, certain elements of which are characterized as relevant. In that one selects certain elements as relevant and not others, the principle is determined at least partly with reference to this concrete situation. It is chosen according to its appropriateness (Habermas 1993, 154). This prudential process makes syllogistic reasoning open, dynamic, and flexible. It does not prevent prima facie ideas, intuitions, and emotions, which clearly condition concrete problems in concrete situations, from coming into play.

From Thomas's perspective, the cardinal virtues — or even all virtues — form a unity. In connection with the virtue of prudence, the virtue of justice refers to coming to the final judgment, which should do right to others, the virtue of courage to keeping enough strength, when fear for danger or obstacles might block one's way, and the virtue of temperance to holding the passions within the Aristotelian mean. These virtues are important because they do not tame the passions, but order and direct them to the good, which is implied in the principle(s). Paradoxically speaking, as far as moral reasoning is concerned, one has to be educated in the virtues (MacIntyre 1988, 124-45, 183-208).

This prudential syllogistic reasoning perhaps bridges the apparent gap between Habermas and Luhmann, as far as the relation between morality and reason is concerned. Luhmann declares: "Never again Reason!" on the grounds that there is no unified normative reason. Reason is pluriform. Reason is reasons. Habermas does accept reason, but with qualifications. He refuses Reason hypostatized, but acknowledges reason in the mode of rationality, which is the self-reflective version of reason. Rationality reflects the plurality of reason/reasons without losing sight of unity. From this perspective, prudential syllogistic reasoning takes the situational fragmentation of reason, the Babel of reasons, into account. It relativizes reason because of its contextualization (Arnaston 1994).

To my mind the modern approach to practical rationality takes these aspects even more adequately into account than does the traditional approach. I call this the imaginative approach, combining insights from advanced neurobiological research and research on imagination in second-generation cognitive psychology. Both of these reject the Cartesian separation between body and mind, "the *res cogitans*" and "the *res extensa*." Obviously, neurobiology and second-generation cognitive psychology have their own unique perspectives. But they also have much in common. I focus here on what takes place in the human mind during practical-theoretical reasoning.

Let me begin with what advanced neurobiology can tell us about practical rationality. This modern discipline has its basis in three essential points. First, the human organism is an indissociable unity of body, brain, and mind. Second, this organism interacts with its environment as a unity. Third, the mind's functioning can be understood only in the context of the organism's interacting with its environment. Neurobiology is interested in the reciprocal influences between body and brain, and thus in the mental images stemming from the neural representations in the neural systems. These mental images can be described as the awareness or consciousness of these representations. The first phenomena by which humans become aware of their environment are internal images of shapes, colors, movements, tones, or unspoken words. Thinking and reasoning can be understood as thoughts about those images. Concepts come later; they belong to secondary processes. Physicists and even mathematicians tell us that they think primarily in images. Within this thought in and about images we compare the images, predict what the consequences might be of the situations, events, and actions to which those images refer, then choose and plan. All this happens in our mind, but not separately from our body. The mental images and thoughts trigger all kinds of bodily reactions, like visceral, muscular, and chemical reactions. Emotions are the product of the cognitive evaluations we make with regard to the situations, events, actions, persons, or circumstances to which the images relate: good and bad, attractive and ugly, advantageous and disadvantageous. Feelings are the awareness, the experience, of these cognitive evaluations. Feelings prompt our fight or flight behavior and accompany our physical responses. All of these neurological, mental, bodily, and emotional processes are connected through a myriad of directly and indirectly intertwined feedback and feed-forward mechanisms. Compared with this neurobiological understanding, the way in which Kant sees rationality operating in the realm of morality is meager and bleak, to say the least. From a neurobiological vantage point one would agree that "the cool strategy advocated by Kant, among others, has far more to do with how the patients with prefrontal damage go about deciding than with how normals usually operate" (Damasio 1994, 172).

This rich interconnectedness of neurological, mental, bodily, and emotional processes, all of which play their part in human thought, may be deepened by drawing on the insights of second-generation cognitive psychology. In opposition to the first generation of cognitive psychology, which conceives of the human brain as an intelligent machine, or computer, the second generation focuses on the human mind as connected with the body, and being in search of meaning in its cultural tradition and context. Images, metaphors, experiences, narratives, emotions, associations, prototypes — all of which have their basis to some extent in "corporeal imagination" — play a key role. As Johnson says: "Without imagination, nothing in the world could be meaningful. Without imagination, we could never make sense of our experience. Without imagination, we could never reason toward knowledge of reality" (Johnson 1987, ix). Imagination accompanies our acts, and one can even say that through imagination our behaviors become acts, because imagination embeds them and weaves around them meaning-giving stories, and because the plots of these stories set out the good reasons by which causes of behaviors become intentions of acts. Therefore one may speak of the acts of meaning, meaning both the "pure" acts and the narratively told acts, as interconnected (Bruner 1990).

Prototypes are especially important with regard to practical-rational reasoning in the realm of morality. Prototypes in the moral realm are those cases in which moral choices, decisions, and actions are self-evident, such that everybody would unhesitatingly agree on them. Examples of prototypes are the absolute prohibition against killing an innocent person in cold blood; the absolute condemnation of the killing of innocent civilians in war; the intrinsic evil of racism in the former Nazi regime, of the Gulag Archipelago in the former Soviet Union, or of the apartheid system in South Africa before 1994; the injustice of the desperate poverty of millions and millions of people in so-called Third World countries, caused by Western neocolonialism. These prototypes refer to extreme crisis situations, the moral response to which imposes itself without question.

Why are prototypes important? Moral reasoning begins with the prototypes and moves from there to nonprototypical cases, the ones with which we are most commonly confronted in everyday life. In order to respond adequately to these concrete moral problems, one has to stretch the moral principles that are implied in the prototypes and apply them to the real situations. This happens with the help of images, metaphors, and stories about other, different, but to some extent comparable cases, the plots of which are explored for the meaning they might hold for the moral case under consideration. This involves the phenomenon known as frame semantics. The various stories, images, and so on place the case under consideration in different interpretative frameworks. For example, the moral interpretation of an act such as cutting someone with a knife will differ dramatically depending on whether it is placed in the framework of war, murder, revenge, accident, self-defense, or medical surgery.[16] Lastly, these metaphors and stories are the embodiment of emotions and feelings, which stimulate the flow of images and direct human imagination in all possible directions (Johnson 1993).

In other words, moral principles and rules do not exist, at least not as hypostatized entities. What do exist are prototypes, or at least imagined prototypes, which may be understood as imagined versions of crisis situations, the moral response to which everyone would spontaneously agree on. Or, to put it less sharply, moral principles and rules only exist as embodied in these imagined prototypes, never apart or isolated from them. When one confronts moral problems in everyday life, imaginative thought begins with these prototypes and runs through all kinds of images. While people mentally review all these images, their problem is not that they do not have enough moral principles, values, and norms, but that they have too many: "My problem was that I had too many ideals, goods, commitments, laws, arguments, and motivations, and that some of them were quite incompatible with each other" (Johnson 1993, 186). For example, from interviews we know that the first thought of many teenagers upon discovering they are pregnant is to reject the idea of abortion, because the prototypical image that spontaneously comes to their mind is that of a fetus in a relatively advanced stage of development, almost a full-term baby. From this initial prototypical image,

---

16. According to the so-called intrinsically evil acts set out in *Veritatis Splendor* (1994), cutting someone with a knife can never be justified. This reading, however, takes such acts in isolation from their circumstances. This makes no sense, because especially this example of cutting someone with a knife makes clear that the circumstances are absorbed into the act itself and even constitute it. Thus the act will be interpreted differently and will in fact be different depending on whether it is an act of war, murder, revenge, accident, self-defense, or medical surgery. The encyclical wrongly rejects proportionalism, which connects acts and circumstances, because "pure acts" do not exist without being embedded in circumstances. Still, "all proportionalists would admit that some acts are intrinsically evil from their object 'if the object is broadly understood as including all the morally relevant circumstances'" (Hoose 1994, 139).

they then go through a series of other images, having to do with their life story, socialization, personal identity, the boy by whom they became pregnant, the relationship between them, parental families, present living situation, and the future. Most often, these images weaken the initial rejection of abortion or make the thinking more flexible. A dynamic weighing process develops, the outcome of which, at the beginning, is uncertain.[17]

To summarize, neither theoretical rationality nor practical rationality unambiguously transcends the plurality of principles, rules, values, and norms that characterizes modern life or perhaps even life in general. Theoretical rationality requires all kinds of additional information from other sources in order to be able to guide moral decision and action. Practical rationality, in its traditional version, is confronted with the variety of relevant principles, which are explored by analyzing the concrete moral situation to determine which principle is appropriate to it. In its modern version, practical rationality is the process of examining and weighing all the aspects of concrete moral problems in concrete situations. This process is characterized by a thinking through of all kinds of different images, referring to multiple and often conflicting values, experiences, and principles, which makes these situations irreparably and irredeemably ambivalent (Bauman 1995, 43). The modern recognition of this plurality can be said to be the result of a conscientization process that began relatively late in human history and led to awareness of a phenomenon that has always been there: the existence of moral plurality in the ambiguous and even "messy" situations of real life. In the face of this plurality, individuals must perform their own moral choices, compromises, decisions, and actions. They themselves have the obligation to "moral self-constitution." This "moral self-constitution" has existed since the beginning of time, "only we did not know about it" (Bauman 1995, 19).

4.3 Moral Complementarity

The insight that people have the obligation to "moral self-constitution" does not answer the question as to which content — principles, values, norms, and so on — is to be transmitted in moral education. It even sharpens the question,

17. Catholic moral doctrine holds that abortion is always intrinsically wrong. But in the tradition of Catholic moral theology, the stage of fetal development has been taken into consideration in connection with the infusion of the spiritual soul, which was supposed to take place forty or even eighty days after conception. This differentiation has been eliminated from doctrinal statements since Pius XII up to the Catechism of the Catholic Church (cf. Beemer 1970).

because "moral self-constitution" confronts us with the plurality of moral convictions and rules and, accordingly, with the plurality of moral selves.

To my mind, Ricoeur's theory of the moral self[18] offers a perspective from which one can adequately deal with this plurality. This theory combines insights from what I have earlier called "substantive" and "procedural" rationality as well as from what I described under the heading of "practical rationality." It takes the form of the three-stage model that was presented in Chapter 1. This model connects Aristotelian teleology of the good and Kantian deontology of the right in a complementary way and adds certain insights from situation ethics (Opdebeeck 1995, 85). The first stage is the search for the good. It is characterized by a substantive approach. In the second stage the good, which has been provisionally identified, is critically tested and purified according to the criteria of the right. This testing is procedural by design. In the third stage the good, after having been found in the first stage and tested in the second stage, is critically applied in the concrete situation in its singularity, contingency, and fragility, in the light of a context-oriented *phronesis* or practical wisdom. This three-stage model values the good over the right, but not without according the right its testing, purifying, and relatively autonomous position, and then wisely applying it in the concrete situation. This three-stage model can offer a guideline for answering the question of what is to be transmitted in moral education. Let us now go into the details of this model (Ricoeur 1992, 169-296).[19]

First Stage: Searching for the Good Life

Ricoeur emphasizes that the desire for the good life, which includes the common good life *(bonum commune),* comprises three dimensions, as I already indicated in the previous chapter: to live well, to do so with and for others, in just institutions. Together they form the tripartite structure of the good life. This structure is related to three dimensions of the self, that is, the self in the first, the second, and the third person: I as my self, you as another

18. Like other philosophers, Ricoeur, by convention, distinguishes between ethics, which from the Aristotelian tradition teleologically aims at the good life, and moral theory, which from the Kantian tradition deontologically emphasizes the norm of the right and the just (Ricoeur 1992, 170-71). Taking them together, Ricoeur might speak of the ethicomoral inquiry into the self (p. 187). In this study I take the term *moral* as an overarching category, as I already indicated in Chapter 1.

19. From this point on I refer to Ricoeur's *Oneself as Another* (1992; English translation of *soi-même comme un autre*) by page numbers only, except where intervening references to other works would cause confusion.

self whose face constitutes my self, and lastly he/she as another self, "each." These three dimensions are associated with three moral attitudes: self-esteem, solicitude, and equality. Self-esteem concerns my self, solicitude concerns you as another self relative to me, and equality concerns him/her as another self, that of "each," the third party, the anonymous "other," who is part of my people, nation, region, or neighborhood (pp. 169-202).

The first dimension has to do with desiring the good life for oneself, living well. It means aiming at living one's life according to standards of excellence, from an Aristotelian point of view. These standards can be described in terms of the various life projects that may relate to family life, professional life, leisure time, community life, or political life. Examples of these life projects would be becoming a caring life companion, parent, child, family member; becoming a skillful swimming instructor, mechanic, teacher, doctor, or pastor; becoming a fine tennis player, chess player, or pianist; becoming a responsible community member or political represen-tative. Living up to these standards of excellence is of intrinsic value: it is an end in itself. In other words, it is done out of personal interest and gives satisfaction, which must not be confused with pleasure. But desiring to live well according to these standards of excellence is something different from the concrete actions and deeds that must be chosen and decided upon in the course of everyday life. The bridge between the ideals, which are embodied in the aforementioned life projects on the one hand, and the day-to-day activities on the other, is built by *phronesis*, meaning prudence or practical wisdom. This practical-theoretical capacity mediates between the ideal and daily life. With the help of *phronesis* a person is able to select from all possible actions those that optimally fit both his/her ideals and the concrete situation in its singularity. I intentionally say "optimally" rather than "maximally." Chance and fate in human life make the individual from the outset a patient who suffers life and is at the same time its author, the one who constitutes life. Suffering and acting go hand in hand, which makes human life tragic (Ricoeur 1970, 2:42-57). This tragic connection of suffer-ing and acting results in an optimal relation between life projects and concrete actions, not a maximal one. The good life is determined by what Nussbaum (1986) calls "the fragility of goodness."

The characteristic mark of Ricoeur's interpretation of *phronesis* is its hermeneutical perspective. For him, *phronesis* is not only a noetic means of building a purely cognitive bridge between life projects and day-to-day activities, because it is embedded in his hermeneutics of the self. That is, in the process of building a bridge, the self constitutes its own being by narrating its story in the present, which stretches from the past into the future, and in this way writing its own life text.

In this self-interpreting activity, the self is engaged in a continuous dialogue with other selves outside and inside itself. This dialogue is continuously conditioned by "the conflict of interpretations." Some urge it to act in this way or that way. Some claim it must do this or that in order to accomplish its life project. The relation between the self and its text is dialectical: it writes the text and is written.

To the extent that the self truly invests itself in its activities or life projects and derives satisfaction from this, it experiences self-esteem. And this is the moral attitude that is critical in the stage of searching for the good life, especially living well. In self-esteem I appraise and value myself as the author of my good text, my excellences, myself.

The second dimension refers to desiring the good life with and for others. Before entering into the question what this statement means, I must mention that the prepositions *with* and *for* refer to a fundamental distinction in Lévinas's philosophy, a distinction that Ricoeur does not explicitly refer to in his *Oneself as Another*. Commenting on Heidegger's *Mitsein*, Lévinas rejects "being with others" as a moral category: "being-with-another is but a moment of our presence in the world. It does not occupy central place. *Mit* means to be aside of . . . it is not to confront the Face, it is *zusammensein,* perhaps *zusammenmarschieren*."[20] For the Jewish thinker Lévinas, who personally suffered from Nazi persecution, this *zusammenmarschieren* betrays his utmost contempt. Being with others means only that one finds oneself in the same time and space with them: on busy streets, in waiting rooms, office buildings, factory floors, on the beach, or in a dance hall. Mostly we keep others whom we are "with" at arm's length, but occasionally we engage in some sort of entertainment "with" them. However, these contacts are episodic, inconsequential, topical, well-mannered, civilized, polite, and of ad hoc interest (Bauman 1995, 44ff.). "Being for" is something fundamentally different. It refers to the appeal by the other to take responsibility. This appeal happens in and through the other's face, which reveals the summons "Thou shalt not kill." This voice goes directly against the conventions of being with others and commands me to commit myself for the other. It morally obliges me to devote, dedicate, and even surrender myself to the other. The answer that I have to give is not in the nominative, "Here I stand," but in the accusative, "It's me."[21]

Perhaps Ricoeur has this distinction between being with and being

20. E. Lévinas, "Philosophie, justice et amour," in *Entre Nous: Essais sur le penser-à-l'autre* (Paris, 1991), 135 (quoted in Bauman 1994, 49).

21. E. Lévinas, *Humanisme de l'autre homme* (Montpellier, 1972), 110 (quoted in Burggraeve 1987, 29).

for others in mind when he starts explaining his thought by referring to Aristotle's three kinds of friendship discussed earlier. For Ricoeur, the first two kinds of friendship, which are oriented toward utility and pleasure, are not real friendship, because they are based on some expected advantage or experience. They may be understood in terms of being with, but not for, others. What they lack is mutuality.

This mutuality consists in my desiring the good life for the other as I desire it for myself, and vice versa, the other's desiring the good life for me as he/she desires it for himself/herself. The emphasis on the good life makes friendship a moral virtue — an excellence — by which it transcends the psychology of affections and becomes part of the realm of moral theory. The mutuality of this friendship implies a reciprocity of giving and receiving on both sides. But friendship goes even further than that. In the course of this reciprocal giving and receiving I give some good not only to the other but to myself as well, and in the same way the other gives some good not only to me but to himself/herself also. In giving myself I am a good for the other, just as in giving himself/herself the other is a good for me. As Aristotle says: "For when a good man becomes a friend to another he becomes that other's good" (*EN* 8.5). In giving myself, I also receive myself, and in giving himself/herself, the other also receives himself/herself. In this giving and receiving we take part in each other's life; we share life. The summit of this friendship is determined by solicitude and sympathy. Solicitude is the exchange of self-esteem (Ricoeur 1992, 221). In sympathy we give our weak, vulnerable, suffering selves to each other. This sympathy ends in mutual solicitude, which expresses itself "in the shared whisper of voices or the feeble embrace of clasped hands" (p. 191).

From this perspective of mutuality, Ricoeur is able to transcend the aporetic question of what is ontologically earlier or prior: love for oneself or love for the other, self-love or other-love. If friendship is based on utility and pleasure, then, by definition, self-love has priority over other-love. But if friendship is based on my desiring good for the other and the other's desiring good for me, self-love and other-love go hand in hand. They do not exist apart: I find myself in giving and receiving my feeble self to and from the other, just as the other finds his/her self in giving and receiving his/her fragile self to and from me. To put it more simply: to the extent to which I am another's friend, I am my own friend.

This friendship is characterized by three aspects. The first one is reversibility: The "I" who I am is "You" for the other, while his/her "I" is "You" for me. When I am addressed as "You," I experience this as being addressed as an "I," and the other way around. We fundamentally exchange our roles in the first and second person. The second aspect is nonsubstitutability. It refers to the anchoring of the roles in the person whom I am in this body, in this texture of place and time. Whereas roles are replaceable, a person is not. From the perspective of roles only, I am replaceable, from that of friendship I am not: "It is first for the other that I am irreplaceable" (p. 193). The third aspect is similitude. It refers to "you too" and "as myself." Just as by being the other's friend I am my own friend, my self-esteem ensures that I esteem the other as myself.

Through this approach to friendship, Ricoeur nuances Lévinas's philosophy of the other. For Lévinas, the other takes the initiative in making me responsible for him/her. In revealing his/her face and commanding me not to kill him/her and to do justice, the other calls me into being and constitutes my self. The relation between me and the other is not based on the reciprocity of equal giving and receiving: "And the summons to responsibility has opposite it simply the passivity of an 'I' who has been called upon" (Ricoeur 1992, 189). This passivity must be considered as one-sided compared with the idea of friendship and its mutuality of passivity and activity on both sides. Ricoeur thinks that Lévinas uses the philosophical technique of hyperbole, in which a profound idea is dealt with in an exaggerated way. He notes expressions used by Lévinas like "obsession of the Other," "persecution by the Other," "hostage to the Other," and even "substitution of the I for the Other." The face of the other has become the master of justice who teaches, and even the offender, who accuses and requires pardon and expiation (pp. 337-39). This approach negates the fundamental mutuality that exists between friends, and their reciprocity in giving and receiving their selves to and from each other. Here is no place for the intimacy of the "shared whisper of voices or the feeble embrace of clasped hands."

The third dimension of the good life is desiring to live well within just institutions. Ricoeur considers institutions separately because they represent a moral category. Morality is not restricted to the personal and interpersonal domain. Let us look at what institutions are and what "just" means in this context.

Institutions regulate our living together in communities as peoples, nations, regions, neighborhoods and so on. The institution transcends interpersonal relationships, which are characterized by friendship, and reaches the other as another self — not as a "you," but as a "he" or "she," an "each," an anonymous being. The anonymous other belongs to the moral domain because, even though I have no personal relationship with him/her, even though he/she has no face and will probably never have one, he/she nevertheless belongs to my community and is another self, a self in the same way I am another self. We do not have only close relations with another self as a "you," but also distant relations with another self as a "he" or "she," which are mediated by the institutions we participate in (Ricoeur 1968).

Ricoeur offers what he calls "a distributive interpretation of the institution" (Ricoeur 1992, 201), where the adjective "distributive" is essentially taken from the classic term *distributive justice*. That is, institutions aim at and have to aim at organizing and maintaining community life in such a way as to ensure that distributive justice is served. What does this mean? Commutative justice refers to the just character of actions and transactions between individuals in the private or interpersonal domain, while distributive justice regulates the actions of individuals from the point of view of the relationships they have in common in a given society. Is this society an ontological entity in the same way as an individual person can be said to be an ontological entity? Here Ricoeur mediates between two extremes. The first stresses that only individuals exist and nothing else, and that these individuals can have relationships between them. The second emphasizes that communities and society are real entities, which live their own life, and even have their own "soul," "character," or "personality." In Ricoeur's opinion, the ontological status of the individual cannot be denied. However, the relationships between individuals are more than the sum of the individuals: "from the individual to society, there is no continuum" (p. 200). At the same time these relationships do not exist on their own, but only to the extent that individuals actually and effectively take part in them. Distributive justice is the basis of this dialectical relation between individual and society. Distributive justice entails two aspects. The first is equality in taking advantages and burdens. It aims at the Aristotelian mean by preventing people from taking too many advantages and/or not enough burdens. It keeps an eye on the greedy and the lazy. The second aspect is proportionality. Distributive justice takes into account the nature of the parties involved as well as that of the things shared. It refers to four terms at least: two parties and two shares (p. 201). In Ricoeur's view, it is important to interpret justice from this idea of equality. The proportional nature of this equality prevents distributive justice from being identified with egalitarianism. In other words, unlike judicial justice, in which everyone is arithmetically equal, distributive justice is identical not merely with equality but with proportional equality (Ricoeur 1990, 27-39).

Distributive justice as proportional equality is more a regulative idea than a descriptive or analytical one. It stimulates people and orients their actions from a community point of view. Moreover, it is more a negative regulative idea than a positive one. The reason is that it emerges primarily when we are confronted with concrete situations of injustice and we cry out: "But this is unjust." It would be better to speak of the "sense of justice," from which emerges the awareness of concrete situations of injustice, according to Ricoeur (1992, 198). I should say that it is in and through the contrast experiences of unjust situations that this sense of justice is awakened.[22]

Second Stage: The Critical Tests

The first stage of Ricoeur's three-stage model of the moral self contains the three dimensions of desiring the good life for myself, desiring it for you as another self, and desiring it for all other selves within the setting of just institutions. The first dimension is characterized by self-esteem, the second by solicitude, and the third by the sense of justice. Ricoeur also identifies three corresponding dimensions in the second stage. In the first of these, self-esteem is critically tested according to the Formula of the Universal Law to determine whether it complies with the criterion of autonomy. In the second, solicitude is assessed according to the Formula of the End in Itself to determine whether it meets the criterion of respect. In the third dimension, the sense of justice is critically evaluated according to the notion of the "kingdom of ends" to ascertain whether it satisfies the criterion of the rules of justice.

This testing process performs two functions. It functions as a critical judge, which may have a purifying effect. But in and through this judging process it also has a transformative effect. Desires become constraints, the good becomes the right, and optatives become imperatives.

In Ricoeur's opinion, however, there is yet another side. The criteria that are applied in this testing process emphasize the human being as agent only and not as patient, as doing and not as suffering, as active and not as passive. This is fundamentally different from what happens in the first stage. Self-esteem is affected by a text that is written by me and others, solicitude consists of the whispering of the weak among themselves, and the sense of justice emerges from injustice experienced. The criteria for second-stage testing, which, as I shall explain, are autonomy, respect, and the rule of justice, leave no room for being written and affected, for chance and fate, for weakness and tragedy, for evil and guilt. Let us have a closer look.

The first dimension in the first stage consists of desiring the good life,

---

22. I borrow the term *contrast experience* from E. Schillbeeckx (1989, 24-26), who probably coined it (cf. Borgman 1986, 249-52; Jeurissen 1993, 95-98; Tavernier 1994, 25-29).

which I aim at for myself. It is based on living up to the standards of excellence in various contexts, such as the family, the professional organization, leisure activities, and public life. Success in living up to those standards develops my self-esteem. Now, however, the critical test is whether those goods I am aiming at are truly good and whether that self-esteem is really right. But what is right?

For Kant nothing in the world is morally good without qualification — the good as such — except a good will.[23] This good will is not adhered to for the sake of some specific material good. It even does not aim at some particular definition of the good like "excellence" in the Aristotelian tradition or virtues in the traditions of Stoicism or Christianity. The good will is of a formal nature.

According to Kant, the good will is the universal will. Something cannot be good if it cannot be the will of all.[24] From here the first categorical imperative in the mode of the Formula of Universal Law can be understood: "Act only on that maxim through which you can at the same time will that it should become a universal law" (Kant 1964, 88). In other words, the good I am aiming at must be tested by the law of universalization. It may be called "the royal gate of universality" (Ricoeur 1992, 206).

When the good successfully passes through this royal gate, it takes on the form of an obligation, a moral constraint. According to the principle of universalizability, for example, the maxim that one must not make false promises is morally required, as the maxim of making false promsies is morally forbidden. In other words, the making of false promises must be rejected "out of duty." Consequently, the law of universalization appears in the mode of the imperative, which one is compelled to obey. Command and obedience are correlates. They are embodied in the same person, because he/she both orders and obeys (or disobeys).

Because of the correlation between ordering and obedience in the same person, the obedience is not obedience to another but self-obedience. It emerges from the free will of self-legislation or autonomy. Autonomy differs fundamentally from heteronomy, in that the latter obeys external authority, whereas the former accepts only internal authority. Autonomy

23. Ricoeur explains at several points how Kant, in his moral theory, connects his deontological concepts with teleological ideas or at least presupposes them. I merely mention this without going into a detailed analysis, which would transcend the scope of this book.

24. This negative formulation, "if it cannot be the will of all," suggests that the categorical imperative is a criterion for what is morally forbidden, not for all that is morally one's duty. In other words, it indicates what is necessary for maxims to be moral, not what is sufficient, as Frankena (1978, 35-38) suggests.

as self-legislation implies that one prescribes a rule to oneself, as if making a contract with oneself. The moral self is the self-obedient autonomous self.

From these three aspects, that is, universalization, obligation, and autonomy, the ethical self-esteem from the first stage can be tested. After this self-esteem has passed through the golden gate of universalization, which results in obligation, which in turn arises out of self-legislative autonomy, it takes on the form of self-respect. Self-respect represents the victory of reason over all heteronomy, which grounds in external authority and affection. Self-respect implies self-authority and self-affection.

Self-esteem and self-respect in this sense clearly differ from what Kant calls self-love, which he defines as excessive benevolence toward oneself, presumption, self-conceit. By contrast, self-love in the Aristotelian tradition presupposes desiring the good life for oneself, which consists of living up to the standards of virtuous excellence, as I indicated. Self-love in the Kantian tradition is self-elevation and self-glorification. From the concept of self-respect, self-esteem can be purified of aspects of self-conceit that may occasionally be associated with it.

Although Ricoeur criticizes Kant on several points, one specific point is worth mentioning in the context of this chapter. This is Kant's concept of autonomy and self-respect. Ricoeur suggests that this concept leaves too little room for passivity and suffering, which structurally determine human existence from the beginning. Self-authority and self-affection are blind to fate and chance in human life, to contingency and finitude, to tragedy and tragic wisdom.

The second dimension of the first stage of the three-stage model, which is that of desiring the good life for the other as another self, who also desires the good life for me, leads to mutual solicitude and sympathy. This symmetry is expressed in the Golden Rule, as Ricoeur points out. He quotes the Babylonian Talmud: "Do not do unto your neighbor what you would hate him to do to you. This is the entire law; the rest is commentary." He also cites the Gospels: "Treat others as you would like them to treat you" (Luke 6:13), and emphasizes the continuity between the Jewish and Christian Bible: "the commandment we read in Leviticus 19:18, which is repeated in Matthew 22:39: 'Love your neighbor as yourself'" (Ricoeur 1992, 219).

But the symmetry of the Golden Rule develops (so Ricoeur) against the background of dissymmetry, in which one is the agent, the one who does, and the other is the patient, the one who is done to and suffers. This is the dissymmetry of violence, which may be understood in terms of the distinction between "power-to-do" and "power-over." "Power-to-do" means the capacity of individuals or communities ("power-in-common") to act, live and live together, and constitute themselves. "Power-over" hinders or even destroys this "power-to-do." It can be seen and recognized on the slippery slope leading from false promises, ruses, threats, betrayal of friendship, and stealing, to physical abuse, torture, and murder. Violence is a product of "power-over." Humiliation is nothing other than a particular form of violence, spiritual violence, by which another's self-esteem and self-respect are destroyed, and the boundaries between "mine" and "yours" are erased.

This dissymmetry has its correlate in the negative form of the prohibitions stemming from the Golden Rule: "you shall not lie, you shall not steal, you shall not torture, you shall not kill." This is because "to all the figures of evil responds the *no* of morality. . . . It is what, ultimately, arms our indignation, that is, our rejection of *indignities* inflicted on others" (p. 221). It is what I would call the contrast experience of this dissymmetry that stimulates us in the direction of the symmetry implied in the Golden Rule.

Kant's second formulation of the categorical imperative, the Formula of the End in Itself, can be seen as the formalization of this Golden Rule, as I already indicated in Chapter 1: "Act in such a way that you always treat humanity, whether in your own person or in the person of any other, never simply as a means, but always at the same time as an end" (Kant 1964, 96). It may be understood as an absolute criterion against which every claim that appeals to the popular wisdom of the Golden Rule can be tested. I add that it not only can but must be tested, because the Golden Rule itself is imperfectly formulated,[25] in that it refers only to what shall be done to others from my perspective ("Treat others as you would like them to treat you"), and not from their own perspective, that is, what they like to be done to them, as noted in Chapter 1. Here the purifying function of the critical testing from the second stage comes in.

This formulation of the categorical imperative has a negative as well as a positive aspect. First, it states what shall not be done: "never treat humanity, whether in your own person or in the person of any other, simply as a means." Here the principle of utility is categorically rejected. As rational beings, humans do not exist merely for arbitrary use, and therefore they must not be treated that way. Kant's deontology is antithetical to utilitarianism in any form, at least as far as human beings are concerned. It is certainly antithetical to rational and ethical egoism. Treating people as a

25. Kant rarely cites the Golden Rule and does so only disdainfully (Ricoeur 1992, 223).

means always rests on dissymmetry and power-over, which is prerequisite to violence.

The second, positive aspect says: "always treat humanity, whether in your own person or in the person of any other, as an end." This aspect also rests on the insight that humans are rational beings, and rational nature exists as an end in itself. This aspect of the rule rests on the difference between humans and things. We obtain, exchange, and use things, but humans cannot be obtained, exchanged, and used. Things have a price but persons have worth.

This formulation of the categorical imperative transforms the Golden Rule in the direction of universalization. The neighbor is transformed into the abstract category "humanity": "treat humanity never simply as a means, but at the same time as an end"! Love is transformed into respect for the other, thereby objectifying what might otherwise depend on subjective feelings of sympathy and preference or loathing and hate. Every person, as an embodiment of humanity, is worthy of that respect. Respect indistinctively and indifferently is respect for all.

Here Ricoeur sees a fundamental problem, because this indistinctiveness and indifference overlooks the respect that I owe to individuals in their diversity, specificity, and uniqueness. He pinpoints this problem in the second formulation of the categorical imperative itself, in the tension between the two main nouns, "humanity" and "person." "Humanity" indistinctively and indifferently refers to all. "Person" relates to particular selves, here and now. They demand solicitude in their unique otherness. They ask for friendship.

The third dimension of the first stage is that of living together in institutions. It is characterized by the sense of justice, which grows out of the contrasting experience of injustice. In the second stage this sense of justice is critically evaluated from the perspective of the "kingdom of ends" to determine whether it is in accordance with the rule of justice. In the "kingdom of ends" each person is simultaneously legislator and bound by law. Each is an autonomous self-legislator on the condition that what is legislated is respectful of all other people in their common status as legislators.

The rule of justice is based on procedure. By its working, rights and obligations are established. It is based on the contract idea. The contract idea is commonly supposed to have its origin in the so-called state of nature. And this "state of nature" is commonly supposed to be neither the paradisiacal garden nor the Hobbesian "war of all against all" in which the principle of *homo homini lupus* rules. Whereas Hobbes describes the "state of nature" as an "unjust state" *(status iniustus)*, Kant describes it as a "state that lacks justice" *(status iustitia vacuus)* or a lawless state, because it lacks any power or facility to arbitrate between opposing individuals or parties and their claims. Because of this lawlessness, people join together to protect their individual interests as much as possible, establishing a *pactum unionis*. Protection is afforded by what is called the *pactum subiectionis*, meaning that they abdicate individual rights and abide by the contract agreed on between the ruler and the ruled, or the state and its citizens. They accept the constraints and compliances that this contract imposes on them, because they see it as the rational means of ensuring peace, security, and survival. The contract idea is meant not as a historical description of the origin and history of states, but as an analytical model, with the help of which political obedience can be legitimized.[26] This political obedience is balanced against the civil liberties the citizen receives from the state precisely because every citizen obeys the state. But the contract idea does not function only as legitimization, which is always backward, as it were, but also as a criterion relating to the present and future, that is, as a criterion that can be applied to test any law for its just character. The criterion is that any law must be backed by the common will of the entire population and must have the agreement of each citizen. This criterion is expressed in the saying *salus publica suprema civitatis lex est*. The state's task, therefore, is not to ensure the good of each individual citizen, or to make people happy. The state's task is only to establish the conditions for people to pursue their own ideas of happiness in liberty (Manenschijn 1985). One might say the criteriological function of the social contract separates the good from the just and lends the rule of the just its procedural character.

As rational as this procedural rule of justice might seem to be, it leaves a fundamental question painfully unanswered. Is the idea of the social contract able to bind people together? Is it sufficiently fundamental to serve as the basis of living together in institutions in a given community? Does it integrate people in these institutions or alienate them? Or, to put it another way, how is it possible that a social contract guarantees the individual's autonomy, especially self-legislative autonomy, and at the same time binds the individuals who together form their community? Is the social contract the only integrating factor? Does community equal social contract, and the other way around? If this is the case, what kind of community do we live in? Is this still a community?[27]

26. Nevertheless, it seems to be used frequently to refer to events that never actually took place. Insofar as this is the case, Ricoeur and many others refer to the contract idea as the contract fiction (pp. 228, 229, 239).

27. Etzioni (1988, 210) notes that a contract is always embedded in a precontractual, social-emotional frame of reference, without which no contract can be established.

Rawls's solution to this problem does not satisfy Ricoeur at all, as I shall explain. Rawls also starts with the state of nature or "the original position," as he calls it, in which the participants know nothing of social status, because they find themselves behind the "veil of ignorance." In this condition, they rationally consider and negotiate the principles they need to agree on to make their common life function well. In the process they identify two principles. The first is that of the equal liberties of citizenship. Its first formulation is: "each person is to have an equal right to the most extensive basic liberty compatible with a similar liberty for others" (Rawls 1971, 60). The "most extensive basic liberty," according to Rawls, includes political liberty (the right to vote and to be eligible for public office), freedom of speech and assembly, liberty of conscience and freedom of thought, freedom of the person along with the right to hold (personal) property, and so on.[28] This list of liberties is then enlarged and the elements in it are formulated in terms of goods. Rawls lists natural primary goods — health, vigor, intelligence, and imagination — and social primary goods — rights and liberties, powers and opportunities, income and wealth, and lastly self-respect (1971, 62). Whereas the first principle is about equality, the second principle agreed on by the individuals in the "original position" concerns social and economic inequalities. In its first formulation it is this: "social and economic inequalities are to be arranged so that they are both (a) reasonably expected to be to everyone's advantage, (b) attached to positions and offices open to all" (Rawls 1971, 60). This second principle shows that one may officially declare that justice shall be based on equality, but what one is confronted with in reality is inequality. Rawls justifies these existing inequalities as long as they satisfy two criteria. First, he admits inequality insofar as it is to the advantage of all. This would not be the case if an equal distribution of, for example, income and wealth would cause a decline in society's general economic level, which would be detrimental to all, including the poor. Rawls borrows this idea from decision theory and its "maximin" rule for choice under uncertainty, which is that everybody at least aims at maximizing his/her minimum share (1971, 152ff.). All this makes Rawls a leftist in the eyes of some conservative thinkers, because he advocates egalitarianism of a sort, and a rightist in the eyes of others, because he legitimizes inequality. The second criterion, that inequalities be attached to positions and offices open to all, is an admission that some positions of responsibility and offices of command will of necessity be associated with

28. Ricoeur argues that Rawls's theory suffers from a circular argument, because certain ideas introduced at the very beginning later on become conclusions (1992, 232n.47, 236n.54).

differences in wealth and income. This makes Rawls a rightist in the eyes of egalitarians. According to Taylor (1994, 37ff.), however, Rawls is not rightist enough, because he has no place for a just distribution by merit. Rawls tries to evade the traps of both capitalism and socialism, but without success (Ricoeur 1992, 235).

Ricoeur sees in Rawls's contractualism a clear individualism at work. The "original position" is a position of individuals: "Contractualism and individualism thus move forward hand-in-hand" (p. 230). Moreover, Rawls's distinction between natural and social primary goods, in his discussion of what constitutes "basic liberty," shows that there can be no "pure" procedural contractualism. Procedural contractualism cannot do without a substantive approach. Procedural justice sooner or later is about goods! Finally, Rawls's treatment of social and economic inequalities amounts to a kind of utilitarianism. He rejects utilitarianism because it implies, in his view, some teleological theory of the good, as evinced in the thought of some utilitarians who see the supreme good in pleasure, or happiness, or social welfare, and so on. It is striking that Rawls rejects utilitarianism for the same reason that he introduces it in his own theory, namely, it is a substantive approach to the good.[29] The difference lies in that Rawls posits that every human being desires the greatest good for himself/herself according to his/her long-term life plan, but accepts that these plans all have different ends and aim at different goods, so that a substantive approach is inappropriate (1971, 92-93). Moreover, Rawls's second principle introduces another utilitarian idea, which is implied in the balance between inequality and benefit for all. This way of thinking is typically utilitarian, because it contains the idea of the sacrifice. Lower pleasures must be sacrificed to higher ones, individual to social ones, and here, with Rawls, the entire lower social stratum to the whole of society. Ricoeur calls it the strategy of the scapegoat. Here human beings are treated as means only, not as ends in themselves.

What then is the meaning of the "kingdom of ends," the "community of autonomous self-legislators" in the second stage of critical testing, in which the claims for the sense of justice from the first stage are evaluated or assessed? Whereas this "community of self-legislators" functions on the basis of the social contract, it investigates the quality of justice that prevails in the equal distribution of advantages and disadvantages. In doing so, it looks at every

---

29. Here it becomes clear how complex the relations among the various moral systems can be. Habermas (1993) distinguishes between teleology and procedural utilitarianism, which he connects with consequentialism. Ricoeur is right in indicating the connection between Rawls's procedural theory of justice and his utilitarian outlook, from which some teleology emerges.

citizen as a free and equal citizen with the same human rights, implying the same claims to the same natural and social primary goods.

But the weakness of this critical testing has to do with the choices that must be made between the different goods when they conflict as well as with the inequalities that arise from these conflicts and choices. Ultimately, the substantial sense of justice from the first stage cannot be perfectly transformed into the procedural rule of justice on which the social contract relies. Substance transcends procedure; procedure does not correspond to the fullness of substance. Ultimately, procedure is negative: it can indicate only what should not be done, not what should be done.

The overall conclusion should be that the "critical test" of the second stage of Ricoeur's three-stage model constitutes a necessary, albeit not a sufficient, criterion that can be used to test for which maxims must not be followed and what action must not be done. In terms of the three dimensions, if the maxim damages the individual's autonomy, it must be discarded; if it is detrimental to respect for others, one must refrain from it; and if it conflicts with the just distribution of equalities and inequalities, one must desist from it.

The other half of the conclusion is that the person's autonomy must be related to the conditions of human existence, which relation is determined to a profound degree not only by acting but also by suffering, not only by intervening but also by being the subject of intervention, not only by achievement but also by fortune and fate, chance and destiny, contingency and tragedy. Further, the respect owed to other people needs to be embedded in the virtue of friendship and mutual solicitude, because humanity's very existence transcends pure reason. It has its roots in the passions of human life: the mystery of good and bad, virtue and vice, grace and evil. Finally, procedural justice is about the distribution of goods, about which all kinds of conflicts arise time and again. How to deal with conflicting goods is a cardinal question, which can only be answered negatively in the second stage.

Third Stage: *Phronesis*

As we have seen, *phronesis*, practical wisdom, plays a crucial role in the first stage of Ricoeur's three-stage model. Now, in the third stage, it reappears. The difference between these two instances goes back to the testing of the second stage. *Phronesis* from the first stage must undergo this critical testing in order to pass to the third stage and be elevated to another level, situated above its starting point (Ricoeur 1992, 290). Let us try to list some characteristic aspects of it now.

To clarify the first aspect of *phronesis,* which is that it happens in a situation, I must return to a distinction made earlier, concerning the two ways in which principles in premises are connected with concrete moral problems in concrete situations. The first way is to analyze the situation, select its relevant aspects, and then link them with the appropriate values and norms. This can be called the regressive way, because the solution found is justified retroactively by subsuming it under a higher principle. The problem inherent in it is that of moral plurality, because it depends on the personal selection of relevant situational aspects and connected values.[30] The second way, no less complex, is progressive, in that it starts from the principle concerned and then reasons from there toward the concrete case. In the process, the specific circumstances and context that determine this case in its singularity must be taken into account. By drawing on additional, specific information applying to the case, it delimits, restricts, or even corrects the principle in question. A relatively simple case may illustrate this. In general the moral principle regarding killing is that killing is prohibited. But the additional, specific information, which shows that in this particular situation there was no other way of protecting a third party who was in danger of being killed, limits the prohibitive principle. Both the regressive and the progressive method require what Ricoeur calls a moral judgment in the situation. It is the response to the concrete problem in the concrete situation, which, for reasons of its singularity, requires a particular and unique moral activity. Such a problem can be approached adequately only if the deliberation fully takes into account its singularity. "Of *phronēsis* we retain the fact that its horizon is the 'good life,' its mediation deliberation, its actor the *phronimos,* and its place of application singular situations" (p. 290). In this context, the distinction by Dewey (1986, 105-22) between "application-to" and "application-in" is interesting. "Application-to" refers to a way of moral reasoning, which does not take into account the situation in its singularity, contingency, and fragility. "Application-in" relates to the deliberation process, by which the principle is not applied "to" the situation by the person involved, as if this situation were something extrinsic or external to him/her, but "in" the situation by taking into full consideration all the relevant aspects that determine its singularity. In the same Aristotelian perspective Gadamer (1960, 290-323) understands the term *Anwendung* (cf. Browning 1991, 38-39).

The second aspect of *phronesis* refers to the very basis of moral plurality, which *phronesis* has to take into account. In itself plurality is a term

---

30. In his discussion of Habermas, who, in Ricoeur's opinion, strongly emphasizes the regressive way, Ricoeur himself does not mention this problem of moral plurality (pp. 280-83).

that may suggest some indifference with regard to the moral stance to be taken, as if it were all the same which moral solution is chosen. But this is to ignore the implicit tragedy of plurality. Human decision and action in a situation are always latently or manifestly determined by the conflict of powers, claims, risks, estimations, and interpretations. A large number of examples might be given here, as Ricoeur indeed does. Let me indicate just a few of them. Take for instance Sophocles' *Antigone,* which Ricoeur presents as a model of tragic action.[31] Antigone's fight to give her brother a sepulcher against the will of the city's ruler Creon exemplifies the many-sided tension between family and nation, brother and sister, father and son, man and woman, friend and enemy, individual and society, custom and rationality, the living and the dead, humans and gods. This complexity of powers that dramatically express opposing claims cannot be satisfied by one person. It requires a tragic choice to be made, in one way or the other. Antigone, being a woman, chooses for her family, her brother, the nation's enemy, the individual, the custom, the dead, and the gods; and Creon, being a man, chooses for the nation, society, the living, rationality, and against his son, and above all against the enemy. Anyone who partakes in this tragedy is dramatically introduced into what is termed the "agonistic ground of human experience," the unavoidable nature of conflict in moral life, "the aporia-producing limit experiences" (Ricoeur 1992, 243). Such a moral conflict of life and death faces us not only in the theater, where it attracts our attention, imagination, and passion, because it symbolizes our own tragic self-woundedness, but also in the so-called life events of every biography. At certain crucial moments we are called on to decide between life and death. At the beginning and at the end of life, for example, we make this choice for ourselves. Abortion for a daughter who has been raped, euthanasia for a mother who is in the terminal stage of a painful illness, and support for a sister who is going through deep depression because she has cancer, her marriage is ended, she has lost her job, and she wants to die: what should we do, how are we to act in these dramatic situations? Here principles, rules, and values such as respect for life and pity, integrity and authenticity, creation and salvation, collide. Who dares to maintain to have found the right answer? Who is not in doubt? Who is not making guesses and estimations? Who is not calculating consequences, unintended effects, or risks? Ricoeur's comment on political deliberation in concrete, singular situations applies to moral debate in general: "Political discussion is without conclusion, although it is not without decision" (p. 258).

31. See further chap. 8, where I offer a narrative account of character, drawing especially on Greek tragedy.

The last aspect of *phronesis* that I want to mention relates to this decision and what Ricoeur connects with it: "attestation." As complex as the singular situation may be, the *phronimos* makes a decision, after weighing all the relevant aspects and carefully weighing the consequences. He/she preferably does so in dialogue, because "the *phronimos* is not necessarily one individual alone" (p. 273). This decision embodies his/her conviction, which, after having gone through the process of testing and deliberation, is now a "considered conviction."[32] "Considered conviction" differs from plain conviction in that it has passed through a process of argumentative communication. Ricoeur rejects Habermas's idea, presented as part of his discourse theory, that this argumentative communication takes place above the level of the conversation in which we exchange and critically respond to our mutual convictions. Whereas Habermas places this argumentation process at a higher level, from which all conventional convictions are looked down upon, Ricoeur sees this process as occurring within this conversation, connecting it with the stories, examples, or models we admire or disdain, and within the thought experiments and fictions we venerate or reject. Argumentative communication, Ricoeur maintains, is not the opposite of conventions and convictions, but the critical agency that operates in the midst of and from within the conventions and convictions we exchange with each other. This, ultimately, makes these convictions "considered convictions" (p. 288). Nonetheless, as authentic and strong as this attestation may be in view of the situation that is to be acted upon in its singularity, it never possesses the certainty of a dogma or ultimate foundational knowledge. Attestation is about truth, it reveals the truth in the light of which a specific action should be done, it is alethic in nature, but it is so in the mode of belief, that is, the mode of "I believe-in," not "I believe-that." This is both the greatness and weakness of attestation. It makes it strong and vulnerable, powerful and fragile at the same time (pp. 21-22).

Phronesis plays a key role within the third stage in relation to the aspects of situation, conflict, and attestation. Let us examine how it functions within the three dimensions in the third stage, that is, living well in personal, interpersonal, and institutional life.[33] Following in Ricoeur's footsteps, I

32. Ricoeur (1992, 237, 288) borrows the term *considered conviction* from Rawls (1971, 19).

33. In his discussion on the third stage, Ricoeur reverses the sequence of the three dimensions, dealing first with institutional life, then interpersonal life, and lastly personal life (1992, 250). For reasons of clarity, I maintain the sequence of the two previous stages in the third stage as well.

especially emphasize the conflict aspect, because it greatly determines and permeates the other two.

In the first dimension, that of personal life, Kant stresses the individual's autonomy. But in doing so, he overlooks the multitude of factors in concrete situations that mitigate or even principally relativize the individual's self-legislative concern. These factors collide with autonomy when this autonomy is related to concrete problems in concrete, singular situations. Autonomy is an abstraction. It is always contaminated by (a term redolent of Kantian thought) or (more descriptively) dialectically related with heteronomy. Heteronomy has to do with the fact that humans are indeed rational beings, as Kant teaches us, but are also influenced by inclinations, desires, and passions, which may pull them loose from "acting only on a maxim of which you can at the same time will that it should become a universal law." Humans never act from rational insights only, because they always are confronted with all kinds of struggles within themselves between theoretical reason and practical reason, rationality and emotion, positive and negative emotions, fight and flight, self-concern and other-concern. Human beings are agents and patients at the same time, they do and are done to, they drive and are driven, they tell and are told. Human beings find themselves in a situation that they construct and act upon at the same time. And this situation, which they are confronted with and at the same time create, is characterized by evil, which they suffer from and commit at the same time.[34] Humans also act from the penchant toward evil, as Ricoeur says (p. 275), because the human condition itself is determined by the inclination toward evil, as the myth of original sin tells us (Wils 1996).

The second dimension is that of interpersonal life, which, from a Kantian point of view, is determined by respect for the other person. But respect does not determine every aspect of this interpersonal life, which is characterized not only by activity but — in a dialectical way — also by passivity. The face of the other reveals his/her need to be taken care of and appeals to my solicitude, in the same way that my face shows my weakness and woundedness. In the "shared whisper of voices" in which we exchange our tragic selves, doing and being done to go hand in hand. In this reciprocity of giving and receiving lies both our strength and our weakness.

Ricoeur illustrates the dialectical tensions within this face-to-face friendship by reflecting on some problems at the beginning and at the end

---

34. From this perspective, Ricoeur (1971, 103) analyzes evil in terms of its dialectical relationship between action and passion: one does the evil that one finds; one commits the evil that is already present, outside and before oneself.

of life. He shows that Kantian respect may lead to aporetic situations, which can only be adequately dealt with from *phronesis*. Take abortion, for example. If one accepts the progressive ontology of the embryo, the human fetus, and the human child, what then is to be done when a woman seriously and authentically asks for an abortion? Much is uncertain here. At which stage of progressive ontology do which changes in the intermediary zone between organic things and persons play which role? Which moral stances shall be taken with regard to which progressive-ontological developments? Which estimations may be said to possess which moral load? Which respect for which "life" must have priority and for what reasons? Ricoeur's answer is: "In this complex play between science and wisdom, the weighing of risks run with regard to future generations cannot help but temper the audacity encouraged by technological wonders. The fear of the worst, as Hans Jonas forcefully asserts in his 'imperative of responsibility,' is a necessary component of all the forms of long-term responsibility demanded by the technological age" (Ricoeur 1992, 272). This tempering of audacity is a product of the moral judgment in situation, *phronesis*. Another example is the case of a patient who finds himself/herself in the terminal stage of illness, and who has been promised that he or she will be told the truth about his/her condition. Ricoeur looks at the moral implications of such a promise in this particular case. If the promise is kept in a straightforward manner, the patient may not receive the message. The opposite course, that of intentionally lying, may be chosen so as not to upset the patient and weaken him/her further. Again, *phronesis* is needed to find the adequate way: "In such cases, one must have compassion for those who are morally or physically too weak to hear the truth. In certain other cases, one must know how to communicate this truth . . . But there are also situations, more numerous than is thought, where telling the truth may become the opportunity for the exchange of giving and receiving under the sign of death accepted" (pp. 269-70). Ricoeur also emphasizes the fragile character of *phronesis*, which he describes as the "stumbling search for solutions" (p. 285).

The third dimension is that of institutional life that, from a Kantian/Rawlsian perspective, must be morally guided by the rules of distributive justice. Here, in the area of institutional life, many conflicts arise that cannot be solved solely with the help of these rules. These conflicts concern, first, which goods — a teleological, not a deontological term — are to be distributed. This problem is a serious one because there are various kinds of goods. For example, Rawls divides them into natural and social primary goods. But social reality is more complex than this division suggests. There are economic goods, like the goods of products and services to be bought and sold; socioeconomic goods, like the goods of welfare and social security, education and qualifications, jobs and career; political goods, like the goods of state membership to be distributed among state citizens, foreign residents, immigrants, and political exiles; social goods, like the goods of family, neighborhood, association, and community; and cultural goods, like the goods of science, literature, and the arts. Second, in what way are these goods to be interpreted? This question also is a serious one, because severe conflicts can arise between the many possible interpretations. For example, what is good housing, good food, good health, good employment, good education, good schooling? Every group and political party have different opinions about what "good" means in this or that area, for this or that people, in this or that case. Third, which priority has to be given to which goods in which area to which group and to what extent? Does proportional distributive justice mean that the most disadvantaged should be taken as the term of reference for the purpose of the "option for the poor" (p. 274)? The practical meaning of this option for the poor in terms of employment and health, housing and education, social welfare and social power must be decided in every concrete situation. The conflicts of interpretation become political conflicts as soon as real choices — financial choices — have to be made between the competing claims of different groups and parties. By definition, politics is about dealing with conflicts through struggle and negotiation. It is about power and domination. It is about distributive justice. But this justice cannot be realized by deductively applying the procedural rules of justice only. It requires entering into the singular situation, participating in it, and weighing its various aspects. It requires dialogue, deliberation, estimation, calculation. It asks for judgment in the situation — in short, *phronesis*.

For this *phronesis* to happen, a fundamental question about the relation between the individual and society must be addressed. Is society a collection of competing individuals and groups, or do the individuals and groups have the common good *(bonum commune)* in mind? Do they aim at the individual maximal minimum (maximin) or the common optimum? Do they work in isolation or in cooperation? Or to put it in more general terms, is society only the sum of its members or something more than that? If so, what is this "more"? As we saw, Ricoeur rejects the idea of society as an ontological entity with its own personality, its own soul. Instead, he stresses the idea of relationship that binds individuals together. What then, one is entitled to ask, comes first: the individuals or the relationship? From Rawls's perspective, we are distinct individuals first, then we form relationship (cf. Sandel 1992, 53). From Ricoeur's perspective, the individuals and their relationship go hand in hand and realize themselves in and through each other. They form a dialectical compositum. The relationship exists only to

175

the extent to which concrete individuals participate in it, and the individuals exist only to the extent to which they participate in each others' lives. By living and acting together, they have power-in-common. This dialectical compositum is connected with the Aristotelian point of view, which is implied in the concept of proportional distributive justice. According to this concept, advantages and disadvantages are to be distributed proportionally.

Here again, the judgment in situation, *phronesis,* comes into play. The academic fiction of the "state of nature" or "original position" is of little help in deciding how to satisfy the requirements of proportional distribution. This requires that one really delve into the situation, which is thoroughly contextualized in terms of time and space, and by deliberating and weighing all of its aspects find the contingent solution for this contingent situation. What constitutes good health, good housing, good procedure, good education, good family life, good parenthood, or good associational life varies from situation to situation, from community to community, from state to state, from context to context. There are no universally good houses, no universally good procedures, no universally good schools. Everything is historical. Political life, like the whole of life, is determined by what Ricoeur, following Lefort, calls "fundamental indeterminacy" (Ricoeur 1992, 260).

Moral Complementarity in Transmission

Let me summarize Ricoeur's thought as it applies to the transmission mode in moral education. I do so by going back to the fundamental question that needs to be answered about the transmission mode: Which values are to be transmitted, and according to what moral criteria shall these values be evaluated? These values and criteria refer to the three stages elaborated by Ricoeur: the good, the just, and the wise. Within each of these stages, three dimensions are distinguished: the relation to oneself, the relation to the other, and the relation to the whole of society. From the analysis of these dimensions emerge the values and criteria that must play a key role in the transmission mode in moral education.

In the first stage the emphasis is on desiring the good life in the personal, interpersonal, and institutional settings, in other words, living well oneself, for and with others, in just institutions. From this teleological perspective within moral education three groups of values are of central relevance: self-esteem in personal life, friendship and solicitude in interpersonal life, and the sense of justice in institutional life.

In the second stage the good, having been discovered in the first stage, is tested from a deontological perspective that emphasizes rationalization, formalization, and universalization. The good is assessed to determine whether it can be justified in rational terms, so that irregular inclinations, passions, and prejudices can be eliminated. This means that the maxims derived from them must be capable of becoming a universal law, applicable to every human being. For every human being, whether it be oneself or any other person, must be treated equally as an end in himself/herself because of his/her nature as a rational being. On this basis the state and its institutions can work in a just way. They embody the common status of all citizens as equal legislators. Each law, whether it distributes rights or obligations, must be tested according to the procedural idea that it represents the common will of the people. This is the basis of true democracy. From this deontological perspective within moral education three groups of criteria are important: autonomy in personal life, respect for others in interpersonal life, and procedural justice in democratic institutional life.

In the third stage the good, after having been discovered in the first stage and tested in the second stage, must be applied in the concrete situation. This application *in* the situation differs fundamentally from application *to* the situation — to use Dewey's phraseology — because it takes into account the situation in its singularity, contingency, and fragility. This fundamental insight applies to personal, interpersonal, and institutional life, referring, respectively, to emotional and other irrational, especially evil inclinations, the shared life face to face, and the context-bound political interpretation of conflicts and power processes. This combining of activity and passivity requires Aristotelian *phronesis*, practical wisdom, "judgment in the situation," as Ricoeur consistently calls it. This *phronesis* is the fundamental virtue to be dealt with in the transmission mode in moral education.

The criteria for determining and evaluating the content of what is transmitted in moral education can be easily summarized. They are implied in the three stages, the good, the just, and the wise, each of which contains three dimensions: oneself, the other, and society. All this leads to the following values: (a) within the stage of the good: self-esteem, solicitude, and the sense of justice; (b) within the stage of the just: autonomy, respect, and democracy, including human rights; (c) within the stage of the wise: *phronesis* as a virtue, which takes into account the intrapersonal irrational inclinations, the interpersonal tragedy of the "shared whisper of voices," and the institution-oriented, political, weighing processes.

Knowing what to teach is one thing; knowing for what purpose one teaches it is another. From an educational perspective, content and aim have to be distinguished, as I said while critically treating the traditional transmission mode. Here I distinguish between three groups of aims, the cognitive, affective, and volitive (see section 4.1)

The cognitive aims can be divided into two groups, those that seek to develop knowledge and those that seek to develop cognitive abilities. While the traditional transmission mode restricts itself mainly to the aim of developing knowledge through recognizing and memorizing, to my mind the modern transmission mode invests more time and energy in developing cognitive abilities. The reason is clear. One must critically reflect on the different values in Ricoeur's first stage: self-esteem in personal life, friendship and solicitude in interpersonal life, and a sense of justice in institutional life. The same applies to the different perspectives in Ricoeur's second stage: autonomy in personal life, respect in interpersonal life, and democratic justice in institutional life. Both stages call for teaching/learning processes that purposefully, systematically, and intensively develop and promote higher analytical abilities. This applies especially to the relationship between the first and the second stage, because the second stage essentially consists in critically testing the results of the first. Ricoeur's third stage requires an even higher ability, that of synthesis, which allows one to compose one's own vision and formulate one's own judgment about the concrete situation in its singularity. It is precisely because of this singularity that the judgment cannot be reduced to knowledge one already possesses. In a sense, new knowledge must be created for every new situation. This is done by selecting and then combining relevant aspects from various levels of abstraction and concretion into a unique composition of one's own. I here refer to the synthesizing ability, because forming and formulating a practical judgment in the situation resembles other activities that require this ability, such as writing an essay, a story, a poem, a melody, or a composition (cf. Bloom et al. 1956, 177-80).

The affective aims can be divided into motivational and attitudinal groups. The importance of motivation is self-evident, because without attention and the will to respond, no learning can take place. The attitudinal aims constitute a serious problem, because their meaning is not always clear. To my mind it is necessary to distinguish between two groups of attitudes. The first are attitudes that are purposefully, directly or indirectly, prescribed or imposed. They recall what I said about indoctrination at the beginning of this chapter (section 4.1). The second group are attitudes that are desired and chosen freely by students themselves. In this last case the aim of attitudinal development is not a communal but a differential aim, which the individual student decides to pursue of his/her own free will

(De Koning 1974; van der Ven 1982, 530-43; 1985, 236).[35] To the extent that the teacher ignores the student's own choice in this respect and pushes him/her to adhere to the teacher's or the school board's or the society's attitudes and convictions, he/she severely violates the student's liberty of conscience and freedom of thought, which are at the very core of universal civil rights. For that reason I can accept only the student's own decision to be initiated into attitudes he/she personally favors and reject all attitudinal teaching that is at odds with that choice. The limit of the student's own decision would be attitudes that clearly violate the human rights of others, for example, racism or neo-Nazism.

The same applies to the volitive aims. To the extent that the student himself/herself wishes to maintain firmly the attitudes he/she favors, to practice them in his/her everyday life, and to exercise some self-discipline with respect to them, this choice should be respected, if and only if these attitudes do not violate another's human rights. But the moment the teacher tries to strengthen and discipline the student's will in an area chosen by the teacher and not the student, there is once again infringement of the universal rights of liberty of conscience and freedom of thought.

---

35. The demarcation line here is between category 2.3 (satisfaction in response) and 3.1 (acceptance of a value) from the taxonomy of educational objectives within the affective domain by Krathwohl et al. (1964).

5

Development

The structural problem of moral education in our time involves a real dilemma, the first horn of which is indoctrination and the second, relativism. Indoctrination often effectively dominates some of the modes of moral education on which I elaborated in previous chapters: discipline, socialization, and transmission. Relativism is often the outcome of value clarification, which I discuss in the next chapter. The first alternative, indoctrination, is a theft of freedom; the second, relativism, implies a neglect of the growing self. Educators faced with the choice between these two alternatives become uncertain and confused. They do not wish either to rob the child of his/her freedom or to abandon him/her, but they have no positive alternatives to these negative courses of action. An experienced junior high school teacher says: "My class deals with morality and right and wrong quite a bit. I don't expect all of them to agree with me; each has to satisfy himself according to his own convictions, as long as he is sincere and thinks he is pursuing what is right. I often discuss cheating this way but I always get defeated, because they still argue cheating is all right. After you accept the idea that kids have the right to build a position with logical arguments, you have to accept what they come out with, even though you drive at it ten times a year and they still come out with the same conclusion" (Kohlberg 1981, 7). In other words, it seems that rejecting indoctrination and leaving the student free to make his/her own moral judgments about norms and rules necessarily leads to value relativism and moral neglect. In this direction lies moral emptiness.[1]

1. One of the sources of moral relativism lies in the confusion regarding the

The psychologist Kohlberg tries to find a way out of the dilemma between indoctrination and relativism, or between the theft of freedom and moral neglect.[2] First, in order to ensure that moral education does not become a process of indoctrination, Kohlberg seeks to identify moral processes that naturally take place in every child, in order to allow educators to work with these processes and build on them. By starting at the child's level of moral development and tailoring moral education to stimulate the child along the lines of the moral processes he/she naturally goes through, educators avoid the problem of violating the child's freedom. Second, in order to prevent education from lapsing into moral neglect, Kohlberg proposes no longer teaching specific moral norms and rules because this smells of indoctrination and paradoxically leads to neglect, but instead focusing on the underlying structures, that is, on moral principles. Whereas norms and rules depend on particular, contextually conditioned institutions, com-

definition of a value or norm. Here I do not deal with the relation between values and norms (values are sometimes said to be more abstract while norms are more concrete; others define norms as the result of conflicts between values, thus making a norm a value-preference judgment; see Stachel and Mieth 1978, 158ff.) because I am more interested in the paradigm from which these terms, both values and norms, are approached. Is it a descriptive or a moral paradigm? In a descriptive paradigm, values and norms may be defined in terms of the meaning that is attributed to people, animals, the rest of nature, things, and events. The meaning itself is not important. It does not matter, for example, whether we see foreigners as fellow human beings whose human rights we must respect, as profiteers, or even as enemies. It is the meaning-giving action as a formal criterion that counts, not the substance of its content. From a moral paradigm, some meanings that are attributed to people, nature, things, and events are good, others are bad; some are just, others unjust; some are permitted, others prohibited. These meanings are based on a moral theory or a set of moral criteria that provide a basis from which to decide what constitutes the good life and which course of action to take. Whereas the descriptive paradigm makes meaning meaningless, the moral paradigm evaluates the meaning of meaning. According to Kohlberg, the descriptive paradigm is becoming increasingly dominant within Western culture. It permeates moral education in families and schools, leading to a growing attitude of moral relativism, which ultimately results in moral and educational neglect. Moreover, Kohlberg distinguishes between cultural and moral relativism. Cultural relativism occurs at the level of facts and is based on the observation that moral principles, rules, and norms vary from context to context and from time to time. Moral relativism holds that nothing can or should be said about the intrinsic, absolute, or universal value or validity of moral principles, rules, and norms. Kohlberg accepts the first but rejects the second. He interprets the confusion between the two forms of relativism as a sign of a naturalistic fallacy, in which "ought" (moral relativism) is deduced from "is" (cultural relativism) (Kohlberg 1981, 63ff.).

2. Logically, Kohlberg might deny any dilemma between indoctrination and relativism, since relativism itself can be seen as a substantial moral theory, the blind and fanatic teaching of which leads to indoctrination (cf. Kohlberg 1981, 98).

munities, groups, or social classes, these principles are assumed to be of a universal nature, applicable to any person, anywhere, at any time. Thus Kohlberg's deep concern is to find universal structures of morality in the child's development, so as to be able to work with and build on them for the purpose of furthering moral education.

With this in mind, Kohlberg developed what is known as the developmental stage theory of moral education, in which development is seen as passing through a sequence of three levels, each consisting of two stages, beginning with the concrete and specific principles and moving to more abstract and inclusive ones. To measure moral development, Kohlberg devised a series of moral dilemmas that present conflicts between moral norms. In the classic Kohlberg dilemma, Heinz, whose wife is dying, needs a certain drug to save her life, but he cannot afford to buy it. The moral dilemma is: should Heinz steal the drug to save his wife? The initial response, whether yes or no, is not important. The key to determining the subject's level or stage of moral development lies in the underlying structure of the reasoning by which the answer is justified.

The educational side of Kohlberg's theory holds that the child should be stimulated to reach the next higher level or stage of moral development. This has been labeled the "N + 1" theory, where N represents the actual level or stage of the child's development, and "+ 1" symbolizes motivating the child to strive for and reach the next higher step. Thus when a child is at stage 3, he/she is placed in an experiential-educational environment that encourages him/her to make the transition from stage 3 to stage 4.

Over the course of almost three decades, Kohlberg and his associates presented many versions of the moral stage theory. Here I summarize the last version of it by Kohlberg (1981, 409ff.; 1984, 174ff.).[3] The three levels in Kohlberg's theory are the preconventional, the conventional, and the postconventional, each consisting of two stages, as table 1 (p. 184) shows. Each stage refers to the principle from which the child establishes his/her judgment regarding the question of what has to be done in a given situation.

At stage 1 the child's judgment is based on the principle of mere obedience, or avoidance of punishment. "Yes, Heinz should steal the drug because it is only a minor offense, which he will be punished for very mildly, and his wife will reward him later on." "No, Heinz should not steal because stealing is forbidden, and he would be put in jail."

---

3. Kohlberg (1984, 1, 5) calls his earlier version(s) obsolete and out of date. K. Bergling (Moral Development: The Validity of Kohlberg's Theory [Stockholm, 1981]) gives an overview of the different versions in a table (cf. Kavathatzopoulos 1988, 18).

Table 1. The Six Moral Stages

Level A: Preconventional
    Stage 1: Obedience and avoidance of punishment
    Stage 2: Individual instrumental purpose and exchange

Level B: Conventional
    Stage 3: Mutual interpersonal expectations
    Stage 4: Social system and conscience maintenance

Level C: Postconventional
    Stage 5: Social contract
    Stage 6: Universal ethical principles

At stage 2 the child's judgment is largely determined by self-interest; the interests of others are viewed in the context of mutual instrumental exchange. "Yes, Heinz should steal the drug because his wife needs it, and he wants his wife to live." "No, the pharmacist should not be prevented from making money by selling drugs."

At stage 3 the child's judgment is based on the desire that the person conform to other people's expectations in order to maintain interpersonal relations. "Yes, Heinz should steal the drug because his wife expects him to be a good guy for her." "No, if he stole, people in his community wouldn't like him any more."

At stage 4 the child judges actions in terms of the functions and roles the person must perform in the wider system of societal institutions in order to maintain social order and satisfy his/her conscience and sense of self-respect. "Yes, Heinz may steal the drug because he has a duty toward his wife, but he must repay the pharmacist later." "No, rules are rules; they have to be followed, otherwise society as a whole would collapse."

At stage 5 the child's judgment takes into account the laws and constitutional arrangements that are part of the social contract between different groups with different interests and values. "Yes, Heinz may steal the drug because the law, which we all agreed upon, does not deal with extreme emergencies of this kind." "No, because he may not take the law into his own hands."

At stage 6 the child reasons from universal ethical principles of justice, including the equality of human rights and respect for the dignity of human beings as individual persons. "Yes, Heinz is allowed to steal because here the principle of respect for life applies." "No, because other people may need the same drug, and they also have the right to live."

This three-level/six-stage scheme has been the subject of theoretical reflection and empirical research in hundreds of books and articles all over the world, and its impact on thought and action with regard to moral development and moral education has been tremendous. The scientific tradition Kohlberg established in the late fifties did not end with his tragic death in 1987, but continues to flourish and explore new ground. The seed Kohlberg sowed is still yielding an abundant harvest.

Yet Kohlberg's moral stage theory has by no means always been accepted in its entirety. On the contrary, several assumptions he made in his research, several arguments on which he based his own, several hypotheses he deduced from his reflections, as well as several assertions he thought he was justified in making from his empirical work have been the object of serious doubts, objections, and attacks. Kohlberg, however, entered into a public discussion with his critics, weighed their arguments, clarified their perspectives and evaluations as well as his own, introduced some new refinements and distinctions, narrowed his previous claims to more limited ones, incorporated some of his critics' insights, and sometimes explicitly corrected his own views. Kohlberg's work is an outstanding example of the forum, a gathering of scientists who discuss and criticize each others' work in order to learn from one another, thereby contributing to scientific progress. Thus in the second part of his last book, Kohlberg reports on the current state of his theory by drawing comparisons with earlier versions and responding to his critics (Kohlberg 1984, 207ff.). This is not a defensive but rather an open response in which he admits that, for example, Habermas from his hermeneutic point of view or Gilligan from her feminist perspective are right in their objections, as we shall see later on. The criticisms of Kohlberg's work can be divided into two categories. The first concerns Kohlberg's moral theory per se, in particular the relation between morality on the one hand and rationality, universality, and procedural justice on the other. The second category of criticisms concerns the area of human development and education, particularly the distinction between development and stage-based development, as well as the relation between cognitive, affective, volitive, and practical aspects of development in the context of moral education.

This does not mean that Kohlberg is always right in presenting and evaluating his critics' views. For example, the accuracy of his statement that "none of the critics rejects the idea of stages of moral reasoning, . . . all the critics . . . accept the legitimacy of a psychology using a hermeneutic approach to interpreting an interview text," depends on how the terms *stages* and *hermeneutic approach* are defined, as we shall see. As far as the present study is concerned, the open interchange between Kohlberg and his critics means that our present discussion cannot be limited to Kohlberg's theory, including his responses to his critics, but must include a critical evaluation of those responses as well.

With this in mind, in this chapter I first present Kohlberg's theory in greater detail (section 5.1). I then proceed to examine the moral character of his theory as well as the main objections to his assumptions and thoughts in this area, especially those concerning conceptions and functions of justice (section 5.2). Finally, I deal with the main objections that have been raised with respect to his ideas about development (section 5.3).

5.1 Stages of Moral Development

Kohlberg's academic work on moral development was rooted in his dramatic experiences as a Jew during the Shoah, the Holocaust. He once recounted rather humorously how, as a seaman volunteer after the Second World War, he helped Jews who had survived the extermination campaigns in southern Europe and transported them to Israel, an activity that earned him a stay in a British internment camp. These experiences sparked his lifelong interest in morality, moral development, and moral education, and led him to develop his theory of moral stages and conduct his research among various populations (Peukert 1988, 181).

At the beginning of his academic career, Kohlberg leaned heavily on Piaget's studies of moral judgment. To fully understand Kohlberg's research, it is necessary first to describe and reflect on Piaget's work.

Moral Types and Moral Stages

Piaget observed and interviewed young children in order to study their use of rules in games, and their ideas about responsibility, truth, punishment, and justice. Based on his observations of children playing marbles, which was a common game among children in Switzerland at the time, he distinguished three types of actions: a merely motor action and two moral ones.

The merely motor action consisted of the child handling the marbles according to his/her own wishes and his/her own motor habits, which are conditioned by the particular situation. From the scheme that underlies these habits, these actions become rituals. They can be called individual rituals, because the child plays alone.

Between the ages of three to six years, the child begins to play with other children. This social interaction leads to the first social actions. The child sees older children playing and imitates their actions, which are based on specific rules. The child accepts the rules, because they are recommended or commanded by adults: parents, educators, teachers, and so on, and therefore loaded with moral authority, which the child obeys from a sense of respect. This respect for moral authority is what Piaget calls moral realism (Piaget 1932, 138ff.). But this respect is unilateral and egocentric: The child follows the rules insofar as he/she feels it is to his/her advantage to do so, because following the rules is rewarded with the adult's attention, reward, protection, and affection. At the same time the child will change the rules to satisfy his/her own whims, needs, and desires, unless the adult forbids and condemns it.

Still later, between the ages of 7 and 10, mutuality and cooperation develop. This culminates at 11 to 12 years of age, when the child follows the rules because he/she feels they have some value for the game. The child's respect for the rules is no longer the result of the egocentric weighing of reward and punishment to be expected from the adult's overwhelming power, but the outcome of seeing the game with peers as intrinsically worthwhile and the cooperation that the game entails as intrinsically rewarding. From this perspective, rules may be changed if the change, by mutual agreement, contributes to the aim, which is joyful playing with peers.

Thus the baby may be said to be asocial, the younger child egocentric, and the older child and the adult cooperative. These stages are associated with three types of actions: motor, egocentric, and cooperative action, which operate on three types of rules: motor, unilateral, and mutual rules. Piaget notes, however, that every action or rule is always motor, individual, and social, so that all depends on the accent *(dosage)* that is laid on a specific action or rule (Piaget 1932, 62).

Looking at children's attitudes toward trust and lying, responsibility, punishment, and justice, Piaget also sees these three types of actions and rules as being present in the moral domain. The first stage he calls premoral. The egocentric configuration of social interaction he labels heteronomy because the obligation in this interaction comes from outside. The cooperative configuration, which is based on the obligation from inside, he calls autonomy. Heteronomy is marked by unilateral respect, autonomy by cooperative respect. Heteronomy implies a moral conscience of fear, autonomy a moral conscience of ideals (Piaget 1932, 320).[4]

4. Piaget's ontogenetic distinction between heteronomy and autonomy within moral psychology mirrors his phylogenetic distinction within sociology. Following Durkheim, who distinguishes between societies determined by "mechanic solidarity" and "organic solidarity" (Durkheim 1984; cf. Giddens 1978; Coser 1984), Piaget historically distinguishes between two types of society, primitive and modern (Piaget 1986; Bertram 1986).

On this basis Piaget subjects some of Kant's moral theories to a critical examination. Moral conscience, says Piaget, does not emerge from within the individual without any influence from outside. Following the psychologist Bovet, Piaget mentions two conditions for conscience to develop. The first condition is that the individual must encounter another individual who confronts him/her with a certain obligation. The second is that the first individual must accept this obligation, which he/she does out of respect for the other individual. On this point Piaget criticizes Kant, because for Kant an obligation has validity for the individual only, independently of the intersubjectivity between at least two individuals. Moreover, for Kant respect is directed at another person, insofar as this person universally represents the whole of humankind. Piaget, however, shows that a seven-year-old child has the ability to respect another person, not because this person is a symbol for all humankind—the child would not be able to grasp such a concept—but simply as an individual (Piaget 1932, 78). This respect has two sides: on the one hand the child is attracted to the obligating other, and on the other the child fears him/her. Respect is a combination of attraction and fear. This two-sidedness is important because mere attraction does not oblige, and obligation without attraction leads to mere submission (Piaget and Inhelder 1978, 119). Without the obligating other, there are no moral rules; and without respect, there are no obligations (Piaget 1932, 301). Both Kant and Durkheim interpret respect as a consequence of duty, whereas Piaget understands this relation as reversed: duty is a consequence of respect (Piaget and Inhelder 1978, 119). This, at least, applies to the first type of moral action and thought, which is characterized by unilateral respect toward another person whom the child considers his/her superior. In the second type, moral rules and thought are based on cooperation, which has its source in mutual respect.

So far I have spoken of three "types" of moral actions and thought, premorality, heteronomy, and autonomy. A fundamental question, which concerns the relation between Piaget and Kohlberg, is whether Piaget considers these types to be stages. Piaget himself used the word *stade,* which Kohlberg translates as "stage." Piaget explicitly warned that the *stades* should be taken only for what they concretely refer to. "For the sake of exposition, it is handy," he says, "to divide the children into age classes or *stades,* but reality presents itself as a continuum without any interruption" (Piaget 1932, 13).[5] In other words, *stades* do not form structured, separate

5. "Il est commode, pour les besoins de l'exposition, de répartir les enfants en classes d'âge ou en stades, mais la réalité se présente sous les aspects d'un continu sans coupures" (Piaget 1932, 13).

wholes that can only be reached by a kind of transformative jump from one to the next. Moreover, according to Piaget, children and adults may be in the *stade* of autonomy with regard to a particular group of moral rules, but in that of heteronomy with regard to another group (Piaget 1932, 61). Piaget continues: "Moreover, the content does not have any linearity, and its general direction only appears for the sake of schematizing things and neglecting fluctuations, which endlessly complicate the detail" (Piaget 1932, 13). Kohlberg is well aware of Piaget's caution, for he mentions that Piaget's *stade*, which he translates as "stage," is not a strictly structural or "hard stage" but an "ideal type," and that Piaget's "stage theory" is in fact a theory of types or a typological theory in the sense of Max Weber. It focuses on only two contrasting moral mentalities, heteronomy and autonomy, which are in a polar relation to one another. Both occur in children and in adults, for adults may remain in the heteronomous orientation (Kohlberg 1984, xxix, 652-53).

Cognitive, Affective, Social, Moral, and Religious Development

Although Kohlberg says that he leans heavily on Piaget, in fact he bases himself not so much on Piaget's theory of "moral types" as on Piaget's general cognitive theory of development and general cognitive stage concept. In other words, Kohlberg directly applies Piaget's general cognitive theory and general cognitive stage concept to the moral domain, whereas Piaget is more hesitant to do so, as is apparent from the aforementioned distinction between "stage" and "type" (cf. Kavathatzopoulos 1988, 24).[6] In order to understand Kohlberg better, however, I deal here with the basic assumptions that Kohlberg claims to owe to Piaget's general cognitive theory of development and general cognitive stage concept (Kohlberg 1984, 8-25).

First, according to Piaget's general cognitive theory, development is not based on socio-affective processes that take place in the child, as Erikson (1968) believes, but primarily on transformations of the child's cognitive structure. The term *structure* refers to the pattern and form of organization of

6. In a fictional conversation between Erik Erikson, Jean Piaget, and Lawrence Kohlberg, Fowler (1981, 49-50) makes Kohlberg say that he applies Piaget's stages of scientific logics to the domain of "moral logics," without referring to Piaget's own weaker claims in the moral area, as they appear from his remarks regarding the term *stade*. In his own theory of religious development, Fowler (1980, 143) defines his stages of religious development as different styles of cognitive organization in the religious area, which are passed through in an invariant sequence.

cognitive behavior, whereas cognitive behavior itself relates to connecting experienced events by paying selective attention to them, information gathering and processing, rule formation, motivated thinking, and so on. The most fundamental means of connecting experienced and interpreted events can be found in Aristotelian categories like substance, space, time, quantity, quality, inclusion or implication, and causality. From Piaget's research, it appears that children undergo cognitive transformations in their abilities to perceive and comprehend relations of space, time, quantity, causality, and so on. Empirically, therefore, Piaget found that the cognitive structure of time is a function of that of space, although Kant speculatively believed it is the other way around (Piaget 1975, 127ff.; Piaget and Inhelder 1978).

Second, the transformation of the child's cognitive structure is not purely a function of innate tendencies, maturational drives, or environmental stimuli, but depends on the interaction between the child and his/her environment. Thus nativism, maturationalism, and environmentalism are rejected as being false theories. Piaget's theory transcends the nature/nurture opposition. In the interaction between the child and the environment two processes can be distinguished: assimilation and accommodation. Assimilation refers to the extent to which the child absorbs characteristics of the situation in which he/she finds himself/herself, integrates them into his/her own cognitive structure, and makes them similar to his/her own cognitive schemes, as it were. In accommodation, the child continuously adapts his/her cognitive schemes to the characteristic object(s) that determine the situation. From this perspective, development can be seen as the change over time in the direction of an increasing balance or equilibrium between assimilation and accommodation. For this equilibrium to develop, the schemes of assimilation and the forms of accommodation must continuously undergo processes of transformation. At the highest level of this transformation, equilibrium does not imply a motionless standstill, but "an equilibrium between the accommodation, which imitates each new modification of reality, and the assimilation, which connects with the previous transformation" (Piaget 1975, 159).

Third, transformative cognitive development takes place in a sequence of cognitive stages. In each of these stages the child relates in a qualitatively different way to his/her environment. This quality is not a simple aspect of the child's relating to the situation, but rather permeates all of his/her aspects of this relating and forms the pattern of relationship. Each of the stages that Piaget distinguishes is a structured whole from which the child deals with physical objects, social subjects, and his/her own self, and solves problems within these areas in an all-encompassing, qualitatively unique way. The stages are characterized by differences in the child's capacities for differentiation and integration. Differentiation is the making of distinctions in the real world and forming mental representations of the distinctions, while integration is the connecting of these distinctions within a higher mental unity. The stages can be seen as a hierarchical sequence of these differentiation and integration capacities, with a higher stage being more differentiated and integrated than a lower stage. This hierarchical sequence also means that the higher stage integrates — or rather reintegrates — the capacities of the previous one(s). One of the fundamental assumptions in this theory is that a person prefers to function at the highest level available to him/her.

Piaget distinguishes among four main stages and ten substages. Here I will mention only the four main stages. In the first stage (0-2 years), called the sensimotor stage, the child acquires knowledge of his/her environment by sensory stimulation and motor activity, and develops preverbal behavioral schemes. The second stage (2-7 years) is labeled the preoperational stage. It begins with language acquisition, symbolic play, imitation, and imagination. These processes, which all involve activities like representing, make-believe, and anticipating, indicate that the child is capable of symbolic behavior. The child not only reacts to environmental stimuli, but internal activity is apparent. Nevertheless, this stage contains a number of deficiencies. Preoperational thinking tends to be egocentric — in an empirical, not a moral sense — which means that the child is not able yet to take the perspective of the other. It is very centered, meaning that the child, when faced with a complex situation, concentrates on only one aspect. It is also irreversible, meaning that the child is not able yet to reverse a chain of actions or thought. An example can be found in the following conversation. "Peter, do you have a brother?" "Yes." "What is his name?" "John." "Does John have a brother?" "No!" (Mönks and Knoers 1982, 159). The third stage (7-11 years) is called the concrete-operational stage. The child's thought is now characterized by a decentric, rather than egocentric, perspective, which allows him/her to observe and meet other people from their own point of view. The child also has the ability to cope with more complex situations, and is able to reverse relationships between people, acts, and thoughts. Whereas the preoperational stage is characterized by precooperative behavior and the conversation at that stage by collective monologues, at the concrete-operational stage children really listen to the other with whom they are communicating. The word *concrete* refers to the deficiencies in the child's dealing with his/her environment, in the sense that the child develops his/her knowledge from direct contact with objects and subjects, and not by establishing and testing general hypotheses independently from them. The last stage is called formal-operational, which is characterized by

191

the capacity for inductive and logico-deductive thinking (from 11 years onward). The child is now able to conduct logical operations of implication (if . . . then), disjunction (either . . . or . . . or both), exclusion (either . . . or), incompatibility (either . . . or . . . or neither . . . nor). The child is also familiar with the concept of probability and the relevance of experimental testing (Piaget and Inhelder 1978, 131).

Fourth, the sequence of stages is claimed to be invariant, irreversible, and universal. Invariance means that no stage can be missed. Although cultural or educational influences may speed up or slow down the sequence, they do not change the sequence itself. Irreversibility and universality may be seen as implications of this invariant sequence. Irreversibility means that once a stage has been fully achieved, there can be no regression to a lower stage. Universality implies that this invariant sequence is the same for all people in all cultures at all times. This also applies to the moral stages within Kohlberg's moral theory. They, too, are said to be invariant, irreversible, and universal.

Fifth, although development is based on cognitive stages, their function is not restricted to the cognitive domain because there is a basic relationship between cognitive development on the one hand and moral development on the other. According to Kohlberg, this basic relationship is a parallel one, which means that as cognitive development occurs in the form of structural changes, processes of moral development take place in the moral domain. This parallelism can be termed isomorphism, in the sense that each new stage, for instance, in the domain of cognitive development, entails a particular set of cognitive operations that are characteristic for a particular stage in the moral domain. In other words, the cognitive stage sequence is paralleled by an isomorphic moral stage sequence. This does not mean that a particular moral stage is merely the result of the application to the moral domain of the cognitive operations belonging to a particular cognitive stage. This isomorphism must be qualified by emphasizing that cognitive development is not a sufficient but a necessary condition for development in the other areas. As Kohlberg says: "Although moral stages are not simply special applications of logical stages, logical stages must be prior to moral stages, because they are more general. In other words, one can be at a given logical stage and not at the parallel moral stage, but the reverse is not possible" (Kohlberg 1981, 138). One of the most striking examples is found in Kohlberg's scoring of Adolf Eichmann's moral judgments: 58 percent of Eichmann's judgments remain at stage 1, 33 percent at stage 2, and 8 percent are at stage 3 (Kohlberg 1984, 54-55).[7]

7. In general, at least 50 percent of judgments must fit into a particular stage for the person to be localized in that stage (Kohlberg 1984, 61).

Sixth, this parallelism not only applies to the relationship between the cognitive and the moral domain but also encompasses other aspects that play an important role within the moral domain, that is, social, affective, volitional, and religious aspects. In other words, the general cognitive theory of development and the general cognitive stage concept are not restricted to the cognitive area or even to the cognitive aspects of the moral domain, because they relate to some noncognitive aspects within the moral domain as well. Let us have a closer look at these social, affective, volitional, and religious aspects.

The relation between cognitive and social development within the moral domain cannot easily be overlooked. Kohlberg explains this relation in terms of George Herbert Mead's theory of symbolic interactionism. According to this theory, defining the situation the person is in together with other people takes place through communicative processes in which the definitions are established by borrowing and combining symbols from the common cultural environment. In this communication, role-taking plays a key role. According to Kohlberg, this role-taking is the very basis of moral development. Role-taking happens when the child is able to react to the other as another self with his/her own viewpoints and interests, to treat the other as he/she likes to be treated himself/herself (the Golden Rule), and to treat the other from the other's perspective as an end in himself/herself (categorical imperative). This social development can be seen not as a sufficient but as a necessary condition for moral development. Children vary in their moral development because of the variety of opportunities for role-taking they have had in their family, school, and especially peer group. Children with few opportunities remain at a lower moral stage than children with plenty of opportunities.

With regard to the affections, Kohlberg rejects the idea that cognitions and affections are two entirely different things. He argues that cognitive processes always entail affective aspects and vice versa, especially in the moral domain. Again, the basis for this mutual entailment, according to Kohlberg, lies in the theory of symbolic interactionism. The cognitive definition of the situation, which is socially communicated among the agents in this situation, results in particular sentiments and attitudes (Kohlberg 1984, 67). In his moral stage sequence theory, all kinds of affections color the various stages and place them in different affective perspectives. In other words, cognitive-moral development implies the development of sentiment. For instance, guilt colors and shapes stages 3 and 4 in different ways. In stage 3 the feeling of guilt is a result of the anticipated disapproval of significant others, who expect the child to be a good boy or nice girl. In stage 4 guilt results from anticipation of institutional blame for failures to do one's duty. Thus the child cognitively differentiates between one form of guilt, in stage 3, which relates to informal group disapproval, and another form, in stage 4, which refers to formal, institutional dishonor (Kohlberg 1981, 121).

The relation between cognitive and volitional or practical aspects within the moral area is also based on the theory of symbolic interactionism, as Kohlberg points out. The person's readiness to act according to his/her cognitive-moral stage depends to a high degree on his/her symbolic definition of the situation in terms of the rights of one person or group and the duties of another person or group. Moral judging requires that rights and duties be distributed among two or more people in a situation that is determined by a moral dilemma, and this distribution is done by defining the situation and the roles and responsibilities of the people in it. Kohlberg claims that only a certain kind of definition — one characterized by judgments characteristic of stage 6 — ensures with a high degree of probability that moral cognition and moral action will be congruent. In other words, to the extent to which a person exhibits stage 6 judgments, he/she will act in accordance with these judgments. Kohlberg claims that only a "principled person," who thinks according to stage 6 principles, is ready to act in a principled way. A stage 5 person may be prevented from doing so by contractual hindrances, a stage 3 and 4 person by obstacles of a conventional nature, and a stage 1 and 2 person by egocentric concerns (Kohlberg 1984, 68-72).

Later, Kohlberg both relativizes and broadens his thinking concerning the relationship between cognitive and practical aspects in moral development. He relativizes the connection between stage 6 and moral action for the simple reason that stage 6 is found only in exceptional people such as, for example, Martin Luther King. He reframes his theory by broadening the concept of a "principled person" to include not only stage 6 but stage 5 as well. At stage 5, the "contractual" stage, moral reasoning is based on the principles of the social contract that forms the foundation of a given society. By reasoning from these "contractual principles," a person can criticize the conventional habits, disciplines, and norms that are the basis of stage 3 and 4 judgments, by appealing to higher, more abstract, principled rules. Kohlberg and his associates then find relevant correlations between stage 5 judgments and moral actions: the higher the stage 5 score, the higher the frequency of moral action. Kohlberg asks why it is that respondents at stage 5 are more likely to act morally. His answer is that a "principled person" at stage 5, who judges a specific situation on the basis of (contractual) principles, at the same time judges this situation in terms of his/her responsibility to act. In other words, from a deontic perspective, one sees

194

the action to be performed as a universal human duty, that is, one sees this action as one's own duty (Kohlberg 1984, 257-60).

Kohlberg not only broadens the definition of a "principled person" to include stage 5 but also extends this concept to what he calls the B substages within stage 3 and especially stage 4. Substages 3A and 4A correspond to Piaget's heteronomy, which is characterized by conventional morality on the basis of obedience in the small community (3A) and in the larger social system (4A). Substages 3B and 4B correspond to Piaget's autonomy, which refers to conventional morality on the basis of principles applied to the small community (3B) and to the larger social system (4B). In other words, a "principled person," in contrast to a "conventional person" (Kohlberg 1984, 69), can be a person at stage 6 (although this stage is rarely seen in reality), at stage 5, and at substages 4B and 3B as well (ibid., 260-61). Generally, the chance of a "principled person" engaging in corresponding action is greater than the chance of a "conventional person" doing so.[8]

How does Kohlberg's general cognitive stage concept, as outlined here, relate to Piaget's, specifically in the moral domain? One fundamental difference between the two is that Piaget applies his cognitive stage concept in only a general way to the moral domain, separating the preoperational stage from the two higher operational stages, that is, the concrete operational and the formal-operational stage. He does not differentiate these higher stages any further in a morally relevant way. Thus at the preoperational stage, the child's moral thinking is determined by heteronomy and unilateral respect, and from the age of 7 to 8 he/she is gradually developing an autonomous type of moral judgment based on mutual respect (Piaget and Inhelder 1978, 118-25). Furthermore, as we saw, Piaget qualifies his concept of "moral *stade*" by defining it as a "type," meaning that the notion of sequence, and especially its implications like invariance, irreversibility, and universality, are relativized. For his part, Kohlberg applies Piaget's general cognitive stage concept systematically to the moral domain and considers the moral stages, which he thinks to have found empirically, in terms of a hierarchical sequence of increasing differentiation and integration, and emphasizes the sequence-related aspects that Piaget clearly relativizes: invariance, irreversibility, and universality.

8. Rest (1980, 119-23) sees moral judgment as only one of the factors on which moral action depends, with other factors complicating, mediating, or modifying the relationship between judgment and action. He mentions seven kinds of factors: ego strength or self-regulation, situational and performance factors, other values besides moral values, the distinction between operative and reflective plans of thought, deliberate misrepresentation, etc.

Kohlberg tries, at least twice, to integrate Piaget's typology of heteronomy and autonomy into his own theory. At the beginning, in his doctoral dissertation, he transfers the heteronomy/autonomy dichotomy to the whole series of his six stages. He localizes heteronomy in his first stage, which is determined by avoidance of punishment and obedience, and extends autonomy to his fifth stage (social contract) and sixth stage (moral principles) together (Kohlberg 1994, 152-55, 182-85). But he fails to find empirical evidence for this construction (cf. Kohlberg 1984, 45). Later, he restricts the heteronomy/autonomy dichotomy to the conventional level, consisting of the third and fourth stages (mutual interpersonal expectations and social system). As I noted above, he theoretically views stages 3A and 4A as corresponding to Piaget's heteronomy, and stages 3B and 4B as corresponding to Piaget's autonomy. He then subjects this theoretical distinction to several empirical assessments, the findings of which lead to the overall conclusion that the A and B stages do empirically exist, albeit not as "hard" stages but only as "soft stages," because the A and B stages do not appear to exhibit the sequence-related aspects of invariance, irreversibility, and universality.[9] Remaining in A or B stages, as well as moving from A to B and from B to A, which is contrary to the claim that the sequence of stages is irreversible, appears to depend strongly on social and familial environments (Kohlberg 1984, 652-83). In the later versions of Kohlberg's description of moral stages, he leaves out the A and B stages (1981, 409-12; 1984, 174-76), which raises the (rhetorical) question of whether Piaget's moral typology of heteronomy and autonomy still plays any meaningful role in Kohlberg's stage theory.

Another noteworthy phenomenon in Kohlberg's stage theory is what Kohlberg called stage 4½. Initially he described this as the "B/C transitional level," where B refers to "Level B: conventional" and C to "Level C: postconventional" (1981, 411). Stage 4½ was added to account for some empirical data which show that many young people, especially college students, have left behind the conventional level, including its obligations arising from community expectations (stage 3) and societal roles (stage 4), but are not yet willing to accept responsibilities arising from the concept of the social contract (stage 5) and universal moral principles (stage 6). Kohlberg calls this stage relativism, and the young people in it relativists.

---

9. Kohlberg distinguishes between soft and hard stages. The former, which are also called "existential stages," are characterized by self-reflection in terms of the personal meaning of life and worldview, like those of Fowler (1981) and Gilligan (1982). The latter have a limited scope because they are restricted to discrete domains, which are part of and integrated into the "existential stages" (Kohlberg 1984, 236ff.).

Later, Kohlberg rejects the transitional meaning of this stage, which is probably why he eliminates it from his stage sequence scheme (1984, 174-76). Relativism does not fit into the sequence of stages because it does not directly refer to any substantial moral position or any substantial moral argumentation.[10] Relativism, Kohlberg decided, is metamoral in nature, in that it says only that no moral norm or rule can be attributed intrinsic obligatory value. Thinking in relativistic terms does not mean that one is moving from the conventional to the postconventional level (the meaning of the 4½ transitional stage); it functions merely as a metaposition. Its only meaning within the stage sequence is that it is a necessary, albeit not sufficient, condition for change — a condition, not a change or transition in itself — from stages 3 and 4 (group and society expectations) in the direction of stages 5 and 6 (contract thinking and universal moral principles). In other words, if and only if one sees through the context-bound, relative character of the moral obligations in one's own group, community, and society (conventional level) can the ability to distance oneself from them emerge, as a prerequisite to taking a critical stance toward them (Kohlberg 1984, 440ff.).[11]

Kohlberg's supplementary stage 7 is treated in much the same way as stage 4½. Stage 7 is a religious stage in which the moral principles that underlie the moral process at stage 6 are integrated and justified in religious terms, that is, from the perspective of life's ultimate meaning.[12] This religious stage, while not taken up in Kohlberg's last stage scheme, is necessitated by the conflicts and questions that are engendered by dealing with the moral principles of stage 6. It lends a cosmic orientation to the doubts, skepticism, and despair that endanger the equilibrium of universal principles of moral justice, thereby transcending the fragility, contingency, and finitude of all human endeavor. Dramatic and tragic questions like "How can one find real justice in the world?" and "How do we establish a world community based on human rights?" are interpreted in a cosmic frame of reference, in which human activities in quest of justice and peace are seen as part of a greater and endlessly continuing whole. This stage 7 not only deals with such questions of doubt and skepticism, but also with more

10. Although relativism does not fit into the stage sequence, Kohlberg continues to refer to it as "stage 4½" (1984, 440ff.).

11. This relativism can take on different forms, such as radical, personal, egoistic, political, or decisionistic relativism (Kohlberg 1984, 442-43).

12. While Kohlberg's stage 7 is a religious one, Habermas's stage 7 remains in the moral domain, referring to the implementing of the universal moral principles that characterize stage 6 in dialogue and argumentative communication (cf. Kohlberg 1984, 385-86).

fundamental ones, such as "Why engage in this work of justice?" "Why seek to be moral?" "Why live?" and "How should we face death?" The willingness of Socrates and Martin Luther King to die for moral principles was partly based on religious convictions (Kohlberg 1981, 318). Sometimes these convictions are expressed in terms of faith in God, but faith in God is not a prerequisite.

Kohlberg gives the example of the Roman emperor Marcus Aurelius, whom he considers to be a noble representative of religious faith in the universe, and one who stands outside the Christian tradition. Kohlberg admires Marcus Aurelius for his pantheistic sayings about the principle of the universe, which he calls sometimes God, sometimes nature: "Your destiny you cannot control. Even the vagaries of chance have their place in nature's scheme. You yourself are part of that universe. Remember always what the world-nature is and what your own nature is and that your nature is such a small fraction of so vast a whole. Then you will recognize that no man can hinder you from conforming each word and deed to that nature of which you are a part" (1981, 346-47).

Another writer whom Kohlberg refers to in this connection is Spinoza. This Dutch Jewish philosopher sees human self-realization in terms of the discovery of the unity of the body and the mind with the whole of nature. Spinoza is willing to call this universe, which as a system is more than the aggregation of its elements, by the name of God. God, as the order of this universe, surely transcends the aggregation of parts, but is inseparable from what unites them. Kohlberg says of Spinoza: "He is arguing, in effect, that his own God has as much personality as the God of tradition, if by personality is meant a personal relation on the part of human beings toward God as it expresses itself in the attitude of love. Spinoza is saying that if we understand Life or nature we cannot help but love it and all things in it" (1981, 364).

Stage 7 may also be informed and oriented by Christian thought. Kohlberg cites as an example a seventy-eight-year-old woman, Andrea Simpson, whose Quaker faith in a loving God is translated into a supererogatory agape, which leads her to perform acts of self-giving love and sacrifice that go beyond justice or duty. Religion and moral action in this case are interdependent, with moral action taking justification, inspiration, and orientation from religion, and religion taking form in this moral action. According to Kohlberg, this faith-informed agape is not an alternative to the universal principles of justice that determine stage 6, but a higher stage, because it presupposes and integrates these universal principles. Agape goes beyond them, takes them up into a transcendent perspective, and transforms them.

Although it is needed as an answer to the moral doubts and questions of stage 6, stage 7 is not a real stage. Rather, it is a soft stage, even a soft hypothetical stage (Kohlberg 1984, 249). It is a metaphor (Kohlberg 1981, 344) in which the figure and ground — in Gestalt psychology terms — are switched. Whereas at stage 6, the moral principles function as figures in the foreground, at stage 7 these figures move to the background to make room for what was previously their ground, that is, the cosmic, religious perspective. This shift from figure to ground not only is cognitive but also involves emotional and volitional processes of engagement, surrender, and agape. Because the structure and content of this stage are much less sharply definable, it cannot be called a hard stage. It is, instead, a level of existential and reflective awareness (Kohlberg 1984, 213).

5.2 Whose Justice? Why Justice?

Justice plays a key role in Kohlberg's stage theory of moral development. Each of the three levels (preconventional, conventional, and postconventional) and each of the six stages is described in terms of justice. Justice is so central to this theory that the six moral stages can be called stages of justice reasoning (Kohlberg 1984, 212-36) or justice judgment (ibid., 620-39).[13] The levels and stages comprise progressive degrees of development

---

13. A major objection against Kohlberg's theory is that he reduces moral development to the development of moral reasoning. "In these classes youngsters learn, at best, to argue about moral issues, but no attempt is made to enhance their moral commitments. Moral commitments require helping young people feel more strongly about those values they already have (or acquire in schools), which can be achieved by using stories, drama, role-playing, videotapes, 'courts,' visiting places where homeless people hang out or a polluted lake, and other such educational devices that are evocative and not merely informative" (Etzioni 1994, 97-98). The objection is that moral reasoning does not offer any insight into the direction human action should take. It only teaches students to discuss moral issues. Etzioni illustrates this point by the following example: "Thus, in one case, prepared by the University of Minnesota and used in a discussion of ethics, a social worker visits the home of an ill person. The patient tells her visitor that if her condition deteriorates further, she will use her gun 'long before anyone puts me into a nursing home.' The question is, should the social worker report the suicide threat to the authorities and have the gun removed? It is then suggested that because of 'the principle of autonomy, the client's wishes are to be respected' and the social worker is not to intervene. But if someone puts more weight on beneficence, the gun would be removed" (1994, 98-99). This emphasis on moral reasoning not only reduces the student's moral development to the development of moral reasoning, but also reduces, so Etzioni says, the teacher's educational task of being an active transmitter of values to that of being a passive discussion facilitator.

of justice, culminating in the sixth stage, at which moral thinking is directed by the universal principles of justice. This highest stage is not only the culmination of the previous stages of moral development but also stimulates the progression through the sequence of these stages. Not only is stage 6 the last in time and sequence, but it inchoatively and progressively informs the preceding stages through the mode of anticipation. Thus the relation of stage 6 to the preceding stages is dialectical in the sense that it is simultaneously the culmination and the starting point. It is necessary therefore to go into the question of what Kohlberg means by this justice, and how it informs the previous stages. Subsequently, I examine how Kohlberg's justice reasoning concept can be evaluated, especially in terms of "whose justice?" and "why justice?"

Justice

Kohlberg's writings are not entirely clear on this point, but I think it is safe to say that his concept of justice is based on the fact of conflicts of interest and competing claims among individuals. Such conflicts, which are part of everyday life, disturb the equilibrium on which social life depends. In the more general view that Kohlberg adopted from Piaget, the equilibrium in the interaction between the individual and his/her environment is a key factor in human functioning, especially when this environment is a social environment consisting mainly of other people. Disturbances must be intelligently dealt with in order to restore the equilibrium at its previous or a higher level. Conflicts in social interactions between people have to be solved by restoring or establishing just relations: "A moral situation in disequilibrium is one in which there are unresolved conflicting claims" (Kohlberg 1984, 194). In other words, justice is a kind of conflict management.

Interpersonal conflicts can be divided into two groups, entailing two kinds of justice. The first group has to do with relations between the state and its individual citizens, institutions and their individual members, or communities and their participants. Conflicts within the state systems, social institutions, schools, and families center on equitable distribution of rights and duties. Justice that is concerned with resolving these conflicts is called distributive justice *(iustitia distributiva)*, which is based on the principle of equality.

The second group of conflicts arise out of the relations among individual citizens. These relations may be disturbed by a lack of balance between punishment and reward or bad and good action, by unfair contractual exchanges, or by imbalances between work accomplished and financial recompense. Justice that addresses these conflicts is described as commutative justice *(iustitia commutativa)*, which is based on the principle of reciprocity (Kohlberg 1981, 142-47).

Elsewhere Kohlberg adds a third type of justice: corrective justice. It is concerned with "private transactions which have been unequal or unfair and require restitution or compensation. In addition, corrective justice deals with crimes or torts violating the rights of an involuntary participant and in this sense requires restitution or retribution" (Kohlberg 1984, 622). In the history of the justice concept, commutative justice is closely connected with restitution. Thomas Aquinas, for example, calls commutative justice *restitutio*, which indicates that commutative justice is an ideal that has to be established time and again by the restitution of unfair relations among individuals (Pieper 1960). Kohlberg's concepts of commutative and corrective justice may appear to be closely connected, but that is not the whole story, from some other examples Kohlberg gives. The basic principle of corrective justice is equity, which comes into play when unequal distribution of compensation is morally required because of previous inequality, as in affirmative action policies with regard to women, ethnic minorities, and so on (Kohlberg 1984, 623). These examples illustrate that corrective justice also functions within the distributive relationship of state and society to its individual members. In my opinion, therefore, corrective justice is not just a third type of justice alongside distributive and commutative justice because it also refers to the equity dimension of compensation within both of them.

Kohlberg even adds what he himself calls a fourth type of justice: procedural justice. In fact it is not really a fourth type next to the other three, because it prescribes the procedures by which distributive, commutative, and corrective justice are realized. These procedures culminate in the principle of universalizablity: moral obligations must be applicable to everyone in the same (class of) situation(s). This principle can be called procedural because it requires the formal question to be asked with regard to any moral obligation: "Would you judge this action right if everyone were to do it?" (Kohlberg 1984, 622).

The principles of justice mentioned, that is, equality (distributive justice), reciprocity (commutative justice), equity (corrective justice), and universalizability (procedural justice), can be seen as the result of transferring social reversibility to the moral domain. In this process, social reversibility is transformed from a description into a prescription, which implies that people not only in fact take on, but morally must take on each other's perspectives: they are morally obliged to do so. Each of these four principles presumes all the others, and in this sense they can be seen as the ultimate expression of social reversibility in the moral domain. From Kohlberg's point of view, these principles constitute the very existence of his stage 6, which embodies perfect social reversibility in the moral domain. Kohlberg underlines Piaget's argument that "just as logic represents an ideal equilibrium of thought operations, justice represents an ideal equilibrium of social interaction" (Kohlberg 1981, 145). In other words: "Justice recognized as a 'balance' or equilibrium corresponds to the structural moving equilibrium described by Piaget on logic" (Kohlberg 1984, 184).

Stages of Justice Reasoning

From this point of view, stages 1 and 2 at the preconventional level, stages 3 and 4 at the conventional level, and stage 5 at the postconventional level can be seen as progressively approximating the ultimate perfection of social reversibility at stage 6. Each stage brings a shift toward greater equilibrium between the individual and his/her social environment thanks to an increasingly developed justice reasoning and a concomitant ability to manage conflict. The motor of this progressive development lies in the conflict to be solved, which functions as the mechanism that, when triggered, stimulates the upward movement: "stage change depends on conflict-induced reorganization" (Kohlberg 1981, 146). The conflict arises from the individual's lack of cognitive capacity to cope adequately with competing interests in the concrete situation, of which the individual is aware (Walker 1986, 136-40).

To illustrate this progressive development toward stage 6, Kohlberg shows how each of the four above-mentioned principles of justice — equality (distributive justice), reciprocity (commutative justice), equity (corrective justice), and universalizability (procedural justice) — functions at each stage.[14] He also uses the three first types of justice, that is, distributive, commutative, and corrective justice, to describe each stage in terms of justice reasoning. In this description of stages he appears to neglect what he calls procedural justice, probably because this type of justice is not really a type like the other three, but rather a dimension that is present in all three. Here I shall not extensively describe how Kohlberg defines each of the six stages in terms of both the four principles and the three types of justice, but refer only to some typical characterizations of them (Kohlberg 1984, 624-39).

14. Kohlberg sometimes distinguishes between the procedural and the universalizable principle, which then results in five principles instead of four (1984, 623).

At stage 1 (heteronomous morality), the individual sees equality as strict equalization in the distribution of goods to persons without any exceptions based on specific needs or deservingness. Therefore equity is absent, and corrective justice is exclusively understood as retaliation and retribution. A norm is a norm, a rule a rule. From this perspective of what both Piaget and Kohlberg call moral realism, these norms and rules have to be maintained without exception, for better or worse.

At stage 2 (individualistic, instrumental morality), moral realism is replaced by a pragmatic approach, in which the self's needs, interests, and strivings for goods are exchanged for the other's wants and desires in order to maximize one's own satisfaction. Here equality means recognizing all individuals, including oneself, as people with needs and desires to be satisfied. Reciprocity takes place in the mode of instrumental, tactical exchange, whereas universalizability is taken into account inasmuch as some order is required to prevent chaos and risk of damage to the instrumental exchange.

At stage 3 (interpersonally normative morality), the instrumental exchange is transcended in that the I and you perspectives, which already are operating at stage 2, are complemented by a third-person perspective that stems from the group or community one belongs to and functions as the perspective of the "generalized other." Equality means engaging with others as equal members of one's group or community. Equality is equality within and from the perspective of the group. This results in reciprocity among people. Here the universalizability of the Golden Rule applies for the first time: "Do to other members of your group as you want them to do to you."

At stage 4 (social system morality), the individual takes the perspective of the social system as the "generalized other." The informal norms and rules at stage 3 are transcended by formal roles, codes, and procedures, which ensure an impartial distribution of goods and burdens among the members of society. They concern every member (universality), which means that they must be impartially interpreted and applied. The Golden Rule is extended to all members of society: "Do to other members of society as you want them to do to you." Equality is equality before the law, which means that people have formalized and standardized rights and obligations toward one another. Reciprocity is defined in terms of this formal equality: people act from the perspective of belonging to the same social system and having the same rights and obligations. Equity is realized as far as laws are seen as not sufficiently sensitive to specific, individual exceptional circumstances.

At stage 5 (human rights and social welfare morality), the "society-maintaining" perspective of stage 4 is transcended by a "society-creating" perspective. The social system is critically evaluated from the "prior to society" perspective of the social contract, based on commutative justice, which is meant to protect the human rights and the welfare of all members, especially minorities. From this perspective, the Golden Rule can be interpreted as "Do to other participants in the social contract as you want them to do to you." The conventional point of view, which characterizes stage 3 and stage 4, is replaced by a rule-utilitarian frame of reference, from which the long-term consequences of institutions and systems for the welfare of all members, including minorities, are calculated and weighed out.[15] Equality means that the laws of society guarantee the same human rights and the same human dignity for all. This implies, for example, the rejection of capital punishment.[16] The retributive or retaliative meaning of corrective justice is given up.

At stage 6 (morality of general moral principles), the real "moral point of view" is taken, which Kohlberg describes as "a point of view which ideally all human beings should take toward one another as free and equal autonomous persons" (1984, 636). What makes stage 6 different from stage 5 is not so much the content of the principles as such (e.g., human rights), but the deliberate reflection on these principles, so that these become "self-conscious principles." This reflection is exemplified in the "musical chairs" with regard to "Heinz's dilemma": not only does Heinz take the perspective of the wife, the druggist, and himself, but each of the others (wife, druggist) also does so. It takes place in what Habermas calls, as Kohlberg says, the ideal communication situation, in which the principles themselves are made the subject of discourse. Here Kohlberg speaks of a second-order interpretation of the

15. Utilitarianism can be defined by the principle of promoting usefulness, but the question is, useful for what? Based on this question, several types may be distinguished: hedonistic utilitarianism (promoting pleasure and avoiding pain), preference utilitarianism (promoting what people prefer to be promoted), and welfare utilitarianism (striving to satisfy basic needs like food, shelter, health, employment, etc.). Kohlberg here understands himself as a welfare utilitarian (cf. Goodin 1994). Moreover, Kohlberg sees himself as a rule welfare utilitarian, which can be clarified on the basis of the distinction between so-called act and rule theories. Act theorists think that a moral judgment regarding an act to be performed in a specific situation needs only specific knowledge about that specific situation, whereas rule theorists think that such knowledge is a necessary but not a sufficient condition for a moral judgment to be adequate. What is needed is the knowledge and application of one or more general moral rules (cf. Munsey 1986, 94-96). Within deontology, an analogous distinction between act and rule theories can be made (cf. Frankena 1977, 26-32).

16. Together with Donald Elfenbein, Kohlberg wrote a whole chapter about capital punishment, including theoretical conceptions, critical reflections on the role of the U.S. Constitution and the Supreme Court, and empirical research on moral stages in judgments about capital punishment (Kohlberg 1981, 243-93).

Golden Rule, which, according to him, lies behinds Rawls's theory. Ricoeur is wrong in his ironic comment that, according to Kohlberg's interpretation, the Golden Rule belongs to the conventional level (Ricoeur 1992, 286n.78). In Kohlberg's theory, the Golden Rule is interpreted in various ways from the conventional to the postconventional level, that is, stages 3, 4, 5, and 6 (Kohlberg 1981, 203-4; 1984, 676).

Whose Justice?

Having explained Kohlberg's conception of justice and how he sees it operating in a progressive developmental sequence of moral stages, I now want to evaluate his approach by asking two questions: "whose justice?" and "why justice?"

The question "whose justice?" (which I owe to the title of MacIntyre's 1988 book) cannot be ignored because Kohlberg's idea of justice stems from a specific theory of justice, that of Rawls (1971). Kohlberg's stage 6 embodies the main relevant aspects of Rawls's theory, as Kohlberg frequently acknowledges, and because of the culminating character of this stage in relation to the previous stages, this theory dominates Kohlberg's whole developmental thinking. For that reason, it is necessary to deal with Rawls's work in order to arrive at an understanding and evaluation of Kohlberg's work.

According to Rawls, the answer to the question "whose justice?" seems to be derived from the so-called original position from which people participate in the debate about how society is to be ordered. In this original position, the participants are unaware of their social position; they know nothing at all of their property, talents, sex, cultural background, and so on. They are behind a "veil of ignorance." They ask only how liberties, rights, income, or welfare should be distributed and try to come to some agreement with one another — in other words, to establish a social contract. This social contract can be seen as a set of procedures agreed on by all, and according to which all competing claims derived from individual self-interest can be ordered in a right way. Thus the answer to the question "whose justice?" would seem to be: "everyone's justice."

But one must ask whether Rawls's theory is so context-free that his "original position" experiment does not reflect any prior idea about human and social life whatsoever.[17] The answer is no, for Rawls himself admits

---

17. Ricoeur points out the circlular reasoning in Rawls's theory. Indeed, Rawls introduces some ideas about justice before having treated his systematic conception of justice (Ricoeur 1992, 232n.47).

later on that his study was meant to establish a theory of justice for the modern democratic society, and did not claim to be relevant to societies in different historical and social contexts. Rawls sees the modern democratic society as developing from the religious wars that followed the Reformation. The principle of tolerance, he believed, was their effect, and the development of constitutional governments and large industrial market economies their long-lasting outcome. It is for these political, economic, and social institutions that he designed his concept of justice (Rawls 1994). In other words, Rawls's theory can be seen as an example of liberal thinking about justice, and the answer to the question "whose justice?" must be "liberals' justice."

Although Rawls belongs to the liberal tradition, it would be unfair not to mention the specific character of this belonging.[18] Classic liberal thought strongly emphasizes unconditional respect for individual liberty, without making allowance for the human and social disadvantages that can flow from competitive individualism. The so-called classic human rights, like the right of assembly or of religious liberty, were designed to protect this individual liberty from the state and the state's apparatus. Rawls apparently chooses liberalism, as evidenced by his giving priority to liberty over equality, as noted earlier.[19] In the list of primary goods to be equally distributed, however, he includes not only classic goods, like civil liberties, but also what he calls social goods, that is, powers and opportunities, income and wealth, which have to do with the so-called second generation of human rights: economic, social, and cultural rights (Rawls 1971, 62; cf. Van Genugten 1992). The reason for including social goods relates to the "original position" behind the "veil of ignorance" that Rawls posits. People in this thought experiment can go one of two ways, depending on whether they adopt the "maximax" rule or the "maximin" rule. The first rule implies striving to maximize the advantages of the most profitable social arrangement, while the second seeks to minimize the disadvantages of the most unprofitable arrangement. Rational people, claims Rawls, borrowing from economic rational choice theory, will prefer the maximin rule: "The maximin rule tells us to rank alternatives by their worst possible outcomes: we are to adopt the alternative the worst outcome of which is superior to the worst outcomes of the others" (Rawls 1971, 152-53). Thus the original

18. MacIntyre (1988, 326-48) rejects the notion that liberalism has no historical consciousness or tradition, arguing that it is itself a tradition and is as much contextualized as Plato, Aristotle, Augustine, Thomas Aquinas, or Hutcheson.

19. The first principle of Rawls's justice, liberty, overrules the second, equality (Rawls 1971, 60-61).

position will be dominated by this "maximin" rule, because everyone seriously considers the possibility of being affected by the worst arrangement rather than by the best one, and believes that it is worse to fall into the former than not to achieve the latter. In other words, out of a certain kind of well-conceived self-interest, people choose for both liberty and economic, political, and social equality in order to prevent the worst outcome from coming into being for themselves. They do not do so out of a sense of solidarity because they are "rational and mutually disinterested. This does not mean that the parties are egoists, that is individuals with only certain kinds of interests, say in wealth, prestige, and domination. But they are conceived as not taking an interest in one another's interests" (Rawls 1981, 13).[20] Their social orientation is self-interested because, in case of emergency, they want a social safety net for themselves. Thus the answer to the question "whose justice?" would have to be "the justice of social liberals acting out of well-conceived self-interest."

This answer seems to be relativized, however, by Rawls's final statement about the second principle of justice. Whereas the first principle refers to each person having an equal right to equal basic liberties, the second principle says that "social and economic inequalities are to be arranged so that they are . . . to the greatest benefit of the least advantaged" (Rawls 1971, 302).[21] In other words, although the liberals' social orientation is based on each individual's well-conceived self-interest, this does not seem to preclude a "preferential option for the poor," which is a fundamental principle in the moral traditions of various religious communities and institutions. Therefore one must ask whether and to what extent social liberalism within the context of modern Western society is compatible with this "preferential option for the poor."

But caution is in order because in legitimizing the so-called difference principle, Rawls is referring not to the inequalities that directly benefit the poor in the form of some kind of affirmative action, but to the rich. In his reasoning, the rich may expect more and receive a greater share of distribution — profiting directly from inequalities — because their greater wealth is to the benefit of all, especially the poor: "The higher expectations of those better situated are just if and only if they work as part of a scheme

20. Cf. Rawls 1971, 126-30.
21. Rawls adds that the greatest benefit of the least has to be consistent with the just savings principle, which refers to the degree to which the welfare of future generations has to be taken into account while establishing the social minimum for the present generation. This relates to the problem of justice between generations (Rawls 1971, 284-93).

which improves the expectations of the least advantaged members of society" (Rawls 1971, 75). Thus the difference principle relates directly to the difference of the rich at the top, which is justified because it does not further lower the status of those at the bottom (cf. Rawls 1971, 300-301).

Whether Kohlberg follows in the footsteps of Rawls's self-interested, social liberalism is a question not easily answered. The only place in Kohlberg's writing, to my knowledge, that one might see as a critique against Rawls is his reference to affirmative action as a compensation for inequalities in the form of "reverse discrimination" (Kohlberg 1984, 623). Generally speaking, though, Kohlberg seems to respect Rawls's social liberalism and even accept it as the embodiment of highest moral thought. Demonstrating what later on is called "Kohlberg's liberal bias" (Kohlberg 1984, 335), he devotes a whole chapter to the history and future of liberalism, to explore whether it is possible to establish stages of liberal thinking along the lines of the moral stages in his sequence theory. From cross-sectional samples of various societies as well as from generational studies, he concludes that the liberalism of the average American is at stage 4, while the Declaration of Independence and the American Constitution, as well as the decisions of the United States Supreme Court, can be localized at stage 5. Some protests against the Vietnam War as well as some arguments in favor of the rejection of capital punishment show evidence of an emerging stage 6. It is not the rejection itself that is an indication of stage 6, because it could be based on procedural stage 5 principles, but the argument that it violates the person's human dignity "because it treats members of the human race as nonhuman. It is inconsistent with the fundamental premise that even the vilest criminal remains a human being, possessed of 'common dignity'" (Kohlberg 1981, 242). Kohlberg concludes by formulating the suggestion, which stems from his reading of Rawls, that the "veil of ignorance" would preclude the participants in the original position from advocating capital punishment, because they do not know whether they themselves will be the murderer or the victim. In other words, based on the maximin rule, it is more rational to reject capital punishment because one might be caught in the "worst possible situation" oneself.

This way of thinking, in which the social orientation of justice depends on a kind of well-conceived self-interested liberalism, evidently differs from the idea of loving one's neighbor, one's compatriot, the stranger in one's midst, or one's enemy. It stands in stark contrast to the solidarity with the least advantaged that dominates some moral traditions in religious communities and institutions, especially the Jewish and Christian prophetic tradition. Why then does Kohlberg, following in Rawls's footsteps, choose justice as the core of morality and moral development, and especially this so-called social-liberal conception of justice?

Why Justice?

The fundamental reason why both Rawls and Kohlberg choose this type of justice would seem to be that they start from the premise that people are continuously in conflict because of conflicting claims arising from conflicting interests. These interests are not only material, for example, financial or economic, but also spiritual. Individuals have different ideas about the aims of human existence, the aims and goals of society, the nature of the good life and good action. They think differently about the meaning of life and death, suffering and mourning, or sex and love. How does one bring order into this disorder of conflicting needs, wants, desires, and preferences? Moreover, people are in conflict not only with one another but also with themselves, because they have to play different roles in various societal and institutional settings. There is no single overriding good that applies to all the spheres and segments in society in which they function, and the compartmentalized areas of economic, political, congregational, familial, educational, and religious life offer a heterogeneity of goods. Thus there is no overall ordering of goods, either for people's relations with one another or for their own lives. Whether this was the case in premodern times is for historians to determine, but in modern Western society there is "no overall good supplying any overall unity to life" (MacIntyre 1988, 337). How might this chaos be transformed into cosmos?

In this situation, Rawls's distributive justice, which is of a procedural nature, may offer a solution. It allows individuals to have their own, even fragmented, desires and preferences and to implement them as effectively as possible, while ensuring that they do not hinder each other, or at least do so as little as possible, in the pursuit of their own notions of happiness. This justice is procedural in that no moral or legal decision is taken unless it is agreed on by everybody who participates in the "original position." And as noted above, the maximin rule prevents the disadvantaged from being excluded from the social contract. The disadvantaged get more from it than they would without it, and even profit from it, according to Rawls.

From Rawls's perspective, the debates within the original position lead to a common agreement among the participants. There is no room for bargaining, forming of coalitions, or persuasion in favor of individual causes, because of the simple fact that the participants operate behind a veil of ignorance, meaning that they know nothing of their social position or special interests, or of what would be to their own advantage. What they decide on, therefore, is to everybody's advantage. This is even true of intergenerational relations. Because the participants do not know to which generation they belong—all generations are virtually represented—they decide on that which is just for each generation.[22] In other words, they are "forced to choose for everyone" (Rawls 1971, 140).[23]

It is this idea of common agreement or universal consensus that intensely attracts Kohlberg because it is the only way to overcome the dilemma between indoctrination and relativism-based neglect within moral education that I referred to at the beginning of this chapter. In Kohlberg's opinion, moral education, especially in public schools, can be legitimated only when no individual's or group's interest overrules any other's. Rawls's conception of justice offers the procedure by which domination of one group by another is prohibited. It is this conception of justice, stemming from the original position, and its inherent principle of universalizability that provide a basis for "the consensual values of society" (Kohlberg 1981, 37). It also satisfies the philosophic ideal of consensus, a consensus that is reached by using rational procedures in the same way as in scientific rationality (Kohlberg 1984, 272). In other words: "Morality as justice best renders our view of morality as universal. It restricts morality to a central minimal core, striving for universal agreement in the face of more relativist conceptions of the good" (ibid., 306). One might call this moral minimalism: a minimum grammar of morality everybody can agree on (cf. Zwart 1993, 75ff.). Later on, however, Kohlberg admits that his theory in which stage 6 defines the morally highest principles in terms of the "original position" concept of justice is controversial, as the critical debate shows (Kohlberg 1984, 216). It is a theory about consensus that arouses dissension.

Should arousing dissension be viewed as bad? In situations in which instrumental reason is used in order to achieve previously established objectives as effectively and efficiently as possible, dissent might be seen as frustrating, undesirable, or even damaging. But in moral situations, in which practical reason plays the key role, dissent can be enriching, in that it complements or even corrects certain views that have undeservedly been

22. At the beginning, Rawls (1971) emphasizes that the participants "know they are contemporaries (taking the present time of entry interpretation)" (p. 140), but later, while presenting the so-called savings principle, he elaborates on the veil of ignorance in the sense that "no one knows to which generation he belongs" and that "all generations are virtually represented in the original position" (p. 288).

23. MacIntyre (1988, 337ff.) is wrong in his suggestion that in Rawls's original position the competing interests and claims are resolved by bargaining processes that occur at the marketplace, where the preferences of individuals and groups are weighed against one another. Habermas's (1992, 175) distinction between conflicts of values or spiritual interests, which must be solved by mutual understanding and consensus building, and conflicts of material interests, which are the object of bargaining, does not fit with the assumptions of Rawls's original position either.

held to be true for too long. Neither effectiveness nor efficiency is the central criterion for moral thinking and action, but moral truth is. The core question is not how to get what we want with the highest benefits for the lowest cost, but whether getting there is good for me/us. Answering this question or, rather, approximating the answer(s) requires that one be continuously in dialogue with different voices both inside and outside oneself, which must be made to speak from both the past and the present. Moral thought does not arise from rational consensus building, but from conversation, which has its very basis in objecting, arguing, and contradicting. Truth in moral conversation is not approximated from striving for consensus; because truth transcends agreement, it continuously requires disagreement.[24] Truth can only be approximated by striving for truth (cf. Zwart 1993).

Kohlberg was confronted with this kind of disagreement himself when he was attacked by people who find Rawls's concept of justice to be too narrow — to say the least — to build a theory of moral development and moral education on. Justice is only part of morality, they maintain, not the whole of it, as Kohlberg suggests, referring to Plato's and Socrates' idea that virtue is ultimately one, and calling this oneness "justice" (Kohlberg 1981, 30).[25]

From his reading of Rawls, Kohlberg should have known that Rawls himself explains that his conception of justice has two fundamental limitations. First, Rawls's study is concerned with societal institutions, especially economic, political, and social institutions. Therefore it does not focus on other dimensions of the moral domain: the relations to oneself, significant others, other individuals, small groups, or communities. Kohlberg's life, however, prevails over his doctrine, so to speak, as two examples from his work may illustrate. Both of these transcend the sphere of distributive justice. First, the Heinz dilemma evidently entails some institutional aspects, such as property and stealing, but its focus is on the intimate relationship between Heinz and his wife and the danger that she may die and be lost to him. The nature of this relationship and what it means to lose a significant other are not the subjects of any theory of distributive justice. Another example is Kohlberg's treatment of tragedy in terms of moral development. In his opinion, tragedies are moral dramas, in which

24. Here I object to Habermas's conception of consensus truth (Habermas 1982; 1983), which was the basis of my previous work in moral education (van der Ven 1985).

25. The Socratic thesis of the unity of the virtues does not establish justice as the name for this unity, as Kohlberg says, but the knowledge of the good, which in turn comprises qualities like courage, self-control, justice, and so on (Crittenden 1993, 80).

moral characters perform moral (or immoral) acts of justice (or injustice), especially murdering another member of the family, which arouse moral emotions of pity, shame, and guilt in the spectator, and moral catharsis as well.[26] Whereas in Sophocles' tragedy *Antigone*, both Creon's civic morality and Antigone's divine morality embody a kind of institutional justice, Shakespeare's characters, says Kohlberg, are more concerned with personal justice (cf. Kohlberg 1981, 373-99).[27] Again, this personal dimension is not (sufficiently) covered by the institutional concept of justice.

The second limitation that Rawls points out is that, although his theory is about societal institutions, it is restricted to only one, albeit a fundamental, dimension of them: that of justice, especially the principles of procedural distributive justice.[28] It does not take into consideration other moral aspects that are necessary for a society to be ordered "for the pursuit of happiness," as the U.S. Constitution says. It refers only to a particular part of the complex social ideal that gives direction to a society, motivates its members, and binds them together (cf. Rawls 1971, 9-10). Again, one must ask whether Kohlberg's choice of Rawls's theory as a basis for his own theory of justice reasoning and progressive moral stages provides an adequate explanation of the broad realm of morality, even social morality. Is justice what social morality is all about? Is the just the only relevant social-moral category, and has the good, with all its implications regarding self-love, love of others, brotherhood, and sisterhood, no moral significance at all? I think that Kohlberg would agree that it does, but he does not explicitly and systematically address these concerns in his work, although, in later writings, he admits that justice is not the whole of morality, by allowing for "soft stages" (as distinct from the " 'hard stages' of justice reasoning"), which reflect concerns about responsibility, the good life, and faith (Kohlberg 1984, 317-18, 375).

One of the most powerful voices to assert that morality and moral

26. Here Kohlberg makes another distinction, this time between stage 5A (the social contract legalistic orientation) and stage 5B (the human justice conscience orientation). The first refers to the laws of society and the second to the higher values of the moral self (Kohlberg 1981, 381-82).

27. According to Kohlberg, almost all characters in classical and modern tragedies find themselves at the conventional level (stage 3 and stage 4). He sees Bolt's *A Man for All Seasons* as one of the exceptions to this statement because the hero, Thomas More, expresses principles of conscience that belong to stage 5B (see n. 26 above) or stage 6 (Kohlberg 1981, 387).

28. Rawls calls this distributive justice "social justice," which must be distinguished from what I further on call "social justice," meaning justice with a special concern for the least advantaged, including the so-called preferential option for the poor.

development cannot be assessed in terms of justice alone is that of Carol Gilligan. Based on her interviews of men and women, she identifies two different modes in which people define moral problems and moral conflicts. She calls these modes justice and care, or the ethic of rights and the ethic of responsibility. In the first mode, moral conflicts arise from competing rights, whereas in the second mode they are seen as the result of competing responsibilities. Justice is related to developing autonomy, whereas care implies connection. Justice has to do with interest, contracts, and power, whereas care is concerned with not hurting other people, helping and supporting them, and loving them. Justice is based on rules, care on relationships. In a justice or rights ethic, the self and the other are independent and opposite; in a care or responsibility ethic they are interdependent. Justice asserts, care serves. In these interviews, Gilligan sees justice as having to do with separation, individuation, self-enhancement, and achievement, and care with attachment and intimacy. "The morality of rights is predicated on equality and centered on the understanding of fairness, while the ethic of responsibility relies on the concept of equity, the recognition of differences in need. While the ethic of right is a manifestation of equal respect, balancing the claim of other and self, the ethic of responsibility rests on an understanding that gives rise to compassion and care" (Gilligan 1982, 164-65).[29] From her empirical observations, she concludes that the first mode is manifested most commonly among men, the second among women. In order to prevent an endless gender debate, let me immediately quote one of the first statements in her study: "The different voice I describe is characterized not by gender but theme" (Gilligan 1982, 2). Indeed, men and women can exhibit either of these modes or both of them, because they are or can be seen as complementary.

Gilligan is right in her criticism of Kohlberg's use of justice and justice reasoning as the exclusive criterion of moral development. Rather than prematurely agreeing with her that justice and care are opposites, and therefore complementary, I would like to reflect a bit further on the relationship between these two modes.

From an Aristotelian perspective, the relation between justice and care — as embodied in Aristotelian friendship — is dialectical in the sense that friendship both entails and transcends justice, while friendship at the

---

29. It is interesting that the psychologist Hermans distinguishes between two basic motives in human life, the self-directed motive (self-maintenance, self-expansion, self-determination) and the other-directed motive (self-surrender, interdependence, caring, intimacy) or, alternatively, autonomy and homonomy (Hermans and Kempen 1993, 147; Hermans and Hermans-Jansen 1995, 21ff.).

same time forms the bed of justice (Ricoeur 1992, 330). From this perspective Aristotle says: "Between friends there is no need for justice, but people who are just still need the quality of friendship; and indeed friendliness is considered to be justice in the fullest sense" (*EN* 8.1). Pure benevolence, which emerges from the attitude of care and friendship, cannot be adequately repaid, as would be required by (commutative) justice, because it transcends the exchange of tit for tat (cf. Van Asperen 1985, 122ff.).

Aristotle's discussion of the phenomenon of complaint also provides an illustration of the transcendent quality of friendship based on care rather than justice. Complaint can arise only in one form of friendship, that is, friendship based on utility, because the basis of such friendship is the hope of gaining some advantage from the association. In the other forms — friendship based on pleasure and friendship based on goodness — complaint does not occur because the friends get what they want when they enjoy each other's company (pleasure) or benefit one another through an attitude of benevolence (goodness). The first form of friendship is grounded in bargaining, the other two in just being together (*EN* 8.13). In the last form of friendship, which Aristotle calls perfect friendship, friends do not complain because they get what they desire, that is, the good of their friend for the friend's sake, and even feel that it is more important to love than being loved, to give than receive affection (*EN* 8.8). One might say that what is a motive for complaint in utilitarian friendship is a motive for gratitude in perfect friendship.

These ideas of care and friendship, which transcend justice, are not entirely absent from Kohlberg's theory because he deals with them in his discussion of Gilligan's criticism. He does not, however, accept them as a basis for an alternative sequence of stages, not even as an alternative basis for stage 6. Kohlberg argues that while care both contains and transcends justice, emphasizing care does not mean eliminating justice because it presupposes justice. The care mode can be covered by creating a stage that goes beyond stage 6 of principled justice. This is a "soft stage," stage 7, which places justice in the context of a broader and deeper worldview of the good life, the meaning of life, and the divine horizon of life. This stage transcends justice, because justice is about rights, which can be claimed, and duties, which are prescribed in correlation with these duties, whereas care and love cannot be demanded or required, because they are "acts of grace from the standpoint of the recipient" (Kohlberg 1981, 352).

The picture becomes somewhat confusing, because Kohlberg admits that care is so important within morality and moral development that it should not be delayed until "soft stage 7," but must be incorporated into the concept of justice at "hard stage 6." He then decides that justice and care — or benevolence, as he calls it — are two aspects of the more abstract concept "respect for the human person," which will determine stage 6 more explicitly. This respect, says Kohlberg, is the highest universal principle, from which both justice and care stem; and care, at this stage, can be seen as care for principally everyone, as principally universal care or "just care" (cf. Kohlberg et al. 1986). From his side, Habermas (1986) seems to agree with Kohlberg, but he likes to complement care, which he sees as directed to the individual human person, with solidarity, which is directed to all members of society from the perspective of the general welfare.

It is interesting to note that Kohlberg at least tries to connect justice and care by adding "soft stage 7" (or even building care into stage 6), while criticizing Rawls, whose theory of justice is the very basis of Kohlberg's, for not doing so: "In this way, our view is somewhat different from that of Rawls" (Kohlberg 1981, 352). In my opinion, Rawls's idea is more nuanced than the one Kohlberg presents here. According to Rawls, the individuals in the "original position" agree on institutional and natural duties that must be fulfilled in accordance with the principles of justice. Institutional duties apply only to those participating in the particular institution, while natural duties, which stem from human nature, apply to all. Natural duties are, for example, the duty of mutual aid, the duty not to harm or injure another, and the duty not to cause unnecessary suffering. These can all be seen as aspects of care and love. Along with institutional and natural duties, Rawls distinguishes permissions, which we are free to do or not to do. One class of these permissions are the so-called supererogatory acts, like benevolence and mercy, heroism and self-sacrifice, which "bring about a greater good for others whatever the cost to ourselves" (Rawls 1971, 117). In other words, according to Rawls, some aspects of care and love are natural duties, which one is required to perform on the basis of the principles of justice (!); other aspects belong to the supererogatory acts, which cannot be demanded or required.

Thus the question of the relation between the just and the good appears to be a complicated one. Does the good, for example in the sense of care and love, belong to a "soft stage," which finds itself beyond the proper "hard stages" of the just, as Kohlberg argues? Or are some aspects of the good, like the natural duties, covered by the principles of the just, as Rawls suggests? What then is the relation between justice and Rawls's supererogatory acts, of which the self-giving forms of love, like mercy and self-sacrifice, are the paramount example? Another way the problem might be phrased is: What is the relation between justice and love? From the perspective of moral development, this question is a fundamental one because the answer will determine on which basis — justice or love — moral development is built.

Justice and Love in the Christian Religion

Kohlberg's idea that the just (stage 1 to 6) is embedded in a wholeness of lifestyle, worldview, and religiosity, in which it at the same time finds its culmination (stage 7), leads us to turn now to a religious tradition. Thus Kohlberg himself points to the relation between justice and religion, in which he explicitly includes the Christian religion, as noted earlier. Let us therefore look at some relevant aspects of the relation between justice and love from a Christian perspective — not "the" Christian perspective, because Christianity exists in historical, contextual plurality. The question is: Should moral development be built principally on justice or on love? We shall look for an answer to this question in the Christian religious tradition.

Beginning with justice, let us ask in which terms justice is defined. While Rawls and Kohlberg principally define justice in terms of the right to liberty, the key words here are *right* and *liberty*. They note that this right must be compatible with the liberty of others, which means that one person's liberty is limited by the liberty of another. The concept of liberty, however, is qualified by a second concept, equality, in their phrase "equal right to liberty." In other words, society is conceived of as a collection of self-interested individuals who strive to satisfy their own basic need for liberty, but this liberty is limited because as they encounter others, they are confronted with the strivings of those others in the same restricted area of space and time.

For Thomas Aquinas, who follows in the footsteps of Aristotle, this conception is fundamentally mistaken. Aristotle's horizon, from which he develops his moral theory, is the polis, which is the community one lives in and lives for. This polis is directed toward all goods for its citizens — the common good. Thomas is of the same opinion, referring to the *bonum commune,* which he sees as the ultimate goal of community, society, and state (cf. *STh* II-II, 42,2; cf. MacIntyre 1988, 201). Within this *bonum commune,* justice never refers to the person's own rights and liberties, but always to the other's: "justice is always to the other," "it only has to do with things which refer to the other" (*STh* II-II, 58.2). The just is formulated in terms of the good of the other, which is, cumulatively, the common good.

Like Kohlberg, Thomas Aquinas distinguishes between two forms of justice: commutative and distributive. He also adds vindicative justice, along the lines of Aristotelian corrective justice (*EN* 52ff.), which Kohlberg acknowledges as well (cf. Wils and Mieth 1992, 49). However, the context in which Thomas makes this distinction is quite different from Kohlberg's and Rawls's, who think from a perspective of liberalism, in which individual self-interest is the leading principle, whereas Thomas stresses the whole of

216

community in which these forms of justice are executed. He speaks of the whole and its parts, describing commutative justice in terms of the relation between the parts within the whole and distributive justice in terms of the relation of the whole to the parts (*STh* II-II, 61.2).

From this point of view, Thomas could not but give a *bonum commune* answer to the Heinz dilemma. He would say that Heinz is allowed to steal the drug because — and in view of Kohlberg's emphasis on justice reasoning, the argumentation is fundamental — his wife desperately needs to survive, and this need cannot be satisfied otherwise than by treating the drug as part of the common property of human beings (*STh* II-II, 66.7). As intensely as Thomas would agree with Kohlberg regarding the cognitive dimension of justice and the importance of reasoning that is implied in it, he would just as strongly oppose the idea that only the method of reasoning — the formal aspect — is important, while the content — the substantial aspect — is trivial. Because of the *bonum commune* orientation, a purely formal, procedural conception of justice that would admit either a positive or a negative answer — as Kohlberg explicitly does — would be abhorrent to him in principle.

This *bonum commune* orientation differs from Rawls's and Kohlberg's conception of justice in still another way. This is the treatment of the least advantaged, if I may use the word *treatment* here, because it connotes that the poor are objects of justice instead of subjects. Rawls acknowledges that the poor must be seriously taken into account because — and this is important — the people in the original position cannot be sure that they themselves will not fall into a state of poverty at some time. Thus the "greatest benefit of the least advantaged," as Rawls observes, is a matter of self-insurance. The patristic stream in the Christian tradition sharply contrasts with this approach. It transcends this self-interestedness by stating that a person who fails to help a hungry neighbor when he/she has the means to do so is a murderer. The reason for this severe judgment is that this person refuses to give back that which, because of the *bonum commune*, rightly belongs to the poor. As Abelard said in the twelfth century, giving food to the hungry and helping the poor is a matter not of mercy but of justice; it is restoring the right relationships within the community as required by the *bonum commune* (Rottländer 1988, 77-78).

It is not surprising that Abelard's idea of justice has recently been reawakened in Christian memory, because for the last several decades, in its research into the life and work of Jesus, theology has been emphasizing that Jesus' proclamation of the kingdom of God is directed toward God's justice and the special place of the poor. The verse "But strive first for the kingdom of God and his righteousness" (Matt 6:33) belongs to the oldest layer of the Q tradition (*Quelle* or "origin") in the gospel, referring to Jesus' historical words and deeds. The "kingdom of God" is a Jewish way of referring to God, pointing not to any space or territory but to the phenomenon that God is sovereign in his justice, while transcending human conceptions of justice. Being king means being sovereign in justice.[30] The context of the foregoing verse indicates that the kingdom of God as a metaphor is sapiential rather than apocalyptic, because it is said that when this kingdom and its justice are sought, "all these things will be given to you as well" (Matt 6:33). It emphasizes the sapiential aspect of the kingdom of God in that it focuses on the here and now to be done and lived through (cf. Crossan 1992, 292).[31] But what are the things that "will given to you"? The answer is found in the preceding verses: food, drink, and clothing — in short, everything human beings need to exist: "Look at the birds of the air: they neither sow nor reap nor gather into barns, and yet your heavenly Father feeds them. . . . Consider the lilies of the field, how they grow; they neither toil nor spin; yet I tell you, even Solomon in all his glory was not clothed like one of these" (Matt 6:26-29). This sapiential kerygma focuses on the pivotal role of God's justice. Or, to put it in other words, justice is first and foremost a characteristic of God, not of men and women, and if one is open to that justice, one will live abundantly.

Here God's justice functions as the ideal form of justice, transcending human justice, as the parables in particular illustrate. "Justice" first and foremost is the name of God and his action; it is not a name that men and women can claim for themselves.[32] The commutative and distributive forms of justice are turned upside down in the parable of the laborers in the vineyard, in which those hired in the eleventh hour were paid as much as

30. Because of its hierarchical connotations, modern people have difficulty understanding the metaphor of "the kingdom of God." For this reason proposals have been made for translations that would bring it closer to modern notions, for example "God's federal republic," as Everett (1988, 171ff.) puts it. But this sounds too anthropomorphic and concrete, while at the same time running the danger of functioning as an ideological legitimation of existing political structures. Understanding "the kingdom of God" as a narrative phrase for "God," indicating a web of narrative meanings, which stem from Jesus' parables within a storytelling community, is more appropriate, while referring to God's sovereign justice and its sapiential implications for human life (Schillebeeckx 1974, 115ff.; 1977, 495ff.; 1989, 130ff.).

31. According to exegetes like Crossan (1992, 265-302), the sapiential aspect overrules the eschatological and apocalyptic aspects of the kingdom of God because of the intense relation between "kingdom" and "wisdom."

32. The Old Testament frequently refers to God in terms of justice. MacIntyre (1988, 198) shows how Plato already conceives of God as "Justice," and how Augustine and Thomas Aquinas follow his lead.

those who had been laboring since the first hour, to whom the householder said when they grumbled: "Friend, I am doing you no wrong; did you not agree with me for the usual daily wage? Take what belongs to you and go; I choose to give to this last the same as I give to you. Am I not allowed to do what I choose with what belongs to me? Or are you envious because I am generous? So the last will be first, and the first will be last" (Matt 20:13-16). The divine form of justice emerges even more sharply from the parable of the prodigal son (Luke 15:11-32). The fundamental truth is that nobody is left out of the kingdom of God or God's sovereign justice. This sovereignty is characteristic of God, in his divine initiative, leaving the 99 sheep to search for the one lost sheep. One might say that this divine justice differs from human justice in that it is informed by unconditional love: it is not conditioned by individual, group, or national characteristics or by any special moral, religious, or ecclesial achievement. Divine justice is justice embedded in unconditional, universal mercy and solidarity. Divine justice is unconditionally loving justice, justice informed by love. This justice does not primarily look at what people deserve, owe, or claim, but at the deficits and shortages they suffer. It looks not only at the needs people have, but also and especially at the needs they are.[33]

On the basis of this divine justice, informed by love, people are able to act in a just, forgiving, merciful, and loving way toward one another. They are able to do so because they are surrounded by God's forthcoming benevolence and solidarity, which precede, initiate, and evoke human beings' care for each other. This makes their actions of justice and love essentially passive. They receive what they do, owe what they perform, and channel what they let pass. Before carrying out justice, they undergo it (cf. Jüngel 1982, 500). This makes justice a grace, a gift, an infused virtue *(virtus infusa)*, as traditional school theology says, a virtue that people receive before passing it on to another and among themselves. Hobbes's *homo homini lupus,* which implicitly or explicitly is at the base of liberal thought, can be opposed by an evangelical phrase, *homo homini homo,* emphasizing human connection because of God's connection with human beings, as Jüngel suggests (cf. Tafferner 1992, 262). This means that claiming one's own rights, which evidently is a part of justice, must be done from a deep insight into the gift of this justice by God. From this perspective, justice is not absolutely due.

33. Browning (1989) is justified in criticizing modern psychologies and therapies, insofar as they favor a restricted definition of commutative justice in cases like marriage counseling, where costs and benefits are weighed against each other, while the potential richness of healthy self-surrender and self-sacrifice is intentionally ignored.

In the meantime, the human individual, especially the Christian, is called on to do the work of justice and love toward the other person or group(s) of people, because justice, as I mentioned, is for the other, as is love. Here the love of God and the love of the other are intrinsically connected, as expressed in the famous text in the gospel: "You shall love the Lord your God with all your heart, and with all your soul, and with all your mind. This is the greatest and first commandment. And a second is like it, 'You shall love your neighbor as yourself'" (Matt 22:37-39). This connection between the two forms of love is anticipated in the Torah, especially in Leviticus (e.g., Lev 19:18), Deuteronomy (Deut 6:4ff.), and the Decalogue (Exod 20), albeit not in explicit terms (Mathys 1986). The first explicit formulation can be found in the so-called intertestamental literature, in which Greek Jews brought together love for God and for the other (Schillebeeckx 1974, 206).[34] Because of this connection, in the New Testament, love of the other is understood as the most fundamental moral virtue. This stands in contrast to Kohlberg's conception that justice is the virtue of virtues (Kohlberg 1981, 30). Love is the very essence of God, and thus the very basis, core, and synthesis of morality. God is love, and love is God (Rahner 1965).[35]

Within the love for the other that is implied in this identification of God and love, certain others or groups of others need special concern and care, particularly the suffering other, the poor other, the alien other, the hostile other, and the dead other. Let us look at these more closely.

The gospel makes special reference to the suffering other, that is, the hungry, thirsty, naked, ill, and imprisoned, through whose face Jesus' and God's face radiates. Feeding, clothing, and visiting them means feeding, clothing, and visiting Jesus himself, however unwillingly, unconsciously, or unknowingly. But this helping the suffering other is not an act one can simply do or not do, as Rawls might say, and surely would say if such an act demanded too much self-cost, self-sacrifice, or self-surrender (Rawls 1971, 117). On the contrary, while justice is informed by love, love, too, is informed by justice, as the gospel indicates, for at the very end, Jesus will judge: "and he will separate people one from another as a shepherd separates the sheep from the goats, and he will put the sheep at his right hand and the goats at the left" (Matt 25:32-33).

34. Schillebeeckx (1974, 207-8) points to the ritual-critical orientation of the parallel text in Mark 12:28-34, an orientation that is not present in Matt 22:37-39 and Luke 10:25-28.

35. Jüngel (1982, 453ff.) would not concur unqualifiedly with the saying "love is God," but would link this love to belief in God. Thus he would say when one believes in God, love is God.

The poor other, too, is in particular need of our concern and care, be it in the West or in the so-called Third World. The position of the poor at the margins of society cannot be rendered tolerable or even legitimated by the idea that their inequality is for the benefit of all, including the poor themselves, as Rawls argues. Their suffering — from structural poverty, oppression, and alienation — cannot and should not be deemed acceptable because an economic weighing compares the institutional attack on their human dignity with other costs. There is no more fundamental cost — if the economic word *cost* can apply here at all — than losing one's self-respect and especially self-esteem. It is worth noting that Rawls refers to human self-respect as belonging to what he calls "primary goods." This self-respect equals one's sense of one's own value as well as confidence in one's ability, so far as it is within one's power, to realize one's own life plan, goals, intentions: "Without it nothing may seem worth doing. . . . All desire and activity become empty and vain, and we sink into apathy and cynicism" (Rawls 1971, 440). This is exactly what the legions of poor in the Third World go through. Their loss of faith in their own dignity is not something that can be weighed against other factors in an accounting, because it is the primary factor, which must of itself tip the scales. This insight is sharply brought to the Christian consciousness by liberation theology. Liberation theology is not based on distributive or procedural justice, but on what Paul VI in the encyclical *Populorum Progressio* (1967) called "social justice" or even "prophetic justice," and John Paul II in the encyclical *Centesimus Annus* (1991) termed "the preferential option for the poor" (Houtepen 1992). This "preferential option for the poor" is at the very heart of the Christian identity (Schillebeeckx 1988). One should say that it constitutes today's Christian creed.

In some Jewish and Christian traditions, the alien other has always been a subject of great concern and sympathy. The alien, or stranger, is part of the triad familiar from numerous ancient texts, which are commended to the special care of the religious community: widows, orphans, and strangers. Following in the footsteps of the Old Testament prophets, Jesus transcends the boundaries, walls, and gaps between mutually unfamiliar and warring parties. He accepts each person he meets, townsperson or peasant, citizen or outcast, military or civilian, Jew or Samaritan, Greek or Roman, religious or pagan, saint or sinner. He accepts each of them in his/her otherness, strangeness, or alterity. At the same time he appeals to his fellow people to reform their own patterns of thought and action. For example, when Jesus praises the officer from Capernaum who asks Jesus to heal his slave, and says that even in Israel he has not found such faith, he stimulates the faith of his own people as well (Luke 7:1-10). The same happens when he tells the story of the merciful Samaritan who comes to the help of the man who fell among thieves on the road from Jerusalem to Jericho, after the priest and the Levite, who passed that way first, would not. He holds up the Samaritan's love as a model for his own people: "Go and do likewise" (Luke 10:37). He instills positive attitudes toward strangers and relativizes his own people's pride. Jesus proclaims that "God is king in his kingdom," which means that God's sovereignty transcends sociocentrism in the direction of universal solidarity.

Coping with the hostile other, the person who is hostile to me/us or to whom I/we are hostile is a challenge that every person faces many times in a lifetime. Christian theologians long thought that the evangelical counsel "love your enemies" was a sapiential incitement exclusive to the New Testament. From his exegesis of Leviticus 19, however, Mathys comes to the conclusion that Leviticus 19:18 already refers to loving one's enemies: "You shall not take vengeance or bear a grudge against any of your people, but you shall love your neighbor as yourself: I am the Lord." Other verses in Leviticus relate to the more general love for the other, especially the stranger or alien: "the alien who resides with you shall be to you as the citizen among you; you shall love the alien as yourself, for you were aliens in the land of Egypt; I am the Lord your God" (19:34). Furthermore, according to Mathys, Leviticus 19:18 refers explicitly to the particular question of how to deal with the neighbor who treats one badly (Mathys 1986, 81). The first part of this verse condemns revenge and the second part condemns accusation; the third part appeals to love, thereby adding a positive injunction to the preceding prohibitions. As Mathys says, "From its context, the commandment of love says: do not think you fulfilled the law if you do not revenge and accuse your brother; you have to come to a positive attitude toward your brother: love him as yourself" (Mathys 1986, 69).

Finally, the commandment of love also applies to the dead, to whom we owe what Peukert calls anamnetic solidarity. That is, the dead live with us in our memory, which is part of God's memory, and God does justice to all who innocently failed, suffered, and died. The good life cannot be achieved or even approximated if the dead are forgotten in an attitude of indifference and neutrality. Cultivating the memory of the dead belongs to the very nature of love-informed justice. Jesus' own suffering and his final cry on the cross, "My God, my God, why have you forsaken me?" may serve as a model of expressing the need for justice, while the paschal stories of his living with God and his solidarity with humankind point to the love that transcends death (Peukert 1978, 308-10, 329-32).

In sum, Kohlberg's conception of morality, which is based on Rawls's social liberalism, is too restricted to function as a basis for moral development and moral education, because it does not cover all dimensions of moral life outside economic, political, and social institutions. For example, it does not allow for issues such as self-identity, family life, intimacy, friendship, neighborhood, or community life (cf. Flanagan 1991, 108ff., 195). From the perspective of the Christian tradition, its deficiency goes deeper in that it does not take into account the dialectical connection between justice and love. There is no justice without love and no love without justice. Justice is love-informed justice, as love is justice-informed love. For future research this means that the idea of moral development must be built on the dialectical relation between justice and love.

5.3 Development Revised

Having examined what can be meant by the adjective "moral" in "moral development," we now turn to the concept of "development" itself. In general, "development" is one of what may be called the family of words of change, which also include "growth," "maturation," "awakening," or "burgeoning." All these terms have three common characteristics. They refer to change as something that (a) happens in time, (b) is irreversible, and (c) is positively evaluated. Development differs from the other terms insofar as it relates to qualitative rather than quantitative change. Development occurs when qualitative change takes place, that is, when something new originates. Consequently, at least two stages of development can always be distinguished: one before and one after the qualitative change. The transition from one stage to another does not necessarily involve a disjunction, however, because qualitative change can also happen gradually. Some metamorphoses are not accompanied by any sudden crisis at all (cf. Van Haaften 1986, 26-28).

Conventional Morality

Kohlberg's moral development theory entails not two but six stages, spread over three levels, resulting in two preconventional, two conventional, and two postconventional stages. Thus conventionalism plays a key role in Kohlberg's work. Kohlberg's point of departure lies in the conventional roles a person has to fulfill within small groups at stage 3 and within societal institutions at stage 4. At stage 1 and stage 2 the child is not able yet to play these roles, whereas at stage 5 and stage 6 the person critically evaluates these roles in the light of moral principles (cf. Habermas 1983, 142).

An obvious question is at what stage or level morality starts: at the preconventional, the conventional, or the postconventional? Surprisingly, Kohlberg fails to develop a theory of the relation between convention and morality, although all of his theoretical and empirical research is based on this relation. Nowhere does he elaborate on these terms in more than a few lines; it is as if the relationship between convention and morality were unproblematic, when evidently it is not.

An example of such a thin description is: "The term 'conventional' means conforming to and upholding the rules and expectations and conventions [here 'convention' is used to define itself] of society or authority just because they are society's rules, expectations, or conventions [idem]. The individual at the preconventional level has not yet come to really understand and uphold conventional [idem] and societal rules and expectations. Someone at the postconventional level understands and basically accepts society's rules, but acceptance of society's rules is based on formulating and accepting the general moral principles that underlie these rules. These principles in some cases come into conflict with society's rules, in which case the postconventional individual judges by principle rather than by convention [idem]" (Kohlberg 1984, 172-73).

Again, where does morality start? Does it begin only at stage 6, the last and highest stage, at which the individual's thinking is determined by universal principles of justice? Or does morality include stage 5, which relates to social contract principles and human rights? Or does it already start at the conventional level, including stage 3 and stage 4, or perhaps already at the preconventional level with stage 1 and stage 2? In short, what does "morality" mean in relation to "convention" and its derivatives "preconventional" and "postconventional"?

Stage 6 might be called the stage of real morality, because only at this stage do the universal moral principles of justice come into play. According to Habermas, the moral character of judgment and action depends on the extent to which it is oriented to the moral universality of justice and can be legitimized from this universality as well (Habermas 1983, 169ff.).[36] In Kohlberg's own explanation, "One may define an act as moral if it is in accord with stage 6 principles in a particular situation" (1981, 172). An example can be found in his criticism of American societal

36. "Dieser scharfe Begriff von Moralität kann sich erst auf postkonventioneller Stufe ausbilden" (Habermas 1983, 174). In this statement Habermas seems to see stage 5 as the beginning of morality, but a few pages further on he criticizes stage 5 because of its overly narrow, Western, liberal, utilitarian content and denies its universal character (Habermas 1983, 185).

and political institutions, which are not able to solve the moral problems of today's world because they are based on "the more utilitarian or more laissez-faire individualistic views of social contract liberalism found at stage 5" (ibid., 241). Kohlberg mentions racial segregation, treatment of minorities, capital punishment, and the degradation of the natural environment as examples of such moral problems that can be solved only from the perspective of universal principles of justice. Unfortunately, only a very few people, such as Socrates, Jesus, and Martin Luther King, have achieved this stage. Even the judges of the Supreme Court do not fit in this stage. According to Kohlberg, they rule against segregation and capital punishment, but they do so uncertainly on grounds of formal procedural justice, which is based on the stage 5 social contract principle of utilitarianism, not on the substantial stage 6 principles of universal justice (ibid., 241).[37]

From this point of view, morality starts at stage 6, but the problem is that this stage exists more in a virtual than in a real sense, as Kohlberg admits explicitly in his later work. Only a few people, who function more or less as moral theorists, are actually at this stage. Their reasoning fits into the moral theorists' argumentation, as Habermas (1983, 185) says. Yet as moral theorists, they are exceptions, as Kohlberg indicates while admitting that his cross-sectional and longitudinal research has not provided him with enough empirical data that verify the existence of stage 6 (Kohlberg 1984, 270).[38] However, if stage 6 is the stage of "real" morality, and this stage does not exist in a practical sense, then morality does not exist in a practical sense.

This conclusion is too bizarre to be accepted, however. Kohlberg might be right in saying that only a few people have reached stage 6 in the sense that 50 percent or more of their utterances fit into the ways of reasoning and argumentation that characterize this stage. But this does not mean and cannot mean that critical moral thinking based on universal

---

37. Crittenden (1993, 77) criticizes Kohlberg for defining stage 5 in terms of utilitarianism and stage 6 in terms of deontology. Here two problems emerge. First, Kohlberg's stage theory is not a formal one in that it embodies at least two specific traditions within Western moral liberalism, utilitarian and Kantian ethics. Second, in what sense can a transition from utilitarian ethics (stage 5) to Kantian ethics (stage 6) be called a "development"? Is it possible to "develop" from utilitarianism to deontology? And is deontology morally better than utilitarianism?

38. At the beginning Kohlberg thought he had found subjects who were clearly at stage 6, but later on, with his improvements in scoring procedure and manual, he had to reclassify the same subjects into stage 5, 4, or even 3, or stage 4B or 3A (1984, 270).

principles of justice is in itself an exceptional phenomenon. One must assume that many people frequently take such a critical stance with regard to moral problems, albeit not in all situations at all times. When faced with instances of racism or sexism, their reasoning would be based on the principle of the human dignity of ethnic minorities or of women; in cases of structural inequality they would reason from the principle of social justice; and in other cases of human rights violations their moral arguments would flow from the principle of respect for the human person. It might be the case that reasoning from universal principles takes place only to the extent to which people are confronted with experiences of severe contrast, which evoke strong feelings of protest, anger, or even revolt. It may also be that the dilemmas, like the Heinz dilemma, with which Kohlberg assesses his interviewees, are too artificial, too verbal, and too far removed from emotional crisis situations to be the stimulus that triggers this critical moral thinking.[39] Assuming, therefore, that many people critically react to situations of oppression and alienation with moral reasoning based on universal principles, I suggest that "postconventional stage 6" be replaced by another term with no "hard stage" connotation. The critical moral perspective that people actually take looks more like what Kohlberg calls "a soft stage," which is a type, configuration, or style of thinking, as Piaget puts it, rather than a specific, discriminate breakpoint of change in time. In its place, I propose "convention-critical reflection," meaning a distantiated stance or reflective position from which all kinds of conventions, all kinds of institutions, or all kinds of status quo can be critically evaluated. The advantage of this new term is that it might eliminate a misunderstanding to which the term *postconventional* sometimes gives rise. With regard to this term, Ricoeur thinks that Kohlberg is driven by an antinomy between convention and argumentation, as if convention implied the absence of argumentation, and critical thinking were restricted to the postconventional level only (Ricoeur 1992, 286n.78). Kohlberg, however, does not reject convention as something that stands in contrast to reason, and he does not see postconventional convictions as purely established on reason beyond all convention. In my opinion, the term *postconventional* is misleading, as all *post-* words probably are. When people, according to Kohlberg, find themselves at the postconventional level — whatever "postconventional" may mean — they accept conventions if these can be seen as an embodiment of some moral universal principles (cf. Kohlberg 1984, 173). Thus in order to eliminate this misunderstanding it might be better to speak of "convention-critical reasoning" instead of

39. Many of Kohlberg's critics object to the artificial character of these dilemmas.

"postconventional reasoning," and understand it as referring to taking a reflective stance (cf. Habermas 1983, 183-87).[40]

Convention-Critical Reflection

The expression *convention-critical reflection* may answer some objections that have been raised with regard to Kohlberg's theory. These objections center on whether stage 6 represents a fixed, closed kind of teleology, within which the universal moral principles lie waiting to be discovered, or an open morality, in which people can construct their own moral principles based on their particular tradition, their situation, and the broader social and cultural context that influences them. Does it refer to an objective morality, the basis of which already exists in nature, or a constructive kind of morality, which must be shaped and created by people themselves? This constructive and creative activity is evidently only relative, because a *creatio ex nihilo* (creation from nothing) is impossible: one always needs motives, images, stories, concepts, and theories from moral and religious traditions in order to put the elements together hermeneutically in a new integration.

Nevertheless, the question is fascinating, because it places the two alternatives in sharp contrast to each other. On the one hand, Piaget clearly chooses the "constructive model," which means each person must arrive at his/her personal judgments and develop his/her own arguments. On the other hand, Kohlberg, according to some interpreters, seems to lean toward what is called the "natural model," in which the individual must "discover" the moral principles that exist somewhere in ready-made form. Because of this, Kohlberg is sometimes labeled a "moral realist" (Kavathatzopoulos 1988, 22-26), and one might ask whether he does not step into the trap of what he himself calls the "naturalistic fallacy" (Kohlberg 1981, 101ff.). Kohlberg admits that his description of stage 6 is not always as clear as it should be; but, after being challenged, he states explicitly that this stage must be interpreted according to the "constructive model" (1984, 300-304). Nevertheless, one wonders whether the strong connections between stage

40. Habermas also proposes replacing "postconventional stages" in the structural-genetic meaning of the word by "stages of critical reflection," without any structural-genetic reference, whereas he doubts whether the liberal political tradition, which is embodied in stage 5, including the social contract and the idea of the most welfare for the greatest number, justifies assuming this universal stage's existence. In essence, Habermas has left only something like "a critical-reflective stance," which connects the critical citizen with the moral theorist's sphere of argumentation (Habermas 1983, 185).

6 and its universal principles of justice on the one hand and the liberal, Rawlsian perspective from which Kohlberg looks at humanity and society on the other hand do not preclude this stage from being understood in the sense of a constructive morality. Although liberalism comprises a plurality of traditions, its fundamental principles are more or less established and fixed, because they are based on axioms like individual liberty, self-interest, rights, and the social contract.[41] My proposal to speak of "convention-critical reflection" instead of the "postconventional level" to some extent transcends the dilemma between the "natural model" and the "constructive model," because "reflection" is based on the "reconstruction" of elements that are available to people from the various moral traditions in the various moral communities.

But does morality really begin only at Kohlberg's stage 6, which I have now termed the stage of "convention-critical reflection"? Might not stage 5 already function as the beginning of morality? Furthermore, why does Kohlberg classify stage 5 as belonging to what he calls "the postconventional level"? Is the social contract principle not part of the status quo of today's economically and politically institutionalized convention? It would surely be more appropriate to classify stages 3, 4, and 5 as belonging to the conventional level. In this way the three stages would represent a broadening perspective, a progression in logical abstraction along the varying conventions of the status quo. Stage 3 refers to the least abstract conventions of the group, including the expectations that determine its social processes. Stage 4 covers the more abstract conventions of the greater society and institutions, including the functions to be performed and the roles to be played therein. Stage 5 takes into account the most abstract conventions, having to do with the fundamental principles of society from a comparative point of view. At this stage, it is as if one were to ask: based on the social contract on which our society has established itself and the principles underlying it, how could we ameliorate this society while learning from the ways in which other societies have organized their social contracts? In other words, stage 3 represents the conventions at the microlevel of people's individual lives, stage 4 the conventions at the mesolevel, and stage 5 refers to those at the macrolevel. Thus the conventions at the microlevel would refer to communication in the family, the neighborhood, associations, the congregation, or the local community; the conventions at the mesolevel would relate to the social processes within institutions, corporations, and

41. Boyd (1980, 206-7) offers a benign interpretation of stage 6 in terms of the constructive model by pointing at the role conscience plays in Rawls's and Kohlberg's thought.

bureaucracies in economic, political, and societal life. The conventions at the macrolevel can be seen at work in constitutional debates about issues such as abortion, pitting right-to-life and pro-choice advocates against each other, or in constitutional discussions about the value of the jury system like those surrounding the trial of O. J. Simpson, who was acquitted of two charges of murder in the fall of 1995. In other words, communications at stage 3 are characterized by arguments referring to microconventions, those at stage 4 by arguments relating to mesoconventions, and those at stage 5 by arguments dealing with macroconventions (cf. Selznick 1992, 392-409).[42] Even Rawls, who inspires Kohlberg's thinking about justice to a very large degree, and who in turn is inspired by Kohlberg on the matter of moral development, suggests that stages 3, 4, and 5 be taken together and treated as a unity (Rawls 1971, 461-79, 495-96).[43]

From the connection that I have now made between stages 3, 4, and 5, all of which can be called conventional stages, the question of whether stage 5 can be the starting point of morality must be rephrased as: Is convention the starting point of morality? In other words, does Kohlberg distinguish between convention and morality? He appears to, for instance, when he refers to the theory of Elliot Turiel, who distinguishes explicitly between convention and morality. According to Turiel, people appear empirically to attribute different properties to norms that stem from convention than to norms that refer to morality. These differences are that, first, conventional norms are seen as arbitrary and context-bound, and respected from an attitude of community-oriented relativism, whereas moral norms are respected because of their universal character. Second, conventional norms are seen as stemming from orders based on hierarchy, whereas moral norms have their foundation in equality among people. Lastly, conventional norms are seen as being oriented toward conformity, whereas moral norms encourage and oblige people to stand up against conformity and authority (Turiel and Smetana 1986, 122-23).[44] Kohlberg,

---

42. Kohlberg himself admits that stage 5 starts from well-established general rights (Kohlberg et al. 1986, 233).

43. Rawls, who distinguishes among three stages (authority, association, and principles) that correspond to Kohlberg's three levels (preconventional, conventional, and postconventional), indicates that his second stage (association) is parallel to Kohlberg's stages 3, 4, and 5 (Rawls 1971, 461-62n.8).

44. Turiel and Smetana not only distinguish between convention and morality as types of action orientations, but also refer to a third orientation, actions based on personal decisions. Based on their research, it appears that people reserve a domain of actions in which they can decide for themselves whether to act and how to act, without intervention from society's conventional or moral orientations. It is interesting that the

229

as I said, makes the distinction between convention and morality, but he relativizes it on grounds of culture- and context-boundedness. Kohlberg notes that the fact that students at school call their teachers by their first names is understood in the United States as a question of convention, whereas in Arab countries it is seen as a question of morality and is felt to be morally wrong, harmful, or unjust. This example seems to suggest that Kohlberg interprets the distinction between convention and morality as a matter of convention (cf. Kohlberg 1984, 235)!

Does this relativization mean that Kohlberg identifies convention with morality? In his view, is being a nice guy (stage 3) the same as being moral? Is acting in accordance with the rules of modern corporations and bureaucracies a moral action (stage 4)? Is an act performed in accordance with the principles of the social contract on which all citizens agree a moral action (stage 5)? It all depends, according to Kohlberg, on the reasons one gives for performing these actions, and the criteria that determine whether an action is moral hinge on the principles of role-taking and reversibility.

At stage 1, the child is not yet capable of role-taking; he/she wants only to avoid punishment, and for that reason he/she obeys. At stage 2, the child is able to take the other's perspective, but does so in an instrumental or strategic way. The child considers how far the other's interest prevents him/her from satisfying his/her own interest, and tries to overcome this hindrance as smoothly as possible, without actually identifying with the other person in the process. This is egoistic role-taking without reversibility. Reversibility comes into the picture at stage 3, and characterizes this stage and the following stages. In a way, one might say that all convention depends on our ability to take the perspective of the other, be it an individual or a

---

pro-life and pro-choice debate over abortion can be explained from this distinction. The pro-life advocates see the fetus as a living human person *in statu nascendi* and defend this developing life. The pro-choice advocates do not see the fetus as a human person during the first months, and reject any societal intervention in a domain that they reserve themselves, precisely because the fetus does not yet have human status. The crucial question therefore is when the fetus takes on the status of a human person (Turiel and Smetana 1986, 131-35). In the meantime, the question is whether the pro-choice advocates are sufficiently cognizant that the private domain of personal decisions is influenced by structural factors from society. Do they sufficiently take into account that the emphasis on economics in liberal-capitalistic politics seems to require expanded opportunity for abortion and almost structurally to compel and coerce both men and women to have more recourse to this option more readily than they would under a different economic system? Such a critical-political analysis would give a more solid basis for the moral reflections on abortion by the pope in his encyclical *Evangelium vitae*, which is at present in danger of being understood as merely a religious-moral outcry or even a kind of moralism (cf. *Evangelium vitae* 12-13, 58-63).

generalized other, and to act from the principle of reversibility. The child acts as his/her significant others want him/her to act (stage 3). The student at school plays the roles the teachers expect him/her to play (stage 4). The adult fulfills the societal duties the state's social contract requires him/her to fulfill (stage 5). All of these actions are based on the principle of reversibility.

Does this mean that Kohlberg identifies convention and morality, inasmuch as convention stems from this principle of reversibility? If this were the case, moral perception would be reduced to social perception, moral reasoning to social reasoning, and morality to sociality. Kohlberg himself regularly refers to the sociomoral perspective, which he defines as "the point of view the individual takes in defining both social facts and sociomoral values, or 'oughts'" (1984, 173). Here Kohlberg alludes to two different aspects, that is, social facts and sociomoral values, indicating that morality cannot be reduced to role-taking and reversibility, as important as these are. In other words, taking the social perspective is a necessary but not a sufficient condition for taking the moral perspective. From the social perspective social facts are perceived as what they are, whereas from the moral perspective these social facts are evaluated according to what they "ought" to be. This "ought to be," or moral convention, is described by Kohlberg as follows: "The conventional individual subordinates the needs of the single individual to the viewpoint and needs of the group or the shared relationship" (ibid., 177). This social subordination is absent at the preconventional level, because at stage 1 and stage 2 the individual child perceives himself/herself as the center of his/her social world, and is not yet able to subordinate his/her own needs.

Interestingly, Kohlberg interprets the term *postconventional* — which I replaced by "convention-critical reflection" — as a return to the individual perspective or, more precisely, the individuals' perspective, since it can refer to any human individual in any place at any time. The awareness of universal moral principles leads the individual to protest against society's unjust laws and conventions for the sake of his/her own welfare and that of all other individuals.[45] I might add, however, that in doing so the protester

---

45. Kohlberg is right in pointing out that not all protests against society are postconventional (or convention-critical), because particular forms of protest may be seen as postconventional (convention-critical) from the point of view of the dominant culture, but as conventional within a particular subculture, like the resistance of some religious sects, such as the Jehovah's Witnesses, to particular laws (1984, 179). In general Cohen (1980, 82) says: "Knowing that an individual's moral reasoning corresponds to Stage X or Y may tell very little about whether that person will become the loyal soldier or restless revolutionary."

does not really take an individual perspective, because the aim is to correct the social system as a social system. He/she wishes to renew the social system in order to be able to subordinate his/her individual interests and that of others to it in a morally responsible way. He/she wishes a morally responsible subordination.

As the principle of reversibility suggests, morality consists of two poles, the conventional and the convention-critical pole, each of which contains elements of the other in two respects. As far as the conventional pole is concerned, one might say that the norms, rules, and principles that underlie the conventions at the micro-, meso-, and macrolevels themselves contain inherently critical points of view. Moral and religious traditions, to which people consciously or unconsciously adhere out of convention, include critical voices, teachers, prophets, and schools that may challenge those very traditions from within. As pointed out in Chapter 4, it is too simplistic to conceive of these traditions as uniform, monolithic entities, when they are in fact composed of a plurality of mutually competing streams. Furthermore, the focus of these traditions is not restricted to the conventional members of their own communities, as Kohlberg seems to think; they also are concerned with marginalized people, outcasts, and strangers, as I have shown above using the example of the Christian tradition. Thus they possess a kind of built-in criticism and incorporate provisions for social change (cf. Crittenden 1993, 84). At the other end of the spectrum, that of the convention-critical pole, one might say that all critical reflection, analysis, and evaluation that aims at improving, complementing, or correcting society arises from the more or less autonomous use of the critical insights, concepts, ideas, or stories that can be found in the existing moral traditions.

The two moral poles, the conventional and the convention-critical pole, can also be understood as two stages in the sense of "soft stages" or what Piaget calls "states" or "types," that is, styles of thinking, ways of thought, or cognitive configurations. The difference between the two is not one of nature, but of emphasis. Piaget would call it a difference of *dosage* (see 5.1). The first stage, which I now call the conventional stage, can be seen as paralleling Kohlberg's stages 3, 4, and 5, while the second stage, which I refer to as the convention-critical stage, parallels Kohlberg's stage 6. A fundamental reason for describing these stages as "soft" is that the absence of any teleology in the critique of convention is not compatible with the definition of a "hard stage," which requires a definite point toward which development proceeds. But because there is no definite goal or end, there is no "hard stage" (cf. Crittenden 1993, 85).

The development that takes place between the conventional and the convention-critical stage involves a change from concrete, limited moral thinking to formal, abstract, broader moral thinking. Here I concur with Piaget's concept of moral development, which emphasizes a process of increasingly logical thinking in the moral area, from the concrete to the abstract, the material to the formal, the limited to the broader (cf. Kavathat-zopoulos 1988, 37ff.).

There is no sudden discontinuity between these stages. In a structural sense the relation between them is characterized by overlap, in that the criticism that is present within conventional traditions in turn feeds the convention-critical perspective. Temporally, their relation is marked by a gradualness of change from the conventional to the convention-critical stage, generally without any abrupt transition from one to the other.

This way of understanding the relation between the conventional and the convention-critical stage corresponds in many respects to Rest's concept of moral development. Rest sees moral development not as a sequence of discrete qualitative stages, as Kohlberg does, but as a continuous variable, which measures the extent to which children, students, and adults appear to use postconventional judgments and arguments (in Kohlberg's terms) or convention-critical judgments and arguments (in my terms). Because for-mal-operational capacities in the Piagetian sense are required for conven-tion critique, Rest's test of moral development cannot be used with subjects younger than thirteen or fourteen.[46]

Premoral Aspects of Social Development

What does all this mean for Kohlberg's stages 1 and 2? They appear to have been accorded comparatively little attention by researchers (Crittenden 1993, 86, 283 n. 46). Speaking from a theoretical point of view, however, one can say the following. Morality consists, as Kohlberg says, of a combination of taking the social perspective, in which social facts are perceived in accordance with the principle of reversibility, and taking the evaluative perspective, in which one (critically) decides how these social facts ought to be. Since the combining of the social and moral perspectives begins only with Kohlberg's stage 3, we have to consider stages 1 and 2 as premoral stages. They lack the principle of

---

46. Although Rest designed his Defining Issues Test (DIT) on the basis of Kohlberg's six stages, the most frequently used index in DIT research works with the so-called P score, which indicates the extent to which the subject exhibits judgments and arguments that fall under the "principled morality" of Kohlberg's stages 5 and 6 (Rest 1980).

role-taking (stage 1) and that of reversibility (stage 2), which are said to be necessary, albeit not sufficient, conditions for morality.[47]

To sum up my reflection on Kohlberg's concept of moral development, one can say that, first, moral development must be seen as a kind of irreversible change over time from concrete and limited moral thinking to abstract and broader moral thinking. Second, this development must be understood as stage-based development, where "stage" is used in the sense of Kohlberg's "soft stage" or Piaget's *stade* or "type." Third, the transition from one stage to the next does not involve a sudden break or discontinuity, but rather is a gradual and continuous process. Fourth, three stages may be distinguished: the premoral stage 0 (which parallels Kohlberg's stages 1 and 2), the conventional stage 1 (which parallels Kohlberg's stages 3, 4, and 5), and the convention-critical stage 2 (which is another name for Kohlberg's stage 6). This three-stage pattern appears to be the object of what has been called a "consensus . . . with a certain air of inevitability" among scholars (Crittenden 1993, 265), and is analogous to Piaget's three moral stages or *stades,* that is, premoral stage 0, heteronomy stage 1, and autonomy stage 2, although it is formulated in different theoretical terms. Fifth, the third stage of moral development, the convention-critical stage, is open in that it does not imply any fixed or closed teleology. The convention-critical reflection is not a set of principles or attitudes that are waiting to be discovered, but rather is the result of a reconstruction of elements from the various moral traditions in various religious and moral communities.[48]

47. Here taking the other's perspective and social reversibility are the criteria by which Kohlberg's stages 1 and 2 are distinguished from the other stages. Some of Kohlberg's interpreters do not appear to have a solid grasp of what social reversibility is. For example, Dykstra (1980, 7-29) believes that social reversibility implies the ability to manipulate the other subject. He forgets, however, that both Piaget and Kohlberg make a fundamental distinction between the world of objects, in which reversibility refers, for example, to the ability to look at a series of dates not only from first to last, but also in the reverse order, and the world of subjects, where reversibility is the ability to look at situations not only from one's own perspective but also from the other's. This is a necessary precondition for empathy and sympathy.

48. Crittenden (1993, 265) mentions "three broad stages: a pre-moral (or perhaps proto-moral) stage; a middle stage in which one's moral beliefs and practices are based mainly on the authority of others and are not thought about in a very adequate way (heteronomous morality, to make use of Piaget's terminology); and a mature stage in which a person is able to assume responsibility for meeting certain standards of behavior associated with virtues or rules (cooperative, autonomous morality in Piaget's terms)." Rawls (1971, 462-78) also distinguishes among three broad stages: the morality of authority (Kohlberg's stages 1 and 2), the morality of association (Kohlberg's stages 3, 4, and 5), and the morality of principles (Kohlberg's stage 6) (cf. n. 43 above).

6

Clarification

"The work of the teacher and educator, like that of the therapist, is inextricably involved in the problem of values. The school has always been seen as one of the means by which the culture transmits its values from one generation to the next. But now this process is in upheaval, with many of our young people declaring themselves 'dropouts' from the confused and hypocritical value system which they see operating in the world. How is the educator — how is the citizen — to orient himself in relation to this complex and perplexing issue?" (Rogers 1969, 239).

Who are these dropouts about whom Carl Rogers, one of the founding fathers of humanistic psychology, expresses his concern? Raths, Harmin, and Simon, the creators of the value clarification method, express the same concern as Rogers. As a result of their research into values, they identify two groups, or at least two extremes on a continuum, which they call the clear and the unclear. The clear have a positive, purposeful, enthusiastic, and proud approach to life, both privately and publicly. They know what they value and want in life and how to work for it. The unclear are described as apathetic, flighty, uncertain, and inconsistent. They are drifters, over-conformers, overdissenters, and poseurs or role players. In short, the unclear are confused in the area of values. They are characterized by "a perfection of means and a confusion of goals" (Raths et al. 1966, 7).

How does this confusion arise? The answer has to do, once again, with moral plurality. Because children and young people are confronted with such a multitude of convictions, principles, rules, values, and norms, they no longer have a firm grasp of what morality is, that is, who they are, what

235

they have to live for, how they should act, what they ought to do. Behind this doubt and confusion are weaker moral bonds in the family, value neglect in the schools, the declining influence of the church, increasing horizontal and vertical social mobility, continuous exposure to TV soap operas, movies filled with sex and violence, and bare-all talk shows.

The value clarification mode aims at helping the unclear and confused. It comes into play when the other modes I have dealt with — traditional discipline, socialization, transmission, and cognitive development, which stress institutionalized and culturally fixed values — have failed. The emphasis therefore is not on the values as such, but rather on the process of valuing that every individual goes through, and on the main values as far as they are involved in this process, which need to be unearthed, explored, and clarified. This clarification can take place in dyadic encounters and group meetings, be they in the family, at school, in clubs and organizations, or in the parish. It happens when people are asked to intuit, become conscious of, and justify the values they hold, and are challenged to cherish and act on those values.

This does not always require formal teaching/learning arrangements, because all situations in which adults and children meet provide an opportunity for this clarification process, if these meetings are handled in an adequate way, as demonstrated by the following conversation between Jerry and his teacher.

> *Jerry:* When I save up the twenty dollars, I'm going to buy that guitar....
> *Teacher:* Can you play a guitar, Jerry?
> *Jerry:* A little, but I'm going to really learn when I get my own.
> *Teacher:* Is playing the guitar important to you, Jerry?
> *Jerry:* Yes, very.
> *Teacher:* What are the possibilities for making the twenty dollars?
> *Jerry:* Not too good right now, I'm afraid.
> *Teacher:* Any chance of cutting down on what you now spend and saving it?
> *Jerry:* You mean giving up smoking?
> *Teacher:* That's one alternative.
> *Joe* (Jerry's friend): Or staying out of the bowling alley for three weeks.
> *Teacher:* Well, good luck to you Jerry. See you later. (Raths et al. 1966, 76-77)

Through this dialogue, Jerry is supported in his value of buying and playing the guitar and given two alternative ways of getting there.

It is not surprising that value clarification is very popular in schools and other educational settings, including local congregations, because it seems to offer an answer to the problem that permeates moral education in general: moral plurality. It solves the problem of what content, that is, which principles, rules, values, and norms, should be transmitted by letting the students or other participants in the process answer the question themselves. It is they who give the answer by becoming conscious of and clarifying the values that they themselves hold and cherish.

There are other reasons for this popularity as well. One of the main reasons I can think of is that our times are characterized by declining church membership, weakening of institutional ties of religiosity, and a concomitant confusion about morality and moral traditions. Value clarification as an approach to moral education is not built on religious traditions and the moral traditions associated with them, but on a secular basis, which has its origin in humanism, humanistic education, the human potential movement, and humanistic psychology. Thus value clarification fills a gap that arose when the religious traditions, and their moral traditions, decreased in plausibility and were replaced by a humanistic approach.

It is a widely held perception that the human potential movement and humanistic psychology, which began in the sixties and seventies at the same time as the hippy counterculture with which they were connected, reached their peak in the eighties, only to fade away after a few decades. The rise of the Moral Majority and the Christian Right focused attention on abortion and other life-and-death issues instead of on general humanistic issues; cognitive psychology emerged and gained influence all over the world. Despite these perceptions, humanistic education and especially the value clarification movement have continued to develop and are more popular today than ever before, even in religious schools and congregations (Clouse 1993, 325-29). Three members of a research team who observed nine elementary and nine high school classrooms in the midwestern United States over a period of two and a half years reported that no value clarification sessions were held (Jackson et al. 1993, 4). But this observation refers to moral education as a formal, autonomous part of the curriculum. If one looks at moral education as it occurs within classes such as religion, social studies, or English, or as part of other processes that take place in regular school life, then value clarification is seen to happen with great frequency. As Milton Rokeach, who criticized value clarification for its deficient definition of what a value is and for its value neutrality, said already in 1975: "All such reservations about values clarification notwithstanding, I believe that the values-clarification movement has made an extremely important contribution to modern education. It has succeeded in getting across the proposition that beyond making students aware of facts and concepts it is also important to make them aware of their own values. Such a broadening of educational objectives now has universal validity, largely because of the pioneering work of proponents of values clarification."[1] It has become so popular that it is almost universally understood and accepted. For example, Kirschenbaum can say, "Thus, the term 'value clarification' will appear more and more without credit, footnote, reference, or elaboration" (1977, 149). Dutch research indicates that value clarification is the mode of moral education with the highest preference among teachers, even in Catholic schools (Hermans and van der Ven 1996).

Most importantly, this humanistic approach is not transmitted directly to the students in moral education. Instead, they are asked to search for and discover, bring to the surface and clarify. Nothing is inculcated from outside; everything is meant to grow and ripen from within. The students decide for themselves what is good and bad, right and wrong. This point leads me to a second reason for the popularity of value clarification, which is that it is in tune with today's cultural atmosphere and our present-day "habits of the heart." The phrase "habits of the heart" is taken from the title of an influential book that argued that while public life today is determined by the symbol of the manager, private life is characterized by that of the therapist (Bellah et al. 1985). The therapist does not transmit values and norms, but listens empathically in order to help the client allow those values to emerge from within. "Clarifying questions," "the clarifying interview," and the emphasis on emotions are all important elements of value clarification. "This is not psychotherapy, but rather a process that focuses on the conscious elements involved in decision making, including one's readily accessible feelings" (Kirschenbaum 1977, 22-23). Indeed, value clarification is not psychotherapy, but it does use the Rogerian therapeutic method in an educational context, something that Rogers himself argued for (Rogers 1969). It is used and appreciated not only in the realm of psychotherapy and education, but also in organizational life, particularly where human relations are concerned (Vossen 1967). It permeates the whole of culture, including the area of morality (MacIntyre 1984, 30).

Still, value clarification is not without its critics. "The courses in 'value clarification' springing up in schools are supposed to provide models for parents and get children to talk about abortion, sexism or the arms race, issues the significance of which they cannot possibly understand. Such education is little more than propaganda, and propaganda that does not work, because the opinions or values arrived at are will-o'-the-wisps, in-

1. M. Rokeach, *Towards a Philosophy of Value Education*, quoted by J. Meyer et al., eds., *Values Education* (Waterloo, Ont., 1975). Sometimes the plural "values clarification" is used instead of the singular "value clarification."

substantial, without ground in experience or passion, which are the bases of moral reasoning. Such 'values' will inevitably change as public opinion changes. The new moral education has none of the genius that engenders moral instinct or second nature, the prerequisite not only of character but also of thought" (Bloom 1988, 61).

The occasionally cynical but always literary and lettered voice of Allan Bloom is joined by others. For example, Etzioni complains:

> In a typical lesson, students are asked to list what is dear to them — money, reputation, and power — and then to rank these pursuits in terms of which they hold most important. They fail — and are thus considered in need of moral tutoring — only if they have difficulty in deciding what is up and what is down in *their* scale of interests.
>
> They are further helped to clarify their preferences through exercises such as the lifeboat drill. In this exercise students are told to imagine that they are in a lifeboat with a group of people that includes a scientist, an artist, a teacher, and a general (the list may vary). The boat is overloaded, and they must decide whom they would cast overboard first, second, and so on. In this way the students' values are revealed. For instance, do they rank art higher than arms? (Usually the teachers are cast off first and the kids themselves last.) As long as the pupils are clear on their preferred tossing order, and hence by implication their values, their moral education is considered properly advanced.
>
> Under moral reasoning per se, nobody is supposed to discuss the question whom they *should have* cast overboard first or ask why there aren't enough lifeboats to begin with. (Etzioni 1994, 98)

Etzioni's criticism is not surprising, because he represents the view that human behavior is not determined only by utilitarianism-oriented happiness in a Benthamite sense (increasing pleasure and decreasing pain), but also by deontology-oriented duty, even in the economic area. According to Etzioni, deontological factors play a key role in developing the goals, selecting the means, and forming the societal context in which economic policy takes place (Etzioni 1988, 238).[2] In his view, the clarification mode in moral education fails when it emphasizes utilitarianism-oriented pleasure and eliminates the moral obligation out of duty.

In the same way, the authors of *Habits of the Heart* warn of the real danger in stressing what they call "the therapeutic ethos," which leads to a celebration of the self or the individualistic cult of self-worship, and thus

---

2. Because of the codetermination of pleasure and duty, Etzioni (1988, 12) calls his approach "moderately deontological."

encourages us to forget that we depend on one another. Later Bellah is even more critical: "And so we may ask whether today there exist in America, in the midst of our triumphant individualism, mores in the sense of 'Sittlichkeit' that would resist our proclivity to become a collection of atomized individuals who would be easy prey to administrative despotism" (Bellah 1992, 124).

To what extent, then, can the clarification mode be properly called a mode in moral education? In the following, I begin with a more detailed look at what this mode is all about, and raise some critical questions with regard to its internal consistency. The intention of this critical analysis is to assemble those elements that need to be kept in mind for the further development of the value clarification mode (section 6.1). In the rest of the chapter, I look at some problems that arise when value clarification is considered from the outside. One of these has to do with value clarification as a hermeneutical process (section 6.2). The other relates to value clarification as a communicative process, especially in the context of the multicultural society in which we live (section 6.3).

6.1 Consistency in Value Clarification

In this section I present the main features of value clarification as developed by Raths, Harmin, and Simon, and add some critical questions pertaining to its consistency. The reason for doing this is to gather the main elements of value clarification to be taken into consideration for its future development.

Valuing and Clarifying

First, what exactly is value clarification? Although the first impulse is to define "value" and "clarification" and then combine the two, the proponents of this method explain that they are not interested in the term "value" as such, but in "value" insofar as it stands for "valuing" as a process. Thus it becomes clear that "valuing" and "clarifying" are closely connected. Because people are confused about values, valuing almost equals clarifying.

Let us first see what "value" is not. The "value" in "value clarification" does not refer to institutionalized and culturally fixed principles, rules, and norms that have been transferred from one generation to the next in the context of the family, the school, or the religious community.

240

Values do not have an ontological, objective, or even societal status, which causes them to exist autonomously and precede the individual person's choice and commitment. They have nothing to do with traditional transmission, by which people are initiated into a specific moral system, inspired by a limited number of moral models, persuaded when expressing questions and doubts, and even manipulated or directly indoctrinated when this persuasion does not appear to succeed (Raths et al. 1966, 39-40). It is not denied that such things exist, but they are not called "values" in the value clarification framework.

Furthermore, from the point of view of value clarification, a value does not equal a goal or purpose, aspiration, attitude, interest, feeling, belief or conviction, activity, or worry. All of these things do have aspects in common with values, but are not themselves values. For instance, a goal can be merely a stated goal, not a goal that one lives by and acts on, which is necessary for it to be considered a value. An aspiration is a value only when it is put into practice in daily life according to certain criteria. Similarly, attitudes often are not concretized in actions. The gap between attitudes and behavior has been known for some decades already. Moreover, attitudes may exist without having been the object of deliberation and critical thinking. This also determines a value: that it is carefully thought over. Nor does interest cover the whole meaning of value, because it may only mean that at some time it would be nice to think and talk about something that we now call "interesting." Feelings may emerge from deep emotional inclinations and passions, but unless they have been accorded thoughtful consideration, they are not values. Beliefs may also fall short because one can have beliefs without cherishing them. An activity may be a necessary but never a sufficient condition for a value to exist. One never knows for sure which value an activity comes out of. A verbalized worry might refer to what someone values, but a verbal statement may be superficial and lack the experiential depth from which a value emerges (Raths et al. 1966, 30-33).

From this list of what values are not, we may indirectly develop some insight into the main aspects of what a value is in a positive sense. Raths, Harmin, and Simon see values, or rather valuing, as based on three processes: choosing, prizing, and acting. Choosing contains three elements. It means that (1) one chooses one's value freely, (2) from among alternative values, (3) after thoughtful consideration of the consequences. Prizing consists of two elements. It means that (4) one cherishes the choice that has been made and is happy with it, and (5) is willing to affirm this choice publicly. Acting again contains two elements. It means that (6) one puts the value choice into practice and (7) does so repeatedly, thereby establishing

241

a value pattern in action. In short, a value is something that one chooses, prizes, and does. It consists of three processes and seven elements.[3]

Before we look separately at the three processes of choosing, prizing, and acting, let us focus on what these three processes together constitute, and ask what then the content of a value actually is. Can everything in the world be a value if it satisfies the criterion that it is chosen, prized, and acted on?

To answer this question, let us look at the following example:

Teacher: So some of you think it is best to be honest on tests, is that right? (Some heads nod affirmatively.) And some of you think dishonesty is all right? (A few hesitant and slight nods.) And I guess some of you are not certain. (Heads nod.) Well, are there any other choices or is it just a matter of dishonesty vs. honesty?

Sam: You could be honest some of the time and dishonest some of the time.

Teacher: Does that sound like a possible choice, class? (Heads nod.) Any other alternatives to choose from?

Tracy: You could be honest in some situations and not in others. . . .

Teacher: Is that a possible choice, class? (Heads nod again.) Any other alternatives?

Sam: It seems to me that you have to be all one way or all the other.

Teacher: Just a minute, Sam. . . . I'm going back to ask that each of you do two things for yourself: (1) see if you can identify any other choices in this issue of honesty and dishonesty, and (2) consider the consequences of each alternative and see which ones you prefer. . . .

Ginger: Does that mean that we can decide for ourselves whether we should be honest on tests here?

Teacher: No, that means that you can decide on the value. I personally value honesty; and although you may choose to be dishonest, I shall insist that we be honest on our tests here. In other areas of life, you may have more freedom to be dishonest, but one can't do anything at any time, and in this class I expect honesty on tests. (Raths et al. 1966, 114-15)

Is the teacher's approach reported here not, in a sense, both inconsistent and shocking? Inconsistent because the teacher acts against the very idea of value clarification by limiting the students' freedom to act on a

---

3. I am speaking of three processes and seven elements here, whereas Raths et al. (1966, 28) speak of three processes and seven criteria, and Kirschenbaum (1977, 139) of three processes and seven subprocesses.

value that they understandably want to choose and cherish, that is, the value (!) of dishonesty, and shocking because the teacher completely ignores the content of the value, that is, honesty or dishonesty, in situations outside the classroom? The teacher's instruction is only that one cannot be honest and dishonest at the same time, because human beings can perform only one act at a time.

The question needs to be asked very seriously whether this opens the door to total value indifference and absolute value relativism. Proponents of value clarification complain that their opponents are continually making the same objections: "superficial," "relativistic," "value free," and "devoid of any cogent theoretical base" is what they hear time and again (Kirschenbaum 1977, 7). Are these objections entirely groundless, given that the students' answers in the above example are not judged as better or worse? Instead, their ideas and values are treated respectfully and equally, regardless of content. "There are no right answers," says Kirschenbaum (1977, 92). Taking this reasoning to its logical conclusion means that everything between heaven and earth can be a value: everything and anything that an individual chooses, cherishes, and acts on, regardless of its nature and content. This opens the door to that which is undesirable, irrelevant, impermissible, bad, and wrong

The proponents of value clarification refer to the U.S. Constitution, which cites three core values: life, liberty, and the pursuit of happiness. It is on these, they say, that their approach is based. They do not, however, attempt to define these values or how they relate to each other. Liberty, they point out, can be broken down into three other values: justice, equality, and freedom. Again, however, the content of these three values and the relation among them are not defined. The authors of value clarification say that value clarification "does not propose to answer all questions of human existence, including the origin and design of the universe. It does attempt to describe a valuing process and to say that if people use the process they will experience more positive value in their living and will be more constructive in the social context" (Kirschenbaum 1977, 13). Again we must ask, what does it mean to experience "more positive value" in one's living and to "be more constructive in the social context"? What beliefs about human life and its relation to values, or valuing, are implied in these statements?

This is indeed a fundamental question, which we may answer as we try to understand and explain as carefully and patiently as possible what "valuing" is. Let us go back to the three processes that valuing consists of, choosing, prizing, and acting, and see if they provide some insights into this question.

243

The first process is choosing the value. Choosing implies that (1) the student chooses his/her value freely, (2) from among alternative values, (3) after thoughtful consideration of the consequences.

Here the word *freely* is paradigmatic and comprises two aspects, a negative and a positive one. The negative aspect is that the value, to be chosen, may not be imposed or even transmitted from the outside. The student is not to be initiated into or even introduced to any moral tradition outside him/herself. "Freedom" here means freedom from. Instead, and this is the positive aspect, the student must make his/her own choice. For this to be a true choice, it must be weighed in terms of alternatives and consequences. Thus choosing freely means two different things. First it means choosing among and from a variety of possibilities. Free choice here is part of an alternate conception of freedom rather than, for example, a commitment conception of freedom in which I choose to commit myself even more intensively to a value in which I am already engaged, without first considering all possible alternatives. Second, freedom means taking all relevant consequences into account. This can be described as a consequentialist conception of freedom rather than a teleological one, as in the unconditional solicitude between lovers, or a deontological one, as in Kant's self-legislative freedom. Where does the teleological summons to friendship — "Love one another" — apply, or the half teleological, half deontological Golden Rule, "You shall treat your neighbor as yourself"?

If the values to be chosen are not drawn from religious and moral traditions — for example, "Love one another" or "You shall treat your neighbor as yourself" — then what is the nature of the values that are to be found through value clarification? The simplest answer perhaps is: experiential values. One of the basic assumptions of humanistic psychology and education is that for values to become one's own, they must emerge from one's own experience rather than being imposed from outside through socialization and then internalized. It is by listening to one's own experiences and feelings that one's own values become clear and conscious, instead of being merely the echoes of those of one's parents, siblings, neighbors, coreligionists, teachers, and so on. For people who have not clarified their own values and who suffer from values imposed from outside, the contact with one's own experience needs to be restored. This is not an easy task because individuals, in order to be loved and accepted, introject values pressed on them by their significant others. Rogers illustrates this by giving an example of a boy who "senses, though perhaps not consciously, that he is more loved and prized by his parents when he thinks of being a doctor than when he thinks of being an artist. He comes to want, above all, to be a doctor" (Rogers 1969, 244). After repeatedly failing chemistry, however, the boy sees a counselor. In the counseling sessions he begins to come close to his own experiences and realizes, "I don't value being a doctor, even though my parents do; I don't like chemistry; I don't like taking steps toward being a doctor; and I am not a failure for having these feelings" (Rogers 1969, 248). In this respect, value clarification is a result of self-clarification. The example illustrates the difference between the discipline, socialization, transmission, and development modes on the one hand and the clarification mode, which Rogers calls the "modern approach to the valuing process," on the other.

How do such "experiential values," which is what "choosing freely" refers to, relate to institutional or cultural values? In the previous chapters I already referred to the relationship between society and the individual. There, following Ricoeur, I said that the individual person plays a fundamental part in society, and that society must not be seen as an ontological entity on its own. Conversely, people exist only in relationships with others, who are constitutive of their very being. These relationships are also the basis of institutions and culture, as well as of friendship, solicitude, the sense of justice, and the rules of justice, such as autonomy, respect, and civil rights. These values are not at the student's ad libitum. If the student never mentioned or referred to them, they would have to be brought into the clarification process from the outside. I am not concerned here with the best time or the best method of introducing such cultural and institutional values. That is a matter of educational judgment and pedagogical wisdom. The point is that if clarification were exclusively restricted to what students themselves directly experience in the realm of values, their humanity and morality would be severely damaged.

Let us now go to the second process, that of cherishing the chosen value. This has two elements: (4) one cherishes the choice one has made and is happy with it, and (5) one is willing to affirm this choice publicly.

The element of happiness does not necessarily come as a surprise here, since we have already seen that Kirschenbaum believes that value clarification may lead people to experience more positive value in their life. The relationship between values and happiness is discussed more fully in the first handbook on value clarification. "When we value something, it has a positive tone. We prize it, cherish it, esteem it, respect it, hold it dear. We are happy with our values. A choice, even when we have made it freely and thoughtfully, may be a choice we are not happy to make. We may choose to fight in a war, but by sorry circumstances make that choice reasonable. In our definition, values flow from choices that we are glad to make. We prize and cherish the guides to life that we call values" (Raths et al. 1966, 29).

Two aspects of this quotation are especially noteworthy. The first is the distinction between values and choices. Choices form the genus, and values the species: values are a special kind of choices, namely, choices that evoke positive feelings. Does this mean that choices that arouse negative feelings can never be values? But that is a form of overly simplistic nominalism. If we accept this definition, it would mean that all kinds of choices we make in our lives that are connected with negative feelings like sorrow, worry, shame, and guilt are not values. Caring for one's child in the hospital for months on end, surely a distressing experience, would not be a value. Going through a painful divorce for the sake of one's own self-esteem would not be a value. Accepting deep and long-repressed feelings of mourning for a sister who committed suicide would not be a value. Confessing one's guilt to a friend whom one has betrayed would not be a value. Value clarification appears to take a kind of suffering-free perspective on life. Of course, I do not argue that suffering, illness, death, and mourning have intrinsic value. I am saying, however, that human beings are not only agents but also patients, that they not only do but also are done to, not only active but also passive. The great challenge of life is to struggle with this circumstance and find reconciliation. The relation between this suffering and values is not final, meaning that we need not seek that suffering as a value in itself. That would be masochism. Nonetheless, without seeking out suffering or justifying it, the process of dealing with suffering can be an instructive and enlightening experience. This distinction is important because religious traditions, or at least interpretations within and about these traditions, have not always avoided confusion between suffering as an end in itself and suffering as a process that can lead to valuable insights (van der Ven 1993, 157-224; van der Ven and Vossen 1995). As with the relationship between experiential and cultural values, here again one could certainly argue that confronting students only with life values that are connected with positive feelings will mutilate their humanity and morality.

The second notable aspect of the quote from Raths's handbook is the absence of any ambivalence in or about the prizing and cherishing. Are there really any values that are associated purely and solely with positive connotations? Perhaps very abstract ideas like freedom, justice, or solidarity might arouse only positive feelings. However, such abstract concepts are without contact with concrete life; by contrast, value clarification sees precisely this situation-bound contact with concrete life as its necessary condition, as we saw. The goal of value clarification is to help students discover and develop concrete values out of concrete experiences, values that are prized precisely because they make a difference in their actual life, as the aforementioned abstract ideals do not. These concrete values, because they do emerge from real life, do not exist in a vacuum, a happy island: they are always linked with their contrasts and opposites. Advantages go with disadvantages, pleasures with pains, benefits with costs. Life is essentially ambivalent; it is contingency and finitude, fate and chance. Human beings therefore have to make the best of positive as well as negative experiences and feelings. Life is lived in fragments. We do not have an overarching moral design or great narrations, but instead we know of moral ambiguity, uncertainty, shame, and guilt (Bauman 1994; 1995). To suppress this negative side would be to damage the young person's psychic and spiritual health. It would alienate the person from himself/herself, trigger all kinds of defense mechanisms, and prevent him/her from achieving that which the clarification method seeks to effect: experiencing what is going on inside oneself (Freud 1986; Uleyn 1969). Need I repeat that ignoring this aspect would mutilate the students' humanity and morality?

Then there is the element in value clarification that says that the value chosen must be willingly affirmed publicly. The authors give a descriptive reason for this prescriptive rule: because when one cherishes the values chosen, one is glad and proud, eager to affirm the choice when asked about it, and even willing to champion it.

Without taking this missionary statement too seriously, I feel that it is nevertheless necessary to ask how this public affirmation is to be understood. I see two aspects to this statement — the first conceptual, the second societal.

By the conceptual aspect I refer to the relationship between humanistic psychology and education on the one hand, which form the basis of value clarification, and on the other, behavioristic psychology, which dominated academic psychology during the time that value clarification developed, and Freudian psychoanalysis. Humanistic psychology sees itself as "the third force" alongside behavioristic psychology in the universities and Freudian psychoanalysis in psychiatry and psychiatric hospitals (Maslow 1964). It rejects both the stimulus/response deterministic model of human life posited by behaviorists like Watson and Skinner, and the intrapsychic conditioning of human existence held by (some) Freudian thinkers. It claims that healthy human beings have the capacity to organize and structure their life freely if they truly commit themselves to doing so. Rogers quotes psychiatrist Viktor Frankl, who survived the Nazi concentration camps: "Everything can be taken from a man but one thing: the last of the human freedoms — to choose one's own attitude in any given set of circumstances, to choose one's own way" (Rogers 1969, 268-69). The strength of commitment depends on three stages that the individual must pass through: desire, will, and decision, as Rollo May, another leading personality in humanistic psychology and education, suggests (cf. Clouse 1993, 329). The transition from desire to will involves becoming conscious of one's desire, which leads to consciousness of intention. To be conscious of one's intention is to will. The transition from will to decision requires that one react and respond to this intention, thus leading to the intended action and action patterns. From that perspective, human beings are not rulers of their fate but cocreators (May 1986, 262). The public affirmation in value clarification can be seen as based on these three interrelated processes of desire, will, and decision.

Connected with this conceptual aspect of protest against academic behavioristic psychology and Freudian psychiatry is also a societal aspect. The plea for public commitment and firmness may be understood as a response to the diagnosis that today's society is marked by value confusion, which is considered to be detrimental to both youth and society. Value clarification aims at encouraging the student to choose in a societal context in which choices, at least in the area of values, are not encouraged or reinforced. Thus it encourages the student to commit to and stand for the values chosen. But it does not do so in what one might call the Victorian way, in which a kind of blind willpower is brought to bear on values that other people, outside authorities, consider worthy of being put into practice, regardless of the circumstances. Value clarification differs from this Victorian approach in that it encourages the student to commit to values he/she has chosen after having considered the attendant consequences.

My reservations on the point of public affirmation are rooted in the same aspects mentioned previously. Is it wise, I wonder, to affirm publicly what is essentially ambivalent, embedded in a combination of positive and negative feelings, rooted in the essential features of the human being as both agent and patient? Or to use Ricoeur's words, is it adequate to affirm publicly one's attestation, which is the result of the practical moral judgment in a situation that is both convincing and fragile? Perhaps, instead of "public affirmation," the somewhat softer "mutual sharing and narrating" would be more fitting for milder attestations in weaker contexts.

Finally, the third process, acting, again contains two elements, which are that one (6) puts the value choice into practice and (7) does so repeatedly, thereby establishing a value pattern in action. The reason for including acting in the definition of value clarification, according to the authors, is that "nothing can be a value that does not, in fact, give direction to actual living. The person who talks about something but never does anything about it is dealing with something other than a value" (Raths et al. 1966, 29). Thus acting is intrinsic to what a value is. A value is something that makes a difference. It must have a "cutting edge."

This interpretation of value appears to have its origin in American pragmatism, which has been a major current in American thought since the golden age of American philosophy at the beginning of the twentieth century. Its most important thinkers were Peirce, James, and Dewey. According to James, Peirce introduced pragmatism in 1878. Peirce's pragmatism strongly influenced James's thought, which in turn stimulated Dewey, who was one of the sources of inspiration for the authors of the value clarification method. Although I do not suggest that there is a linear relationship from Peirce through James and Dewey to the authors of this educational approach, I do suggest that the notion that values must have practical relevance has its roots in this philosophy.

Several years ago I came across a beautiful sentence by James, who suffered bouts of severe depression throughout his life, and it has remained in my mind ever since. Speaking of the many men and women who commit suicide, James asked, "What reason can we plead that would render such a brother or sister willing to take up the burden again?"[4] This quotation illustrates the essence of American pragmatism. Although Europeans sometimes confuse American pragmatism with empty functionalism, sheer instrumentalism, and superficiality, it in fact aims to discover the truth of living together and searching for the good life for all *(bonum commune)*.

Pragmatism is not only a theory of methods and instruments, but also a theory of truth. As a theory of method it is concerned with the practical consequences of values. If, for example, two alternative values A and B are in competition and it is found that A influences the mood and behavior of people involved while B does not, then A will remain under consideration and B will be rejected. Pragmatism as a theory of truth implies a combination, one might say, of coherence truth and problem-solving truth (Murphy 1989). In other words, there must be a "fit" between values and other values ("coherence") in order to find strategies for solving (multi- or inter-) disciplinary puzzles ("problem solving"). James clearly set out this conjunction of the coherence dimension and the problem-solving dimension of truth: true "ideas 'agree' with reality." But what does this mean? True ideas "lead us, namely, through the acts and other ideas which they instigate, into or up to, or toward, other parts of experience with which we feel all the while — such feeling being among our potentialities — that the original ideas remain in agreement" (James 1975, 97).

This conjunction of the coherence dimension and the problem-solving dimension of truth is found in Dewey's work too. Dewey says that truth is what is fitting with other truth (coherence), while also being applicable in practice (problem solving).

4. I found the quotation in Dean 1986, 70.

Dewey identifies five steps in problem solving. The first step is that one finds oneself in an actual situation that is so complex and confusing that one does not know what to do. The second step is to structure this complex situation by formulating the underlying problem. Defining the problem of itself will suggest various possible courses of action. The third step is to choose the right or best course of action to resolve the problem. Let us take, as an example of a complex and confusing situation, a marriage crisis. The problem is how to resolve the crisis in such a way that my own self-esteem and my care for my spouse can be (re)established. Some possible courses of action would be to get a divorce, seek therapy either alone or as a couple, work on strengthening the marriage, throw oneself into work outside the home, change accustomed role patterns, or strengthen intimate friendships with others. Let us imagine that the option I choose to pursue is to strengthen my relationship with my spouse. To do so, I must consider whether this course of action will in fact solve the problem, what consequences it may entail, and how the various aspects of the situation will be affected by it. This brings us to Dewey's fourth step, which is to "ground" the option that one has selected by thinking through the idea, connecting it with similar ideas that apply in similar situations, and comparing it with other models and prototypes. In this way the idea is placed in a context of related ideas and arguments. In the example of the marriage crisis, one looks, for instance, at similar couples who may have faced similar situations — one's parents, siblings, friends, or acquaintances — and compares their actions and outcomes with one's own situation. Finally, after the idea has been grounded, the fifth step is to enact it in practice in an experimental way. "Experimental" means that the idea is tried out a number of times, and the outcome evaluated to determine whether, how, and to what extent it works, whether to continue with that particular course of action or to try a different one (Dewey 1986, 105-22).

Looking at this sequence, one notes that the first three of Dewey's five steps are preparatory; the fourth, the "grounding" step, corresponds to the coherence dimension of truth; and the fifth step, the experimental one, corresponds to the problem-solving dimension. Thus Dewey's pragmatism combines both dimensions of truth.

The authors of the value clarification approach refer frequently to Dewey and his ideas as one of the fundamental sources of their own theory. How then does value clarification compare with Dewey's emphasis on coherence and problem solving as fundamental elements of pragmatism?

The coherence dimension of truth is conspicuously absent from value clarification, and indeed it must be absent, because it would contradict the authors' assumption that values must emerge from the students' own experience. By contrast, Dewey's grounding transcends direct experience, drawing on the experience of others and requiring the ability to analyze and draw conclusions from that experience. My objection is not that the children "are not old enough," as many critics of value clarification have complained (Raths et al. 1966, 41), but that they are not yet educated enough. "Grounding," as Dewey uses the term, presupposes some knowledge of other experiences, values, value systems, and moral traditions, as well as the ability to relate them to one another. This knowledge and ability should be acquired by students in moral education classes, and requires systematic teaching/learning processes that intentionally aim at developing this ability. As long as such teaching/learning processes do not really take place, value clarification shall continue to be confronted with objections that it is "empty" and "superficial."

With regard to the problem-solving dimension, a comment is in order as well. Dewey explicitly favors replacing what he calls the "application to the situation approach" by the "application in the situation approach." The first is deductive because it reasons from truth (convictions, ideas, or values) to the situation, whereas the second is inductive in that it experiments with truth within the situation and tests it in relation to the situation. The value clarification method in fact uses the "application to the situation approach" by encouraging students to choose and cherish their values first and then apply them to the situation by putting them into practice. By contrast, Dewey makes the final choice only after experiencing what relevance the conviction, idea, or value appears to have in the particular, actual situation. For these reasons, the claim by the authors of the value clarification method that the criteria by which they define what values are have been borrowed from Dewey's thought needs to be substantially relativized (Raths et al. 1978, 286; cf. Van der Plas 1981, 33).

Having explained and evaluated the three processes and seven elements that make up value clarification, I believe it is now appropriate to ask what the ultimate aim of this approach is. The student's task of choosing the value — freely, from among alternative values, after thoughtful consideration of the consequences (first process) — suggests a utilitarian orientation to the entire value clarification approach. The student has an ultimate aim in mind, for example pleasure or happiness, then calculates what things, in this case what "values," can best achieve that aim. The calculation takes into account alternatives — which choice might be more useful — and consequences — the balance of potential benefits over potential costs. The other two processes can also be understood in this context. If one has chosen a value that is well suited to achieving that ultimate aim, one will prize it and even champion it (second process) and will not pass any opportunity to apply it to the situation one is in (third process).

251

Now I want to qualify this utilitarianism a bit, since utilitarianism can have different contents and shapes. It is not economic, commercial, or political utilitarianism that is at stake here, but what I would like to call experiential utilitarianism. I already introduced the terms *experience* and *experiential* when I referred to Rogerian humanistic psychology and education as the very basis of value clarification. As I said then, from this experiential perspective, values become your own when they emerge from your own experience instead of being socialized from the outside and then internalized.

From a close study of the value clarification method, the ultimate aim of this experiential process seems to be self-actualization. Self-actualization can be described as the ultimate aim of experiential utilitarianism, which dominates value clarification from beginning to end.

Self-actualization is at the top of Maslow's hierarchy of the five basic needs or values.[5] The first basic need is physiological, that is, the need for food, drink, shelter, and clothing. The second is for safety, that is, to belong to a safe, orderly, predictable, organized world. The third is the need for belonging and love (belonging to a family, community or other group, sharing affection with parents, friends, children, or significant others). The fourth need is for esteem (strength, competence, mastery and prestige, reputation, status, recognition, dominance). The last and highest need is the need for self-actualization (aliveness, wholeness, truth, goodness, justice, honesty, beauty, playfulness, freedom). Maslow argues that a lower need must always be satisfied to a certain degree before a higher need will express itself (Maslow 1954; 1962). Although value clarification may deal with all values in all five domains, from physiological needs to self-actualization, the ultimate aim of the value clarification process itself must be seen in terms of self-actualization: by clarifying one's values and valuing process, self-actualization is advanced. As confusion and apathy decrease, aliveness and wholeness increase, together with truth, goodness, justice, honesty, beauty, playfulness, and freedom (cf. Clouse 1993, 299-307).

A careful reading of Maslow's work on needs and values and his analysis of self-actualization suggests that beyond mere naked, albeit experiential, utilitarianism, a certain teleological orientation informs his concepts. Maslow's theory reaches into the area of higher, ultimate, spiritual values and peak experiences, which also include religious experiences. He argues that these ultimate values and peak experiences, together with self-

---

5. Maslow identifies needs and values, as does Rokeach, for example, because values may be seen as expressions of basic human needs. In other words, I value something when I have a need for it (cf. Schotsmans 1982, 470, 474).

actualization, should play a key role in education, but that modern education, regrettably, is shaped by educational technology and characterized by value confusion. One of the aims of education must be to advance people's capacity to answer questions like: What is the good man and the good woman? What is the good society? What is good for our children? Who are my brothers and sisters? To what should I commit myself? What should I prepared to die for? What are illness, suffering, and death for? What are truth, virtue, justice? What are my obligations to society? What should be my relation to nature? (Maslow 1964).

There is some doubt, however, whether such a teleological orientation is present in value clarification, for two reasons, having to do not with the vagueness and confusion that often characterizes Maslow's hierarchy of needs, but rather with the moral quality of the hierarchy of needs. First, Maslow's hierarchy appears to have been established and developed within a specific societal and cultural context, the white middle class of Anglo-Saxon America and other Western countries. Thus the hierarchy — and specifically the "higher" needs — represents the good life and values that are held by this middle class to be worthy of striving for, and underrepresents the huge underclasses, both in Anglo-Saxon America and elsewhere. Empirical research shows that self actualizing values are found in the top quartile of educational and occupational levels in Western societies (Inglehart 1990, 22, 163, 165). One may wonder whether this self-actualization orientation has any room whatever for the most disadvantaged, and whether it can be taken as the frame of reference for all just distribution (Ricoeur 1992, 274). It is appropriate only for those who have already satisfied their lower or, as Inglehart calls them, material needs, that is, physiological and safety needs. Those who are struggling to meet those material needs do not have the luxury of worrying about what he calls the postmaterialistic needs, for belonging, esteem, and self-actualization (Inglehart 1990, 134).

The second reason for doubting the moral quality of Maslow's hierarchy and its influence within value clarification springs from an insight offered by Charles Taylor in his brilliant overview of the history of Western moral thought. Taylor indicates that what he calls the source of the modern moral self is no longer to be found in some transcendent reality (i.e., God) or some othe · reality that is outside human existence (i.e., nature). Today neither the nature of God nor the nature of cosmic creatures but the nature within, the human soul, is the source of the moral self. We find truth within us, we hear our inner voice speaking, we listen to our experiences, and we take seriously what our feelings tell us about life.

But in value clarification this experiencing from within as the source of the moral self takes on a specific character: it is not the content of our experiences that is important, but the fact that they are ours: coming from within, emerging from inside, that is all that counts. Not substance but emotion counts. In a way, the emphasis on experience qua experience reduces ethics to aesthetics (*aisthesis* equals "experience"). Ethics becomes the "aesthetics of the self," to use a concept from Foucault. Taylor sets out the parameters for value clarification: "If our access to nature is through an inner voice or impulse, then we can only fully know this nature through articulating what we find within us" (1989, 374). This approach can be labeled as a kind of expressivism: "My claim is that the idea of nature as an intrinsic source goes along with an expressive view of human life. Fulfilling my nature means espousing the inner élan, the voice or impulse. And this makes what was hidden manifest for both myself and others" (Taylor 1989, 374). This self-articulation advances self-actualization, and the causal relationship between them is based on a biological model of growth. This explains why humanistic psychology and education often speak of the goal of individual growth through self-clarification: "There is an organismic base for an organized valuing process within the human individual. . . . This valuing process in the human being is effective in achieving self-enhancement to the degree that the individual is open to the experiencing which is going on within himself" (Rogers 1969, 251).

The unique originality of my experiences, which advance my self-actualization if I carefully listen to and clarify them, makes my good life different from everybody else's. Each person must follow his/her own inner voice: "Being true to myself means being true to my own originality, and that is something only I can articulate and discover. In articulating it, I am also defining myself" (Taylor 1991, 29). The "expressive individuation" that emerges from this "ethics of authenticity" can be seen as the cornerstone of modern culture (Taylor 1989, 376).[6]

Various social scientists agree with this diagnosis. In the sociology of culture, modern society is labeled an "experiential society" *(Erlebnisgesellschaft)*, characterized by an increasing aestheticization of ordinary day-to-day life *(Ästhetisierung des Alltagsleben)*. The market has become more and more an "experiential market" *(Erlebnismarkt)*, and rationality is no longer

---

6. Some critics reject the personalism that, they say, permeates American society, and with value clarification, they argue, this "personalism goes to school" (T. Lockona, *Educating for Character* [New York, 1991], 10). However, this individualistic personalism is fundamentally different from Buber's "I and Thou," Marcel's "Having and Being," or Ricoeur's anthropology of "self and other" (cf. Laurent 1985; 1987). Schotsman (1982, 556; 1983, 117) refers to the dramatic conversation between Rogers and Buber, in which Rogers appears not to understand Buber's philosophy at all.

substantial rationality but instrumental rationality, which is, however, not directed toward improving means to achieve specific ends, as it is with Weberian work ethics, but to experiencing and feeling life to an ever greater degree, that is, "experiential rationality" *(Erlebnisrationalität)*. Not the substance of life counts, but the lifestyle: how life looks, the image it creates, the impression it makes, the enjoyment and pleasure it delivers (Schulze 1992).[7]

While style of self-actualization, which is at the basis of value clarification, may evoke some teleological connotations, its substance cannot be understood other than from the perspective of experiential utilitarianism. The criterion, ultimately, is that one experiences one's inner self, not what one experiences. The teleological perspective of goods that are desired and aimed at, the sense of seeking the good life, is lost.

Furthermore, this experiential utilitarianism can even be called naive in that it completely neglects, as I said, the ambiguity of the light and the dark, contingency and fate, responsibility and shame, fragility and suffering in human life. Because of its biological organistic orientation it provides no acknowledgment of or inoculation against evil, either structural or personal. It does not acknowledge the role of guilt, nor does it pay any attention to the dialectical phenomenon of being an agent and patient in both good and bad things at the same time, that is, that I do the good that I encounter as well as the wrong that confronts me (Ricoeur 1971, 103). It does not take into consideration the institutional or structural dimension of human life. It provides no analysis of the societal conditions that at least codetermine the course of all individuals' lives as well as the way in which those lives are understood and clarified. Maslow's humanistic psychology and education suffer from a salutary anthropology, which does not take into account the personal and structural ambiguity, passivity, and negativity of humans (Jackers 1983; Bulckens 1994).

Future Development of Value Clarification

At the beginning of this section I promised to analyze critically the value clarification methods of Raths, Harmin, and Simon from the point of view

---

7. This experientialism is a by-product of increasing consumerism, which, at least in the Netherlands, refers to three different kinds of goods: material goods (material consumerism), welfare goods by the state (social consumerism), and intimacy goods from personal relationships (relational consumerism), all of which exist independently of one another (cf. Ester and Halman 1994, 11-38).

of consistency, and to obtain from this analysis elements that one should take into consideration for future development of this method. Let me summarize the foregoing critical comments by placing them in a constructive perspective. Once again, we will look at each of the processes that make up value clarification — choosing, prizing, and acting — as well as at what I see as the ultimate aim of this method.

In themselves, the three processes represent three important aspects of what the clarification mode in moral education ought to be. However — and this applies to all three processes — it seems to me that they should apply not in a linear but in a circular sense. It would be even better to conceive of them as a spiral, in which each process, carried out at successively higher — or deeper — levels, builds on what the other two processes have already led to.

To look now at how value clarification might be improved, we can say that the first process, choosing, must be directed toward the complementary relationship between the teleological good and the deontological just, or in Ricoeur's terms, the good desired and tested. This means that the student's choice, whatever it may be, must be interpreted by the student in terms of how it relates to the good and the just. This process must focus not only on individual but also on institutional values, especially insofar as they are related to each other. To bring about an awareness and understanding of these connections will no doubt require substantial help and support from the teacher.

The alternativity conception of freedom, which I alluded to earlier, needs to be complemented with the commitment conception of freedom. That is, values that the student has already been introduced to and even initiated into through the modes of discipline, socialization, transmission, and development must be subject to further exploration, understanding, internalization, engagement, and so on, even without necessarily being weighed against the alternatives. Tradition and freedom are not opposites, any more than are rationality and convention.

The consideration of the consequences, one of the elements of the choosing process, can be seen as a first reflection on what certain value(s) might mean in "real life." It is important, however, to stress the provisional nature of the conclusions because, as Dewey's "application in situation" reminds us, these consequences need to be experienced and tested in actual life.

The second process, prizing and cherishing, should be located within a moral frame of reference that renders it softer, more provisional, and more fragmentary, and this for two reasons. The first reason is that allowance must be made for negative aspects inherent in human life and morality, such as suffering, sorrow, frustration, and disappointment. Values, as positive as they may be, also require endurance, perseverance, compassion, and sacrifice. Second, making choices in moral life is always surrounded by uncertainty, ambiguity, ambivalence, questions, and doubts. It is important to develop in students an appreciation that morality is surrounded by a cloud of unknowing, because that is what they will be confronted with later on in life.

Although stressing that the will is important, especially when it is formed according to the three-stage model of Rollo May (from desire through intention to decision), the aspect of will that is expressed in public affirmation might have certain undesirable consequences. First it might prevent the student from correcting his/her own decision when such correction is necessary, especially when it is the student's own insight that makes apparent the need for correction. Second, when public affirmation is done — metaphorically speaking — too loudly, it could prevent other persons, especially students, from going their own way and weighing and deliberating the personal choices that they need to make on their own.

The third process, acting, needs to be intrinsically connected with the processes of choosing, as discussed earlier. Acting is applying values not to the situation but in the situation. It follows from what Ricoeur calls judgment in the situation, which equals Aristotelian *phronesis*. This means that choosing essentially takes place through acting and is therefore essentially provisional.

Lastly, with regard to the ultimate aim of value clarification, I believe that inasmuch as this approach is based on a naive kind of experiential utilitarianism, it must be complemented. But by what? In essence it can be argued that the clarification mode is not intrinsically different from the transmission mode, with the exception that the clarification mode emphatically stresses the student's input into moral education, whereas the transmission mode similarly stresses the contribution of the moral tradition or traditions. Together these two modes represent the dialectical relationship between *educandus* (student) and content, which is at the root of all education. Each of these modes emphasizes one of two poles. If that is true, then the ultimate aim of the clarification mode must be to create the optimal conditions for students to introduce themselves to the dialectics of the good, the just, and the wise, and to do that freely as far as possible.

6.2 Clarification as a Hermeneutical Process

To find out how students might best be helped to introduce themselves to clarification as a hermeneutical process, we first need to ask what really happens when students ask themselves which values are important for them. Taking the imaginative approach to human functioning to which I referred in Chapter 4, one would say that the process of experiencing and thinking that is triggered by such a question evokes all kinds of images, symbols, stories, narratives, associations, and prototypes. These images, symbols, and so on form and mold the ideas and thoughts that then emerge; they stimulate a variety of feelings, connotations, reasoning, and evaluating (Johnson 1993).

Where do these feelings, images, symbols, stories, and thoughts come from? According to the interactionist perspective dealt with in Chapter 1, they are not innate but the result of the exchange between the individual and the environment. They are embodied in what symbolic interactionism calls the "me," in contrast to the "I." The relation between "I" and "me" is dialectical, as we saw in Chapter 3. The "me" is shaped by one's significant others and the generalized others, and the traditions these generalized others represent. It consists of the expectations others have of me, and which I introject as principles, values, and norms. When the student asks himself/herself what values he/she believes are important, he/she delves into this "me," that is, into the values and norms that other people, based on the traditions they cherish and act on, wish us to cherish and act on. Is there not, as Rogers claims, a primitive, innocent, noninfluenced, "real me" that is in possession of itself, as it were? From the point of view of symbolic interactionism, the answer is no, because the "me" is exactly the deposit of what I expect others to expect of me. In symbolic interactionism there is, however, the "I," which time and again transcends this conventional "me" and establishes and shapes its own "experiencing" — to use a Rogerian term. This "experiencing I" does not operate separately from the "conventional me," but rather reconstructs, reorganizes, and reconfigures what the "me" has to offer. Thus what the student does in the clarification mode is to reconstruct, reorganize, and reconfigure what his/her significant others and generalized others, from the context of their cultural and moral traditions, expect him/her to value and do, but he/she does so in his/her own way, from his/her unique perspective, adding to it, complementing it, and even correcting it. Clarification is always "self"-clarification.

This "self"-clarification may be interpreted in a hermeneutical sense. While the "I" is restructuring the "me," one asks: Who am I? Who would I like to be? What do I live for? Which values should I commit to? What should I do? These questions are inextricably interwoven with one's own individual identity. They refer descriptively to what and where one is (the ego), and normatively to what one desires to be or become (the ego-ideal). The clarification mode tries to bridge the gap between the ego and the ego-ideal by searching for and exploring what is appropriate to aim at in this situation, here and now. It is a mode of moral self-understanding. This is done by taking up, questioning, and critically reflecting what biography, community, and tradition have said that one is, must commit to, and ought to do. As Habermas says, "self"-clarification is a hermeneutical process (Habermas 1993, 4-5).

One might say that this interpretation of a seemingly simple daily classroom reality goes too far in that it places a burden of clarification activity on the student that is too heavy for him/her to carry. I do not believe that this is the case, but let us have a closer look at what the student actually does when he/she is asked to indicate what values are important to him/her. What students then bring forward is a collection of oral texts that has been inscribed in their biography by the family, the neighborhood, the school, and so on. This collection is an ensemble, because the people who relate and read these texts unconsciously treat them as a kind of coherent whole, almost as a canon. The texts are embodied in habits, customs, conventions, rules, and rituals. At the same time, they broaden and deepen these texts by including not only parts from small traditions like family or community stories, newspaper reports, and TV programs, but also parts from the great traditions, like classic texts from literary, moral, and religious traditions. In all these oral and written texts, the Burkian pentad can be seen at work, that is, an actor, an action, a goal, a scene, and an instrument, each of which plays its narrative role (cf. Burke 1966; Bruner 1990). In telling stories, people make all kinds of connections between these oral texts as well as between oral and written texts. This is what is known as intertextuality, meaning that the storyteller reconstructs the story that is told to him/her by weaving it into a web of other texts (Van Wolde 1989). Thus the students delve into their small and great traditions and come up with their personally, intertextually reconstructed stories. In the process of telling their stories, they develop a concept of their own identity, possible futures, and actions to be performed. In short, they perform their own hermeneutics.

Hermeneutical Criteria

I would now like to elaborate on four hermeneutical criteria that must be satisfied by this storytelling process, so that these can be incorporated within the clarification mode. The first criterion refers to the so-called hermeneutical circle. This circle contains the tension between the otherness of the texts and the prejudice with which the reader, here the student, approaches these texts. I take the term *prejudice* here in the sense Gadamer attributes to it, meaning both the legitimate preformed judgment with which the reader reads and retells the texts, all texts, and the illegitimate preformed judgment that is distorted in advance by some ideological alienation of the text from itself by the reader. The only way to prevent such distortion is to be as open as possible to the text, and as conscious as possible of one's own prejudices, so that the text can be given the optimal opportunity to present its own meaning. The reader must bracket his/her judgment, so that the *mensuratio ad rem* can be realized (Gadamer 1960, 247) and the hermeneutical circle closed. How does one establish the conditions by which the student is challenged to thus bracket his/her own prejudice? There are two answers, which in essence might be reduced to only one: the student has to encounter hermeneutical models from which he/she is able to experience what it means to bracket one's judgment, and these models can take one of two forms: written texts, in which this bracketing is concretely performed with regard to other texts, or the teacher, who demonstrates this bracketing *in actu.*

In order really to understand the meaning of a text, a second condition must be satisfied: the fusion between the horizon of the text and the reader's own horizon. This fusion is realized by putting oneself and one's horizon within the horizon of the text, and not the other way round, which would be to place the text's horizon within one's own horizon. In this way, from within its own horizon, the text can say what it has to say to the reader in his/her own horizon. Only this procedure leaves the text and its meaning intact (Gadamer 1960, 284-90). Again, for students to learn this procedure, some teaching models would have to be arranged, so that they can experience and practice it.

Discovering the meaning of the text in real life is not something that comes after one learns to perform hermeneutics, because applying the meaning of a text, which is what this discovering is all about, is an intrinsic part of the hermeneutical process itself. This is the third criterion. We already have been confronted with Dewey's distinction between the application of a value "to the situation" and its application "in the situation." In the hermeneutical field there is a similar distinction. Insofar as a value is woven into the web of the text—which is always the case to some extent—understanding this value always means applying it in the situation one lives in, or else it does not reveal its true meaning. Truth and application correlate with each other (Gadamer 1960, 290-323). As there is no understanding without application, there is no truth without application (cf. Ricoeur 1973). If students are to learn this application, the clarification mode needs to deliver the tools for reflecting on what they have gone through in concrete life situations in which they tried "to live their texts and values."

The fourth and last criterion refers to what I might call the "hermeneutics of the good" or what Van Tongeren has described as the "hermeneutics of moral experience." The text that addresses me must intrinsically appeal to me or oblige me to perform an action in such a way that I understand this action as taking part in the good life (cf. Van Tongeren 1991, 12; Zwart 1993, 151-57).

Hermeneutics of the Good

This "taking part in the good life" is a crucial aspect. In all moral or at least morally relevant texts, an indication can be found that the concrete good they refer to implicitly or explicitly points to a good, or the good, that is broader, deeper, or more comprehensive, in other words, to the good life in all its dimensions and aspects, which may be seen as the limit of all concrete goods. Let me call it the transcendent good. This transcendent good is ultimately shrouded in mystery. Nobody knows exactly what it is, and yet it appeals, summons, and evokes. It is anticipated by the concrete goods at which we aim in ordinary life, and still it escapes. It is present and absent at the same time. It reveals itself by hiding itself, and it must be that way (Fleischacker 1994, 59-70).

But this transcendent good is not only anticipated in a direct way by experiencing the concrete goods we aim at, but also in an indirect way by experiencing the bad things we reject and abhor. The transcendent good can be negatively foreshadowed by the contrast experiences in which we resist the wrong actions, situations, and structures by which we are confronted. In this resistance are active a longing, desire, and hope for the transcendent good (cf. Schillebeeckx 1972; 1974; 1977; 1989; van der Ven 1995).

The stories that students pick up from the small and great traditions can be divided into positive and negative. Stories about mothers holding their babies to their breasts and being madly in love with them sow the seed of a dream that all babies will be treated that way, something that is by no means a foregone conclusion, especially in the poor areas of large cities, where drug abuse prevents addicted mothers from behaving this way. And stories about boys killing other boys evoke horror that something like this can happen. The horror is indicative of a belief and hope that something should and will be done to prevent such things from happening again in the future. These stories can be seen as the anticipation of something that is not yet real but will come, or at least is hoped for. In a sense the stories transcend their own limits in the direction of the ultimate, common good, even though that common good is not achieved in tangible form. The transcendent good is only inchoatively present in these stories. Without the perspective of the transcendent good, cultural hope and critique, which characterize these stories from a moral point of view, would be incomprehensible — "A culture cannot maintain its claim to be directed toward the good unless it makes room for this possibility" (Fleischacker 1994, 182). Therefore hermeneutical interpretation of moral texts must take into account this perspective of the transcendent good, and thus satisfy the fourth criterion, that of the hermeneutics of the good.

Moral Authority

Which conditions have to be fulfilled within the clarification mode in order to satisfy this last criterion? At this point it is necessary to introduce a term to which I did not refer in the previous chapters in this study, but which now needs to be brought into the discussion: authority. Following the definition by Max Weber, I distinguish authority from power. Power empirically consists of the ability to make others do what you want them to do, occasionally even against their own will and desire. Authority implies a kind of leadership by which other people wholeheartedly do what you want them to do, because they acknowledge and respect your leadership (Weber 1980, 122-76). Thus power is "naked power," while authority is power acknowledged and respected. Ricoeur would describe authority as the "power-to-do," which has its basis in the "power-in-common," whereas he would equate "naked power" with "power-over" (Ricoeur 1992, 220). Here I use the term *authority* in the Weberian sense, or in the sense of Ricoeur's "power-to-do," based on "power-in-common."

For people who are familiar with value clarification in Raths, Harmin, and Simon, it is not surprising that I introduce the term *authority* at this point, since this approach can readily be interpreted in terms of the relationship or even struggle between freedom and authority. It is not by chance that the very first process and the very first element of this method are indicated by the words *choosing freely*. The value clarification method has its roots in humanistic psychology and education, which are, almost by definition, characterized by freedom, that is, resistance against authority. This resistance grew out of the studies on authoritarianism by representatives of the Institut für Sozialforschung in Frankfurt, including Adorno, Fromm, and Rokeach, all of whom had had to flee Europe for the United States during World War II. These studies indicated that authoritarianism is linked with totalitarian, fascist, racist, ethnocentric, and anti-Semitic styles of thought and action in family, school, church, and other social institutions. These insights greatly influenced the founders of humanistic psychology and education, especially Maslow and Rogers, who argue for what Rogers calls the nondirective personality as opposed to the authoritarian personality. To encourage the development of this nondirective personality, the emphasis in education within family and school is on the experiencing process from within, out of which the human being is able to grow organically. This experiencing process can take place only when three attitudes are developed by the educator: empathy, congruence (realness or genuineness), and acceptance. Empathy means that the parent or teacher accurately senses the feelings and personal meaning that the child or student is experiencing and communicates this understanding to him/her. Congruence, realness, or genuineness means that the educator communicates what he/she experiences himself/herself at certain moments. Acceptance means that he/she unconditionally loves both the child or student and himself/herself (Rogers 1969). All this tends to downplay the specific essence and role of authority in educational processes in family and school. Perhaps authority should be eliminated altogether? This is a pivotal question in humanistic psychology and education (cf. Schotsmans 1982; 1983).

Against this background it is advisable to be as cautious as possible when reintroducing the concept of authority in the context of value clarification, and yet I must do so, because without attributing an appropriate role to authority, the fourth criterion, that of the hermeneutics of the good, cannot be fulfilled. "Authority" here is not used in an institutional sense, because my argument is restricted to moral education as a process, and in particular to the clarification mode. Here I focus only on the hermeneutical dimension of this clarification mode, in order to explicate the dialectical relationship between concrete goods and the transcendent good. I believe that for this explication to be successful, moral-hermeneutical authority must be brought to bear.

This moral-hermeneutical authority can be seen as having three positive and three negative aspects, which I owe to a Jewish philosopher of culture and morality, Fleischacker. The first of the positive aspects is the expression of joy, which is characteristic of real authority. The joy is functional in that it arises from the interpretation of the meaning of the moral text. Second is the expression of commitment, which springs from insight into what the texts means within one's actual day-to-day life situation ("application in the situation"). The third positive aspect is passion for the meaning of the text and for communicating that meaning to people who are confused. The three negative aspects are the obverse of the positive aspects. The opposite of joy, then, is blind dogmatism; commitment stands in contrast with obsession with details; and passion can be seen as the other side of single-minded devotion (Fleischacker 1994, 92-95).

In real life, one occasionally sees the three positive aspects of authority functioning in a pure way, at other times one may be terrified by the three negative aspects, but in most situations the positive and negative aspects occur side by side. To the extent that the positive aspects outweigh the negative, moral-hermeneutical authority may have both therapeutic and prophetic qualities. The authority may act in a "therapeutic" way by helping others existentially to process, reconcile, purify — in a word, clarify — the confusion of values, the conflicting norms, and the aporias they would otherwise be overwhelmed by. Authority can be "prophetic" when it helps to enlighten "my text," my biography, with the light of the hidden but transcendent good that evokes, summons, and appeals to me to continue to pursue the good life for myself and for others in just institutions — the common good life for all past, present, and future generations.

Moral education, especially in its clarification mode, needs this balanced moral-hermeneutical authority. It can fulfill this need by offering models, which may take the forms I noted earlier: the model of texts and the model of the teacher. These models must have definite qualities, which are, first, that they speak the students' language; then, that they knowledgeably and sensitively interpret "great" texts; and, third, that they reflectively judge what must be done in the concreteness of life (Fleischacker 1994, 96). These authoritative — not authoritarian — models (for the difference between "authoritative" and "authoritarian" see Chap. 2) do not replace the students' texts. On the contrary, the students' texts and the authoritative texts need to be clarified by mutual exchange of perspectives, or, as Ricoeur might say, by inscribing the students' texts into the authoritative texts, through which the meaning of both texts is broadened and deepened.

Yet the question remains: Does the appeal to some kind of moral-hermeneutical authority not impose limits and thus damage the students' freedom and free choice? Can authority and freedom coexist? This extremely serious question can be said to be the crux not only of the clarification mode but of moral education in general, and even of education as such. It points to a fundamental paradox of education, which is that education by its nature implies having authority over children, but if it uses this authority to free children from authority, it puts an end to education itself (Snik 1990, 25-33). How do we authoritatively deal with freedom? Or freely deal with authority? In a sense this question is unanswerable. The relationship between authority and freedom can best be viewed as a dialectical process.

In Freudian terms, authority has to do with the relationship with the father as a character in the play of life and with the Oedipal complex, which is part of the child's relationship to both the mother and the father. One of the ways in which this complex can be resolved — if "resolved" is the right term — is by psychologically killing the father character and metaphorically stamping with one's feet on his grave. The father's death is the child's freedom (Freud 1986). As is frequently the case with Freudian thought, three aspects must be distinguished: the diagnoses Freud made of his patients, the therapy he developed for them, and his (sometimes highly speculative) interpretation of the data observed from both the patients and the therapeutic practice. In his clinical work, Freud saw people suffering from many kinds of negative feelings, moods, and attitudes. He diagnosed some of these in terms of individuals wrestling with their father or father figures. He then interpreted this wrestling in terms of the Oedipus complex, which involves not only the relation with the father but also and even more so the intimate relation with the mother, as well as the competition between the two parents. In some cases this might be the right interpretation. But the range of interpretations that can arise from the observed data and the variety of ways these interpretations can be elaborated on in therapeutic treatment become clear when one reads Freud's magisterial analysis of Leonardo da Vinci's Mona Lisa (Freud 1985).

Coming from a Jewish background, Fleischacker posits that wrestling with the father character should not be exhaustively interpreted as metaphorically killing the father in order to liberate oneself from him, which is a process that does not end before one's own death. The father character also embodies a good that is consciously or unconsciously accepted and respected by the individual, but also has to be transcended. Here I speak of "transcended" in the sense of "the" good as a limit, the transcendent good. The good that the father character carries with him may inchoatively and anticipatorily indicate the transcendent good, which is in part incarnated in the father character's good and in part goes beyond it: "You need to go beyond your biological, literary, and ethical fathers not (just) because they are psychological hindrances to your independence, but because their function is to teach you a truth that by its nature goes beyond anything they can embody" (Fleischacker 1994, 108).

This wrestling with the father, or authority, can never be given up but must continue, because otherwise one falls existentially into slavish obedience and culturally abandons the very idea of the transcendent good as inchoatively and anticipatorily incarnated in the concrete goods within our fathers and ancestors, who metaphorically embody our communities and traditions. Wrestling with the father, then, is both the expression of and the process of coming to terms with the tensions between authority and freedom. It is this lifelong wrestling that the students need to learn in moral education, especially in its clarification mode.

6.3 Clarification as a Communicative Process

So far I have not mentioned the distinction between "traditional" and "post-traditional" value clarification that Kirschenbaum makes (1977, 148). Whereas Raths *cum suis* focuses only on the individual students, Kirschenbaum also considers the communication among students. This communication has three aspects: transmitting one's own message as clearly as possible to the others in the group, communicating empathy by taking the others' perspective, and developing the ability to resolve conflicts between competing values. In connection with that, he also stresses the affective dimension of this communication process: he emphasizes not only the students' values but also negative and positive aspects of their feelings. Denying one's feelings can interfere with understanding and acting on one's values, while being aware of and accepting one's feelings can advance one's capacity to realize one's values (Kirschenbaum 1977, 10-11).

The Dutch educationist Van de Plas (1981) elaborated on this affective and communicative dimension by developing a model of educational phases that each value clarification process must undergo: (1) explicitly formulating one's own values and feelings, (2) explicitly formulating others' values and feelings, (3) relating one's own values and feelings to those of others, and (4) validating values and feelings. The affective dimension is present in all phases, because the values are always connected with the feelings and vice versa. The communicative dimension is emphasized in the second and third phases. In the second phase, the student has to take the others' perspective and to develop empathy. In the third phase, the student has to combine his/her own "I" perspective and the others' "you" perspective, and coordinate these two perspectives. The fourth phase consists of putting values and feelings into practice, as in the "traditional method" found in Raths, Harmin, and Simon.

Models of Communication between Multicultural Moral Traditions

The communicative dimension, which essentially consists of understanding the values and feelings of others by taking these others' perspective, carries a fundamental problem with it that has not been mentioned in the literature

266

on value clarification so far. What does it mean to take the others' perspective, when the others come from different cultures and subcultures? Students come from all kinds of families, neighborhoods, and classes, and bring into the classroom all kinds of stories that grow out of all sorts of small and great traditions. How shall they relate the values and feelings that are associated with these various small and great cultural and subcultural traditions? Do they simply leave them as they are, juxtaposing them, as it were, without attempting to relate them to one another? Inasmuch as the processes on the microlevel of the classroom mirror those on the macrolevel of society, seven different models of relationship can be distinguished, which may be relevant to the development of the clarification mode up to this point. I call them the monocultural, multicultural, autocultural, enlightened autocultural, crosscultural, intercultural, and supracultural models.

In the first model, the monocultural, one's own culture is the final criterion for evaluating and judging all other cultural or moral traditions. To the extent that the other culture contains elements or aspects that are similar to those in one's own culture, the assessment will be positive. Those cultures that are not similar are not believed worthy of any serious attention. This model develops from the so-called in-group and out-group idea. The cultural in-group and the tradition it represents are highly respected, while the cultural out-group is met with neutrality, neglect, or even hostility. These attitudes readily lead to cultural prejudices and ethnocentrism, and are more common than one sometimes expects, even among children and young people (cf. Eisinga and Scheepers 1989).

The second model, which I call multicultural, is the opposite of the first one. In this model other traditions are seen merely as other cultural traditions, and no effort is made to interact with them, one way or the other. They are simply put alongside one's own culture, that is, alongside one another. They evoke no feelings and attitudes other than a kind of passive tolerance, neutrality, and curiosity, in some circles perhaps some academic zeal for objective, distant knowledge. In this model, one's own culture and the other cultures form a multicultural mosaic. This model easily leads to a kind of relativism, a recognition that because of the different contexts in which they emerge, develop, and continue to exist, all cultural traditions are so different that a rational debate or choice between them is impossible. This relativism in turn leads to perspectivalism, which holds that no truth claims or moral claims about goodness or justice can be made, because claims always are perspective-bound, because they are tied up with their specific contexts. The result is cultural indifferentism, agnosticism, skepticism, and cynicism (cf. MacIntyre 1988, 352). In his *Closing of the American Mind,* Bloom cynically calls this attitude of relativism and perspectivalism the virtue of openness, which is, in his opinion, essentially closed (Bloom 1988, 26).

In the third model, the autocultural, one's own culture serves as the starting and ending point of the relationship with other cultures. Other cultures are always interpreted in the context of one's own (auto) culture. This means that the other culture is seen from and in a sense incorporated into one's own perspective, perhaps even incorporated into one's own culture. Such an approach is not necessarily negative. Some scholars maintain that this is indeed the only one possible relationship one can have with another culture, and that the other models described here are illusory. This is a strong claim, and one that perhaps sounds excessively conservative in our multicultural society. Nevertheless, the argument is one that merits closer analysis, for it is honest and stringent. MacIntyre, whom I refer to here as representative of this autocultural model, distinguishes three stages in the development of cultural traditions.

In the first stage, the stories that form part of the tradition of a culture, as well as the convictions, values, and norms that they contain, are totally characterized by what is called their plausibility structure (cf. Berger and Luckmann 1967). There are no hesitations, no doubts, no questions, no problems, no conflicts. Although changes may take place in this stage, they are legitimized in practice by their continuing obedience to "the dictates of immemorial custom."

In the second stage some difficulties arise. These have to do with incompatible, conflicting interpretations and incompatible, conflicting courses of action justified by competing interpretations. Members of the culture may come to realize that these problems cannot be solved using the traditional methods and tools that were helpful in the first stage. Some new ideas may creep in and new alternative interpretations may be put forward. However, these do not yet offer an approach that would solve the whole range of problems. The inquiry of interpretation, which is established to bridge the gap between the old tradition and the actual circumstances, ceases to make progress, which leads to what MacIntyre calls an epistemological crisis.

This crisis is dealt with in the third stage, which brings entirely new discoveries and inventions of concepts, from which the old tradition can be retold, reinterpreted, restructured. This stage also brings the capacity to see and understand why the old interpretation was running into problems that it was not able to solve, and why the efforts to solve these problems were not successful. Finally, it bridges the gap between tradition and actuality by reestablishing the continuity of the old tradition in new structures and forms. The classic examples cited by MacIntyre are Aristotle,

Augustine, Thomas Aquinas, and the seventeenth-century Scottish philosophers, all of whom were able to rewrite and renew their traditions in an
insightful, viable way.

They did this by borrowing from the respective rival traditions certain
images, ideas, concepts, and theories that they incorporated into their own
traditions, so that intellectual progress could be made and the seemingly
insoluble problems dealt with creatively. To be capable of this task, they
learned the conceptual language of the rival tradition, which they considered rationally superior. Then they translated the images, ideas, and
concepts of that language into their own. In some cases it took a very long
time before this process of translation made a noticeable contribution to
solving the culture's problems, but over time the impact was significant.

The point of this three-stage theory is that nobody is above or outside
the traditions of his/her culture. Everybody takes part in one tradition or
another, and when true interaction between cultural traditions takes place,
it is by integrating elements from another tradition into one's own in order
to solve one's own problems.

MacIntyre's polemical focus is to make clear that those who take the
modernist point of view that cultural interaction must be guided from a
neutral, third-person, "it" directed perspective that coordinates the "ego"-
based "I" tradition and the "alter"-based "you" tradition do not take into
account that this "third-person" perspective is in fact "ego"-based. The
modernist third-person orientation is in itself an "I" tradition with two
centuries of history behind it with Hume, Smith, Bentham, Mill, Kant, and
the like as its founding fathers. MacIntyre points out that cultural interaction can be undertaken only from the "I" perspective of the tradition one
is part of. In other words, cultural interaction is restricted to processes of
self-understanding or self-clarification, as Habermas (1993, 104) notes in
his interpretation of MacIntyre. MacIntyre stands for an autocultural approach to cultural interaction, which develops naturally from his communitarianism (cf. MacIntyre 1988, 349-69).

A fourth model, next to this strictly autocultural approach, is the
critical, enlightened autocultural model. It arises from an awareness of the
contingent nature of one's own tradition: that this tradition originates in a
certain space and time, in a certain context, that it develops at specific
places at particular times, moving through particular steps, jumps, or loops,
and taking various forms. This contingency can not be stripped away from
the tradition, just as the heart cannot exist without its body, the core without
its margins, the substance without its accidents, *hyle* without its *morphe*.
There is no Archimedean vantage point from which I can look neutrally
at my own tradition and at the same time the other tradition. I am totally

embedded, incorporated, incarnated in my own tradition. What happens when I truly open myself to the stories, values, and norms of another tradition is that I am able to sense this contingency, thus giving me the capacity to see my own egocentricity, sociocentricity, and ethnocentricity, and break through them. By breaking through, my contingent believing and valuing are not eliminated but broadened, and can be further broadened by more moments of cultural interaction. I call this the enlightened auto-cultural model, for although it acknowledges the impossibility of stepping outside one's autocultural "I" perspective, it does allow for the broadening effect of cultural interaction (Rorty 1991a; 1991b).

In the fifth model, which I call crosscultural, a number of different approaches can be distinguished. The first is to look for cultural overlap between the traditions involved, so as to arrive at some cultural consensus. At the request of U.S. President Carter, sociologist Peter Berger came up with a limited set of cross-cultural standards, condemning genocide, torture, enslavement, the forced separation of families, and the desecration of religious and ethnic symbols. He assumed that all cultural traditions, from Hinduism through Islam, could subscribe to these standards. Coming from an entirely different perspective, social scientist Michael Walzer developed a similar idea. He came to the conclusion that a universal and therefore minimal or, as he calls it, "thin" conception of justice could be established: a set of "negative injunctions, most likely, rules against murder, deceit, torture, oppression, and tyranny" (Walzer 1994, 10).

Nevertheless, these efforts are still speculative because all kinds of qualifications may be imposed: "There may yet be room for atrocities if (1) the victims are not considered sentient, human, or the kind of human deserving of or needing compassion, (2) death, torture, expulsion, or slavery is considered to be for the victims' good, a high mode of respect, or a form of compassionate treatment, or (3) death, torture, expulsion, or slavery is considered a regrettable necessity, an unavoidable violation of respect and compassion in the service of some higher or more final good" (Fleischacker 1994, 161-62). The events of the Balkan war in former Yugoslavia in the first half of the nineties provide a dramatic example of these qualifications in action.

A second approach to cross-cultural understanding is based on the claim that the so-called human rights could function as a common ground. These rights can be divided into civic, political, and socioeconomic rights. Civic rights are, for example, the equality of all people independently of sex, race, political conviction, or religion, the right to hold personal property, liberty of conscience, freedom of thought, and freedom of speech and assembly. The political rights concern, for instance, the existence of political parties and the right of citizens and other residents to vote. Socioeconomic rights have to do with, for example, education, employment, just pay, social security, rest and leisure, and collective action (cf. Andrews and Hines 1987).

As influential as these and other rights are, some fundamental problems are associated with them. Let us look at the well-known statement in the U.S. Declaration of Independence (1776), already mentioned, because it is a cornerstone of the value clarification method: "We hold these truths to be self-evident, that all men are created equal, that they are endowed by their Creator with certain unalienable Rights, that among these are Life, Liberty, and the pursuit of Happiness." In this statement human rights are founded in the equality of human beings as creatures of the Creator. Today this foundation is highly disputable, because those who do not believe in God cannot accept it. Thus dissent already exists at the foundational level, which is the very basis of human rights. Moreover, what does the term *right* mean in this statement? This question is relevant because not only the foundation but also the principle from which the human rights derive is anything but clear. Does "right" refer to the principle of human autonomy, from which derives the freedom of will or choice, which has some plausibility within value clarification (as we have seen)? But would this not mean that human beings who are not able to exercise this freedom, like children and the mentally disturbed, do not possess these rights? Or does it refer to another principle, that of human interest? Do human rights mean that material, social, cultural, and spiritual interests have to be protected? Then children and the seriously disturbed would also possess rights, because they also have interests to be protected. The objection that can be raised to this idea is that children and the mentally disturbed then need other people to decide for them what their interests are, something that comes into conflict with the principle of human dignity. Dignity itself rests on self-respect, which could serve as the overall criterion from which all human rights can be justified. But then, one might ask, where are the limits of this human dignity, as in the case of a person in a long-term coma? Lastly, the concrete content itself of human rights is a problem, for these rights emerged in the particular historical context of the rise of Western liberal, capitalistic society in the seventeenth and eighteenth centuries. Historically, the rights referred to by the founding fathers of the United States of America were not universal, nor are they universal today in their actual application in various parts of the world. For example, the right to education and employment in the Western world and the Third World are two entirely different things. Is it possible to find a common ground with regard to human rights? Given the lack of a common foundation, a common principle, and a common content, the answer cannot be an unqualified yes (cf. Veldhuis 1985).

A last approach to cross-cultural understanding is more modest. It

271

consists of conducting empirical case studies in order to determine which convictions, values, and norms occur across all traditions. In other words, one does not start off with some concept of what constitutes common ground, but empirically investigates whether any commonalities actually exist. Let us look at an example. Based on the value of tolerance toward other religious traditions, the Christian tradition created a distinction between universal and nonuniversal law, thereby preventing itself from justifying the coercive imposition of its own laws on Jews, pagan Slavs, Saracens, or Amerindians. For instance, Vitoria argued specifically against coercing the Amerindians because of practices that then were believed to be against human nature, like pederasty, bestiality, or lesbianism. Other traditions, like the Buddhist, Jewish, and Muslim traditions, contain the idea of double standards, meaning that distinctions must be made between laws applying to their own members and those applying to nonmembers. Here the Christian distinction between universal and nonuniversal law and the Buddhist, Jewish, and Muslim conception of double standards overlap and provide evidence of common principles (Fleischacker 1994, 162-70, 237-38).

The sixth model, which I call the intercultural model, is probably the one that Van der Plas has in mind when speaking of coordinating the student's own values and feelings with those of the other. This coordination is based on mutually taking the other's perspective — something that is less simple than this seemingly simple statement suggests. It presupposes six (3 × 2) processes, as I will explain by using the example of two groups of students, A and B, who try to take each other's perspective. First, group A interprets its own values and feelings from its own frame of reference, which is the auto-interpretation of A by A (1). Group B does the same for its own values and feelings, which is the auto-interpretation of B by B (2). Then group A interprets the values and feelings of group B from group A's perspective, which is the auto-interpretation of B by A (3), and group B interprets the values and feelings of group A from group B's perspective, which is the auto-interpretation of A by B (4). Lastly, group A interprets the values and feelings of group B from group B's perspective, which is the hetero-interpretation of B by A (5), and group B interprets the values and feelings of group A from A's perspective, which is the hetero-interpretation of A by B (6). One might object that only the last two processes are, strictly speaking, taking the other's perspective, but in order to fully understand the last two processes, one needs to compare them with the first four processes.

One important question is at what stage of development students have the ability to thus exchange perspectives, and on what anthropological basis this ability is founded. With regard to the first question, the distinction between play and game, which children already make at an early age, may be mentioned (see Chap. 3 above). On the one hand, in play the child develops dialogues with himself/herself, in which he/she takes on various characters, such as a parent, brother, doctor, or himself/herself. The child is by turns the policeman addressing the child and the child responding to the policeman. In other words, the child takes the perspective of the other and also responds to the other from the child's own perspective. From his/her own perspective the child understands himself/herself as "I," and from the perspective of the other, he/she sees his/her "me." In the game, on the other hand, the child does not take the perspective of only one "significant other" but of a number of them, and perhaps even all of them. The child looks at the players in the game from the point of view of the rules of the game and includes himself/herself in that framework. In Mead's words, the child looks at "me," while taking the perspective of the "generalized other." Thus he/she looks at his/her "me" in an objective way, corresponding to the rules of the game. The question is, What rules of which game? There are the rules of the interaction games in the family, the neighborhood, the peer group, the school, and the local community. There are also the rules of the game of the wider community, of the town, county, or state. As the child grows older, he/she is able to take increasingly wider perspectives. The "generalized other" becomes increasingly wider and more abstract, as do the rules of the game.

The question of the anthropological basis of this ability to take the other's perspective is not easy to answer. Most authors would claim that an individual can understand another person or group because that person or group would experience similar feelings or sensations when in a similar situation. The assumption is that there is some likeness or family resemblance, or at least some translatability or commensurability of the other's tradition in the other's local community, as Davidson says (cf. Fleischacker 1994, 15; MacIntyre 1988, 370-71; Habermas 1993, 104). But whether this assumption corresponds to reality is still a matter of debate, thus making the intercultural model a matter of debate as well.[8]

---

8. To my mind, Gadamer also leaves this question open. He rejects the possibility of direct knowledge of the other, which is presented by authors who argue for "empathy" or "sympathy" as the very source of this knowledge. He also rejects the idea of indirect knowledge of the other, which is based on the concept of inferential analogy, which means that I understand the other's feelings from his/her behavior, because I reason from the relation between my own behavior and feelings to the meaning of the other's feelings. Gadamer argues for what he calls the fusion of horizons between myself and the other (text). But it is not clear at all how this is possible and on what it rests (Gadamer 1960, 284-90; Spiegelberg 1960, 259-61; Rosenthal 1991; van der Ven 1993, 130-33).

The seventh and last model I wish to present is the supracultural model. This model holds that some moral rules may be found and formulated that apply universally to all people in all places in all cultures at all times. Therefore these rules are called universal. For any rule to imply a moral obligation, it must be universalizable. This universalizability is based on the conception of justice, as we have seen in the previous chapters. Justice refers traditionally to the part to be given to the other (*justitia est ad alterum*). This conception forms the basis for two different theories: a contract theory and a discourse theory. Although both are procedural, the former is based on the universal principle of distributive justice as fairness and the latter on the universal principle of justice by discourse. Here I take Rawls as a representative of the former and Habermas of the latter.

In Rawls's theory, people first find themselves as individuals in the so-called initial position, from which they will make a contract that is to contain principles and rules that apply to all individuals without exception, in order to initiate and develop social cooperation among them. This contract is based on the principles of liberty and justice, as we have seen in the previous chapters. The first principle is: "Each person is to have an equal right to the most extensive total system of all equal basic liberties compatible with a similar system of liberty of all." The second principle is: "Social and economic inequalities are to be arranged so that they are both (a) to the greatest benefit of the least advantaged, consistent with the joint savings principle,[9] and (b) attached to offices and positions open to all under conditions of fair equality of opportunity" (Rawls 1971, 302). The first principle overrules the second; liberty should be restricted only for the sake of liberty, not for justice. Justice in turn overrules efficiency and welfare, that is, justice is prior to utility and maximizes the sum of advantages. Rawls's general conception is: "All social primary goods — liberty and opportunity, income and wealth, and the bases of self-respect — are to be distributed equally unless an unequal distribution of any or all of these goods is to the advantage of the least favored" (Rawls 1971, 303).

Are these contract rules universalizable? This is an important consideration for determining whether the supracultural model is a valid one for finding common ground between different cultural traditions. According to MacIntyre, these rules are not universal at all, because they mirror and reproduce a specific type of human being and of society: the individual who aims at optimally satisfying his/her interests within the modern Western society of liberalism, and whose principal question is: What kind of

9. The joint savings principle provides for fair investment in the interests of future generations.

social contract with others is reasonable for me to enter into? In response to such criticism, Rawls later admits that his contract theory of justice is not meant to be applicable to any society in any place at any time, but only to the modern constitutional, democratic society, which is the product of historical developments in the Western world that arose out of the religious wars following the Reformation. The contract theory originates in this specific political tradition, which is characterized by religious, moral, and political tolerance. Within this political tradition Rawls develops his political conception of the human person who possesses two moral capacities: a sense of justice and of the good (Rawls 1994).[10] As a result, Rawls shifted from a procedural to a substantive approach (Habermas 1993, 25-29). Once this substantive approach has been established and recognized as such, it may be critically compared with and evaluated from the viewpoint of other substantive approaches. Taylor has commented that Rawls's distributive conception of justice as fairness is not able to take into account the contributive conception of justice by desert in relation to advancing the common good. It contrasts with Aristotle's conception of justice, according to which all must share in the good, but that more is owed to those who make a more signal contribution (Taylor 1994a, 37-42). In other words, considering the distributive conception of justice as fairness, using the supracultural model as a basis for interaction between different cultural traditions would mean making those traditions adapt to the substantive standards of Western constitutional liberalism.

Does discourse theory provide universalizable rules of justice? This theory develops universal claims or even presupposes them, according to Habermas's communicative action theory. The distinction between communication and discourse proper is that the former has a consensual basis of accepted facts, shared values, and agreed-on norms, whereas discourse occurs when disagreement and dissent arise. Then claims as to the truth of fact-oriented assertions, the rightness of moral rules, and the authenticity of subjective and intersubjective expressions are a matter of debate. For discourse to happen, some universal principles apply. These are rules such as: (1) everybody is allowed to take part in the discourse; (2) everyone is allowed to question any claim, to introduce any claim whatsoever, to express one's attitudes, desires, and needs; and (3) nobody may be prevented by coercion inside or outside the discourse from realizing his/her rights pre-

---

10. Sandel (1992) remarks that Rawls's conception of justice, which, from its utilitarian perspective, reduces justice to justice by preference, prevents him from developing a convincing conception of the good, because it reduces the good to individual preferences as well, and so eliminates the good as good.

viously mentioned (Habermas 1983, 99). The underlying principles are principles such as freedom of access, equal rights to participate, truthfulness on the part of the participants, and absence of coercion in adopting positions (Habermas 1993, 31). Reasoning from these principles, Habermas arrives at his universal rule of argumentation (U), mentioned previously: "Every valid norm must satisfy the condition that the consequences and side effects its general observance can be anticipated to have for the satisfaction of the interests of each could be freely accepted by all affected (and be preferred to those of known alternative possibilities for regulation" (Habermas 1993, 32). The objection made to this rule is that unqualified terms such as "general," "anticipated," "each," and "all" make the discourse participants carry the burden of taking into account the unforeseeable multitude of concrete situations. Consequently, Habermas agrees with Günther's re-formulation of U: "A norm is valid if the consequences and side effects of its general observance for the interests of each individual *under unaltered circumstances* can be accepted by all" (Habermas 1993, 37). This means that the question of whether the norms concerned also apply to future situations is left unanswered.

Do these principles and rules actually have a universal quality? Are they able to contribute to building a solid base for the supracultural model, by which the interaction between different cultural and moral traditions can be guided? In a sense, the answer is yes, because in the procedural concern for "each individual" they dismantle the presumptuous claims of universalism made by representatives of the ruling class in Western culture. This dismantling process advances the emancipation of underprivileged groups in the Western world, such as domesticated women and marginal-ized minorities. It also breaks through the habit of justifying the imposition of Western rules on non-Western cultures. It sets the conditions for de-Westernizing rules to be validated by the global community. In this sense, Habermas's U rule contributes to a twofold process of emancipation and solidarity in both the Western and the non-Western world (Habermas 1993, 15).

There is a problem, however. To what extent do underprivileged groups and underdeveloped countries actually take advantage of this rule? Are they able to benefit from it in practice? Do they possess the personal, social, and cultural qualities to speak, argue, and fight for themselves? Do they have at their disposal the national and international institutions that establish the structural conditions that are necessary for advancing these qualities in fact? To the extent that the answer is no, then the reaction should be that (groups in) the Western world must take up the role of advocate to the non-Western world. The U rule, then, becomes a universalism-directed advocacy rule. Here the universalism perspective that characterizes the supracultural model is not a neutral, impartial, observer-bound, "third-person" perspective, an Archimedean point from which one looks at the world below. It is an engaged, committed, participatory, "first-person" perspective, from which one strives for the common good of all people, especially those people in Western and non-Western societies who suffer from claims of bourgeois superiority and universalism (Habermas 1993, 48).[11]

Still further, we must ask whether this advocacy orientation fits in with the interests of those who suffer, in the West, from bourgeois standards of discourse and, in the south, from Western discourse practice. Is this discourse procedure anything other than the product of contemporary Western democratic culture? Is it not too class-bound and too Western-parochial in order to be able to serve as the basis for a universal moral theory? (cf. Walzer 1994, 1-21).

What does the preceding discussion of the models for cultural relations mean for value clarification? One thing that should be clear is that the clarification mode should not overlook the fundamental problems created by students from different cultures and subcultures seeking to clarify their own convictions, values, and norms, while communicating them to one another. Considering the seven models dealt with above, we need to ask which models should be rejected and which merit further development. I consciously speak of further development, because we still have a long way to go in this area.

The first and the second models, which I called monocultural and multicultural, do not fit with the general aim of moral education. As I said in Chapter 1, the common denominator of all moral education, including

---

11. Here Habermas distances himself, as I have already said, from the Piagetian psychologist Selman (1980), on whom Habermas relied heavily in both his *Theorie des kommunikativen Handelns* (1982, 2:53-65) and his *Moralbewusstsein* (1983, 127-206). At the time, Habermas saw the "third-person" perspective as the basis for the coordination between the "first-person" and the "second-person" perspectives. His endeavor in his *Moralbewusstsein* to integrate his moral theory and communicative theory with both Selman's theory of social perception and Kohlberg's theory of moral development is far from clear, if not confusing and highly speculative. Moreover, a fundamental distinction has to be made. Selman refers to developmental stages of social perception by babies and children at the microlevel, whereas Habermas is speaking here of cultural interactions at the macrolevel of society, or even societies. One should be very cautious in drawing inferences from the individual developmental microlevel to the collective structural macrolevel of culture/cultures in society/societies and vice versa, as it can easily reduce individual facts to a mirror of social facts and social facts to nothing more than a collection of individual facts (cf. Durkheim 1982, 50-59).

value clarification, is moral communication, which implies not only intrapersonal and interpersonal but also intracommunal and intercommunal moral communication. This moral communication is the infrastructure of moral education, which means that all seven modes have to be built on it. The monocultural and multicultural models do not satisfy this condition.

In the day-to-day practice of moral education, however, many students are consciously or unconsciously committed to either the monocultural model with its ethnocentrism, patriotism, and nationalism, or to the multicultural model with its relativism, perspectivalism, indifference, and even cynicism. The stories and jokes about people from other cultures, which children hear in the family, on the street, from their peers, in school, and which they tell, retell, and laugh about, tell us more about the viability and feasibility of value clarification than any scholarly book ever could. At the same time, they also tell us that there is a real need for value clarification, at least if conducted in a proper way.

What then is the proper way? Although I do not wish to dismiss out of hand the third and fourth models (the autocultural and enlightened autocultural models), I do not like them to be used exclusively. The reason for including them is that real dialogue between people from different cultures always has some repercussions on one's relationship with one's own cultural and moral tradition, and even on this tradition itself. These repercussions may be broadening, widening, complementing, enriching, and purifying, and may serve to correct one's own tradition. In a real dialogue one goes beyond one's own boundaries and plunges into the other cultural and moral traditions for their own sake, for their intrinsic worth, but one always brings something back into one's own tradition.

The last three models — the crosscultural, intercultural, and supracultural — contain a real challenge for the clarification mode in that they are not yet very well developed. Much in them is still vague and confusing, but at the same time they provide some future perspectives that deserve to be seriously studied and reflected on. They provide many more questions than answers, and each possible answer again leads to another set of questions, as we have seen.

Clarification in a Multicultural Context

Nevertheless, we cannot and need not wait for answers to all these questions before we start applying the clarification mode in a multicultural context, because some educational ideas already are developing in the literature. For the sake of discussion, we can divide these ideas into four groups: ideas

278

regarding the aim, content, methods, and moral meaning of the clarification mode in a multicultural context.

The first group of ideas, having to do with the aim of value clarification in a multicultural context, emphasizes the communicative infrastructure of the dialogue between students from different cultures, which I dealt with in Chapter 1. Moral communication, I said, is the ongoing process of moral exchange and understanding in the search of truth. Exchanging means that students clarify and explain their moral convictions and values, relate them to their feelings, and refer them to their strivings and actings. It also means that they have the opportunity to express any doubts, objections, and protests they may experience regarding the beliefs and norms to which they are socialized. Not only are they free to voice their doubts and objections — they are asked to do so. Understanding means that they mutually take the other's perspective, that they look at the other's statements, explanations, and justifications from the vantage point of the other's premises. This understanding is a necessary condition for any dialogue between people from different cultures. But it is not an end in itself, because it is oriented to the search for truth. I emphasize the word *search*, being aware that truth is a limit concept. Truth is the truth of life and of morality, in all its active and passive aspects, its doing and suffering, its contingency and fragility. Truth may be approached by seeking, while anticipatively and inchoatively revealing itself precisely in this search. Value clarification in a multicultural context essentially means learning to ask the right questions about the moral meaning of life: Who am I? What do I live for? What am I committed to? What is the good life? What is the common good? What is good and bad? What is just and wrong? Lastly, what is wise? Learning to ask these kinds of questions presupposes plunging into one's own culture and the other's as well in order to see what answers to what questions they contain, because learning to ask questions comes from learning answers.

This leads me to the second group of ideas, which refer to the content of value clarification in a multicultural context. As we saw, the seven models with which I dealt, from the monocultural through the supracultural model, still entail too many problems to be considered as a sufficiently robust basis for dialogue between people from different cultures. Perhaps it is preferable, at least for now, to leave the study of these models to the universities and replace the search for common beliefs, norms, or standards with a concern for common questions. Perhaps in the end we will have to admit that different cultures do have different values and value systems, but nevertheless wrestle with the same questions. Perhaps the answers will always be different, while the questions the different cultures struggle with will exhibit common structures and denominators.

The literature offers several approaches to the questions that cultures ask. Two examples will give a sense of how the content of value clarification can be dealt with in moral education. The anthropologist Kluckhohn argues for a kind of biological approach by saying that all cultures are concerned with solving questions regarding the existence of the two sexes, the help-lessness of infants, the need for satisfaction of elementary requirements such as food, warmth, and sex, the presence of individuals of different ages and differing physical and other capacities (Kluckhohn 1962, 317-18). A more societal approach is used by a Dutch philosopher of culture, Hofstede, who did research among employees of IBM in fifty countries and three groups of countries, for example, the Arab countries, in 1968 and 1972, resulting in a data bank with more than 116,000 questionnaires. From these data, he discerned four sets of questions that people confront: questions having to do with social inequality, the relation between society and the individual, the social roles of men and women, and lastly coping with uncertainty, including aggression and other emotions. Hofstede investigated the similarities and differences that existed between the countries with respect to these questions as well as the consequences for family, school, employment, state, cultural development, and so on (Hofstede 1991). Thus in these particular examples biological and societal themes were used as a kind of template to identify common patterns of questions, which lead to different answers in different cultures.

The third group of ideas refers to the methods that can help stimulate the dialogue between students from different cultures. These methods aim at developing awareness, knowledge, and skills regarding other cultural and moral traditions. To develop awareness, for example, is to be alert to one's own assumptions and barriers to changing these assumptions, which may be present in stereotypical thought patterns, language structures, and non-behavioral communication reactions. To develop knowledge is to make first contacts, experience dissonance, deal with resistances and rejections in oneself, perform critical introspections, and develop provisional, fragile, and fragmented integrations. To develop skills is, for example, to raise and articulate problems, learn communication styles and methods for recogniz-ing resistance and lessening defense mechanisms, and to cultivate attitudes like empathy, acceptance, and genuineness. The skill of simply interpreting nonverbal communications is a very important one here (cf. Pedersen 1988). From curriculum evaluation research we know that such methods do break down prejudices, which are an important source of ethnocentrism and racism (Van der Lans 1996).

An important method in this context is learning divergent thinking. Divergent thinking contrasts with convergent thinking, in which specific knowledge like theories, concepts, principles, and rules are applied to situations that are relatively familiar to the student.[12] Divergent thinking starts from the insight into the fundamental contingency of cultural and moral traditions, especially one's own. In its Aristotelian sense, contingency deals with the facts, insofar as they are facts — they are neither necessary nor impossible (Brugger and Hoering 1976; Striker 1985). Contingency means that my own tradition is in fact what it is, but without necessarily being what it is, because it could have been otherwise. It has to do with the actual world, with empirical reality, but tells us that this world is only one of all possible worlds, this reality only one of all virtual realities. In other words, contingency means *endechomenon,* which equals "chance" (van der Ven 1994a). By implication, it means that one is prepared to reconstruct totally what one has learned, turn it upside down, replace it in entirely different places and times in order to see how it would "behave," what it might mean, what presuppositions it would need to operate in this new context, and what consequences might derive from it. It implies decontextualizing one's principles, convictions, values, and norms, and recontextualizing them (Joubert 1992). Educationally, developing divergent thinking means developing "as if" strategies with the students, thinking in terms of simulations, in both deconstructions and reconstructions, in both dystheses and syntheses. Divergent thinking is imaginative thinking (cf. Rang 1993). It can be an important way for students to relativize their own cultural tradition and learn to imagine how other cultures would look, how their members would think and act, and how people can be happy in them.

Lastly, I must say something about the moral meaning of value clarification in a multicultural context. Here I refer to a text by Ricoeur (1995a), in which he reflects on the new ethos, based on the relationship between identity and alterity, that is needed in Europe after the fall of the Berlin Wall in 1989, an event that resulted in the nations of Europe, with all their many, diverse cultural aspects, directly confronting one another. In a way, Europe can be said to be an experiment in intercultural dialogue. Ricoeur argues for a change of mentality, which he concretizes in the terms *translating, exchanging,* and *forgiving.*

First, *translating* refers to the process of mutual transposition of the other's stories and experiences into one's own language. This linguistic translation is one element of the deeper ability to translate from one culture to the other, which is done by cultural bilingualists who have the skill to express their thoughts, feelings, and strivings in the terms of another culture,

---

12. For the difference between convergent and divergent thinking see De Corte (1973).

a language that differs from the native language of their own culture. Moral education has to contribute to developing this kind of second language capacity, through which it advances linguistic and cultural hospitality.

Second, if one dives deep enough into the other's language and culture, the point of *exchange* will be reached, especially exchange of memories, meaning the narratives people tell about themselves and their relationships. When people tell stories from their memories, they directly address the other, because their stories are a segment of the other's stories and vice versa; they are "entangled in stories" *(in Geschichten verstrickt)*. In this narrative activity, a plural reading of history can happen, a recounting differently of the main episodes in common history. This crossed reading may lead from linguistic and cultural hospitality to narrative and commemorative hospitality, at the level of which not only sympathy for the other arises but also recognition *(Anerkennung)*.

Finally, translating and exchanging may establish the conditions for *forgiving*, not to be confused with forgetting. Forgiving is not possible without forgetting, because forgiving is grafted onto the work of memory. It realizes the suffering of the others as victims in the past and in the present, and does not abolish the debt but "shatters the debt," does not ignore the guilt but lifts the burden of guilt. Here the logic of the gift transcends — but does not replace — the logic of reciprocity; the economy of abundance complements the economy of exchange. Forgiveness exceeds justice but without substituting for justice. This gift, being a surplus, cannot be required or commanded; it has to be awaited, for there is a time for the unforgivable and a time for forgiveness (Ricoeur 1995a).

It is from this moral perspective, based on the aspects of translation, exchange, and forgiveness, that value clarification in a multicultural context must be developed. It provides a morally appropriate framework for the aim, content, and methods to be used within the clarification mode in moral education.

7

Emotional Formation

E motions frequently play a confusing role within education in general and within moral education in particular. Sometimes they are understood as disturbances of mind or instinctive feelings as opposed to reason, as the seventh edition of the *Concise Oxford Dictionary* tells us. Other times they are viewed as precious vehicles for a healthy and mature development. Let me give a few examples, which refer to various periods of life.

The first example has to do with the importance of basic trust. For a baby to grow up in a healthy way, it is essential that he/she has at least one person who loves him/her unconditionally. A youngster who lacks a strong, nurturing bond with another person can grow up with little sense of what the good life is all about. Most of the time, the importance of such an attachment is interpreted in psychoanalytic or psychodynamic terms, but rather recently it has also come to be understood in terms of neural functioning. The gazing into mother's eyes, the touching and holding, all take place in a period of time in which specific parts of the brain, which govern attachment, are developing. If a baby undergoes an abnormality in attachment experience in the first year, he/she will forever have abnormalities in the way these parts of the brain function, and suffer accordingly. Emotional neglect during the first years of life is almost impossible to erase, says Dr. Perry, a former University of Chicago professor, who has studied children in the city's poorest neighborhoods. He asks: "How can an 11-year-old child kill? When you have that kind of early-life experience, the value another human being has for you is the same value that a chair has for most people. If you were never valued or loved and touched, how on earth can

283

those feelings be expected to come out? It's like expecting me, who has never spent a minute in the Soviet Union, to speak Russian. It's not there; it's not in my head. This is literally the same neurobiological thing. In the same way you learn a language, you learn the language of affection and attachment."[1] In other words, if the baby feels the emotions of attachment and trust, the conditions are set for growing up in the direction of the good life.

Emotions are not only supposed to be vehicles for experiencing the good, that is, living well for and with others, but also for feeling what is just — doing the right and refraining from the wrong, as illustrated in the following example. Emotions inform the child's conscience, says psychologist Kochanska, who in 1992 began to study 103 mothers and their children from the ages of 26 months to 40 months to see how they developed a sense of right and wrong. She looked at the relationship between the development of conscience and aspects such as how easily a child would become distressed when he/she thought he/she had done wrong.

> In a recent session in this long-running study, a research assistant showed 3½-year-old Madeleine a basket full of toys. "When I was just your age, when I was 3½, I used to play with these guys," the researcher said as she removed a stuffed owl, duck, and finally, a kitten. "This," the researcher said, "is my favorite stuffed animal in the whole world. I took him everywhere. He's very special to me. Be really, really careful. He's very special." When the child touched the toy, its head rolled off. Alarmed, Madeleine looked at the researcher, who pretended not to have noticed. Madeleine surreptitiously tried to reattach the head, but it fell off again. The researcher looked up. "What happened to the kitty?" "I don't know," Madeleine said very softly. "You don't know. Well, who did it? Do you know who did it?" "No." "How are you feeling?" "Fine." "How come? Do you know how come?" The child seemed uncomfortable and looked away without answering. In the other side of the one-way mirror, Kochanska grimaced, feeling the stew of emotions cooking within the little girl. "She feels bad," the scientist said. A moment later, the assistant assures Madeleine that the stitching had come loose on the kitten because it was a very old toy, that it could be fixed and it was no one's fault. The major mechanism of socialization is to instill inside a person feelings of right and wrong, even if nobody catches you and nobody sees you, Kochanska said. This is the emergence of conscience. Such internalization is evident in children from 18 months to 36 months old.[2]

1. *Chicago Tribune,* Oct. 30, 1994.
2. *Chicago Tribune,* Oct. 30, 1994.

One might feel at least morally ambivalent about what the research assistant did with Madeleine. Is it morally justifiable to deceive her, even for the sake of research? But in addition to this question, another one may arise: In what sense can conscience be called a mechanism for instilling in a person feelings of right and wrong? Does this emphasis on right and wrong exhaust the concept of conscience and does it not prevent a child from growing up as a free human being, a concept that lies at the very core of morality?

Although these examples of basic trust and conscience raise many difficult questions, the third one, concerning sexual emotions connected with masturbation, exceeds them in this respect. It is interesting that neither the New Testament nor the church fathers in the first centuries, nor even Augustine, refers to masturbation. Thomas Aquinas, however, calls it one of the vices against nature *(vitia contra naturam)* and a sin of impurity, which causes weakness (*STh* II-II, 154.11). Traditional theology condemns it as an intrinsically perverse action, as did Pope Pius XII (cf. Häring 1960, 2:566-68). But this rigid kind of evaluation overlooks that (almost) all young people, at least, frequently practice masturbation. Why do they do so and why is it bad to do so? What should be the aim of sexual education, especially regarding masturbation? In trying to answer these sorts of questions, moral and pastoral theologians began to develop a less restricted evaluation. Because masturbation has to be seen, they said, as being an expression of affective immaturity, anxiety, frustration, or a lack of psychic and spiritual balance, it should not be separately evaluated. It might be seen as a more or less morally indifferent act in itself, which has to be placed in the context of the person's whole character and lifestyle, from which it receives its moral meaning. In other words, as far as psychic and social factors contribute to or even cause masturbation, they decrease moral guilt or even practically neutralize it, as the Catechism of the Catholic Church (no. 2352) says. An entirely different question arises when masturbation is required by medical technology for fertility research and (homologous) artificial insemination. The moral doctrine of the Catholic Church always, after all, emphasized the procreative character of any sexual action, and precisely this kind of masturbation can be said to be "in direct service of the achievement of procreation" (Janssens 1994, 113). Masturbation need not be for such medical purposes in order to be positively evaluated, at least in the view of a task force established by the American Lutherans. This task force concluded that "masturbation as a means of self-pleasuring, is generally appropriate and healthy." Since it was delivered in October 1993, however, this statement has provoked a firestorm of protest and negative publicity. While emotions in general raise ambivalent reactions in the domain of morality and moral education, this applies a fortiori to the area of sexual emotions and sexual education. Should sexual feelings be suppressed, controlled, neutralized, ordered, or intentionally processed?

The fourth and last example is a statement made by Archbishop Desmond Tutu just before the first democratic elections in South Africa in 1994: "If people don't want to forgive, there is no way that we are going to have a new beginning. . . . Had Nelson Mandela and all these others not been willing to forgive, we would not have even reached first base."[3] Tutu contributed greatly to the atmosphere of reconciliation that now makes South Africa so different from its past of apartheid. He did not do so by suppressing emotions of anger, frustration, and disappointment that the white Boers evoked in him: he expressed these emotions and, at times, even cried them out. He allowed these negative emotions to fight with his other, positively oriented emotions, like his longing for freedom and justice and his yearning for peace, and by means of this struggle he worked through and processed them (Pieterse 1995; van der Ven 1995). Tutu's example shows that moral emotions not only emerge spontaneously from the inside, but they are also to be strived, worked, and even fought for. Forgiveness, which equals ceasing to be resentful and pardoning a person by whom one has been offended, is such an emotion, which comes into being only when the negative emotions have been fully worked through. Emotional work is hard work.

What do these examples tell us? First, from a psychological point of view, emotions can be divided into positive ones, like gladness, happiness, gratitude, joy, and forgiveness, and negative ones, like anger, sadness, frustration, and anxiety. They may seem to arise spontaneously, but they also may be seen as the result of hard processing work, which demands a large investment of energy and a specific goal or aim. Second, from a moral perspective, emotions can be seen as good or bad, or at least oriented toward somebody or something that is interpreted as good or bad. They also can be understood as related to something right or wrong. This is not to say that emotions have a stable or even fixed moral meaning over time. Their moral value may vary with both phylogenetic and ontogenetic development, as in the case of the sexual emotions related to masturbation. A more fundamental question is whether or at least to what extent emotions touch, influence, or even limit or remove freedom, which constitutes the very core of morality. In which sense are emotions disturbances of mind, as the *Concise Oxford Dictionary* says, and so disturbances of morality altogether? Does this mean that emotions should be suppressed, controlled, neutralized, ordered,

3. *Chicago Tribune*, Nov. 4, 1994.

or intentionally processed? Third, what does all this mean for emotional formation within the area of moral education? What is the relevance of this emotional formation and how is it to be dealt with?

In formulating these questions, I indicate the structure of the following text. First, I deal with the problem of what emotions are, how they can be understood (section 7.1). Then I look at the morally relevant ways in which emotions are dealt with. I approach this question in a general and a more particular way; I refer to ways of dealing with emotions as well as to specific emotions and their development. The difference between the previous section and this one — to put it succinctly — is that the previous section deals in a psychological sense with the emotions we have and develop, whereas this section looks at the moral question of which emotions we should have and should develop (section 7.2). Lastly, I consider how emotions can be learned in a morally relevant way, so as to advance emotional formation as a mode of moral education (section 7.3).

7.1 Emotions

In order to answer the question of what emotions are and which emotions we have, a theory of emotion is required. Without such a theory, we would not know where to start when speaking of emotions, what to look at, or even what to feel. Is this not an odd statement, to suggest that we need a theory of emotion to feel emotions? But, insofar as feeling emotions always implies an understanding of what emotions are and what specific emotions we are feeling, it is not so odd. There is no feeling of emotions without a cognitive frame of reference from which they receive their meaning. This is not to say that this cognitive framework has to be consciously present. It can be, but it need not be. Whether consciously present or not, this cognitive frame of reference, or web of meanings, channels, mediates, and directs the emotions that are felt, and it does so by, for example, identifying the cause of these emotions (oneself, another person, a situation), and by interpreting, assessing, and evaluating them. A theory of emotion is nothing other than making explicit, elaborating on, and explaining this cognitive embeddedness of emotions.

With this statement I have already opted for a particular kind of emotion theory, one known as the cognitive interaction emotion theory. The term *cognitive* refers to human goals and beliefs, with which emotions are connected and from which they receive their intentionality. The term *interactive* concerns the way in which the person interprets the context he/she is in, appraises the events that take place in this context and change it, copes with these changes, acts from this coping, feels emotions, and expects future outcomes of both the changing context and his/her actions in that context. By combining the terms *cognitive* and *interactive* to understand "emotions," I exclude the idea that the emotions would be considered as separate entities, as if they would live a life of their own, so to speak. Emotions are emotional processes, which are embedded within the inter-action processes of a person with and within his/her contexts and conditioned by his/her goals and beliefs. This description needs further elaboration in order to be fully understood.

Before doing that, however, I need to emphasize the differences between this cognitive interaction theory and other approaches, such as Thomas Aquinas's theory of passions, phenomenology, classical behaviorism, and neobehaviorism, in order to legitimate the choice of this cognitive interaction emotion theory.[4]

Traditional Emotion Theories

First I turn to Thomas Aquinas's classic theory of passions, which we here call emotions. Because this theory has a powerful reputation in the tradition of Catholic theology, we may not and cannot overlook it. Within the passions, Thomas distinguishes three phases: inclination *(inclinatio)* in the beginning phase, movement (moving and being moved) in the middle phase *(motus)*, and quiet rest in the end phase *(quietatio)*. Inclination is characterized by "moving toward" or "moving away from." It culminates in love *(amor)* or hate *(odium)*. Movement, which is characterized by the fact that the object of love is not attained or that of hate not yet removed, can be the movement of desire *(desiderium)* or that of flight *(fuga)*. If the object of desire is difficult to achieve, hope *(spes)* or despair *(desperatio)* comes up. If the object of flight

---

4. Here I do not claim to present a complete overview of all relevant emotion theories. For example, I leave aside psychoanalytic instinct, drive, ethological, and social learning theories; Bandura (1973) has shown how these differ in describing and interpreting an important emotion like aggression. In instinct theories, aggression comes first, because it is understood as an instinct that originates aggressive behavior. In drive theories, it is frustration that comes first, which leads to aggression, which, in turn, results in aggressive behavior. In social learning theories, what comes first is a few aversive experiences, including anticipated consequences, which lead to emotional arousal, which, in turn, results in various forms of behavior like dependency, withdrawal, alcohol and drug abuse, and, occasionally, aggression. In short, in instinct theories aggression occupies first place in the causal model, in drive theories second place, and in social learning theories third place.

is difficult to avoid and conquer, fear *(timor)* or audacity *(audacia)* comes into play. The quiet rest can take three emotional forms: satisfaction *(delectatio)* if the desired object has been achieved, dissatisfaction *(tristitia)* if the object of flight has not been removed or conquered and is tolerated, and anger *(ira)* if it is not tolerated but protested and resisted. In sum, this scheme contains eleven emotions, put together in a logical way, so that each emotion receives its own relevance and meaning (*STh* I-II, 22-48; Peters 1957, 298ff.; Strasser 1956, 152).

Now I present some phenomenological approaches to emotions. These differ from theories like that of Thomas Aquinas insofar as they aim to describe the function that emotions play in daily life and how people experience, feel, and process them. The difference is the difference between an observation- and an experience-oriented analysis, between a researcher- and a participant-guided description, between a third- and a first-person-laden theory. Thus we look briefly at the theories of Lersch, Scheler, and Strasser, to take just a few representative examples. In his anthropology, Lersch distinguishes among vital, individual, and transitive emotions. This distinction is based on three layers that occur in the human person: the layers of the living being, the individual being, and the spiritual being. The first layer of emotions are those with a biological infrastructure; the second group are those having to do with the individual's self-preservation, the drive for power and retaliation, and the need for recognition and self-esteem; while the third group relates to social, esthetic, erotic, moral, metaphysical, and religious emotions.[5] Lersch refers to his theory as a real theory, which goes beyond simply a list of emotions. His study goes beyond such a list in that the emotions are structured according to three layers to which they belong. In this sense, his study can be said to entail a layer theory of emotions (Lersch 1974, 124-31).

Another phenomenological layer theorist of emotions is Scheler, whose ideas greatly influenced Lersch's work on emotions. Scheler distinguishes not three but four layers where the emotions are located: the layer of sensual emotions, of body and life emotions, of psychic emotions, and of spiritual emotions. According to this layer theory, positive emotions such as joy, happiness, and lust differ not in intensity or quality but in essence, just as negative emotions such as the pain of bodily suffering and the pain of sadness differ in essence, because they belong to different layers. This means that these emotions cannot be compared with each other. Scheler uses the layer concept to explain how contrasting emotions belonging to

---

5. Here, in order to give an impression only of Lersch's work, I have selected some of the main emotions he refers to.

different layers can coexist, even though they go in opposite directions. A person can feel deep psychological depression and at the same time have a sensual feeling of bodily lust, and he/she can feel joy while suffering severe bodily pain. The layer concept also explains that emotions from a deeper layer color emotions at a more superficial layer. For example, a person who carries a deep existential sadness can laugh at a joke, but the suffering permeates the laughter, as can be seen from the person's face (Scheler 1966, 332-34). The layer theory also explains how desires that remain unfulfilled at a deeper layer seek to be satisfied at a more superficial layer, as when a person replaces his/her desire for spiritual fulfillment by longing for narcotics. The deeper a positive feeling is, the more it is independent of the vicissitudes of life (Scheler 1966, 347-49). Based on this layer theory, an interesting interpretation can be developed of a phenomenon that frequently takes place when people suffer, that is, purification. This phenomenon can be seen in terms of an emotion at a superficial layer serving as a source for becoming conscious of an emotion at a deeper layer. Thus when a person suffers from bodily illness, he/she can be touched by the insight that he/she already, albeit as yet unconsciously, is enjoying an emotion at a deeper layer, like the emotion of devotion or gratitude. This is called catharsis (Scheler 1966, 349).

A rich phenomenological layer theory of emotions was developed by the then Nijmegen philosopher Strasser. Strasser distinguishes three different main types of layer theories: the evolutionary layer theory, which explains the phylogenetic relation between the animal and the "rational animal" *(animal rationalis)*, the human being; the function-psychological layer theory, which describes emotions in terms of the objective functions of human existence, like Lersch's vital, individual, and spiritual functions; and lastly Scheler's phenomenological layer theory, which describes emotions in terms of how people subjectively experience and feel them (Strasser 1956, 14).[6] Strasser develops his theory from the third type. It provides a way of explaining the coexistence of emotions that are differently experienced and felt.[7] Within this phenomenological approach, Strasser distinguishes three layers, which can be referred to in two different ways. One is in terms of intentionality, so that the first layer, which relates to the organic structure of human existence, is called preintentional; the middle

---

6. Strasser also refers to a fourth layer theory, i.e., the content-psychological theory by, e.g., O. Kroh.

7. Strasser points out that many authors developed a layer theory of emotions, mentioning J. B. Fröbes, J. Lindworsky, K. Schneider, H. C. Rümke, L. van de Horst, L. Bigot, and B. G. Palland.

one, which deals with human existence as being directed toward the world outside itself *(ex-sistere)*, is called intentional; and the last one, which has to do with the human being's orientation toward his/her metaphysical and religious ground, is called supraintentional. One might say that the preintentional emotions are driven by a tendency *(tendere)*, not an intention *(intendere)*, whereas the supraintentional ones emerge from an intention fascinated and overwhelmed by something that transcends them. The other way to identify these layers is in terms of the three different interpretations of emotions. Emotions can be interpreted first as a drive without a clear goal or objective, which functions, so to speak, behind the person's back *(vis a tergo)*; second as a desire and longing that originate from the will and choice of the person and function within the person, from which the true, the good, and the beautiful are strived for; and lastly as an affection, a pathos, by which a person is touched, moved, pulled, and appealed, as though the emotion functions before the person, who is characterized by receptivity. This rich metaphor of emotions, which function behind, within, and before the person, can be exemplarily illustrated from the area of sexuality. Sexual emotions can be felt as a blind drive, a dark instinct,[8] as a matter of will and choice, or as being affected and touched by love (Strasser 1956, 51). An interesting question Strasser considers is the relationship between the three layers on the one hand and the unity of the human person on the other. Does the difference between the layers not nullify this unity? Strasser solves this problem by a kind of hierarchization between the layers. This means first that the lower (or superficial) layers are oriented toward the higher (or deeper) ones, in the sense that the higher layers direct the lower ones, and second that the lower layers are a necessary condition for the higher layers, in the sense that the latter cannot exist without the former (Strasser 1956, 89-90).

The behavioristic approach to emotions can be seen as a clear-cut protest against phenomenological approaches, which are seen as highly subjective, intuitive, arbitrary, uncontrollable, and mutually contradictory. From a behavioristic point of view, such theories perhaps represent beautiful literary essays about emotions, from emotions, or even into emotions, but they do not offer any scientific description and explanation of them. In its extreme form, behaviorism tries to develop a theory of emotions by

---

8. Interestingly, Strasser (1956, 53-71) points to the theoretical construct of the instinct concept, which explains empirical facts in a nonempirical manner. Because it is not a necessary hypothesis at all, he proposes replacing it with a concept referring to people's experience of instinct. This he calls *Drangerlebnis*, or the feeling of being driven forward.

taking into account exclusively that which can be observed and measured, and eliminating all inner mental or even broader intrapsychic processes from the research program. Two forms of critique may be distinguished, classical behaviorism and neobehaviorism, of which the latter at least gives some inner events a relative role to play.

Classical behaviorism considers emotions as the feeling of physiological arousal, which, in turn, is interpreted as the response to a triggering stimulus in the human's environment. This stimulus can be an unconditioned or a conditioned stimulus, as in the case of Pavlov's dog, whose salivary response is caused by the unconditioned stimulus of food or by the conditioned stimulus of the bell's tone, previously connected with the food. In terms of emotions, if one feels hungry and thirsty, eating and drinking cause pleasure; if one feels aggression, acting out gives relief; if one feels sexually aroused, orgasm causes satisfaction. This stimulus/response reaction can also be produced by what is known as operant or instrumental conditioning. Whereas feeding the dog causes a salivary response, commanding your dog with "stay" and "come" does not need a physiological basis. The dog must stay or come for other reasons before it can learn to do what you want it to do. It learns to react on your signal by being rewarded and reinforced. With regard to emotions, this means that emotions are stimulated and learned by reward and reinforcement or extinguished and unlearned by punishment and inhibition. For instance, distress can be reinforced, as joy can be extinguished, or, to use modern examples from the area of behavioral therapy, fears (phobias) and helplessness are learned and can be unlearned by reconditioning. In emotional developmental research babies use an arm pull to produce a reinforcing slide of an infant's smiling face which is shown in front of the baby, accompanied by the sound of children singing the theme song from *Sesame Street*. These babies appear to express emotions of excitement and enjoyment more frequently than babies in the control group, who have not the possibility of pulling the arm in such a way that the smiles and the singing are produced. The babies in the experimental group are systematically rewarded and reinforced, the babies in the control group are not (Lazarus 1991, 328). In both classical and operant conditioning, emotions are based on direct stimulus/response-relationships (S-R); they are functions of behavior, not of intentions, goals, beliefs, or expectation.

In neobehaviorism the directness of the stimulus/response-relationship is replaced by indirectness, which means that the stimulus's causal influence on the response is moderated by the organism's activity (S-O-R). The organism's main activity refers to the person's expectations with regard to punishment and reward. In this theory, the response is not the direct outcome of the stimulus, but the direct outcome of the person's expectation of the relationship between stimulus and response. When a stimulus, let us say professional piano playing, time and again leads to the emotion of enjoyment, in the long run this enjoyment will be brought about merely by the expectation that playing piano sonatas in a professional manner will bring this positive emotion. It is a kind of success expectation, which moderates the relationship between stimulus and response, in the same way as failure expectancy can inhibit the stimulus from leading to the related response. When erotic longing repeatedly fails to be rewarded by emotional satisfaction as a result of a particular intrapsychic or interpsychic inhibition, the disconnection between the stimulus and the desired outcome emotion depends more and more on the failure expectation that the satisfaction will not emerge. In the long run it can even lead to the extinction of the stimulus itself. Here, at least approximately, the mind is moderating the individual's emotional life, although expectancies are not to be identified with intentions, goals, and values; that is, only a specific part of the human mind moderates the individual's emotional life. Expectations are described and explained in the observational mode of the researcher's perspective, whereas intentions, goals, and values are sensed, seen, and understood in the participatory mode of the person's involvement within his/her own life in his/her own context.

It may become clear from the above why a theory of emotion is needed that is different from Thomas Aquinas's scheme of passions, the phenomenological approach, and the behavioristic approach. This is not to say that none of these theories has some positive points, some advantages, or even some richness that is worth maintaining. Thomas Aquinas's analysis is to be admired for its logical clarity, the phenomenological approach for its experiential depth as expressed in the layer concept, and the behavioristic research for its conceptual economy. However, just these strong points have some negative side effects. Thomas Aquinas's theory contains a beautifully logical system, but it is without empirical references. It is an a priori scheme, not an empirical theory in which emotions are described in the way people experience and feel them (cf. Strasser 1956, 153). The phenomenological approach deals with emotions from the perspective from which they are experienced and felt, but as if they were isolated entities that mysteriously happen within the individual person's soul, having no connection with his/her (changing) context. In the framework of behaviorism, emotions are seen in the (changing) context in which the individual exists, but this context is formulated only in terms of a stimulus, which directly or indirectly elicits a behavioral response, and the complexity of inner processes occurring within the person is ignored.

The Cognitive Interaction Theory of Emotions

Therefore, to take this list of advantages and disadvantages together, a theory of emotion must satisfy the criteria of logical clarity, conceptual economy, experientialism, and contextualism. Let me explain these criteria. The criterion of logical clarity implies that the theory has to have a transparent logical basis, resulting in a clear network of concepts. The criterion of conceptual economy requires that the number of concepts in this theory be as small as possible, and the number of conceptual relations between these concepts as large as possible — in other words, few concepts and many relations. The criterion of experientialism means that the theory must take into account the inner processes people go through when they feel emotions, and in which layers the emotions originate. The criterion of contextualism requires that the theory consider the environment within and from which emotions are experienced and felt.

In my opinion, the aforementioned cognitive interaction theory of emotions meets these four criteria. It satisfies the criterion of logical clarity because of its transparent basic structure. It complies with the criterion of conceptual economy because its conceptual model combines simplicity and explanatory power. It fulfills the criterion of experientialism because its cognitive approach emphasizes the inner processes people go through when feeling emotions. Lastly it meets the criterion of contextualism because it interprets emotions precisely in terms of the interaction between the person and his/her environment.

This is not to say that the cognitive interaction theory of emotion extensively and intensively covers all aspects of emotions, such as the three groups of aspects — neurophysiological, motor or behavioral-expressive, and subjective-experiential — that play a key role in them, but at least it contains a conceptual scheme that takes all of these aspects into consideration and adequately localizes them. Nor does the cognitive interaction theory of emotion supply the absolute last word regarding the relationship among emotion, cognition, and context, but at least it starts from the insight that emotions emerge from the interaction with the person's context as mediated by cognitive operations. The emotion-cognition interface may be understood such that the cognitive processes in some aspects are a sufficient condition for emotions to emerge, in other aspects a necessary condition, and in still other aspects one of the causal conditions of the emotion expression (cf. Izard et al. 1984, 5). This description of the emotion-cognition interface does not exclude any of the three basic models representing the relation between emotion and cognition: emotion as a consequence of cognition, emotion as an antecedent of cognition, and emotion and cognition as interdependent, although the last model has a strong family resemblance to the cognitive interaction theory I present below (cf. Zajonc et al. 1986; Lewis et al. 1984).

Within these cognitive operations, a substantial role is played by the so-called appraisal processes, by which (changing) situations and contexts are defined, estimated, and valued according to the meaning they have for the individual. Two groups of appraisal processes can be distinguished: primary and secondary (Lazarus 1991, 149-50). Let me explain these processes by taking an example as simple as the boss entering the secretary's office.

In the group of primary appraisal processes, the person first determines whether the new situation has a certain goal relevance for him/her by estimating whether his/her interests are at stake. When the boss simply goes through his/her usual morning greeting ritual and then leaves again, this event differs from the boss entering the office in order to deal with a serious complaint that someone has made against the secretary. The greeting ritual, which may be identical in both cases, is a convention of politeness without any particular meaning. But the exchange about the complaint might have a strong goal relevance, because the secretary's job might be at stake, and thus may elicit a strong emotion. Second, the person establishes whether there is a goal congruence between the situation and his/her goal. If there is such congruence, a positive emotion will be generated, and if there is incongruence, a negative one develops. If, for example, the person who made the complaint against the secretary is known by the boss as a chronic complainer, then they will laugh together. This reinforces the secretary's relationship with the boss, which makes them both happy. But if the complaint came from the president of the board of directors, then the emotional barometer might go the other way, generating sadness. The last question then is: To what extent does "ego-involvement" come into play with regard to the person's goal? The level of ego-involvement can be low, high, or in between. Ego-involvement may concern different aspects, such as one's self-esteem, social esteem, values, ego-ideals, meanings, life goals, or other people's well-being. If the boss himself takes responsibility for the problem that led to the complaint, the secretary's ego-involvement will be low. But if the boss suggests that the complaint seriously calls into question the secretary's competence, the degree of ego-involvement will likely be high. In sum, the first group of appraisal processes entails three subprocesses: establishing goal relevance, goal congruence, and ego-involvement. I owe these three terms to Lazarus (1991). Frijda (1993, 59-69) summarizes these terms by calling emotions "the promoters of interest."

In my opinion, the layer concept, which, as mentioned above, is developed within the phenomenology of emotions, may be interpreted in terms of this group of primary appraisal processes, meaning that the space metaphor of the layer may be understood in the functional terms of goal relevance, goal congruence, and ego-involvement. That is, a positive emotion at a deep phenomenological layer may be seen as an emotion emerging from the interaction with a new situation, which has a high degree of goal relevance, goal congruence, and ego-involvement. The same is true of a negative emotion at a deep layer, except that then goal congruence is replaced by incongruence. Similarly, emotions at a higher, more superficial level have a low degree of goal relevance, goal congruence, and especially ego-involvement. In other words, emotions do not ontologically exist in layers, layers that in Scheler's case, for example, are associated with ontologically existing, higher- or lower-ranking values, but are the functional outcome of varying interactions with varying situations with varying goal relevance, goal congruence, and ego-involvement arising from varying processes of primary appraisal. The cognitive interaction theory contributes to a justified criticism of the existence of values as a "quasi-object," a "world of values," or even an "eternal entity" (cf. Ricoeur 1975, 324).

In the group of secondary appraisal processes, the person abstracts little by little from the concrete situation, and tries, as it were, to obtain answers to specific questions. First, he/she tries to determine whether somebody is to credit or blame for the new situation that has come into being. If there is a combination of goal relevance, goal congruence, and a high degree of ego-involvement, the positive emotion that is generated takes the form of pride when the credit is to oneself, and of gratitude when it is to somebody else. If the person caused himself/herself the trouble, shame and guilt emerge, and if somebody else is to be blamed, anger arises. If the secretary believes that the boss himself is accountable for the complaint, she gets angry at him. If the secretary was responsible for the problem, she may have feelings of guilt, remorse, or even self-reproach.

Second, the person looks for some coping potential by which the demands of the new situation can be managed and the personal goals and values realized. Two modes of coping can be distinguished: problem-focused and emotion-focused coping. Within the problem-focused coping, actions are taken in order to adjust the situation to one's commitments and/or to adjust these commitments to the situation. These actions arise from certain action tendencies, which are implied in the emotions that the person experiences. The emotions wish, as it were, to be concretized, materialized, put into practice, transformed into behavior. They set in motion various kinds of neurophysiological processes within the glands, muscles, visceral organs, and brain by which the emotions are physically expressed.

From this, certain action impulses arise or, at least, some action readiness comes into being. The emotion in the situation elicits action, but to the extent that the action execution is blocked for some reason, only action readiness develops (Frijda 1986, 83). Some elementary forms of action or action readiness are: moving against (in the case of anger or irritation), moving toward (in the case of joy and love), and moving away (in the case of fear and anxiety). This threefold distinction is reminiscent of Thomas Aquinas's analysis of emotions, which starts from moving toward and moving away, as I explained earlier (cf. Frijda 1993, 61). If the secretary feels endangered, the impulse may arise to threaten the boss by bluffing him, or to withdraw and flee the situation, at least metaphorically. But if the secretary feels glad, she may feel an urge to "jump for joy." If the secretary feels sorry, she may bow her head and indicate with her bodily posture that she would like to hide and withdraw. While problem-focused coping embodies action or action readiness, emotion-focused coping consists of the endeavor to interpret the changing situation, accommodate oneself to it, tolerate it, and accept it. By this second kind of coping the emotion loses some of its "heat" and action readiness. The reason might be that the new situation is unchangeable or, at least, looks as if it were unchangeable, or the problem-focused coping, which is based on taking action, is inhibited by some values, ideals, self-esteem, social esteem, enlightened self-interest, or social control. The secretary would like to attack the boss out of anger, but self-esteem prevents her from doing so. The secretary tries to understand what factors have led to the complaint and how to deal with it in a cooperative way, which lessens the "hot" feeling of aggression. Lastly, the person thinks in terms of future expectancies. Will the new situation change over time without any specific action? Or does an occasionally desirable change require a specific intervention?

This leads to the third question: which intervention would be the most appropriate one and what might its direct consequences and side-effects be? What might happen in future situations if the secretary takes no action at all this time? What might happen if the secretary were to answer back and stand up for the rights the labor union says each employee has? Would the secretary lose social esteem, reputation, or credibility? In sum, the second group of appraisal processes contains three subphases: attributing the cause of the new situation (crediting or blaming), looking for coping potential (problem-focused or emotion-focused), and future expectancies.

In my opinion, the phenomenological concept of purification and catharsis, which I referred to earlier, may be interpreted in terms of emotion-focused coping. It is not necessary to use the layer concept in order to explain what happens when a person is able to tolerate or even accept severe bodily illness and suffering. The person may reinterpret the new situation of physical suffering by relativizing its goal relevance, goal incongruence, and ego-involvement, looking at it from a different perspective, and making new connections between it and other relevant situations in his/her experience. Such situations are the intimate love relationship with significant others like the partner, children, parents, or friends, service to social, cultural, or scientific causes, commitment to the religious congregation, or religious surrender to God. These situations, which may have a high degree of goal relevance, goal congruence, and ego-involvement, enable the bodily suffering to be tolerated. In other words, purification and catharsis can be understood in terms of the primary and secondary appraisal processes.

I owe the terms *primary* and *secondary appraisal processes* to the analysis by Lazarus (1991), whose earlier work on stress and coping subsequently developed in the direction of emotion research. The Dutch psychologist Frijda, whose emotion theory takes the same perspective as Lazarus's, summarizes the concepts that I have presented thus far in terms of emotional laws. The "Law of Appeal" says that emotions depend on the appeal the situation has for the person. The "Law of the Strength of Reality" means that the subjective experience of the situation and the intensity of this experience determine the emotion, not the objective characteristics of the situation. The "Law of Change" refers to the fact that only the changing situation elicits emotions, not the situation insofar as it remains unchanged. This law correlates with the "Law of Habituation," which expresses the phenomenon that situations we are used to do not elicit emotions. Yesterday's anger is disappearing today because we are becoming accustomed to the new situation, just as the joy we feel today will fade tomorrow. All this again correlates with the "Law of Comparative Feeling," which says that emotions emerge from the disparity between what happens and what we think could happen. The greater this disparity, the stronger the emotions. However, habituation does not take place in the same way for negative emotions such as sorrow as it does for positive emotions such as joy and gladness. Generally speaking, emotions decrease in intensity over time because we become accustomed to the new situation; but, whereas gladness disappears over time, sorrow continues relatively intensely — time does not heal all wounds. From this phenomenon Frijda develops his "Law of Hedonic Asymmetry," as he calls it, or the "Law of Emotional Momentum," which refers to the fact that positive emotions fade away, whereas negative emotions like loss do not totally disappear but remain relatively intense (Frijda 1986; 1993, 106-32).

So far, I have spoken of emotions in terms of emotional processes, as

298

being part of and arising out of interactions with contexts. The use of the plural "emotions" and "emotional processes" is meant to suggest that an emotion is not to be seen as a separate phenomenon, in that a particular emotion often coexists with another emotion or several emotions. In this sense one speaks of basic, elementary, or primary emotions on the one hand and complex, secondary, or derived emotions on the other. Which emotions are basic and which are complex is a matter of scientific debate. For example, some psychologists see joy, anger, sadness, fear, and interest as basic emotions, along with surprise, affection, and sexual ardor, and view shame, guilt, envy, and depression as more complex emotions (Campos and Barret 1984, 249-55). Izard's list of ten basic emotions, which clearly differs from Campos and Barret's, includes interest-excitement, enjoyment-joy, surprise-startle, distress-anguish, anger-rage, disgust-revulsion, contempt-scorn, fear-terror, shame-shyness-humiliation, and guilt-remorse. The reason for the variety of lists is that "basic" connotes different criteria: it can mean physiologically elementary, cross-culturally common, original from birth, or adaptationally functional in crisis situations. Thus some psychologists consider basic emotions to be those with an elementary physiological structure, others consider them to be those which are common to all cultures, and so on (Lazarus 1991, 79). Besides these criteria, Frijda emphasizes the criterion of action tendency. According to this criterion desire can be understood as the action tendency of approaching, fear as avoiding, enjoyment in terms of being-with, interest in terms of attending (opening), disgust in terms of rejecting, and so on (Frijda 1986, 88). From his analysis of the primary appraisal processes, Lazarus establishes a list of emotions that is divided into positive and negative emotions. Positive emotions are characterized by goal relevance and goal congruence, and include happiness/joy, pride, love/affection, and relief, whereas negative emotions are characterized by the combination of goal relevance and incongruence, and include anger, fright-anxiety, guilt-shame, sadness, envy-jealousy, and disgust. Next to these two groups he distinguishes borderline emotions like hope, compassion, and aesthetic emotions. Based on these lists, Lazarus speaks of complex emotional states, including, for example, grief and depression; of ambiguous positive emotional states like awe, confidence, and satisfaction; and of ambiguous negative emotional states like frustration, disappointment, helplessness, and meaninglessness. Regardless of the relevance or value one attributes to these and other lists, it is certainly true that emotions often group together, and together determine the person's emotional state. As this grouping together happens over time, it results in a dynamic chain of changing emotional states or emotional processes.

Still another reason for speaking of emotions in the plural has to do with the primary and secondary appraisal processes, each of which, as noted above, consists of three aspects: establishing goal relevance, goal congruence, and ego-involvement (primary), and attributing cause, looking for coping potential, and future expectations (secondary). I described these appraisal processes in a linear way, although in reality they form a cycle or even a spiral, and the six aspects have to be seen as mutually influencing each other. The appraisal processes not only moderate but also mediate the interactions between the person and his/her context. In other words, they not only regulate and direct these interactions but also add new aspects to them. The appraisal processes cocondition each other.[9] To put it more concretely, a particular emotion, which is triggered by the person's interaction with the changing situation, can itself elicit a second emotion, by which the first emotion changes and takes on some of the colors, contents, and orientations of the second one, and vice versa. To return to my earlier example, when the secretary fears that the boss is coming in for a nonritual reason, but then senses that he/she will take on himself/herself the responsibility for the complaint, an emotional change may happen from the simple emotion of fear to that of relief, the more complex emotion of gratitude, or the borderline emotion of hope. When the secretary reflects on these emotions of gratitude and hope later on from a more distantiated point of view, however, he/she may feel anger because the gratitude and hope have led to increased feelings of dependence. Here we may speak of emotional reciprocal causality because, as cognitive processes change, emotions cause emotions within processes of interaction with changing situations. Emotions form streams, flows, or fluxes of mutually inducing emotions.

An important question that should be dealt with here refers to the relationship between the conscious and unconscious character of emotions (cf. Freud 1984, 159-222). Are the appraisals, which play a key role, entirely and exclusively conscious processes? Not at all. Although appraisal processes are cognitive, this does not mean that they always take place in consciousness and that people are always aware of them. Cognitive and conscious processes are not identical. The cognitive must be seen as the genus of both the conscious and the unconscious; the conscious and unconscious are both species of cognition. Many cognitive processes happen in the realm of the unconscious (or the preconscious or subconscious). Typing this text on the personal computer, playing a prelude from Bach's

9. This implies a kind of reciprocal determinism (Bandura 1986, 1-46; Lazarus 1991, 88, 173-76, 204), which transcends the dilemma between freedom and determinism in the area of emotions.

Well-Tempered Clavier, coordinating the accelerator pedal, clutch, and gears while parking my European car in a narrow street in Amsterdam — all these activities imply a multitude of cognitive operations, but they take place (fortunately) at the unconscious level. They are automatic rather than deliberately and volitionally controlled. The same applies to the aforementioned appraisals within the flux of emotions. Most of the time they are automatic processes, which we have been learning to carry out since childhood. In new situations or in situations with a high degree of ego-involvement, however, they may emerge at the level of consciousness. In counseling and psychotherapy these processes can be deliberately made conscious in order to allow them to be reflected on, channeled, and regulated, or to flow spontaneously. Normally, emotions are to be seen as embedded in varying combinations of unconscious, preconscious, subconscious, and conscious appraisal processes (cf. Wegman 1985).

7.2 Emotions from a Moral Perspective

The analysis presented so far indicates that emotions are a combination of active and passive aspects, because they are the result of the interaction between the person and his/her context. This interaction takes place in the form of primary and secondary appraisal processes, in which the person experiences the changing situation and at the same time estimates, defines, and evaluates it. The person is influenced by the situation and at the same time influences it in a dialectical process that results in flows of emotions. This interpretation rules out two other, contrasting approaches. In the first approach, emotions overwhelm the person and make him/her unable to think or act freely. Of course emotions do influence one's freedom to varying degrees, while sometimes even preventing a person from being himself/herself, but generally emotions, as they occur in psychodynamically more or less healthy people, do not absolutely eliminate the person's responsibility. In the other approach, emotions are seen as being totally within the person's capacity to deal with and react to, as if the person were able neutrally to observe, register, control, and distantiate from them. This approach does not take into account that people are always moved, affected, sometimes suffering or even wounded by emotions. In the sense that emotions combine active and passive aspects, they may be said to be similar to all other basic human qualities like speaking and acting. Speaking combines *langage et parole,* that is, using the language structures the individual passively finds in his/her cultural tradition, and at the same time transforming some elements of these structures in a unique, original way in order to express himself/herself as a creative subject, as an *ipse*, as "I." In the same way, acting combines passive and active aspects: the actor adapts to the action patterns that he/she owes to the institutions he/she is in, and at the same time reconstructs some elements of these patterns from his/her own self. Acting is at the same time "instituted" *(institué)* and "instituting" *(instituant)*. In the realm of both speaking and acting, *praxis* always takes place in the traces of previous *praxeis* (Ricoeur 1975, 318-22). Analogously, one might generally say that emotions move the person, while at the same time the person moves the emotions.

Patterns of Managing Emotions

It is important to take into account this dialectical process of passive and active aspects when inquiring into the moral relevance of emotions, especially in the realm of moral education. In literature referring to emotions from a moral perspective in general and from moral psychology in particular, different patterns of managing emotions in a moral sense in the area of education may be distinguished. Let me describe five patterns, which can be conceived of as "ideal types" in the sense of Max Weber, meaning types of which the characteristics are accentuated or even exaggerated as a way of imposing some order on reality. I then evaluate these according to the passive/active dimension, which is relevant to every expression of human existence—not only the linguistic or practical but emotional expressions as well.

In the first pattern, which I call suppression, emotions are seen as both exclusively passive and exclusively negative. Sexual emotions can be seen and were in fact seen in the past as resulting from the sexual instinct, at least in some cultural and religious circles. This instinct is interpreted as a blind mechanism or force that overpowers people's mental, rational, and intellectual capacity and puts one's own and another's psychic and spiritual health at risk. In the same way, anger or rage can be experienced as totally overwhelming, robbing one of rationality and control, and severely damaging one's own bodily and mental integrity and another's. In this pattern, it is held that such emotional drives as life and death, *eros* and *thanatos*, have to be suppressed, so that they are weakened and eventually extinguished. This pattern often goes hand in hand with body hostility. Sometimes the virtue of temperance is misunderstood as referring to the extinction of bodily emotions in particular (van der Ven 1992).

The second pattern of managing emotions, which I call control, is concerned with keeping emotions down, restraining them, and holding them within boundaries. This approach is not concerned with whether emotions are in themselves bad or good, but only with bringing their direct effects and side effects under control in the short or the long term. The blame for the one-sidedness of this mastery is often laid at Kant's feet, because of his strong emphasis on the purity of reason and freedom of the will, which are supposed to guarantee human autonomy in the moral area. Insofar as reason and will depend on emotions, they are thought to depend on something heteronomous. The universal rational duty functions as a regulative constraint. But this rational mastery out of moral duty does not mean that Kant neglects, denies, or even relativizes the positive role emotions may play in concrete moral life. For example, he understands the emotion of compassion as helping us to sense the relevant features of moral situations, to know when people are in need, to do the right thing, to support those in need, or even to model the right attitudes to fellow citizens, who learn to help needy people from this compassion modeling (Sherman 1990). In determining moral duty itself, however, emotions have to be controlled.

The third pattern I call neutralizing. Here emotions are understood as morally indifferent. Kohlberg's theory, which I discussed extensively in Chapter 5, is a clear example. Kohlberg accepts that emotions play a part in morality, but for him they are not morally relevant: they have a moral value of zero. Let us take, for instance, sympathy, which indicates a person's emotional involvement with another person, especially a fellow sufferer. This sympathy is implied throughout Kohlberg's six stages of moral development.[10] In the first two stages (preconventional morality), emotional energy is taken up by the individual's striving to prevent punishment or to obtain reward; in the middle two stages (conventional morality), it plays a part in leading the individual to comply with small-group and community-based expectations; and in the last two stages (postconventional morality), it inspires the individual to look to universal principles of justice. The emotional energy itself does not determine, change, or even influence the cognitive structure of the stages. The universality of the structure is essential; the emotional content is accidental (cf. Kohlberg 1980, 40).

In the fourth pattern, which I refer to as ordering, the emotions are not suppressed, controlled, or neutralized. Instead, their affective flow is directed toward the moral goal or value at which the person is aiming, while their affective energy is purposively used for approximating and reaching it. This especially applies to the relationship between emotions (or passions, as they are called in Aristotelian and Thomist moral theories) and virtues.

10. For my critical comment on Kohlberg's six-stage theory, see Chapter 5.

The emotions are not inspected for their possibly negative influences, but positively taken up into the purposive human striving to perform virtuous actions and approximate excellence in virtue. The emotion of sympathy, for example, is integrated into the orientation toward the virtue of friendship as a concern for the friend's true well-being. Here, reason, emotion and will form one whole, a Gestalt, as it is realized in the orientation toward the common good in the community of the polis (MacIntyre 1984, 156). For sympathy to be integrated as an emotion into striving for real happiness for one's significant others, maturity is an essential condition. Experience, appropriately developed habits, intellectual training, tutored emotions, and character are needed for that. Sympathy and friendship do not emerge spontaneously; they require virtuous intentionality (MacIntyre 1988, 127).

I would like to add an insight by Hume, who by differentiating between calm and violent emotions makes the ordering type both more real and more complex.[11] The calm emotions are, for instance, benevolence, love, and kindness, whereas the violent ones are strong emotional reactions to injury by another or to the threat of a serious disease. Arguing for a balance of the calm over the violent emotions, Hume refers to virtue in terms of cultivating and encouraging the calm emotions and inhibiting the violent emotions, because that is in our well-conceived interest, our interest in the long run. This ordering, which consists of stimulating the positive and relativizing the negative emotions, is not a purely emotional activity, for reason plays a key role in it. The calm emotions, which strive to be fulfilled in order to lead the person into joy and happiness, establish that which is to be satisfied, while reason calculates what kind of actions must follow to achieve this satisfaction under the conditions at hand, not only in the short run but especially in the long run (cf. MacIntyre 1988, 304-9).

The fifth and last pattern I call processing, meaning that emotions are considered a unique source of information, inspiration, and orientation toward the good life, and thus something to listen to carefully and to trust. Emotions are made to take the lead in moral judging and acting. This entails the hard work of digging up and seriously working through emotions that may have disappeared under the phylogenetic or ontogenetic dust of civilization, or which may have been excessively trimmed, disciplined, and domesticated (cf. Freud 1961; Elias 1977; 1982). From the "processing" point of view, emotions possess a kind of "moral gold" that has to be mined, a kind of classical wisdom that has to be cautiously learned from. They possess

11. MacIntyre (1986, 302) points out that Hume speaks not of emotions but of passions. These are not identical because to Hume's mind passions are preconceptual and prelinguistic, whereas emotions imply judgments and beliefs.

biographically old codes, which have to be discovered, broken, and decoded so that they can reveal their unique information about lifelong questions like: Who am I? What do I strive for? What does happiness consist of? If emotions are civilized, inhibited, and suppressed, their increasing compliance results in shame for giving utterance to positive emotions and guilt for expressing negative ones. Both the positive and the negative emotions have to be explored in depth. In the nondirective educational counseling approach, the emotions are processed in such a way that the negative ones can be increasingly accepted and the positive ones sorted and interpreted as a source of direction. In this approach, the emphasis is on becoming fully aware of the emotions that were denied and distorted in one's own biography. By becoming conscious of them, self-caring and at the same time allocentric attitudes can be developed, prerequisites for living a truly authentic life (Schachtel 1959; Rogers 1969). In the psychodrama version of this approach, all kinds of roles that belong to the drama of the person's biography can be played out in order to discover the rich potentialities contained therein. By going into one's own depth, it is possible to make necessary changes and even conversions toward self-growth and self-realization, which are in turn the necessary conditions for creative love and solidarity. In bibliodrama this role-playing is connected with narrative figures from the Bible, the emotional meaning of which stimulates the player's own emotional processing and expressing (cf. Derksen and Andriessen 1985; Andriessen et al. 1995).

How can these five patterns of dealing with emotions in moral education be evaluated from the cognitive interaction theory to which I referred in the previous section? In what sense are they legitimated through the dialectical relationship between passivity and activity within human existence, which is expressed in speech, action, and emotion?

The first three patterns clearly deny, neglect, or undermine what emotions are and how they function from the point of view of the cognitive interaction theory of emotion. The suppressing, controlling, and neutralizing patterns imply that emotions are dangerous, dysfunctional, or at least morally neutral, and therefore have to be extinguished, mastered, or made irrelevant. In the primary appraisal processes, however, emotions provide important information because they are connected with goal relevance, goal congruence, and ego-involvement in the changing situation. In the secondary appraisal processes, emotions are relevant insofar as they function to assign credit or blame for the situation, orient problem-focused or emotion-focused coping, and direct future expectancies. Not only do these appraisal processes evoke emotions, but the emotions themselves can lead, as I said, to new appraisals, new actions, and even new emotions. Emotions are a unique source of defining, assessing, and evaluating the changing situation, and as such, to use Frijda's phrase, are "promoters of interest." And this interest is directly or indirectly connected with fundamental moral concepts like the good, the just, and the wise. This is not to say that all emotions, all varieties of emotions, or all expressions of emotions are morally justifiable. As Hume indicates, in his distinction between calm and violent emotions and his idea that the former should outweigh the latter, some moral differentiation, ordering, and integration processes are needed in the area of emotions. This, however, is the very opposite of extinguishing them, controlling them, or rendering them morally meaningless. Indeed, the suppressing, controlling, and neutralizing patterns of managing emotions have no place in moral education.

Two other patterns remain: ordering and processing. Let us look first at the processing pattern, because the idea that emotions need to be listened to and worked through clearly fits in with the theoretical and empirical insight that emotions contain precious information about the goal relevance and goal congruence of the changing situation with which the person is interacting. For example, anger tells me that the new situation I am in is preventing me from being honest, because the person who influences the situation is urging me to tell white, social, or political lies. My anger gives me the impulse to engage in an open, assertive, and insistent conversation with this person. The emotion of empathy, which I feel when I meet a vulnerable, terminally ill person, urges me to accompany that person on the way in the sunset of his/her life. The emotion of justice make me intuitively aware that someone has not been treated equally or equitably, and that the injustice has to be repaired, corrected, or even reversed.

Emotions are not always to be followed directly, however. In many situations, especially those in which one is deeply involved, some discernment between authentic and inauthentic emotions is needed. This discernment requires introspection, in which one places the emotions in front of oneself, as it were, in order to sense, feel, explore, inspect, reflect on, and evaluate them in as impartial a way as possible. To take emotions, which are intimately connected with one's self and belong to the innermost core of one's being, and to place them outside oneself and look at them in an objective way, sounds very strange. It requires that one combine the stance of the participant and that of the observer, be both subject and object, accused and judge. For some people, it is helpful to write in a diary, especially when they are emotionally confused, or at least not entirely sure whether their authentic emotions outweigh the inauthentic ones. If one feels incapable of being one's own judge, one has the possibility of discussing the matter with somebody one trusts. The result of such conversation can be an enriched insight into one's own emotional life. By discerning between authentic and inauthentic emotions, it is possible to focus more on the former and less on the latter, and to order the emotions in such a way that they support and contribute to the goals, values, and convictions that one stands for. In other words, the processing and the ordering patterns imply, complement, and orient each other. They are dialectically related to one another.

Is it possible to explain this dialectical connection of the processing and ordering patterns from the perspective of the cognitive interaction theory of emotion? The answer can be found in the distinction between conscious and unconscious appraisal processes. Many appraisal processes happen unconsciously, because they take place automatically on the basis of emotional goal/environment interaction chains that we have learned and developed in the past, the past being the last couple of years, the first years of our existence, and everything in between. These interaction chains may be adequate or inadequate. A young child learns to appraise the contact with his/her mother as trustful, and subsequently transfers this emotion to contacts with other people. However, another young child who lacks the necessary emotional attachment to his/her mother and appraises the contact with the mother as nontrustful, because, as a drug addict, she neglects and abuses the child, learns to transfer this distrust to relationships with other people. This interaction chain becomes inadequate when the child does not see that these other people — or at least some of them — really are trustworthy and responds to them in the same way he/she responds to the mother. Inasmuch as these inadequate chains operate at later stages in life, and the inauthentic emotions stemming from them are more or less unconsciously (preconsciously or subconsciously) felt, then a discerning process is needed in which these inauthentic emotions are separated from the authentic ones. I should point out that most of the time the terms *authentic* and *inauthentic* do not refer to different emotions, but to two or more sides of the same emotion. The anger one feels when a situation that is evidently caused by an other person is preventing one from achieving a life goal that one considers highly important can have an authentic and an inauthentic aspect. The authentic aspect relates to the other person causing the inhibiting situation. The inauthentic aspect may stem from the way one was treated by authoritarian, oppressive parents, and engender a grandiose feeling of narcissistic hurt, out of proportion to the objective damage inflicted by the other person. As with neuroses, narcissism has to do not with too many emotions, as one might think, but with suppressed inauthentic emotions (Jacoby 1990). Introspective and/or conversational discernment is needed to separate these two sources and streams within the emotion of anger and to act appropriately on the authentic aspect of the emotion.

As I said, the processing and ordering patterns are dialectically linked. The processing pattern consists of letting the emotions go and allowing them to take the lead, whereas the ordering pattern discerns the emotions and distinguishes between their authentic and inauthentic aspects in order to determine which authentic aspects ought to be acted on in preference to the inauthentic ones.

Summarizing what I have said so far in terms of the passivity/activity dimension, which permeates all human expressing, speaking, and acting, the first three patterns of managing emotions emphasize only the active side of this dimension. Suppressing, controlling, and neutralizing emotions all imply some active intervention in the realm of emotions and do not allow for the possibility of allowing emotions to take their course or to take the lead. The active intervention of extinguishing, mastering, and rendering irrelevant makes the emotions passive. The other two patterns, the processing and ordering, which occur in conjunction, aim at combining, synthesizing, and integrating the passive and active aspects of emotions. In nurturing a dialectical relationship between emotional passivity and activity, they together form the royal way.

Emotional Development

Having dealt with typical patterns of managing emotions, I now look at some specific emotions and ask how their development ought to be interpreted from a moral perspective. I intentionally speak of "emotions from a moral perspective" rather than of "moral emotions." Rawls explains the distinction between natural and moral emotions (or sentiments, as he calls them) by saying that the latter necessarily imply an explanation that "invokes a moral concept and its associated principles" (Rawls 1971, 481). Indeed, he restricts himself to "typical" moral sentiments like guilt, shame, remorse and regret, indignation and resentment (ibid., 485), although he admits that natural and moral emotions may mutually imply each other (ibid., 486-87), from which he concludes that moral emotions are a "normal part of life" (ibid., 489). Because (some of) the moral emotions Rawls refers to are complex emotions, it is necessary to look at their constitutive (natural) emotional basis in order to understand them well. Moreover, although these basic emotions — rightly or wrongly — are not considered moral emotions, they are not without moral relevance. I therefore prefer to speak of "emotions from a moral perspective" rather than of "moral emotions," because the former provides a broader scope and allows for such "natural emotions" as ego-identity, basic trust, empathy and sympathy, sex and love, along with such "moral emotions" as sense of justice, shame, and guilt.

Ego-Identity

Emotions directly involve the ego because they bring to the surface the awareness that says "I feel these emotions," and emotional development is thus tied up with the development of ego-identity. Without ego-identity, one cannot feel emotions. To put this in terms of the primary and secondary appraisal processes I outlined at the beginning of this chapter, it is the ego that sets goals for the person, establishes goal relevance in concrete situations, and determines goal congruence. It is the ego that is involved in the emotions that arise from these activities, not as an impartial observer, a "he" or "she," but as the central participant, the primary agent, the "I." Emotional development is therefore one of the conditions of morality, because morality is about goals, intentions, and actions deriving from ego-identity.

According to Lewis and Michalson (1983), five periods can be distinguished in the development of ego-identity in children. These periods refer to the normative development of the self in the sense that they relate the experiencing of emotions to various values and norms. The precise age boundaries of the periods are subject to scientific debate. Here I summarize their characteristics by connecting them with Lazarus's cognitive interaction theory of emotion (1991, 307-15). Whereas Lewis and Michalson make the transitions between the periods abrupt in a Piagetian way, I prefer to present them in terms of a gradual process.

In the first period, from birth to three months, the infant feels himself/herself to be in undifferentiated unity with the mother and other caregivers. A first sign of ego-identity may be observed when the child perceives and assimilates the connections between his/her own behavior and the reactions of others.

The second period is from four to eight or nine months. The child is able to differentiate himself/herself from others and begins to recognize his/her own actions and goals. In this period rudimentary forms of experiencing emotions begin to occur in relation to appraisal processes, including goal relevance and goal congruence, albeit in an inchoate way. In this period the child already is able to experience vaguely a personal stake in a transaction, to estimate rudimentarily consequences of situations and actions, and to feel sadness, fear, or anger.

The third period, between the ages of nine and twelve months, is characterized by the child's awareness of self-permanence. It does not only differentiate between himself/herself and others in a concrete situation, but also does so independently of the concrete situation.

The fourth period occurs from twelve to eighteen months. In this period the child is able to recognize himself/herself in the mirror, as well as in photos or movies. The child is increasingly grasping the social rules of living together with other people. From this emerges an increasing awareness of emotional meanings and interchanges with the mother and other significant people, especially within the family. Empathy and sympathy with others' distress begin to develop as well as the readiness to try to ease this distress.

The last period begins around eighteen months. In this period the child begins to develop and articulate a so-called categorical self as distinct from others. He/she begins to understand his/her involvement in social relationships and the emotional significance they have for the child's own goals and well-being in terms of goal relevance and goal congruence. The child starts to feel emotions like pride, shame, and guilt, which are involved in more complex appraisal processes, in which crediting and blaming play a key role. These emotions also presuppose an awareness of what is going on between and within people in interpersonal and intrapersonal relationships.

In sum, ego-identity and emotional development are intimately linked in the sense that the child increasingly becomes aware of having and going through emotions. Awareness of emotions and awareness of self manifest themselves both in the child's reacting to changing situations and in his/her influencing "significant others" like parents, other caregivers, siblings, and peers (Lazarus 1991, 314).

Basic Trust

Starting with the first period of ego-identity, the affectionate bond with the mother, father, and other significant caregivers is very important for the emotional health of the child.[12] This bond has to fulfill certain criteria if it

12. The child's attachment is a subject of scientific debate, which has given rise to two different theories: the differentiation theory and the parallel theory. In the former, the child attaches to only one caregiver, especially the mother, until the age of about six years, after which he/she also attaches to other adults, as Bowlby holds. The parallel theory claims that the child attaches to only one caregiver until the age of about one year, after which he/she seeks proximity and contact both with adults and with peers (cf. Mönks and Knoers 1982, 81-85).

is to function as a basis for the child's development of basic trust. These criteria have to do with the child's having a secure attachment to his/her caregivers, as Bowlby (1987) convincingly demonstrates. Attachment means that the child is strongly disposed to seek proximity to and contact with one (or more) of the caregivers, especially when he/she confronts negatively experienced situations, that is, when the child is frustrated, frightened, tired, or ill.[13] It also means that the child strives to maintain this proximity and contact, because they protect him/her from dangerous or at least disadvantageous people, happenings, or situations. In other words, they give the child safety, security, and confidence. Because proximity and contact are alternated with the absence of the caregiver, it is important to observe how the child reacts after the caregiver returns. In the alternation between proximity and absence of the caregiver, two forms of attachment may be distinguished: secure attachment and anxious attachment. The latter may be divided into two subforms: one connected with avoidance and another with resistance. Secure attachment means that when the mother returns, the child again seeks her proximity, and after having been comforted, returns to his/her play. Anxiously attached children do not strive for contact with the mother after a brief separation, but either avoid her in frustration or angrily resist her attempts to touch, kiss, and hold the child (Bowlby 1987, 335-40). Research indicates that securely attached children show significantly higher scores on ego-resilience and moderate ego-control scores, whereas the anxiously attached children appear to be either overcontrolled or undercontrolled (Bowlby 1987, 364).

To the degree that this secure attachment develops, it can be transferred to other relationships and forms the foundation for basic trust, which includes various aspects, as Erikson explains. The first aspect is that the child experiences his/her social world and the people in it as reliable. When the child asks something, people respond, thus allowing the child to trust them. The second aspect has to do with the child himself/herself. What the child does, thinks, and undertakes is experienced as reliable, so that the child learns to count on himself/herself. The child's activities are experienced as effective, and satisfy his/her interests and needs. The child trusts himself/herself. Both aspects result in a positive outlook on the world and oneself, a readiness to give and take in relationships, to receive and maintain.

13. The attachment theory by Bowlby (1987) allows for elaboration on many interesting emotional phenomena, such as separation and loss (see Bowlby's vols. 2 and 3 of *Attachment and Loss*), or homesickness as an indication of too little attachment instead of too much. Bowlby also clarifies in which sense attachment has to be distinguished from concepts like dependence or (striving for) sexual contact.

311

The child values himself/herself and develops a basic feeling of self-trust and self-esteem. The alternative is distrust and suspicion, in which the basic feeling is one of being able to rely only on oneself. It is very important that adults, especially the caregivers to whom the child is attached, possess self-trust and self-esteem themselves, because they socialize to the child who they are, how they are, and what they are. Such socialization of reliability and trust, which in most cases happens quite unconsciously, is more important than manifest signs of caring for the child's food, clothing, and so on, or intentional demonstrations of love (Erikson 1963, 249). The psychiatrist Van den Berg even claims that distrust and suspicion of others and oneself are not the result of too little love from the mother (or other caregivers), but of too much love that is demonstrated in isolation, separate from the person's normal interactions with the child, which can easily be inauthentic, artificial, and inhibiting love (Van den Berg 1958).

What all this means can be illustrated from the happenings during November 1994 in Union, South Carolina, that I read about in the newspapers. Susan Vaughan Smith, a young mother, went to the police saying that her car had been stolen and her two boys, 3 and 14 months, kidnapped by an African-American. After some investigation, she confessed to killing her two toddlers. Strapped in their car seats, the boys drowned after their mother put her car in gear and sent them down a ramp into John D. Long Lake. Remarkably, families with small children have flocked to Union to visit the murder site since. The media have carried stories and photographs. One of them showed a 3-year-old kneeling next to the shoreline, "reflecting," according to the caption. A 5-year-old girl clutched her daddy's hand and stared at the greenish water. "You know what I told my mama?" the child apparently said to the reporter, "I told her, you go out driving and you better take a gun." "We told her it was the mama," the father said, "and she just hung her head. She can believe a stranger would do something bad but not a baby's mama." Here the point is not only the mother's killing but also taking the children to the murder site. Children suffer from irrational fears that can be assuaged only by the confidence that their parents are there for them. In no child's world — in not even his/her worst nightmare — should a mommy kill her children. To deprive them of their single most important connection to trust, hope, and security is to leave them emotionally marooned. Forcing a frightened child to visit the death site is to abandon him/her to nightmares that no one may assuage, especially the people who took him/her there. The media play a key role in that situation because they make money off people's tragedies; by showing the places of emergency time and again, they attach people, including their children, to these places, and this attachment contributes to feelings of insecurity, lack of safety, and distrust.

312

Empathy and Sympathy

In empirical theory and research, empathy and sympathy are seen as fundamental for emotional development in general and for developing specific emotions in particular. They begin to be established at the very beginning of the infant's life. In treating them as emotions, however, I touch on a discussion that I can mention here only in passing. On the one hand, some people say that empathy and sympathy are not emotions because they consist of the cognitive ability to take the other's perspective. Although the other's state may be emotional because he/she may be in a negative state of anger, distress, or disappointment, or in a positive state of happiness, gratitude, or joy, taking this other's perspective is itself a cognitive activity. One cognitively understands the other's emotional state, imagines how he/she feels in that state, and recognizes what factors led to it. One is not affected oneself by these emotions: I do not personally suffer when I understand my neighbor's suffering. Here empathy and sympathy differ from compassion, in which I suffer with my friends and feel the fellowship of the weak. Others see empathy and sympathy as basic altruistic emotions, in which cognitive and affective processes come together and which form the basis for higher moral emotions like pity, compassion, and fellow suffering, as Hoffman (1993) says. A weak point of this argument is that empathy and sympathy have to be distinguished from compassion in the sense that the former may refer, as I said, to openness to a plurality of emotions, including both positive and negative ones, thus perhaps suggesting a merely formal basic cognitive structure, whereas the latter relates to sadness and distress only, thus indicating something substantial that has both cognitive and affective aspects (cf. Lazarus 1991, 289).

The best I can do is simply to refer to Hoffman's empirical description of empathy and sympathy insofar as they relate to another person's distress. This empathy and sympathy for the others' sadness are localized at five developmental levels. They may increase in complexity in the direction of anger, shame, and guilt at the fifth level, as I shall explain. Hoffman's developmental scheme is based on rich theoretical and empirical research, which largely goes beyond the description I give here.[14]

The first level refers mainly to automatic and involuntary affect arousal, albeit possibly mediated by lingual cues. Infants cry when they hear other people (infants, adults) cry. Mimicry, by which the child imitates the other's facial and postural expression, after which the brain processes this

14. Hoffman's latest version of his developmental scheme is summarized here, and the overlap between the levels is left out.

message, produces the emotions of the other in the child. As the child's language mediation develops, verbal cues may evoke emotions that resemble the emotional happenings that were associated with the other's emotions in the recent past. By this language mediation the child is able to take the other's perspective and put himself/herself in the other's place. This can take two forms. The first form is self-focused, whereby the child puts himself/herself in the other's place by imagining what it would mean if the situation of the other were to impinge on himself/herself. The second form is other-focused, because the child imagines how the other feels in this situation. Research shows that children of eleven months are able to function at this level.

Whereas the first level already contains some cognitive aspects, which are implied in the language mediation of emotions, the second level is explicitly cognitive, and consists essentially of two important other-focused aspects. The first aspect is concerned with the other as having internal states that are independent of the child's own internal states. The second aspect goes further than the here and now, and relates to the other as having experiences that go beyond the immediate situation and stem from the other's biography.

The third level is primarily affective in nature. It consists of two important aspects. First, the other is felt as experiencing and going through his/her emotions. The second aspect again goes beyond the other's emotional here-and-now situation. In it, the other's emotions are understood as emerging from biographical experiences from the present on back through early childhood. This empathetic capacity can be found among two- to three-year-olds.

At the fourth level empathy is transformed into partial sympathy. This happens when the child experiences a feeling of compassion for the other who suffers from negative feelings like sadness, unhappiness, hopelessness, grief, misery, or loneliness. Sympathy goes along with the desire to help the other — the child feels sorry for the other. How this transformation from empathy into sympathy takes place is not easy to explain. Perhaps an additional concept like model learning, which stems from social learning theory, may explain it. When the child is treated by his/her significant others, especially the caretaker, who in most cases is (still) the mother, in a sympathetic, caring, and loving way, the child will imitate this behavior with regard to the caretaker and transfer it from him/her to other people (Spiecker 1991, 31-32).

At the fifth level causal attribution takes place, which means that the child is asking who is to blame for the distress the other is going through. The kind of attribution the child makes determines which other emotion or emotions combine with the empathy/sympathy emotion. Three kinds of attributions are possible. The first is that no specific person is held to cause the other's distress, which means that nobody can be blamed for it. The other is considered simply as a random victim, as in the case of illness or a natural disaster. This reinforces the sympathetic distress. Here the idea of fate, which strikes arbitrarily, may emerge. The second possible attribution is that someone else is seen as causing the situation that evokes the distress. This attribution leads to anger. Feelings may alternate between sympathetic distress and sympathetic anger. One might also think that the other already has a long relationship with the person causing this distress, and that by failing to leave that person the sufferer now deserves this hurt. This attributive thinking may decrease the sympathetic distress and anger. The third possible attribution is that one sees oneself as having caused the other's distress. This perception can lead to the emotion of shame and guilt. Shame relates to the perceived loss of self-esteem and social esteem, whereas guilt has to do with the awareness that one has neglected moral values like caring and love and transgressed moral rules in not treating the other humanely. Shame and guilt may also emerge when one becomes aware that one did nothing to prevent the other's distress. In that case we may speak of shame by passivity and guilt by inactivity.

According to this theory, empathy has to be distinguished from sympathy in that the former is more cognitive and the latter more affective in character. This distinction explains the difference between psychopaths and psychologically more or less healthy people. The first group is able to develop empathy only, not sympathy, whereas the second is able to feel both empathy and sympathy. Psychopaths fall short of feeling the emotions of another as an other. They do not emotionally know pity, compassion, and fellow suffering, although they may wear the mask of sanity, suggesting that they emotionally care for other people. They may be driven by Machiavellian values, by which they manipulate others out of intelligently calculated self-interest (Spiecker 1991, 54-65).

Sense of Justice

While empathy and sympathy are already subject to debate because some authors, as we have seen, consider them to be not emotions but rather cognitive dispositions, the question of whether justice is an emotion is still more debatable. Even if justice did have an emotional aspect, this would not exhaust its broad, deep, and rich content, which also contains cognitive, attitudinal, and action-directed aspects. The cognitive aspect refers to, for instance, knowing and being able to apply the principles of distributive and social justice in specific situations. The attitudinal aspect relates to the conviction that it is good to be — or perhaps better, to become — a just person. The action-directed aspect has to do with readiness to act in such a way that one's own good and that of others are promoted in a fair way (cf. Rawls 1971, 472-79). Next to these aspects, the emotional load of justice concerns the desire to become a just person, to act justly and make others act justly, and especially to help and support others who suffer from injustice. The sense of justice is a passion for justice (Ricoeur 1992, 198). It emerges when we are confronted with contrast experiences, as I said earlier, and we cry out: "But this is unjust!" The sense of justice implies a regulative idea, which leads to a cry for change and reform when the concrete situation violates the proportional distribution of advantages and burdens among the members of our community. The sense of justice implies a desire for the good life for all (cf. Ricoeur 1992, 201).

In defining the sense of justice in terms of desire, one may wonder why it is unusual to do so. In the classical tradition of scholastic thought, desires are distinguished into two groups: passional desires and rational desires. The former emerge from the person's vital striving for the good life, whereas the latter refer to striving to realize values like happiness and love (Dent 1984). From this perspective human rationality and human desiring go together, as the term *rational desires* shows. Since Descartes they have tended to lose sight of each other, although Rawls (1971, 567) also sees the sense of justice as a rational desire, albeit in the context of his contract idea of justice. When we consider how, in Kantian thinking over the last two centuries, moral theory has been characterized by justice as a rational principle only, not to be disturbed by emotional arousal, we see that this classical tradition has almost totally disappeared. In the Aristotelian approach to justice as a virtue, it is impossible to overlook the relationship between human rationality, the passions, and the just act. The just act presupposes that the passions are rationally informed and ordered in such a way that they contribute to the telos of the polis. Being rationally informed and ordered implies, first, that the passions do not distract the agent from doing justice. If they did, Aristotle would call the agent a weak person *(akratic):* he/she does not (yet) own his/her passions. Second, and at the other extreme, the passions must not be tamed so strongly that they disappear altogether. Aristotle calls this person too strong *(enkratic)* because he/she killed his/her passions. The "Aristotelian mean" exists anywhere in between these two extremes. The just person acts justly out of his/her passions, which are those of the wholly virtuous person. The passions are part of the person's overall orientation toward virtue — passions are virtuous passions, they are passions for virtues (MacIntyre 1988, 108, 112, 128). All this is implied in the passion for justice.

Still another, more deep-rooted reason why we have lost sight of the emotional dimension of justice has to do with the dialectic relationship between the self and others. When the self is understood as a monadic self, which has its very basis in its isolated rationality, others function only as other selves, with whom I engage for reasons of shared private, albeit well-conceived and enlightened, interests or necessary cooperation, as is the case in utilitarian or Kantian moral theories. However, when the self is a relational self, which is constituted in and through the embedding community with others, then the existential search for answers to personal questions with regard to myself ("who am I" and "what do I live for") and others ("who are you" and "what do you live for") belong to the very essence of living together (cf. Sandel 1992, 133-74). In such processes of mutual self-understanding, which take place in interpersonal and intrapersonal conversations, the passion for justice arises. "Justice is to the other" *(Justitia est ad alterum)*: Justice is what is rightly owed to the other, as Thomas says (*STh* II-II, 58.2). It is a continuous orientation to render to the other the part that is due or owed to him/her (MacIntyre 1988, 198-99). It consists of "wanting to be fair with our friends and wanting to give justice to those we care for" (Rawls 1971, 570), but is not restricted to "me" and "you," because it includes also the anonymous member of my community, the unknown "he" or "she," whom I reach through the mediation of just institutions, for which I desire to take responsibility too (Ricoeur 1992).

The passion for justice quite naturally emerges and develops from these processes of reciprocal self-understanding, which are based on mutual attachment and emotional bonds. It particularly emerges from empathy, especially sympathy. Sympathy is not a detached, neutral, or impartial way of taking the perspective of the other. It allows me to "participate empathically in another's experience: their suffering, pain, humiliation, and frustrations, as well as their joy, fulfillment, plans, and hopes. . . . Passion is the basis of our noninstrumental relations to others, and it takes us beyond fixed character, social roles, and institutional arrangements" (Johnson 1993, 200). It is not restricted to the small, local communities of family, neighborhood, or peers, but extends to the greater community of fellow sufferers beyond the local boundaries. If one restricts justice to a rational principle, and reduces it to a negative procedure aimed at preventing damage to our self-interest, "we lose a great deal of its resonance and promise. We fail to garner the psychological and intellectual benefits that come from receiving justice and doing justice. Most important, we miss the full contribution justice can make to the enrichment and enlargement of community" (Selznick 1992, 431).

317

It is easy to see why the passion for justice emerges, as I said, from the emotions of empathy and sympathy and why they form its very basis. For example, the passion for distributive justice may arise when I feel sympathy for a person who suffers from lack of a social benefit to which he/she is entitled. The passion for commutative justice may arise when I feel sorry for a person who is wrongly treated in an exchange of benefits and costs with another person. The passion for social justice may develop when I feel sad for people whose primary needs are not satisfied, even though all purely juridical regulations have been fulfilled. In these cases in which one is confronted with fellow human beings who have been the victims of injustice, one is likely to stand up, protest, and advocate for them. These forms of justice may also have a clear dimension of caring, solidarity, or other so-called supererogatory acts, which all belong in effect to the sense of justice. In empirical research, a positive correlation is found between the degree of sympathy on the one hand and preferences for need-based forms of justice, say, social justice, on the other (Hoffmann 1993, 168). A possible explanation for this empirical finding is that the passion for justice is based on the emotions of empathy and sympathy, because it relates to the emotional tendency to be affectionately involved in and effectively caring for others' well-being. This process is surely reinforced when caretakers and other adults model this passion for justice and make explicit to children the principles of justice that govern this passion (Spiecker 1991, 32).

Shame and Guilt

Western thought about shame and guilt is strongly influenced by Freud's psychodynamic theory, in which the key role is played by the triune self. This triune self, which consists of the id, ego, and superego, represents three different but interrelated psychic dynamics, which organize one's emotional economy in life (Freud 1984, 339-408).

The id represents the collection of instincts or instinctive drives, which relate to or even stem from the animal, physical side of the human person. These are drives like hunger, thirst, and sex.[15] In a more general

---

15. Whether sex is an instinct or an instinctive drive, and if so, to what extent, is a subject of debate. Some people suggest that religion is also an instinctive drive, which at least partially rules us independently from our rational insights and free choices. But then the term *instinct* is taken in a metaphorical sense, as the adjective *instinctive* already implies (cf. Berger 1972).

sense they also include libidinal and aggressive impulses, like eros and thanatos. When the id satisfies its needs, it operates according to what Freud calls the pleasure principle. Society tries to control and even domesticate the id because its libidinal and aggressive impulses embody an anarchic power that could destroy everything in human culture. Civilization was invented, as it were, to control this power, to refrain and restrict the id by suppressing its impulses, a process that, however, violates the pleasure principle. That is why Freud speaks of "civilization and its discontents" (1961). Civilization does not completely succeed in controlling the id, however, because at an unconscious level the impulses creep out through gaps in the armor of civilization.

The superego refers to the dimension of the self in which the demands of civilized society are internalized and interiorized. This means that they are seen as norms that, although coming from the outside, are worthy of being accepted and integrated in such a way that a coherent belief and norm system emerges and develops. The commandments and prohibitions as well as the positive sanctions (reward) and negative sanctions (punishments) that accompany these norms are seen as precious moral rules. In Freud's view, together they form the moral conscience. This moral conscience ensures that transgression of the norms leads to the emotions of shame and guilt. That is, the punishment that comes from the outside is complemented by the punishment from the inside. In shame and guilt the person punishes himself/herself. This punishment is a complex phenomenon in which the person plays different roles. The person is not only his/her own judge, but by judging his/her own moral crime, he/she looks at himself/herself as his/her own moral victim and imposes his/her own sentence, according to his/her own attorney's request (cf. Fotion 1968).

It is the ego's task to regulate the impulses coming from the id and the internalized demands of society coming from the superego. The ego operates according to the reality principle, by which the libidinal and aggressive drives on the one hand and the internalized norms and rules on the other are held in a dynamic equilibrium. The ego functions on the basis of feedback. When the id pushes too strongly in the direction of eros and thanatos, the ego pulls back with the help of society's principles and rules as represented by the superego, and vice versa. The ego is equally in touch with the id as it is with the superego.

In this theory of the triune self, the development of ego is the key factor in becoming a real self. The ego regulates the interaction between the needs of the id and the superego. It is not identical with the self, but is the ordering principle of the self, which consists of the id and the superego as well as the ego. The ego accepts the drives coming from the id as far as possible. This might very well include delaying satisfying them, but without totally suppressing them. It also accepts societal rules and norms from the superego, but without totally being emotionally dependent on group pressure, cultural convention, and conformity. In freedom, the ego satisfies bodily and societal needs; in sovereignty it rules over their pressures. The ego is "an agency of fulfillment tempered by realism" (Selznick 1992, 156).

From this point of view shame and guilt are, as I said, the expression of inner punishment, which is caused by the pressure of conventional norms and rules taken from the cultural environment. Shame means that I want to hide myself from other people because of the transgression I committed, and guilt means that I blame myself for this transgression. Ego has to liberate itself from the domination of which shame and guilt are the emotional inclination, without however giving up the justifiable demands of society. Shame and guilt must be transformed into realistic engagement in societal tasks and challenges, which are balanced against the needs of the internal drives. Shame and guilt are thus seen as two sides of the same coin, the bill to be paid for group pressure and cultural convention. Shame is self-hiding punishment and guilt self-blaming punishment. Psychoanalysis helps develop a healthy and mature ego by transforming the cultural debt into a credit of freedom and autonomy. Shame and guilt, freedom and autonomy are negatively correlated. The more shame and guilt, the less freedom and autonomy, and vice versa.

Freud's psychodynamic theory, as I said, has been very influential in the definition, interpretation, and evaluation of shame and guilt. They are considered neurotic phenomena, something to be liberated from. But more recent historical and empirical research shows that we need to redefine, reinterpret, and reevaluate the emotions of shame and guilt.

First, shame and guilt are not two sides of the same coin, and they do not have exclusively sexually connotations, as has often been assumed in the past. True, the Greek *aidos*, meaning "shame," is indeed connected to the term for the genitals, and guilt — especially in Roman Catholic confessional praxis — is often associated with sexual lust and abuse. Shame, however, has to do with being seen crying, which may happen when I lose control over myself, as when positive or negative emotions overwhelm me, or when I am in a situation in which I lose social recognition, reputation, and power. Guilt relates to bad, wrong, or unjust acts toward another person, which may take place in many areas, for instance, commerce, education, work, or recreation.

Second, shame and guilt develop in certain stages. Therefore shame and guilt are not necessarily neurotic. Rather, one can speak of stages of development of shame and guilt, and even of the possibility of healthy and mature shame and guilt.

We will look first at the differences between shame and guilt, and then examine the stages of each. These are considered without explicit reference to more general moral developmental stages of emotional, moral, or even cognitive structures. Whereas Kohlberg (1984, 65-66) localizes guilt at the conventional and postconventional stages of general moral development, and Rawls (1971, 442ff., 486) interprets both shame and guilt in the context of the totality of his three moral stages of general moral development, I restrict my analysis to the stages of development of shame and guilt in themselves.

The differences between shame and guilt are, first of all, sense-based, that is, based on the difference between seeing and hearing. Shame arises when one is seen naked, exposed, by the wrong people, in the wrong condition, whereas guilt is rooted in hearing the voice of one's own judgment. Further, shame results in a desire to hide oneself from view and even to disappear, by which shame may decrease and lessen. It emerges from the vital emotion of self-protection. Guilt is different, in that the inner voice would continue to speak even if I were to hide or disappear. Moreover, the other in whose presence I feel shame may express contempt or derision or avoid me altogether. This is not only because I did something wrong or failed to do something, but also because there is some failing, some defect, in me. Guilt results from an act or omission, not a defect. When I feel guilt, I expect to elicit the other's anger, resentment, indignation, or punishment. Lastly, the inclination to hide in shame can be seen as an endeavor to protect one's self-esteem or social esteem. The healing comes from myself, my own external or internal actions. Guilt can only be expiated by reparation of the damage that my act or omission has caused. This reparation can take the form of compensation or healing. This healing can be brought about by forgiveness. Shame, however, cannot be healed by forgiveness. Shame has to do not with the other against whom I did wrong, but with myself, my self-esteem, and social esteem. Forgiveness can silence the inner voice of guilt, but it cannot raise my estimation of myself. However, these differences do not mean that shame and guilt cannot go hand in hand. They often do. For instance, when we let someone down, we may feel shame because we have failed to meet our own standards, upon which our self-esteem depends, and we may also feel guilty because we did damage to the other's justifiable interest. Shame and guilt relate to two dimensions of the self: the former to the relation of the self to the inner world of self-esteem and social esteem, the latter to the relation of the self to the outer world.

Some subtle distinctions need to be made with regard to shame.

Generally speaking, there are two forms of shame. The first is outer-directed shame, meaning that I feel shame out of fear that others will negatively evaluate me, leading to a denigration of that part of my self-esteem which is dependent on social esteem. Thus it is other-directed self-esteem that is at the basis of this shame. The other whose negative evaluation I fear may also be internalized and localized within myself, especially a significant other like my internalized father, mother, wife, husband, friend, teacher, or minister. In that case, however, the shame is still other-directed, even though the significant others are looking at me from within. It is still they who determine me and dominate my emotion of shame. It is an internalized, repute-based form of shame. The second form of shame is purely inner-directed. It is engendered by a failure to meet the standards that I set within myself for myself, and it is detached from how other people, even significant others, might react to me. Even in this pure inner-directed shame, however, my significant others are present. I engage in an internal dialogue with them, intrapersonally pursuing the interpersonal conversation with them about my failure to meet my own standards. In this dialogue they do not impose their expectations on me but exchange their perceptions and ideas with me, as I do with them. I respect them and they respect me. From this dialogue, self-respect emerges, integrity arises, purity grows, honor develops. In this process, the negative orientation of shame as self-protection transforms into a positive orientation as intersubjectivity-based self-actualization (Williams 1993, 88-102).[16]

This analysis explains why some scholars in the field of emotional development distinguish between at least two stages of shame, heteronomous and autonomous shame, or inauthentic and authentic shame. The first element of both of these pairs refers to what I called other-directed shame, in which "the other" includes the internalized other or others who determine my emotion of self-esteem. The second element of each pair relates to the internal dialogue between myself and my significant other(s) within myself, from which my intersubjectivity-based emotion of self-respect and self-esteem emerges (cf. Spiecker 1991, 40-53).[17]

16. This presentation of shame is much more subtle than Rawls's (1971, 444ff.) distinction between natural and moral shame, of which the former relates to the loss of self-respect and the latter to the loss of social esteem.

17. Here I follow Spiecker's (1991, 40-53) dichotomy instead of Kekes's trichotomy of shame related to decency, honor, and value (fatsoen-, eer-, en waardeschaamte), because Piaget's original dichotomy "heteronomy/autonomy" seems more valid to me than any other distinction. This also applies to my criticism with regard to Kohlberg's trichotomy, especially his distinction between preconventional/conventional and conventional/postconventional (see Chap. 5).

Parallel to these two stages of shame, two stages of guilt may be distinguished: heteronomous and autonomous guilt, or inauthentic and authentic guilt. The first element of both of these pairs relates to guilt in which the fear of anger, resentment, indignation, punishment, or recrimination predominates. The second is a sense of remorse for the damage my action or omission caused to the other's justifiable interest and well-being. It implies an inclination to repair the damage and to heal the relationship that has been broken or at least put at risk.[18]

One final remark about shame and guilt must be added here, concerning Freud and his influence into our days. Freud suggests that shame and guilt must be seen as intrapsychic mechanisms or strategies by which the drives or instincts of sex and aggression, eros and thanatos, are suppressed. Paradoxically, because of this Freudian definition and interpretation of shame and guilt, it is not far-fetched to say that in our own time, shame and guilt are themselves suppressed. Indeed, what we see is a remarkable cultural shift. Because Freud warned against shame and guilt suppressing and killing all kinds of emotions, especially libidinal ones, we now have to warn against the suppression of shame and guilt themselves. This suppression can lead to the same pathological consequences that Freud identified in relation to the suppressed libidinal emotions. These consequences may be seen in the products of defense mechanisms such as repression, rationalization, projection, compensation, displacement, and minimization (cf. Uleyn 1969).

Sex and Love

The nature of sex and sexual emotion are difficult to define. Sexual passion covers a broad area, encompassing a number of dimensions, functions, orientations, and approaches. The dimensions of sex are physical, psychic, social, and cultural. Sex may be used as relief for physical arousal, alleviation of psychic distress, play in social encounters, or compliance with a cultural or subcultural convention. The functions of sex are the three Rs: reproductive, relational, and recreational. Its aim can be procreation, intimacy, or lust. Sex may be interpersonal, autopersonal, or nonpersonal in orientation. It may take place in monogamous or nonmonogamous marital, cohabitational or noncohabitational, long-term or short-term relationships, or as autoerotic activity. Approaches to understanding sex may be biological,

18. Here again I follow Piaget's original dichotomy and not Rawls's trichotomy (Rawls 1971, 467); see n. 17 above.

psychological, or sociological. The sexual passion can be seen as a sexual drive, which builds up sexual tension to which sexual satiation functions as an outlet. It also can be interpreted as psychologically learned behavior, which can be gradually reinforced or extinguished. Lastly it can be sociologically studied from the point of view of scripting theory, choice theory, network theory, and life-course theory. Scripting theory emphasizes the culturally or subculturally determined sexual patterns and scripts of sexual emotion and conduct, leaving some space for the individual's own creativity. Economic choice theory explains what sexual goals people aim at, which resources (time, energy, relationships, money) they use to reach them, how they solve problems relating to the scarcity of these resources, what benefit they gain, what uncertainty and risk are involved, and how all this affects their sexual conduct on the market for sex partners. The network theory localizes sexual conduct within the relationships people maintain with others of varying social characteristics. The life-course theory looks at age not as a biological but as a social and cultural factor, in terms of the cohort or generation to which people belong, especially during their formative years (Laumann et al. 1994, 3-34).

One might say that where these dimensions, functions, and orientations, which can be studied according to various approaches, intersect, we touch on the area of sexual passion. However, the question is whether each of these dimensions, functions, and orientations is a necessary and/or sufficient condition for sexual passion to come into being, and if not, which of them can be left out and why. Since this question is too complicated to be adequately dealt with in this chapter, which is concerned with emotions from a moral perspective in the realm of moral education, I restrict myself to discussing sexual passion in general terms, as an area where the aforementioned dimensions, functions, and orientations touch on each other, without any further qualification as yet, and to presenting some moral considerations according to which this sexual passion can be interpreted and evaluated. The moral aspects I refer to here are empathy and sympathy, justice, shame and guilt, and love.

Empathy and sympathy must be considered very important to interpersonal sexual passion. Empathy and sympathy involve taking the perspective of the other in order cognitively and especially affectively to understand and to feel the emotional processes the other is going through. In sex, this can include an understanding of whether and how the sexual activity fits into the partner's ego-identity and personal biography, as he/she experiences them at the moment. Empathy and sympathy are also important in that they prevent the actor from entering into the partner's intimacy when he/she does not wish it. They inhibit psychic violence, coercion, and instrumental use of the partner, ensure respect for the partner, and promote his/her freedom, ego-identity, and self-esteem. They facilitate true equality and mutuality between the partners.

Here the passion for justice can play its role. Justice is about rendering to the other what is due or owed to him/her. This especially refers to commutative and need-oriented justice, which implies cosuffering and fellow suffering. It aims at solidarity and advocacy, and touches the supererogatory act of surrender. Together with empathy and sympathy this need-oriented justice reaches into the realm of love, in which the other as other is respected and celebrated, and his/her well-being is intrinsically cared for as an end in itself, for that person's own sake. Love happens when people whisper into each other's ears, sharing the common finiteness, contingency, and fragility of human existence (Ricoeur 1992).

Although shame is not restricted to sex, as I said, it is not without relevance to sex either. Shame has to do with self-protection in terms of self-esteem, at least in its stage of autonomy and authenticity. All activities that are undertaken out of sexual passion may be evaluated against whether they evoke shame in its autonomous and authentic stage, that is, whether a specific sexual activity hurts or advances the person's own self-esteem. Can one look at oneself in the mirror without wishing to hide or disappear from one's own sight? To which degree are one's own integrity, honesty, and authenticity either promoted or damaged? This is a question that may be asked about all kinds of interpersonal and autopersonal activities.

Let me take masturbation as an example. From history we know that, until the eighteenth century, masturbation was sometimes mildly condemned, sometimes tolerated, and sometimes even recommended. Masturbation among youth in particular was not seen as important enough to be seriously discussed. From the eighteenth century onward this situation changed in that masturbation came to be diagnosed as damaging because it was seen either as a sin in the religious meaning of the word or a moral transgression, or as a psychic weakness or even illness. In the second half of our century, the situation again changes. The social historian Van Ussel, who has conducted historical research into what he calls "the antisexual syndrome," comments on this change: "And in the same way that masturbation in the eighteenth century was fought without any evidence of its harmfulness, so we see today that masturbation is called harmless without the necessary evidence being brought forward for it either" (Van Ussel 1977a, 258). From the most comprehensive sex research, which was conducted in the United States at the beginning of the nineties, we learn that almost 50 percent of women and more than 60 percent of men reported having masturbated in the past year; 7.6 percent of the women and 26.7

percent of the men said they did it once a week. The researchers also found that masturbation is less frequent among young adults age 18-24 than among adults age 25-34, increases with educational level, and does not necessarily decrease when a stable sexual relationship with a partner has been achieved. Among those who masturbate once a week, the percentage who are affiliated with a Christian church is clearly lower than the percentage of nonchurch members — between 9 percent and 18 percent lower — although with liberal and moderate Protestants and Catholics the difference is clearly less than with the members of Protestant evangelical and fundamentalist churches. Nevertheless, the researchers found that masturbation is not without feelings of ambivalence. On the one hand, people gave a number of positive reasons for masturbation: 73 percent of the men and 63 percent of the women said it relieves sexual tension, 40 percent of the men and 42 percent of the women cited physical pleasure, 26 percent of the men and 32 percent of the women said they do it to relax, and 16 percent of the men and 12 percent of the women said it helps them sleep. On the other hand, about half the population — 54 percent of the men and 47 percent of the women — reported feeling guilty after masturbating. Interestingly, men who belong to a Christian church feel more guilty than those who do not belong, whereas with women it is different: women who are Protestant feel less guilty than those who are Catholic or not connected with any Christian church (Laumann et al. 1994, 82, table 3.1). One wonders whether what the researchers call "feeling guilty" is in fact a feeling of shame, especially since, in their more popularized version of their research report, they connect feeling guilty with social condemnation, which, as I explained earlier, is an aspect of shame related to social esteem, not guilt (cf. Michael et al. 1994, 166). In any case, the researchers felt masturbation to be the most sensitive topic in their sex survey, not only because it made respondents as well as interviewers the most uncomfortable, but also because government officials insisted that questions about masturbation be left out of the questionnaire (Laumann et al. 1994, 69). They described their overall finding in this area as follows: "Masturbation has the peculiar status of being both highly stigmatized and fairly commonplace" (Laumann et al. 1994, 81). This observation, made in the mid-nineties, may be taken as an indication of a high degree of ambivalence with regard to masturbation. To my mind, the main question about masturbation is not whether it is a sin, an illness, a sign of social or psychic incompetence, a lack of willpower, or an appropriate form of sexual expression for adolescents and people with or without sex partners. The main issue is to what degree it is free of shame, of authentic shame, of self-directed shame. From a moral point of view, only well-formed, well-ordered, self-directed, self-esteem-based shame is a reliable indicator for evaluating activity related to sexual passion. When one's own integrity, honesty, and authenticity are at risk, the emotion of shame is of informative value. It indicates when one is transgressing the boundaries of self-directed self-esteem. Emphasizing authentic shame as a moral criterion at least relativizes the idea that masturbation is a kind of less perfect sex, as some people say (cf. Spiecker 1991, 80).

Not only shame but guilt too can function as an evaluative criterion for activity related to sexual passion. With guilt, the other enters the picture. We therefore have to distinguish between inauthentic and authentic guilt. Guilt is inauthentic when it is a fear of being punished, isolated, or abandoned because of the sexual activities that I undertake with my partner. Authentic guilt arises when I feel sorry for my harming my partner's justifiable interest and well-being. Authentic guilt is other-directed guilt, which hinges on respect and love for the partner. Moral education must develop this authentic guilt in children, students, and adults, because it can function as a reliable indicator of well-doing or evil-doing, of right-doing or wrong-doing toward one's partner. An especially striking finding of the sex research project was in the area of "forced sex." About 22 percent of the women studied reported having been forced to perform an unwanted sexual act. These women were found to be less happy in general, and reported that their emotional problems interfered with sex in the last year. The disparity between the experience of women who were sexually coerced and that of men performing this coercive sex is apparent from the fact that only about 3 percent of the men admitted to performing coercive sex acts. It must be borne in mind that "coercive sex" is broader than "rape" as legally defined or as experienced by women (Laumann et al. 1994, 333-39).

The most decisive moral point of view for the interpretation and evaluation of sexual passion and conduct is love. My presupposition is that sex and love belong together — as I have already indicated by entitling this section "Sex and Love" — at least in the sense that sex can be a fundamental aspect of love. In this frame of reference, sex can be morally interpreted from the perspective of love, because they constitute a part/whole relationship.

Before deriving conclusions from this part/whole relationship, however, it is necessary to clarify the implications of this insight. In literature three dimensions of love are distinguished: intimacy, passion, and commitment. Various combinations of these dimensions produce different forms of love. The first form contains only one dimension, the second and third each consist of two dimensions, and the fourth encompasses all three dimensions together (Lazarus 1991, 275).

The first form is characterized by intimacy but without passion or commitment. It is called liking, and consists of feelings of closeness, attachment, and warmth toward another person. It may happen among neighbors, colleagues, or acquaintances who feel attracted and attached to each other.

The second form is romantic love, which combines intimacy and passion but without commitment. People "fall in love" and take part in one another's experiences and feelings, but do not deeply engage in the other person's real well-being for a long period of time. Romantic love is described in plays, movies, novels, and poems.

The third form combines intimacy and commitment but without passion, and can be called companionate love. People are companions in life, for better and worse. They affectionately know they are committed to support one another in their dramatic paths through life. This companionate love is characteristic of the relationship between parents and children, or between close friends.

The last form combines all three dimensions, that is, intimacy, passion, and commitment. This is known as consummate love. Although all three angles of the triangle play a role in this type of love, the emphasis may vary from case to case, as couples vary in the sense that intimacy may be deeply or superficially felt, passion strongly or weakly expressed, and commitment seriously or provisionally promised and acted on.

From this analysis, sex can be a constitutive aspect of love, a part of love. This part/whole relationship may lead to and form the basis of the moral insight that sex should be embedded in the wider horizon of love, oriented toward love, and guided by love. For the sake of illustration, I wish to restrict this insight to the claim that sexual passion as an emotion should be connected with love as an emotion. I mean this claim to be a general one, without taking into account all singularities of all concrete situations characterized by human fragility and contingency, in which this claim may be only partially and fragmentarily true.

Nevertheless, this general claim needs some clarification, because it is not immediately clear that love is necessarily an emotion. Is love an emotion or an attitude or, in more traditional terms, something that belongs to the realm of the passions or the will, desires, or virtues? When two people are asked whether they love each other, in a particular situation at a particular moment in time, their answer will depend on how they feel. If their answer is negative, it may be because they feel emotions other than just love. This also applies to couples who have been at least seemingly happily married: "In a genuine love relationship, some of the time — and in spite of the tendency of poets to idealize it — there will be hope, passion, anger, indifference, boredom, guilt, distress, and even love, depending on the moment and day to day patterns of interaction with the partner" (Lazarus 1991, 274-75). In other words, love can be seen as just an emotion among other emotions, although being an emotion does not exhaust the essence of love.

What do we really mean by the general claim "sexual passion should be connected with love as an emotion"? Rather than clarifying all possible aspects of this statement, I will give just a few examples, which show how sexual passion is related to love as an emotion. Let me start with situations in which emotions other than love dominate the relationship, for example, emotions of rivalry such as jealousy and envy. Jealousy refers to another person having and enjoying something or someone that in the recent past belonged to me ("he has run off with my friend"), whereas envy is what we feel when we see another person having and enjoying something or someone that we do not have ("she is popular, I am not"). Both jealousy and envy may cause anger, despair, distress, or hate, and lead to a quarrel between the partners (Frijda 1993, 70-87). A quarrel always has some aspects of a struggle for possession, power, and reputation, which stem from the classic triad of human desires of having *(avoir),* power *(pouvoir),* and honor *(valoir),* which Ricoeur (1968, 183-84) owes to Kant's anthropology *(Habsucht, Herrschsucht, Ehrsucht).* It is always characterized by reproaches the partners make to each other: relative reproaches ("you did something wrong"), absolute reproaches ("you always do this wrong"), character reproaches ("you have a bad character trait" or "you have a bad character altogether"), family reproaches ("your mother was just the same"), or inauthenticity reproaches ("you said this, but did that"). The importance of these reproaches depends not on their seriousness but on the degree to which they inhibit the partner from reacting and defending, the degree to which they overpower, overwhelm, and—as it were—kill the partner (Frijda 1993, 88-105). Although in situations like these the partners may intensely hate each other, this does not mean the end of love, because the opposite of love is not hate but indifference, while hate always presupposes some form of emotional connectedness (May 1986). In this kind of situation, in which the relationship is blocked, longing for sex and making sexual advances neglect and deny the real emotions of the partner—or even both partners. A cooling off is needed, a breakthrough, or a first step toward bridging, which is not possible without some authentic insight into the wrong I myself have committed. This insight requires some degree of critical self-analysis and self-reflection, which in traditional terms is called remorse, and which may lead to breaking through the burden of guilt, forgiveness, and reconciliation. This does not mean that we forget what happened, but demands something difficult and authentic: that we clarify our own and the other's part, how our part and the other's part were mixed up by acts and facts, liberty and tragedy, or freedom and fate, so that we may accept each other as we are in this mixture of strength and weakness. In these situations, this mutual acceptance is the necessary condition for sex to be connected with love as an emotion. This mutual acceptance is love.

Does this breaking through the burden of guilt and forgiving mean abandoning oneself? Does it mean giving up care for oneself, self-esteem, or self-love? Does taking the first step toward reconciliation imply self-effacement, self-abnegation, or self-starvation? These questions touch on the difficult relation between other-love and self-love, between natural love and supererogatory love, as Rawls (1971, 114-17) might call it, or between equal regard and agape, as it is sometimes called in the Christian tradition. Let us examine these last two terms, equal regard and agape, in order to clarify what love might ultimately mean (cf. Browning 1989, 117-60; 1995, 260-62).

The fundamental problem here is that modern psychology, especially humanistic psychology, emphasizes self-actualization and accords great importance to self-regard, as I pointed out in Chapter 6. At the other extreme, some forms of modern philosophy and theology focus on the moral appeal emanating from the face of the other as the other in his/her alterity, and the moral obligation emerging from this appeal. Agape may be understood as taking the appeal of the other as the ultimate perspective from which to live one's life. While humanistic psychology emphasizes self-regard and some moral philosophy and theology accord priority to other-regard, the concept of equal regard tries to bridge both extremes.

Equal regard means that every human person deserves to be respected in his/her dignity as a human person, as an end in himself/herself, not only as a means, as Kant would say. From a Christian point of view, every person deserves this respect because every person is God's own creation and a subject of God's unending love. Human beings are lovable because God loves them. This does not mean that one should love the other in order to love God, as if the other were an instrument for achieving the love of God and not an end in itself. This would negate real love for the other. No, this statement means exactly what it says: people are lovable because God loves them (cf. Rahner 1965).

Because this applies to every human being, including oneself, we can say also that other-regard and self-regard are not opposites but aspects of the same human dignity deriving from the same divine creation and divine love. Because both "I" and "you" are divine creations, we deserve equal regard. But does this equal regard not preclude taking the first step, breaking through the burden of guilt, and forgiving? Does it not preclude agape as a supererogatory act, which is an act of grace that cannot be required but only given and received, and which transcends equality and reciprocity?

Here another aspect of equal regard comes into play, which is the relationship between agape and equal regard. Theoretically one might look at this relationship from two different directions: from agape to equal regard, and from equal regard to agape. From the first point of view, agape is the ultimate form of human and Christian living, and in this sense equal regard is seen as at the very most a lower stage of human and Christian perfection. I say "at the very most a lower stage," because some philosophers and theologians, such as Reinhold Niebuhr, take equal regard to be a lower stage of perfection, while others, like Anders Nygren, who coined the conceptual pair "eros and agape," see it as a sign of imperfection, weakness, or even evil (cf. Tafferner 1992, 146-56). If one takes the other point of view and looks at agape from the concept of equal regard, agape can be seen as a specific form of equal regard. The very basis of human and Christian love is mutual love, from which derives supererogatory or sacrificial love. Equal love, then, implies sacrificial love: "We must regard and love the neighbor equally to ourselves, and we must do this even if the neighbor does not respond and does not regard us equally, and in fact, actively works against us" (Browning 1989, 152).

Lastly we must qualify the idea of self-sacrifice in order to avoid certain misunderstandings. These qualifications have to do with approaching agape from the concept of equal regard and not the other way around. The first qualification is that self-sacrifice does not mean submitting to exploitation by the other, because this would harm or violate our own dignity. The second is that we must protect ourselves from being exploited by the other because this would also do damage to the other's dignity (Browning 1989, 155).

Approaching self-sacrifice in terms of equal regard means that taking the first step, breaking through the burden of guilt, and forgiving the other do imply self-sacrifice, but not in the sense that one's self-regard, self-esteem, and well-being are seriously endangered. The concept of equal regard balances between self-regard and other-regard, between eros and agape.

7.3 Emotional Learning

In this chapter I present a cognitive interaction theory of emotions, in which appraisal processes play a key role. The primary appraisal processes are concerned with goal relevance, goal congruence, and ego-involvement. The secondary appraisal processes relate to crediting, coping, and developing future expectancies. Emotions are antecedent, concomitant, and consequent factors in these processes. They inform the person about the meaning of the changing situation. They can be understood in terms of the cognitive interactions between the person and the context that take place in these appraisal processes. Within this frame of reference, emotional formation, which is the subject of this chapter, means advancing these emotional appraisal processes. This advancement can be brought about by stimulating the children's emotional learning processes, which may be divided into observational learning, learning by experience, and concept learning.

By Observation

It is important that children see adults and peers, especially significant others, dealing with emotions. They experience these adults and peers having, expressing, and acting on emotions among themselves and in relation to the children as well. The most basic experiences, as we have already said, are those of attachment and basic trust. These depend on the development of empathy and sympathy. On the one hand, if a child grows up in a family in which significant adults show genuine interest, care, and love for both each other and the child, the child feels joyfully and happily attached to them and derives from that a basic trust in these adults, other people, and also himself/herself. On the other hand, if the little boy or girl grows up in an atmosphere of disinterest, indifference, and suspicion, and frequently confronts emotions like anger, rage, indignation, annoyance, hatred, resentment, and wrath on the part of adults, he/she will lack the bonds of affection, tenderness, intimacy, and compassion that are necessary for healthy emotional development. In an atmosphere of animosity among adults, the positive emotions with which they address the child are felt as inauthentic, dishonest, and artificial. The child needs adults who are caring of each other and caring of the child as well, in a consistent and continuous way. The child should see, feel, and smell: "They care about each other and about me."

This does not mean that negative emotions must not be expressed. On the contrary, they should be expressed as frequently as they are felt and experienced. It would be wrong to suppress them, especially if that were done so as to avoid damaging the child's innocence or serenity. The child consciously or unconsciously senses and experiences the suppressed negative emotions, which then paradoxically damage the child's integrity. The darker sides of living together, as expressed in negative emotions, are part of life, and it is better to be confronted with these negative emotions, prudently expressed, than to have negative emotions artificially suppressed (cf. Jaschke 1974). It is better not to hide from the child the negative emotions that are present in every relationship, even in the "perfect family."

The important thing is how these emotions are expressed, the atmosphere in which this is done, and with what intention. It is important for a child to experience his/her parents dealing with irritation, frustration, and anger toward each other, taking the first step, looking and reflecting from the other's perspective, understanding the other's goals, ideas, and feelings from within, and coming to a cognitive and emotional agreement, or at least to an agreement to disagree, a compromise, that satisfies both parents' goals, values, and norms for the moment, and in doing so breaking through the burden of guilt and striving for reconciliation. In short, it is important for a child to experience his/her parents managing conflicts in a constructive way (Prein 1976). By constructive conflict management I mean that conflicts are treated, if not solved, in a way that prevents them from escalating and damaging both partners' self-esteem. Constructive conflict management can even advance their self-esteem. It requires balancing the two dimensions that characterize every conflict, that is, the objective dimension, which has to do with the object/theme of the conflict and the intersubjective or relational dimension. Different styles of conflict management can be distinguished according to how they treat these dimensions. Ignoring both the objective and intersubjective dimensions leads to flight or laissez-faire behavior. Overemphasizing the objective dimension leads to a likelihood of forcing, whereas overemphasizing the intersubjective dimensions means giving in. A real balance can be reached only by a solution that the parties themselves see as a solution, or by a partial solution that both parties see as a win/win compromise (Blake and Mouton 1984; Rondeau 1990). It is important that the parents' conflicts are dealt with in the children's presence, because this gives the children a chance to experience the different goals, the different goal relevances, the different goal congruencies and incongruencies, and the different ego-involvements that play a role in the conflicts, and learn how their parents deal with those differences. Quite simply, even the most devoted "kangaroo care" will ultimately benefit the child but little if the adults do not care for each other too, and devote the same "kangaroo care," the same positive, constructive attention, to their negative emotions and conflicts, not despite but precisely with an eye to the children's best interest.

By Experience

It is not enough for children to see adults dealing with emotions and with emotions in conflicts. They need to experience these emotions themselves too, in their relationships with their parents and other adults as well as with siblings and peers. This applies to the emotions mentioned in the previous section, like empathy, sympathy, attachment, care, and love, just as it applies to negative emotions like anger, disappointment, sadness, and to emotional conflicts. By way of example, and to avoid unnecessary repetition, I look now at two emotions I did not mention in the previous section: shame and guilt.

Whereas emotions like sadness, anger, and fear make their appearance in the first three to four months of the infant's life, shame emerges later, probably from the age of 18 months on. Shame presupposes the presence of the second appraisal process, especially the capacity of blaming. Blaming is ontogenetically a complex behavior, because it comprises complex processes like establishing goal relevance, goal incongruence, and ego-involvement. Blaming means that goal incongruence is attributed to a specific person — in the case of shame this person is oneself — in relation to another person or group of people — those who see one "naked." It develops only once the child has developed the ability to experience these complex processes among adults and in the adults' relationships with the child. It presupposes a certain level of social, especially interpersonal, learning (Lazarus 1991, 307-15).

Some scholars find it abhorrent that shame should be learned at all, and that moral education should aim to advance this learning. In their view, moral education ought to place as little emphasis as possible on shame and guilt, or even ignore, discredit, and eliminate them. For example, Kekes says: "My reason for the claim that moral progress leads us away from the shame toward other moral responses is that shame undermines self-direction, reduces the chances of moral reform, and weakens our selves" (in Spiecker 1991, 52). My reaction is that this statement should be accepted for what I call inauthentic shame, in which the person fears for his/her reputation in the eyes of others. This kind of shame, in my interpretation, is based on other-directed self-esteem. Moral progress, however, cannot and must not lead us away from what I call authentic shame, which is shame engendered by a failure to meet my own longing for honesty and integrity, which are based on inner-directed self-esteem. The education of shame means to advance the child's transition from the stage of inauthentic to authentic shame.

The transition from inauthentic to authentic shame cannot be made by the child without educational assistance. It requires educational conversation or even educational counseling, which must include a certain mix of nondirective and directive approaches. Nondirective interventions are, for example, mirroring, supporting, cognitive understanding, and emotional understanding of the child's utterances. Directive interventions are questioning, interpreting, exposing, or advising (Stiles 1978). Two extremes that are to be avoided are indoctrinating and manipulating the child on the one hand and neglecting the desirable, gradual transition from inauthentic to authentic shame on the other. I stress the word *gradual* because the transition process can take a long time, even among certain "adults," who have not yet become adults as far as authentic shame is concerned.

What about guilt? As with shame, children from the age of 18 months on can experience guilt because it is predicated on the same blaming process. In the case of guilt, this blaming is not connected with a wish to hide, as if to protect one's integrity, but with a recognition of having harmed the other's interest and well-being. As with shame, from the point of view of moral education the child needs to be educated from the stage of inauthentic guilt, in which the fear of punishment, abandonment, and isolation prevails, to the stage of authentic guilt, in which one feels remorse for the real damage the other has suffered. Whereas inauthentic guilt is based on self-centeredness, authentic guilt is directed toward the other and is for the other's sake. Here, too, the child needs some adult facilitation, which requires a certain mix of the nondirective and the directive approaches.

I would like to warn here that the education of shame and guilt is a precarious and even perilous task. Once again I distinguish between inauthentic and authentic aspects, but this time as they apply to the area of education itself. The education of shame and guilt is inauthentic education when the educator consciously or even unconsciously uses shame and guilt to attain or maintain control and power over the child. By imposing shame and guilt, he or she pushes and pulls the child back into the inauthentic stage of shame and guilt. Authentic education presupposes that the educator, for reasons of the child's development and not for the sake of his own control and power, engages in honest conversations with the child as a means of facilitating the child's transition to a morally healthy life. To do so the educator must be aware of his/her own emotions, especially shame and guilt, listen carefully to them, and discern time and again between their inauthentic and authentic aspects. The education of emotions, especially shame and guilt, is a precarious undertaking because it carries with it a potential for emotional exploitation and abuse of the child. It must be seen as an educational challenge in which the morally healthy development of the child as a precious human being is fundamentally at stake and which requires morally healthy educators.

By Concept

After what I said about emotional learning by observation and experience, it may seem superfluous to look separately at emotional learning by concept.

335

The general advantage of concept learning, however, is that it gives the capacity to abstract from concrete events, situations, and persons, and look at them in a less subjective way. It therefore may reinforce the observational and experiential learning processes with regard to positive and negative emotions. Furthermore, it can help to purify and correct the errors that always creep into these learning processes because of human weakness and frailty, as well as to clarify certain obscure, incomprehensible, or unbelievable aspects of these processes, which might have raised in the child some irritation, frustration, anger, or even hatred.

In order to be effective, conceptual learning in the area of emotions must cover two different aspects: structures and cases. The structures refer to concepts and conceptual insights regarding emotions, whereas cases are concrete situations that may be clarified by applying the concepts and conceptual insights in these situations.

According to the cognitive interaction theory of emotions, the main concepts that have to be learned are contained in the primary appraisal processes (goal relevance, goal congruence, and ego-involvement) and the secondary processes (crediting, coping, and expectancies). Then the core content, specific appraisal processes, dynamics, action tendencies, and so on must be learned for an appropriate list of positive and negative emotions. My remarks in the previous section with regard to attachment and basic trust, empathy and sympathy, the passion for justice, shame and guilt, and sex and love may be considered as examples, from the perspective of which appropriate curriculum material can be developed. From there one can ask how emotions and emotional conflicts can be handled. Appropriate conflict management styles would need to be treated as well as the conditions under which emotional agreements or at least compromises can be reached.

This kind of teaching contributes not only to developing knowledge but also to critical and creative thinking regarding emotions and emotional development. Critical and creative thinking is extremely important in this area. It provides an opportunity for analyzing and criticizing the emotional status quo, and evaluating the emotional assumptions that determine it in terms of goals, values, convictions, and appraisals. It also stimulates emotionally divergent thinking as a way of coming up with new solutions to problems, and develops the child's imagination. In order to achieve this aim, taxonomies of cognitive objectives may prove to be helpful because they indicate paths to reaching this critical and creative thinking (Bloom 1956; De Corte 1973; van der Ven 1982; 1985). The crucial point is to learn how to disagree emotionally without being emotionally disagreeable.

The advantage of case studies is that the abstract conceptual structures that are implied in the cognitive interaction theory of emotions are applied in concrete situations. This provides an opportunity for questions like "What is my goal?" where goal relevance is concerned; "How does this changing situation interfere with my goal?" when goal congruence and goal incongruence are at issue; and "Who am I, what do I stand for, and how serious is this for me?" when ego-involvement comes up. Along with the aspects of the primary appraisal processes, the secondary processes also may be considered, with questions like "Is it my fault or yours?" as far as crediting or blaming is concerned; "Should I react immediately out of anger or quietly think about taking a different perspective?" when a certain coping strategy has to be chosen; and "Why do I think that this changing situation and my intervention in it have a positive or negative end result?" with regard to future expectancies.

Two classes of cases may be distinguished. The first class consists of cases from the lives of people the children are not acquainted with, but which are nevertheless so concrete, lively, and empathetically understandable that they directly trigger the children's imagination and encourage them to role-play. The second class is made up of cases that represent more or less the children's own situations, for example, situations in their own family, neighborhood, local community, congregation, or school. From my own experience I would say that some caution is advisable when deciding whether examining cases of the second class is appropriate under the children's particular circumstances, for instance, their emotional and social home situation and their emotional and social capability to handle these cases adequately, as well as the educator's capability to guide these learning processes prudently and wisely.

In summary, emotional formation is a very important mode in moral education, and it should be treated as carefully as possible. It includes observational learning as well as learning by experience and concept learning.

8

Education for Character

D aniel, twenty-one years old, was entering his senior year in college as a premedical student when he had a tragic accident. As he lay in his hospital bed, totally dependent on a ventilator, his physical situation deteriorating daily, his family helped and supported him to make the decision he really wanted: to remove the ventilator and thus quickly and effectively end his life. Afterward, his mother wrote about the experience in *Saying Goodbye to Daniel*.[1]

Let me take another example. The day when Tim Shuck can no longer laugh is the day he plans to take his life. A fragile-looking man of 45, he wants to die before AIDS wastes him into someone who does not recognize his own friends and family, before he withers into a state he equates with mere existence, not living. He spent much of his career working in an outpatient surgery center, and he says friends in the medical field have assured him they will get him the lethal dose of medicine needed to end his life when the time comes. The central question is not whether he will take the step, but whether it will be legal. "I have a right to do that," he says in a soft but firm voice; "I would like to have the legal right to do that so the people I care about don't have to worry about being persecuted for breaking the law."

The Death with Dignity Movement defends the right to die, arguing that doctors should be allowed to write lethal prescriptions for terminally

1. J. C. Rothman, *Saying Goodbye to Daniel: When Death Is the Best Choice* (New York, 1995).

ill patients who request them. This movement advocates legalizing physician-assisted suicide, but not allowing lethal injections. Patients would have to take life-ending medication themselves, and they would have to make three requests for the medication, one in writing. They would have to wait at least seventeen days before the prescription was written. A second doctor would have to approve issuing the prescription. And if the patient was believed to be suffering from depression, counseling would be required.

Former U.S. Surgeon General C. Everett Koop wrote a strong criticism of the right to die in his state's official voters' pamphlet: "The medical profession cannot be society's healer and killer at the same time," Koop wrote; "poor, elderly, frail, and disabled patients will be the victims when the "choice" to die becomes the "duty" to die.

"I am a criminal," former registered nurse Patty Rosen asserts in a television ad for the right to die. "My 25-year-old daughter Jody was dying of bone cancer. The pain was so great that she couldn't bear to be touched, and drugs didn't help. Jody only had a few weeks to live when she decided she wanted to end her life. But it wasn't legally possible. So I broke the law and got her the pills necessary. And as she slipped peacefully away, I climbed into her bed, and I took her in my arms for the first time in months," Rosen says, her voice breaking.[2]

Decisions about euthanasia and physician-assisted suicide are made in situations of tragedy, and tragedy and character are inextricably linked, as I hope to clarify in the course of this chapter, which looks at character formation. The choice made by Daniel is a tragic one. The decision that the doctor will have to make with regard to Tim's wish to die is a tragic dilemma between the principle of beneficence, meaning the obligation to help others, and the principle of nonmaleficence, meaning the obligation not to do harm. Is it a sign of character to perform this kind of action or to refuse? In general, the decision will depend on the specificity of the patient's physical state, the expected quality of future life, the nature of the patient's voluntary request, the patient-doctor relationship, the mutual and informed decision-making by patient and doctor, the considered rejection of alternatives, the structured consultation with other medical parties, a durable preference for death expressed by the patient, unacceptable suffering by the patient, and the use of a means that is as painless and comfortable as possible (Beauchamp and Childress 1994, 240). What is character in a doctor, what is character in a patient in cases like this?

Let us look more specifically at the patient, who experiences and feels the situation he/she is in as distressing and hopeless in the very

2. *Chicago Tribune,* Nov. 6, 1994.

highest degree. What is a patient with character in a terminal situation of endlessly inhuman, unworthy suffering? Is it a person who carries his/her suffering to the very end, the painful end, of existence? Or is it the person who decides to leave life because it is inhuman, as the Stoic emperor Marcus Aurelius describes in his *Meditations* (3.1, 7; 5.29; 7.33, 45; 8.47; 10.8, 22, 32)? Character and tragedy are inextricably linked: as the classic Greek tragedies illustrate, there is no character without tragedy, and no tragedy without character. We will examine this in more detail a little later on.

Still, the reader may well ask why "character" forms the subject of an entire chapter, and the final one no less, in a book on formation of the self. Why is "character" so important? What moral meaning does it have?

These questions reveal certain widely held doubts, ambivalences, and objections with regard to the term *character*. Some people equate character with virtues, which they dismiss as old-fashioned ideals that no longer have a place in modern society. The word *virtues* itself already disturbs and irritates them. Others object that *character* implies a distinction between "bad" and "good" character, with "good" character referring to some unworldly, pious, ascetic, mystical saint; or between "weak" and "strong" character, of which the latter is considered the "ideal" character connoting "steel-hard men" and "iron ladies." They might say that what we need today are well-tempered, mildly tuned, understanding, concerned, forgiving, reconciling styles of interaction. Other people argue for the revival of character formation and wish to see it reestablished as the ideal mode if not the very core of moral education. They see the objections brought against "character" and "character formation" as positive aspects, which regrettably have been neglected for too long. Or, if they agree with the objections, they point out that character formation as practiced in the last several centuries has been distorted from its true form as shaped within Aristotelian ethics. Still others hold that an Aristotelian renewal might be beneficial, but that the Aristotelian approach needs to be reinterpreted in terms of today's society, which is a product of the Enlightenment, modernization, and value pluralism. Let me call this last group "enlightened advocates" and try to clarify the positions of the adversaries and the enlightened advocates of character formation from five different aspects.

The first aspect refers to the human person who is considered to be the bearer of character and virtues. The adversaries of character formation believe that it creates "fixed selves" who act on the basis of "fixed virtues," which results in "character rigidity." From the point of view of the enlightened advocates, character formation allows individuals to remain or become "open selves" or "true selves," to operate as self-determined

341

thinkers, develop their own judgments, and cause their own actions, which are their own responsibility, and nobody else's.

The second aspect has to do with the way in which character formation leads people to deal with situations. The adversaries believe that the educational mode of character formation requires people to deduce rules from the virtues that have been inculcated in them and deductively apply them to concrete situations. They are afraid to become tied up with "a bag of virtues," as Kohlberg (1981, 78ff.) calls them, that are no longer appropriate to today's situation. The enlightened advocates criticize Kohlberg for confusing virtue education with behavioral conditioning and indoctrinational transmission (Nicgorski and Ellrod 1986). They point out that according to Aristotelian thought, individuals decide how to act in concrete situations by referring to the virtues that they themselves perceive as salient for these situations. Thus they stress that character and virtue are developed in the interaction between person and situation, which implies an inductive approach.

The third aspect has to do with character and virtues per se. The adversaries see character and virtues as too abstract to function as guidelines for concrete actions in concrete situations. They point to empirical research which suggests that actions depend more on the situations people find themselves in than on the virtues they claim to value. For instance, honesty depends more on the likelihood of dishonesty being detected than it does on the degree to which honesty is favored for its own sake (Casey and Burton 1986, 76-79). The enlightened advocates see the abstractness of character and virtues as an advantage, because this leaves much space for individual and situational differences to influence the choice and performance of moral actions.

The fourth aspect concerns the plurality of virtues. On the one hand, the antagonists see this plurality, the various systems of classification and valuation of virtues, as a drawback. They see an array of confusing distinctions between cardinal and noncardinal virtues; self-regarding, other-regarding, and mixed virtues (Slote 1990); teleological and nonteleological virtues (Steutel 1992); virtues oriented to sense-desires and to passional desires (Dent 1984); the virtues of the moralities of authority, association, and supererogation (Rawls 1971, 478); the virtues of integrity or authenticity like truthfulness and sincerity, lucidity and commitment (Rawls 1971, 519); and more. What is missing in particular is a hierarchy or taxonomy of virtues, at least of the cardinal virtues. For some, the supreme virtue is justice, for others prudence, for still others temperance or courage. Some claim virtues other than the traditional cardinal virtues to be of the highest importance. Beauchamp and Childress give a list of four (again four!) "focal virtues" — compassion, discernment, trustworthiness, and integrity — that are intended especially for biomedical ethics with an eye to the character of health professionals (1994, 466ff.). A handbook of character education published in the first decades of this century suggests self-respect as the most important virtue (Patterson 1927, 146), while honesty appears to be ranked as the most important virtue for oneself and for one's children by all age, income, education, race, and religious groups (Casey and Burton 1986, 76). On the other hand, the advocates view the plurality of virtues as beneficial for free judging, decision making, and acting. Character ethics does not exclude situation ethics but includes it, at least in that it takes the specific aspects of every situation into account. Moreover, it emphasizes the idea of *epieikeia* (mildness), which implies that there is no one-to-one relationship between virtues and situations. Virtues are orientations, not fixed guidelines, and as such guarantee the uniqueness of both persons and situations.

The fifth and last aspect has to do with the educational implications of character formation. The adversaries fear that character formation will take us back to the "dark ages," to the educational methods of the past that were characterized by rigid training programs, fixed rules, punitive habit formation, and inhumane coercion. They suspect character formation of being made up of the "three M's," which are moralizing (by invoking guilt), manipulating (by reward and punishment), and modeling (expecting the child to be as we are and to act as we do). They are the "Three Misleading M's," according to Clouse (1993, 346). The enlightened advocates claim that character and virtue education serve to liberate from these restricting and oppressive rules, norms, and constraints by emphasizing questions like "Who am I, who are we?" and "What is good for me, good for us?" rather than "Which rules do I or do we have to follow?" "What am I or are we obliged to do?" "What is allowed or prohibited?" Virtues make people breathe fresh air, see themselves in a positive light, understand their situations in a challenging way.

Among the enlightened advocates one may distinguish two groups. The first group, the radicals, view character ethics as the fulfillment and culmination of moral education. If this were the case, character formation would have to be seen as the integrative mode, in which the other modes come together. Thus the members of the Foundations of Moral Education and Character Development Project, which was conducted under the auspices of the Council for Research in Values and Philosophy (RVP), say of their project: "The framework may be called an integrative one, for it combines what is valid in several approaches to the moral person" (Ellrod 1986, 3). The question is what is "valid," to whom, and for what purpose,

343

who determines what "morality" is, what the "moral person" refers to, and what it implies. That is precisely what the present discussion is about. If character formation were to be considered as the overarching mode of moral education, it would be overextended, because it would have to make space for all kinds of other ideas that were not originally part of it. At the same time it would do violence to those other ideas by forcing them into the frame of reference of character ethics that is too narrow for them and would detract from their value. The radical advocates, who consider character ethics as the only valid form of ethics and character education as the only valid mode of moral education, fall into this very trap. Anscombe already initiated this line of thinking in the late fifties, and moral philosophers like MacIntyre and Taylor followed in her footsteps. For instance, Taylor argued that we must "once and for all expunge from our thinking the ideas of moral right and wrong . . . and turn instead to the ideas of virtue and happiness" (1988, 55). The Dutch educationist Steutel, who also belongs to this group, squeezes Kantian duty ethics into the mold of virtue ethics, with the result that he treats duty as a virtue and speaks of the virtue of duty (Steutel 1992, 97-143).

The moderates among the enlightened advocates see duty ethics and virtue ethics as complementary. Whereas virtue ethics is oriented toward one's desires in one's own situation within one's own community, which indicates the ends being strived for and the means to these ends, duty ethics is concerned with acts to be performed according to universal moral rules and principles. Virtue ethics is about personal dispositions, duty ethics about universal or at least universalizable norms; virtue ethics has to do with the person himself/herself, duty ethics with the person's acts. The two are not in competition because they are, as Frankena states, "two complementary aspects of the same morality" (1973, 65).

This complementarity may be viewed from two different points of view: that of character ethics and that of duty ethics. From the point of view of character ethics, one first looks at the habits, conventions, principles, or ways of life of the community one belongs to. These are the ethics at home, which have implications for all important sectors of life. Because this is a broad field, character ethics implies maximalism. Duty ethics may be seen as the end result of a comparison of character ethics from all different communities in all different cultures, inasmuch as they have certain principles in common. In terms of an ethical Venn diagram, duty ethics can be conceived of as the intersection of sets of character ethics from different communities. Character ethics come first; duty ethics are both their common denominator and their derivate. Duty ethics are the ethics of the broader world, and because they are by definition restrictive, they imply minimalism. Character ethics is substantive, duty ethics is procedural. Character ethics is thick, duty ethics is thin. Character ethics is particular, duty ethics is absolute. Thick precedes thin, maximal precedes minimal, substance precedes procedure (cf. Walzer 1994).

If one looks at the complementarity between character ethics and duty ethics from the angle of duty ethics, character ethics are sociocentric and ethnocentric in nature. They are language dependent, community bound, context directed, tradition oriented, accidental, and relative. They bind only insofar as their rules and principles are universalizable according to, for example, either Rawls's original social contract position of musical chairs or Habermas's U rule of moral discourse. Character ethics are provisional; they need to be justified. Character ethics have yet to be questioned and tried against the universal criteria of reducing oppression and alienation and advancing emancipation and solidarity. It remains to be seen whether character ethics are able to meet these criteria (Habermas 1993).

As I said in Chapter 1, Ricoeur's perspective on the complementarity between character ethics and duty ethics integrates both points of view by adding a third one: situation ethics. Ricoeur starts from the Aristotelian background of character and virtue ethics, which implies self-esteem, solicitude, and a sense of justice. Then he puts the values, norms, and principles that are part of the cultural traditions of the various communities on trial to test their universal validity in terms of human autonomy, respect for the other, and an ideal society in which individual people, as ends in themselves, together form the universal kingdom of ends. Lastly he explores the concrete situation in which some action has to be performed, from the point of view of its specificity, peculiarity, and fragility, then wisely judges what has to be done in that situation, prudently decides between alternatives from their effects and side effects to be expected, and lastly acts on this decision. In fact, he acts on the guidelines provided by character ethics, but after they have been purified according to the criteria of justice and wisely applied in — not to — the concrete situation in its singularity (Ricoeur 1992, 169-296).[3]

In this chapter, from the perspective of the moderate advocates of character ethics, I deal with three questions. The first is: What is character? Based on insights stemming from Plato and Aristotle and reconstructed in today's terms in light of John Dewey's thought, I attempt to explain what it means to "have character" or to "be a character" (section 8.1). The second question, then, is what kind of character one should have or develop. The aim is to define what is "a good character," which especially implies a sense

---

3. See Chapter 4 above.

for the tragedy in life. I approach this topic from the hyperbole of the Last Judgment (section 8.2). Lastly I try to clarify the implications of character for moral education, an undertaking that leads me to transcend the "three misleading M's" (section 8.3).

8.1 Character

So far I have taken the term *character* at face value. Now I will look more closely at it. What is character? To answer this question, I first borrow some key insights about the structure of the human character from Platonic and Aristotelian ethics. Then I connect these classical insights with some more recent thought by Dewey, which enables us to place them within the interaction between person and situation, which takes place continuously in time. Next I integrate the main aspects of an interactive framework into a narrative account of character, for which I draw freely on the thought of narrative analysts like Ricoeur and Morson. Finally, I take the narrative account of character, focusing on a tragic interpretation. In so doing, I hope to contribute to a reconstruction of some classical ethical concepts, which have much to offer for the challenges of today's moral education.

The Structure of Character

From the point of view of Platonic and Aristotelian ethics, the human character can be said to consist of three interrelated groups of structural aspects, which together form a kind of triangle: desires, goods, and reasons. A person strives for the good life and the goods that it implies, and from this striving rationally informs, orders, and even controls his/her desires in order to direct this whole fabric toward the pursuit of happiness. The term *character* refers to this whole complex (Dent 1984; Sherman 1989; Adler 1991). Let me examine these desires, goods, and reasons one after the other.

According to Dent's interpretation of especially Platonic and subsequently Aristotelian ethics, in his/her actions the person can be motivated by three groups of desires. These groups tell us from which forces and drives the individual acts, and what his/her motives are.

The first group are called "sense-desires." They refer to the desire for pleasure through the senses, such as the pleasure of looking at Van Gogh's glowing colors, hearing a Bach fugue, smelling the scent of roses, tasting a mature, well-rounded wine, or touching the beloved's soft skin.

346

Eating, drinking, and sex are not sense-desires, nor are hunger, thirst, or sexual passion, which are the drives satisfied through food, drink, or sex. Sense-desires are desires for the pleasure of seeing, hearing, smelling, tasting, and touching in themselves, not for the pleasure that comes after the drives have been satisfied. Tasting delicious food is different from eating when one is hungry. In both cases it is pleasant to eat, but tasting a well-cooked meal just for the sake of tasting its delicate flavor is something different from eating because one is hungry. These sense-desires tend to move the person toward doing or obtaining whatever gives the sought-after pleasure, thus motivating his/her action. This motivation is supported by some sort of belief about what would be pleasing to the senses.[4]

The second group are "passional desires." They differ from the sense-desires in that although the sense-desires entail some sort of belief, they do not attach value to the situation, whereas passional desires do. Passional desires valuate the situation as desirable or undesirable. In the case of situations valuated as desirable, the desires are positive; in undesirable situations, the desires are negative. These valuations are associated with active or passive passions. Active passions can be both positive and negative. Positive active passions such as joy, gladness, and gratitude relate to situations that one desires to continue. Negative active passions are anger, fear, jealousy, envy, hatred, pity, and resentment. These negative active passions are evoked by situations that are not what they should be, and aim at changing the situation. In the case of anger, one desires to injure or harm the other person who is blamed for the situation, in order to restore one's self-esteem, which the other person has damaged. Fear evokes an impulse to remove a threat by fighting or fleeing. In the case of jealousy, one desires to change the situation in which one is less favored than another person, for example by regaining one's central place in the loved one's attention. Pity moves one to remove the conditions that cause another to suffer. Passive passions, too, can be both positive and negative. Joy, gladness, elation, and gratitude do not tend to change a situation, because the situation is celebrated as adequate, purposive, and satisfying. They tend to express themselves in smiling, laughter, or jumping for joy. They are the passions of well-being. Negative passions such as sorrow, misery, and despair also

---

4. According to the emotion theory I referred to in Chapter 7, sense-desires and the pleasures that they give are produced by what are called innate sensorimotor reflexes, which are bioneurologically elicited by physical stimuli. They do not belong to the class of emotions, although some writers treat them as emotional states (Lazarus 1991, 55). At least insofar as they are learned, they may imply neurologically transmitted beliefs about the pleasure that the satisfaction of desires might afford (cf. Damasio 1994).

are not aimed changing the situation, but this time because it is thought to be unchangeable. They are passions of ill-being. They are inclined to defend and to preserve what the person holds dear. They do not entail any tendency to direct action.[5] Both active and passive passions are triggered by the emotional valuation of something as desirable or undesirable, that is, as something good or bad for the person concerned.

The last group is called "rational desires." They motivate the actions of the individual on the basis of judgments of good and evil. The person acts in a particular way because he/she thinks and believes it is the best way to act. Such judgment is based on an idea of the sort of life one wants to live, the course to be taken, the project to be chosen, the plan to be followed. The question is asked, To what extent and in what sense does the action to be performed contribute to that project or plan? The person thus has some conception of the good life in mind, as well as of the conditions required for its realization. Such a conception is not a systematic, comprehensive, consistent, and unchangeable one, free of unconnected, contrasting, or even contradictory elements. It is, however, at least a partial picture, containing at least some goods-related considerations. The conception of the good life is not only cognitive but also implies a commitment to implement that conception or at least a concern for it, a sense that it matters. Therefore we speak of "a fabric of rational desires," and not of "a rational fabric." An important difference between passional and rational desires is that whereas passional desires are spontaneous, momentary, and incident bound, rational desires transcend particular moments, because they depend on the larger conception of the good life, however provisional, partial, and sketchy this may be.

What kind of evaluation of situations and actions is implied in this conception of the good life: a "weak" or "strong" evaluation? Taylor holds a strong evaluation to be necessary in order for the self to function as a moral agent. Moral action, in this view, presupposes a strong character with a strong conception of life, from which flows a strong evaluation of all occurrences in life (cf. Taylor 1989, 20, 27, 29-30). This argument for a strong evaluation is connected with a religious argument, because according to Taylor this strong evaluation should be based on some transcendent

---

5. Whether the negative emotions directly or indirectly imply any action tendency, as Dent (1984, 65, 90) suggests, is a matter of psychological debate. The question is whether negative emotions such as sadness and helplessness and mild positive emotions such as gratitude involve some biological impulses and evoke some physiological mobilization (Lazarus 1991, 112-21, 194-203). It also depends on the degree to which the action programs are interpreted as fixed and rigid push-button programs or as open and flexible adaptational agendas with alternative courses of action (Frijda 1986, 83).

ground (Taylor 1989, 520-21). Other scholars, who are more or less empirically oriented, think differently, supposing a weak evaluation to be sufficient in daily life situations, requiring not a strong but a weak conception of the good life (cf. Flanagan 1990). In essence, we must act on belief and take risks, as William James said, because there is no certainty as there is in the sciences (cf. Mann 1986). From a philosophical perspective, the fragmentary conception of the good life is confirmed by Ricoeur's idea of "attestation," which is not a kind of ultimate and self-founding knowledge but a belief — not a belief in the mode of "I believe-that," but of "I believe-in." It has less standing than *episteme* (scientific knowledge), although it is no less alethic owing to its hermeneutical grounds. Attestation is essentially weak, fragile, vulnerable, but at the same time trustworthy, that is, trust giving and trust receiving (Ricoeur 1992, 21-22). Interestingly, Taylor himself sometimes concedes that moral comprehension can be "tentative" (Taylor 1989, 17) or even prearticulate (ibid., 77-78, 91-92).

Let me now turn to the term *the good life* itself, including the goods implied in it. This term does not directly imply happiness, but rather the pursuit of happiness. Happiness per se is unachievable, as it depends on luck.[6] Happiness functions as a limit, as we will see (Adler 1991, 115). What, then, is the pursuit of happiness? In a sense equally formal as general, one might say that the pursuit of happiness is "striving for the totality of goods" *(totum bonum)*. The next question is: What is this "totality of goods"?

According to Aristotle, the pursuit of happiness, which consists of striving for the totality of goods, can be advanced with the help of four sorts of goods: the highest good *(summum bonum)*, which is *theoria;* the internal goods, which are the virtues; and two groups of external goods. The terms *internal* and *external* refer to the relation of the goods to the individual: some goods are inside the person (internal), for example, the virtues; while others are outside him/her (external). These external goods are, for instance, friends, wealth, political influence, good birth, good children, personal beauty, and so on (*EN* 1.8). Looking at this list of external goods, one can say that it contains two groups: extrinsic external goods and intrinsic external goods. Extrinsic external goods do not represent a real good in themselves, although they may contribute to the pursuit of happiness, albeit in a purely instrumental way. Intrinsic external goods constitute a good in

6. Adler (1991, 109) writes: "Aristotle is the only moral philosopher in the Western tradition who makes good luck as well as moral virtue a necessary condition of a life that is morally good as well as one that is enriched by the attainment of all real goods and many apparent goods that are innocuous. That is why I think his *Ethics* is the only sound and pragmatic moral philosophy that made its appearance in the last twenty-five centuries."

themselves because they are not purely instrumental. An example is friendship, which belongs to the very core of character (Sherman 1989, 119ff.). Let us look at these goods in more detail, starting with the external goods and then going from the internal goods, the virtues, to the highest good.

The most important extrinsic external goods are pleasure, money, political connections, fame, and power. They may be helpful at least partly in the pursuit of happiness, although their quality as goods is fundamentally different. I already spoke of pleasure in the context of the sense-desires — the desire to gaze on the beautiful bodies of ballet dancers, hear birds singing early in the morning, smell another's person perfume, taste the Thanksgiving turkey and cranberries, or feel the lover's tender touch. Although this sensual pleasure may be strived for as a good, it forms only part of the good and of happiness. It would be wrong to strive for it as though it were the *totum bonum*. The same applies to health and knowledge. Just like pleasure, they are only part of the good. One may strive for them, but not as if they were the *totum bonum*. As far as money is concerned, Aristotle considers it a good that is a means. It is an apparent good, which means that it is factually desired, although it ought not to be desired. It is wrongly desired when it is strived for as an end in itself and not purely as a means, for it then leads to the vice of greed and avarice. Desiring money is permissible only insofar as money is treated as a means. Fame and power are also apparent goods: they are indeed strived for, but they must not be considered as goods in themselves or as means to happiness. They are not parts of happiness. We have to distinguish fame from honor and from esteem. Both honor and esteem are important, but the virtuous person does not strive for either of them (Adler 1991, 37-53).

The most important intrinsic external good, as noted above, is friendship, at least a special form of friendship. Earlier I referred to Aristotle's three forms of friendship: friendship based on utility, on pleasure, and on goodness. Both the first and second forms are extrinsic external goods, in the same way as fame, power, political connection, wealth, and pleasure. In the third form, one desires the good of the friend for the friend's own sake, because one loves the other for what he/she is, not for any accidental quality such as utility or pleasure (*EN* 8.3).

The internal goods are embodied in moral virtue. They are internal parts of happiness and a means to it as well. They contain aspects of happiness in themselves, while at the same time establishing the conditions for and the way toward it. Moral virtue is a *conditio sine qua non* for happiness.

Among the many aspects of virtue, temperance and fortitude belong to the fundamental ones, according to Aristotle, because virtue is concerned

350

with pleasures and pains: "pleasure induces us to behave badly, and pain to shrink from fine actions" (*EN* 2.3).[7] Temperance, then, is the virtue of relativizing sense-pleasures in order to achieve higher order goods, while fortitude enables us to suffer pain or surmount obstacles that hinder us from doing what we must. Temperance requires distance from oneself, whereas fortitude demands commitment and the willingness to take risks. Both virtues are focused on the pursuit of happiness in the long run, fortitude insofar as hard work is required for attaining happiness and temperance inasmuch as it allows one to free oneself from pursuing momentary pleasures. "Both are aspects of one and the same basic habit of choice — the disposition to prefer a good life in the long run (however hard it may be to work for that end) to a good and an easy time here and now (however pleasant that may be from moment to moment)," Adler says (1991, 185), summarizing Aristotle's thought.

Another fundamental aspect of virtue is justice, which Aristotle deals with in book 5. Justice in general means not to harm another person and to give this person his/her due in his/her pursuit of happiness. In this general sense, it is complete virtue, as expressed in the classic saying quoted by Aristotle: "In justice is summed up the whole of virtue" (*EN* 5.1). Under the broad heading of justice, particular aspects referring to particular human transactions are examined, such as exchange (commutative justice), distribution (distributive justice), and government (legal justice). Interestingly, justice does not fit the Aristotelian mean, in which virtue finds itself between two vices — courage between rashness and cowardice, and temperance between licentiousness and insensibility, for instance — because in the case of justice there is only one corresponding vice — injustice. Injustice, however, can be interpreted from two aspects: doing injustice and suffering from it (*EN* 5.5).[8]

The meaning of these virtues in concrete situations with an eye to the solution of concrete problems is ordered by the virtue of wisdom. As I said, wisdom does not apply principles and rules *to* the concrete situation but *in* the situation. It takes the contingency, particularity, singularity, and fragility of the situation into account. It draws on a hermeneutical ability to understand what universal ideas and values mean in the unique, unrepeatable here and now, populated by unique, unrepeatable people (*EN* 6.7-9; cf. Ricoeur 1992, 240ff.).

---

7. Adler (1991, 185) translates: "it is on account of pleasures that we do the wrong things, and on account of pains that we abstain from doing the right ones" (*EN* 2.3).

8. In the diagram of virtues and vices that illustrates the doctrine of mean, justice is missing (*EN* 2.7).

Together these four virtues form one virtue, because it is impossible to be temperate and not courageous, to be courageous and not just, to be just and not wise, or to be wise and not temperate.[9]

The tradition after Aristotle's moral philosophy since Ambrose holds that these four virtues, while forming a unity, are fundamental or even cardinal virtues. To understand why this is so, one can look at the question from either Plato's or Aristotle's perspective. From Plato's perspective, cardinal virtues are the basis of all other virtues, a statement that may be interpreted to mean that special aspects are present within the cardinal virtues, and that every other virtue, for example trust or piety, can be seen as a specification of one or more of the cardinal virtues. From Aristotle's perspective, cardinal virtues are not general attitudes, which would lack concrete specificity and end in vagueness.[10] They are called "cardinal" because they take priority over all other virtues. Let us take justice, which deals with exchange relationships. Justice is not the only virtue that is relevant in this kind of relationship; gratitude, liberality, and magnanimity may also play a role. Nobody will deny that justice takes priority over these other virtues, however, when the determination of the right price, wages, taxes, or interests is at stake. In such a situation justice rules over gratitude, liberality, or magnanimity. Thomas Aquinas takes Aristotle's position and establishes the priority orientation of the cardinal virtues (*STh* I-II, 61; Steel 1995).

Lastly, Aristotle calls the highest good *theoria*. This *summum bonum* is not identical with *totum bonum*, but is rather only part of it. However it may have been interpreted in the past and however many misunderstandings it may have been subject to, especially as a result of its translation in the Latin *contemplatio, theoria* in its very essence relates to intrinsic enjoyment. This intrinsic enjoyment can be obtained from pure actions done for their own sake during one's leisure time, such as gardening, cooking, cabinetmaking, scientific research, musical performance, or philosophical thought (Adler 1991, 85). It is interesting to note that the "summum bonum" of leisure is a subject of lively debate at the present time. On the one side, MacIntyre interprets the present-day preference for the pursuit of extrinsic goods such as money, power, and fame over the good of intrinsic enjoyment in leisure,

9. The sequence of cardinal virtues may differ. For example, Thomas presents the list in the following sequence, which is based on his own conception of virtue (Schockenhoff 1987, 272ff.): prudence, justice, temperance, and fortitude (*STh* I-II 61.2), while Pieper (1970) amends this list to prudence, justice, courage, and temperance.

10. One may ask why in fact Kohlberg (1981; 1984) leans more toward Plato's conception of justice as a cardinal virtue than toward Aristotle's. He does not seem to see the difference between them.

such as playing chess, as a symptom of moral decline (MacIntyre 1984, 188ff.). On the other side, some of his critics suggest that our times provide more opportunities for intrinsic goods, such as sports and arts, to be accessible to all and not just to a few aristocrats, than any society at any time before (Miller 1994, 252-53). Interestingly, in this debate, a culture is evaluated according to how it deals with its highest good *(summum bonum)*: leisure time *(theoria)*.

The structure of character involves not only desires and goods but also reasons. "Reasons" here refers to practical reasoning, the operations of practical rationality. Its function can be understood in relation to desires and in relation to goods. The interrelation of desires, goods, and reasons together forms the structure of character.

In relation to desires, practical rationality links both the sense-desires and the passional desires with the conception of the good life, which is embodied in the rational desires. It does so by checking and controlling the sense-desires in such a way that they do not form an obstacle to pursuing happiness, which is inscribed in the conception of the good life. Striving for and experiencing too much sense pleasure — as in the case of compulsive eating, drinking, and sexual behavior — would prevent us from achieving the good life. With regard to the passional desires, practical reasoning enables one to perceive the situation in which the passions would tend to move one to act, and to diagnose its salient aspects in relation to one's conception of the good life. It also allows the person to look for alternative actions and weigh their advantages and disadvantages in terms of potential consequences. In this deliberation, practical reasoning assesses the fitness of these alternatives for both the situation and the conception of the good life. After that, it selects the actions or courses of action to be taken, formulates a resolution, and decides to act, with the action following in the short or long term. Whereas practical rationality takes the form of the virtue of temperance with regard to the sense-desires, it takes the form of prudence/wisdom with regard to passional desires.

In its concern with the conception of the good life, practical rationality also is concerned with the totality of the goods: the extrinsic external goods, the intrinsic external goods, the internal goods, and the highest good. The straightforward description of these goods tends to gloss over the fact that in concrete situations they often come into conflict with each other. Unfortunately, in Aristotle's ethics, little attention is paid to this potential for conflict between goods (Sherman 1989, 30). These conflicts occur endlessly between individuals interacting in concrete situations, as well as within individuals. The interpersonal conflicts are rooted in preferences for different goods, such as family, career, money, wealth, political office, fame, power, or friendship. Different people simply see and judge things differently. The intrapersonal conflicts also arise from differences in perceptions and evaluations, but now within the same person. Practical rationality is called on to treat these conflicts by sorting them out, developing dialogues, seeking connections, settling agreements (which occasionally may be agreements to disagree), and reaching compromises. Practical rationality thus operates tactically and strategically. Here again temperance and prudence/wisdom are the key virtues (*EN* 6.5; *STh* II-II 48, 50).

So far I have distinguished among desires, goods, and reasons. But this is only a logical distinction *(distinctio rationis)*, not a real one *(distinctio realis)*. Indeed, the three groups are intrinsically related. As I already said, together they form the structure of character. In sum, according to the goods that make up the conception of the good life for a particular person, the person's practical rationality informs the rational desires, orders the passional desires, controls the sense-desires, and directs this whole fabric toward the pursuit of happiness.

An Interactive Framework for Character

As stated above, I wish to localize the structure of the human character, as it has been analyzed in the light of the key insights of Platonic and Aristotelian ethics, within the interaction between person and situation taking place in time, from the perspective of Dewey's pragmatism. In doing so my aim will be, first, to deconstruct the normative essentialism that underlies these classic insights, and second, to reconstruct the classic insights in such a way that they can contribute to advancing moral education in modern society, especially moral education for character.

What does "interaction" mean here? The term *interaction* simply refers to the fact that the human person as the bearer of character is intrinsically embedded in and constantly exchanging with the situations he/she is in. The human character is not something one has before entering into and finding oneself in a particular situation. It is rather the consequence of one's interaction with and within this situation. Character does not unfold from within the person in isolation, but is called out through interaction with others in the situation, and through the grappling with tasks and challenges that are part of that situation.

As Dewey understood, this seemingly simple idea of interaction has far-reaching implications, which resolve some of the objections that are made against Platonic and Aristotelian ethics for failing to take sufficiently into consideration the aspects of human character that characterize modern thinking on the subject: its interactive, dynamic, unique, and open-ended aspects. I will elaborate on these four aspects, in the process drawing from Dewey's pragmatism (cf. Dewey 1994, 23-163).

First, the human character must not be understood in an individualistic way, as if the traits that make up character belong exclusively to the individual as a separate self. Cardinal virtues such as justice, courage, prudence, and temperance, and other virtues like honesty, kindness, and benevolence, which may be part of a person's character, are not the individual's private property. They are the product of the person's interactions with others who influence him/her, just as he/she influences those others. Traits such as trust, responsibility, and compassion, which are the outputs of these interactions, function as inputs in subsequent interactions. In other words, character traits operate as dependent as well as independent variables.

For this reason, the theory known as character and personality trait theory has to be criticized for its assumption that traits are situation independent and cross-situationally stable. This assumption has proved to be unfounded, because situational differences empirically explain behavioral differences at least as much as or more than character trait differences do. This empirical evidence should not lead to the opposite assumption, however, that differences in situations, say those in the home and the school, solely account for differences in behavior. It is interactionism that satisfies both empirical theorists and researchers who take both character and situation seriously (Hermans and Kempen 1993, 126). This interactionism relativizes and even removes the objections against individualistic and even internalized interpretations of character that have been formulated by some moral philosophers and theologians (cf. Wils and Mieth 1992, 125).

Second, the situations with which the individual is in constant interaction are changing all the time, and the structural aspects of human character, that is, its desires, goods, and reasons, change with them. They are situation bound. Desires do not only come and go, but their directedness, their coordination, and the relative emphasis on some aspects of each of them and neglect of others continuously change over time. The same applies to goods: they are not perennial, they do not exist "out there" forever; they are shaped by situations and fluctuate with them. It also applies to reasons. No matter how free and transcendent they are, they are also situation bound. They are tied to the situations from which they emerge, live, and complete their existence. Reasons operate through their embodiedness in the human body, which is itself fundamentally connected with and conditioned by the fluctuations in and of situations. Even the conception of the good life is situation bound, provided that it is not a strong but a weak conception with its partial, fragmentary, and even fragile evaluations. Because of the vulnerability of the "attestation," which epistemologically constitutes the conception of life, long-term beliefs about the pursuit of happiness change time and again.[11]

The human character is clearly not durable or fixed of nature, as some scholars hold (Steutel 1992, 22). Character is surrounded by history, while at the same time history is within character. It is created by history and at the same time creates history. It does not consist of a stable core, only the accidental aspects of which would be touched by history, but it is in its very core historical. It takes part in the historical process of a particular time and space in a particular culture in a particular context. It participates in the historical flow of the river of human culture, which determines its contingency. The human character passes through a course of historical events and realizes itself in this course of events.

Third, the changing nature of situations lends a uniqueness to the human character, so that no two characters are the same. Aristotle understands human character as a kind of permanent collection of fixed character traits, by which are meant the virtues. At times he appears to speak of only one character for all individuals, referring to the human character in a normative or even moral mode, as the same character that every individual ought to develop. Descriptively speaking, however, people do not have the same character. Each individual develops a unique character, to the point that each individual may be said to be a unique character.

Human character, then, is not singular but plural. There are as many characters as there are people, because each person strives for different goods with different passions and different reasons, with an eye to different aspects of the good life in different situations. Emphasizing certain passions, goods, reasons, situations, and aspects of the good life necessarily means neglecting others. It is interesting to see how even different ethics imply different characters, all dependent on their own times. For example, Aristotle may be said to have developed the character of the balanced wise man (*phronimos*) and Kant that of the severe and earnest teacher of the categorical

11. Taking into account the singularity of situations from a moral perspective transcends the Aristotelian *epieikeia* idea, which entails only "a rectification of law insofar as law is defective on account of its generality" and considers a law "such as the legislator himself would have given if he had been present there, and as he would have enacted if he had been aware of the circumstances" (*EN* 5.10), because "the law is essentially incomplete; no enumeration (*diarithmounta*), no matter how imaginative or far-sighted, could possibly be comprehensive" (Sherman 1989, 16-17).

imperatives. Hume himself described the characters of the Skeptic, the Platonist, the Stoic, and the Epicurean. It is not difficult to typify the characters of the Benthamite calculator, the Millian social planner, or even Nietzsche's anticharacter (Oksenberg Rorty 1992, 48-49).

Lastly, character is open-ended: the final account of character can be given only at the end. This is because, as Aristotle points out, "In the course of life we encounter many reverses and all kinds of vicissitudes, and in old age even the most prosperous of men may be involved in great misfortunes" (*EN* 1.9). We must "look to the end," as Herodotus tells us. What, then, is this "end"? Is it an end of life in the biological sense or an end of character in a social sense? This question is a fundamental one, because character is formed, as I said, through interaction with the social world, that is, other people, while also determining this interaction. This dialectic between character and its social world *(Umwelt)* does not suddenly end at the moment of biological disintegration. From a phenomenological perspective on human relations, the human character stretches from the interaction with the predecessors *(Vorwelt)* through that with the contemporaries *(Mitwelt)* to that with the successors *(Folgewelt)*. It is substantially formed by the time dimension, which permeates all networks of relations (Schütz 1967, XXVIff.). Here a fundamental paradox emerges, which Aristotle expresses thus: "Suppose that a man has lived an exceptionally happy life right into old age, and has ended it in like manner: many changes of fortune may befall his descendants, some of whom may be good and enjoy such a life as they deserve, and other just the opposite. . . . It would surely be absurd, then, if the dead man changed with their changes of fortune, and became at one time happy and turn miserable; but it would also be absurd for the experiences of the descendants to have no effect, even for a limited period, upon their ancestors" (*EN* 1.10).

In other words, time is open; the end of biological life does not close time, because it is not the completion of time. Human life exists in a multiplicity of temporalities. In his Bakhtinian analysis of the Russian novel, the literary critic Morson says: "one's death cannot be an event in one's life. The point is almost tautological, but its implications are far-reaching. My death can be an event only in the lives of others; I can never see my whole life. In Bakhtin's terms, that is because 'finalization' (the sense of a completed whole) demands radical 'outsideness': an end requires an external standpoint" (1994, 38). Time is an ongoing process: "In our own lives, most of us know by experience that there is never a point when all loose threads are tied together, at least not until the end of history or the Last Judgment" (ibid., 8).

A Narrative Account of Character

I will now seek to integrate the interactive, dynamic, unique, and open-ended aspects of character into a narrative account of the human character by showing these aspects in the context of storytelling.[12]

First, in the course of the interaction with our contemporaries *(Mitwelt)*, predecessors *(Vorwelt)*, and successors *(Folgewelt)*, language plays a key role in the formation of character. It is difficult to conceive of any character separately from the language structures it is embedded in and woven into, although I do not like to deny the very existence of such character as a *Ding an sich* either. However, the stories people are told and tell about themselves are clearly central to character formation. And it is only by knowing and participating in this storytelling as both an active agent and a passive patient that one is conscious of, has access to, and shapes one's own character and that of the people with whom one communicates. Through narration we refigure our character in the twofold sense of uncovering its concealed dimensions and transforming its experienced dimensions. Stories come from other stories. As they are retold, recast, and reshaped, the "I," "you," "he," and "she" in these stories are deconstructed from other and deeper layers and their characters constantly reconstructed. In the retelling, the self alternately functions as author, character, protagonist, antagonist, implied listener, real listener, absent listener, commentator, and so on, in the same way as does the partner in the interaction, and the entire process shapes our character. We are both the reader and writer of our stories. In sum, interaction implies character-forming narration.

Second, storytelling is to be seen as a dynamic process that integrates various dimensions of time: on the one hand, objective and subjective time and, on the other, the ecstatic dimensions of past, present, and future, as

12. In the paragraphs that follow, I describe *character* differently from the way Ricoeur defines it. From his sound anthropological insight into the tension between sameness *(idem)* and ipseity *(ipse)* within the self, Ricoeur rightly uncovers the temporal dimension of this tension by looking at the burden of the past weighing on the self, which results in the continuity of the self *(idem)*, and at the future horizon of the promising self, which says "here I am for you," by which the self, in keeping its word, acts as ethical creator *(ipse)* of intersubjectivity. Against this background, Ricoeur equates the *idem* dimension with "character" and the *ipse* dimension with creativity and future. This interpretation, which Ricoeur developed in *Oneself as Another* (Ricoeur 1992, 118-19), goes back to *The Voluntary and the Involuntary*, partly as a warning against "characterology" (Ricoeur 1992, 119n.4; Bien 1995, 289ff.). In my narrative analysis, in which I draw on Morson (1994), "character" implies both the *idem* and the *ipse* dimensions, although Ricoeur also includes at least some *ipse* aspects in character, while giving a narrative account of character (Ricoeur 1992, 122-23).

Ricoeur explains in *Time and Narrative*. In stories, the characters inscribe their biography, fitting their subjective experience of time into the cosmic and cultural coordinates of objective time, from which a third time emerges, narrative time, which integrates objective and subjective time. It reconciles the mortal time we subjectively experience in care — or *Sorge*, to use Heidegger's term — and the impersonal time horizon of nature and culture, which phenomenologically lies outside experience and emotion. This narrative time encompasses calendar time with its regular intervals of days, months, and years and its relation to other time cycles like biological, ecological, and social cycles. It also expresses the sequence of generations by which ancestors, contemporaries, and descendants, all of them with their characteristic social and cultural lifestyles, are narratively connected. It also provides a narrative place for the notion of traces, the vestiges individuals or groups leave as they pass through life, which are recounted as significant and as operating in actual life in a causal mode. But despite the connection between past and present that constitutes narration, storytelling is dominated by the horizon of future expectations, which opens up time and makes all things virtually possible, while stimulating the presence of initiative (Kemp 1995; Stevens 1995).

Third, the uniqueness of character is a product of the open-ended nature of narrative time, because the past reveals its unused possibilities and the future lacks any fixed design, plan, or telos. The character in the story is confronted with the necessity of choosing from alternative relations, paths, and actions. It is his/her unique responsibility to take probabilities as opportunities, contingencies as conscience, and chances as challenges. The human character has a life of its own, in the midst of other characters. It never coincides with itself, because its story always transcends the parameters of past and present, limiting but not eliminating choice and freedom. Stories are full of contradictions because the characters live their own lives, as the subjects of their own directly signifying discourse, as Bakhtin puts it, which creates not a universe but a pluriverse or heteroverse (Morson 1994, 94-95). Characters are surprising, even to themselves; they provoke unexpected events, ideas, and deeds, in which they realize themselves: "Character tends to no goal but rather acquires qualities as life goes on. Unpredictable circumstances and their own actions make heroes and heroines different; they do not live in completed selves. It follows that they are ethically responsible not only for what they do but also for how they transform themselves — not only for their actions but also, over time, for a considerable part of their character" (ibid., 108).

Lastly, the open-ended nature of stories told and continuously retold determines their characters. This again relates to the conception of narrative time, which, at least in the great Russian novels of Dostoyevsky and Tolstoy, is not closed time but open time. By "open time" I mean three things. First, events that happened in the past are seen as contingent; they might not have happened because their happening was not necessary but was caused by chance or by human choice. Second, actions to be done in the present form a subset of a greater set of possibilities, from which a selection has to be made. Third, things that are to be expected in the future are surprising because they do not follow a plan or design, and are neither teleologically directed nor predetermined. There is no predestination because chances and choices are formed into destiny after they happen; therefore this destiny itself remains open-ended because it is not completed yet. The character's destiny is in process; it does not unfold but develops from existing and future alternative attitudes, alternative paths, and alternative actions. Gary Saul Morson together with Michael André Bernstein coined the term *side-shadowing* in order to articulate the meaning of open time. Time can be seen from the vantage point of various shadowing activities: foreshadowing, backshadowing, and sideshadowing. Foreshadowing projects onto the present a shadow from the future, backshadowing reverses this process, being foreshadowing after the fact in that it projects onto the present a shadow from the past, and sideshadowing projects from the "side" and broadens the horizon by taking into account all possible alternatives in the past, present, and future. Only this sideshadowing leads to the character's temporal openness, especially with respect to the future, which makes it open to multiple futures (Morson 1994, 82-116).

A Tragic Interpretation of Character

At this point, the reader may ask the critical question whether and how Plato's and Aristotle's moral thought, which I dealt with at the beginning of this section, can be connected with the narrative insights into character I referred to in the preceding paragraphs. How is the tripartite structure of the classic character, that is, the desires, goods, and reasons, related to the interactive, dynamic, unique, and open-ended nature of character as seen from a narrative approach? How does a conception of the good life, which dominates the classic character, fit into a narrative reading of character? What role do goods, especially intrinsic goods, more specifically the moral virtues, have to play in a narrative interpretation of character? How does the tension between desires and reasons relate to the telling of stories to and about character? My point here is that Plato and Aristotle, especially in Dent's account, offer substantial thought, whereas the narrative analysis of character up until now is purely formal. The challenge, therefore, is to interpret the main substantial insights by Plato and Aristotle within the formal frame of reference of narrative analysis. Perhaps surprisingly, I use the concept of tragedy to respond to this challenge. With the help of this concept, I hope to show how some of Plato's and Aristotle's substantial ideas can be approached from the formal point of view of storytelling.

The first step is to explain how morality and narrativity belong together. In storytelling human imagination is at work, both in the mode of private imagination, by which we convergently or divergently "think out" possible courses of action, and in the mode of social imagination, by which we produce social utopias, that is, "open utopias," since "closed utopias" limit future possibilities and function as anticipatory backshadowing (Morson 1994, 256). In this imagination, various visions are developed, entailing alternative moral choices, decisions, and actions. This imagination can be said to be the source of morality, insofar as morality deals with visions, ideals, and wants rather than with rules, duties, and obligations.[13] Here the tension between the good and the just, which I referred to in Chapter 1, again comes into play. Ricoeur's three-phase model of the good, the just, and the wise offers a balanced explanation of the preponderance of the good that, after being purified by the just, orients the wise (Ricoeur 1992, 169-296). Moral quality must be attributed both to the small everyday stories we tell and are told and the exemplary stories that cultural tradition transmits from generation to generation.

The second step is to realize that tragedy is a special form of narration. It is not superfluous to ask which form, because in the common view tragedy is linked to pain, distress, sorrow, grief, pessimism, or even fatalism. This view arises from a misreading of what tragedy is, at least as exemplified in the classical Greek and Shakespearean dramas. These tragedies do not necessarily end badly. They begin badly, but almost half of the Greek tragedies, as we know them, end well. Tragedy is not a matter of facts, events, or situations as such: "Tragedy, unlike disaster, involves a choice. Tragedy is something harder, infinitely rarer, a challenge thrown in the

13. Ricoeur does not accept or at least relativizes the idea that narrative is the foundation of morality, because we should "not fail to connect the exemplarity of witnessing to a normative requirement that cannot be reduced to its historicity" (Ricoeur 1995, 397). By contrast, Kemp, for example, argues for the moral evaluation of narratives in terms of other narratives, because "there is no Archimedean point" (1995, 389). I think the distinction between narratives as a foundation or as a source of morality is crucial. Even if one agrees with Ricoeur that morality cannot be reduced to historicity, one can agree with Kemp when he says, "Thus, we cannot argue that ethics is experienced in a completely normative manner prior to the poetic story" (1995, 377).

face of the brute facticity of the world. If Hamlet is tragic — and he most assuredly is — then it is not because of what the world does to him; it is because of what he is, what he does, and how he does it. His tragedy derives, in large measure, from who he is. 'Character is destiny,' said Heraclitus, some three millennia ago" (Ruprecht 1994, 16).

Aristotle wrote that "tragedy is not a representation of men but a piece of action, of life, of happiness," adding, "unhappiness comes under the head of action" (*Poetics* 6). This is meaningful if we bear in mind the notion that tragedy involves a choice. In tragedy a story is told of happiness and unhappiness flowing from the moral choices, decisions, and deeds of characters whose lives are permeated by fate and chance, fragility and frailness, vulnerability and woundedness. In other words, tragedy can be said to have a moral status, as far as the tension between will and power, ideals and possibilities, or challenges and opportunities is concerned. Tragedy is about the real life we live from day to day, including its ideals, desires, and needs as well as its facts, chances, and limits. Tragedy is not just a play to be watched in the theater, but a play in which to participate in moral life, because it expresses the depth of moral doubts, struggles, and conflicts between and within its characters.

The moral choice that tragedy centers on is based on the fact that the tragic play tells the story not just of characters but of good and bad characters. Aristotle defines tragedy as "a representation of men better than ourselves" (*Poetics* 15), compared with comedy, which represents "people as worse than they are today" (*Poetics* 2). Through the catharsis that tragedy inevitably results in, the spectator participates in the play in such a way that he/she senses and experiences choices that are the same or analogous to those that he/she must make in his/her own life, including the possibility of moral achievement or failure. Through catharsis tragedy reveals and transforms the moral self (Kemp 1995, 378).

The third and last step is to clarify the intrinsic relationship between tragedy and character by explaining the moral quality of tragedy in terms of passions, goods, and reasons, to which Plato and Aristotle related the notion of morality. This moral quality does not emerge directly from tragedy, as can be illustrated by Sophocles' *Antigone*, the preeminent example of tragedy and one highly admired by Hegel, Hölderlin, and Schelling. The two protagonists, Creon and Antigone, embody two different sets of passions, goods, and reasons, which come into direct conflict with each other. Creon, the king of Thebes, denies burial to Polyneices, Antigone's brother, because Polyneices besieged the city in order to wrest control of it from his brother, Eteocles, and the two brothers then slew each other. Antigone dies for giving Polyneices an honorable burial, intending to perform the

symbolic rites herself. Creon's character is determined by a particular configuration of passion, good, and reason: he is possessed by passion for the
law, which he holds to be the ultimate good for the city and its citizens,
because it will save them from anarchy. Antigone's character is determined
by a different configuration of passion, good, and reason: her passion is for
the bond of blood and nature, which she sees as the ultimate good in human
life and to be devoted to above all others because it represents community
and human solidarity. Each of the protagonists, with their different sets of
passions, goods, and reasons, embodies a main virtue: Creon, justice; Antigone, love. The moral quality of the tragedy, however, does not emerge
directly from these conflicting values. For the moral quality to become
apparent something else is needed: first a negation of both characters and
then a negation of this negation. Let me explain.

The negation of these characters takes the form of the fanatical one-
sidedness that both Creon and Antigone exhibit, a one-sidedness that makes
them almost blind. Creon is so absorbed with the legal aspects of justice,
seeing only the law's "thou shalt nots," that he is unable to see the depth
of the positive dimension of the "thou shalts." He is blind to the intrinsic
limitations of any law when it is confronted with that which transcends law,
that is, the bonds of love, especially natural bonds of love. Unlike Antigone,
who sacrifices her life for her brother's honor, he does not recognize the
limitedness of politics. He is confined to a narrow conception of the city:
"This narrowness of viewpoint is reflected in his estimation of virtues.
Alone is 'good' that which serves the city, 'bad' that which is harmful to it;
the good citizen alone is 'just,' and 'justice' commands only the art of
governing and being governed. 'Piety,' an important virtue, is reduced to
the civic bond, and the gods are called upon to honor only those citizens
who have died for their country" (Ricoeur 1992, 244; cf. Mongin 1994, 75).
He appears to be deaf to his son, Haemon, who teaches him that a polis is
not a single man's possession, for that would make it a desert.[14]

While Creon stands for terror, Antigone represents pity. But her
attitude, too, is one-sided. Although many interpreters in the past have
clearly favored Antigone, we must open our mind and see what strange
fanaticism determines her also. Her love for her older brother has certain
erotic overtones, suggesting incestuous desires, which explain Antigone's
intense, even irrational, feelings for him. According to Ruprecht, the Greek
erao and *keimai*, referring to Antigone's love for her brother, possess "a

---

14. "Creon: Shall I rule this land for an other than myself? Haemon: The polis
is not a single man's possession. Creon: Is the polis not under a single ruler's law?
Haemon: You would rule a desert well — alone" (*Antigone* 736-41).

none-too-subtle erotic implication" (1994, 39n.38; 49n.70). Ruprecht blames Hegel, notwithstanding his sublime reading of Antigone, for not seeing this and instead making Antigone a model of innocence, purity, and chastity in the relation between brother and sister (Ruprecht 1994, 39n.39). Antigone's erotic love for her brother blinds her to other natural bonds she is engaged in. She holds in contempt her sister Ismene, who, like Antigone, denounces Creon's verdict and is willing to share in the condemnation and punishment meted out by Creon, but does not share Antigone's passionate, life-killing piety that leads her to perform the burial rites. In the end, Polyneices' burial leads to a "domino-chain of death": Antigone hangs herself, Haemon kills himself, and Creon's wife, Eurydice, after hearing the news of this calamity, dies by her own hand. Antigone is not destroyed passively; rather, she destroys herself (Ruprecht 1994, 30n.9) — and others too, I would add.

Both Creon's and Antigone's characters may be said, therefore, to be determined by an unbalanced relation among passions, goods, and reasons. Creon is possessed by an "erotic" passion for legal justice, which diminishes the good of justice and prevents him from taking wise counsel from others, for example from Haemon. Antigone is possessed by an "erotic" passion for her elder brother, which diminishes her ability to be aware of what is good for the other people to whom she is bound by bonds of nature and blood as well.

All this adds a deeper meaning to Heraclitus's definition "character is destiny," which I cited earlier. As with Creon and Antigone, passions, goods, and reasons are the material from which individuals shape their lives and destinies, and influence the lives of others and their communities. People have a hand in their own individual life and their living together (Ruprecht 1994, 29, 72).

Now we come to the negation of the negation. What is it, and what moral instruction does it hold? At the end of the play Creon relents and orders Antigone's release. At this dramatic moment, in which Creon's character is balanced against Antigone's, Creon is at least partially restored from a moral point of view. But it is too late, because she has already hung herself. Creon suddenly becomes aware of what has happened to Antigone, her brother, her sister, his own son, and his wife, and condemns himself: "Oh me, me! No other mortal is yoked to these crimes as their cause — only me. For I did this to you. Heedless, I did, I say it clear. Alas, servants, lead me away, quickly, take me away on foot — I who now am nothing more than nothing."[15] The ultimate cause of Creon's misfortune is stated earlier on in the play by Creon's son: "You wish to speak and, speaking, not to

15. *Antigone* 1317-25.

364

listen."[16] Out of this configuration—this negation of the negation—emerges a human being who goes through the most painful conflicts and comes to terms with them, who finds life by losing it.

The story of Creon and Antigone can be formulated in terms of the cardinal virtues I mentioned at the beginning of this section: courage, temperance, justice, and wisdom. What Creon and Antigone indirectly teach us is first of all a conception of courage that transcends the rigidity with which they defend their respective causes, that is, the city's justice and the family's love, and points toward a weak conception of strength, in which finding life consists of losing it. They indirectly teach us also the meaning of temperance, because both of them are possessed by an irrational passion that makes them blind to other goods and other dimensions of the conception of the good life. Further, they indirectly teach us the broadness and depth of justice, by transcending its negative "thou shalt not" and inscribing in us its positive "thou shalt," which refers to that which is due the other in terms of honor, esteem, and dignity for both the living and the dead. Lastly, they indirectly teach us the meaning of wisdom, which weighs and assesses the good of virtues to be applied not to the situation but in the situation, taking into account its uniqueness, contingency, fragility, and brokenness. In sum, human character is a process, a process that undergoes virtuous conflicts and in reconciling these virtuous conflicts in the concrete situation learns what life is all about. This makes the human being noble and gives him/her hope (Ruprecht 1994, 90, 103).

8.2 Good Character from the Last Judgment

What makes a character does not depend ultimately on the judgment made during our own or anybody else's lifetime, but on the judgment rendered at the completion of time, which is in itself a religious theme. The problem, however, is whether the idea of the Last Judgment implies, to take up Morson's phraseology again, either foreshadowing or sideshadowing. If it involved foreshadowing, it would ruin the time- and narration-oriented account of human character as I have described it so far. It would orient all human life and action toward a fixed day when good will be separated from bad and right from wrong in a predetermined way. The Last Judgment would then operate in terms of the preconceived future, from which back-shadowing—because foreshadowing and backshadowing imply each other—would take place, and the present in its presentness would be corrupted.

16. *Antigone* 757.

The idea of the Last Judgment and sideshadowing are compatible only if the Last judgment — negatively speaking — does not entail a closed utopia and if it — positively speaking — strengthens the presentness of the present by making people aware of sideshadowing and encouraging them to look at alternative courses of action. In short, the Last Judgment is compatible with the time- and narration-directed analysis of human character if it does not take the individual and social status quo for granted and instead turns it upside down. In sum, it intensifies the dynamic nature of human character, insofar as it questions foreshadowing and backshadowing and confronts people with the contingency of responsibilities and choices in the presence of initiative and of new beginnings.

At the same time, when the Last Judgment is seen from this perspective of contingency-related responsibility and choice, it also implies a sense of tragedy, an awareness of virtuous conflicts, a feeling of greatness and weakness, and of aporias. Without this aporetic structure, the Last Judgment would probably fall into the trap of foreshadowing and backshadowing, because its very nature would be perfect knowledge and the perfection of the utopian world. However, perfection implies "good" and "bad," and the nature of these is not at all clear, since in each concrete situation "good" and "bad" are tied up with an endless number of singularities of concrete situations, of which there is an infinite variety. Yes, we have virtuous guidelines, which indicate the paths to be pursued in a general sense, the abstract decisions to make, and the general actions to perform. But what is good or bad, is good or bad in these concrete situations, where we meet ourselves, our significant others, our anonymous fellow human beings, in a large number of divergent institutions.

The story of the Last Judgment, especially Matthew 25, which I take as my starting point here, strikes me as an appropriate narration in the context of this chapter. This text contains at least two layers, a moral and a religious one. The moral layer encourages the listener or reader to give food to the hungry, drink to the thirsty, clothes to the naked, and to visit the sick and the imprisoned. The religious layer consists of Jesus' identification with the "least of mine," so that what is done to them is done to him.

One particular reason why this text fits in with the subject of this chapter is that, as Ricoeur (1975, 335) indicates, it falls into the category of hyperbole. Hyperbole can be seen as a rhetorical strategy in which an exaggerated statement is developed, a statement that is not meant to be taken literally as truth but aims to achieve a specific goal in the audience. Hyperbole does not point to a thing to be described, verified, or confirmed, but to an action to be performed. In fact, this action takes place in both the articulation and the hearing of the hyperbole, because a speech in hyperboles is a speech act.

What then is the goal of hyperbole? What is the action it seeks to produce? According to Ricoeur, hyperboles strive to turn the world as it is upside down.[17] They take away the plausibility of the world we take for granted. They turn the conventional world we live in topsy-turvy. They dislocate what seems to be consolidated and indicate a point in time that is "only beyond an abyss of shadows" (Ricoeur 1991, 92). As fictional literature, they establish a distance with regard to everyday reality and open up "the reality of the possible" (ibid., 97). They refer to crisis situations, never to situations we are used to dealing with in our common daily life. They describe a sort of behavior in these crisis situations one cannot really imitate. They connote something new, surprising, and creative. The parables in the Gospels are good examples of hyperboles that recount the aporias or paradoxes of human existence. We can think of the shepherd who leaves the ninety-nine sheep behind in order to save a single lost sheep, or the father who receives his lost younger son more graciously than he ever treated his eldest, or the host who sends away the guest because he does not have his wedding garment on, or the workers of the eleventh hour who are paid the same wages as the workers of the first, third, and sixth hours.

Jesus' eschatological parable about the "least of mine," which is narrated in Matthew 25, is also hyperbole. It leads the listener or reader into the crisis of the last judgment (the word "judgment" in Greek is *krisis,* literally "crisis"). It turns the easy, everyday life upside down and presents convention, even religious convention, in a new and problematic light. In doing so, it leaves the listener or reader with a paradox or even aporia, which by definition cannot be solved. A paradox is a seeming contradiction between two possibilities or ways out, whereas an aporia is a real contradiction with no way out. If one wishes to realize both possibilities at the same time, there is a wide gap, a yawning abyss, between two unattainable, mutually exclusive, shores. The hyperbole of the "least of mine" confronts us with the paradox or even aporia of human life. It opens us to the weakness, fragility, and tragedy of our very existence.[18]

I wish to examine three kinds of paradoxes or aporias with which

17. A few decades ago, Ricoeur distinguished five literary genres within the Bible: prophetic, narrative, prescriptive, sapiential, and hymnic discourse. In more recent years, he distinguishes three genres based on the rabbinical triad (Torah, Prophets, and other books): narrated law, prophetic literature, and sapiential texts (Mongin 1994, 235-49). Hyperboles especially belong to the prophetic texts.

18. Ricoeur emphasizes the specific quality of the referent "God" in these parables and other hyperboles, i.e., being "at once the coordinator of all these diverse discourses and the vanishing point, the index of incompletion of these partial discourses" (Ricoeur 1991, 97).

Jesus' eschatological hyperbole confront us. These three paradoxes or aporias refer to the first person, the "I," the second person, the "you," and the third person, the anonymous "he," "she," or "they." For each one I will inquire into the meaning of the "least of mine," which is the core expression of this eschatological hyperbole, and I will subsequently do so from the perspective of the first, second, and third person. From the perspective of the first person, the paradox or aporia is that of self-care and other-care; from the perspective of the second person it is the paradox or aporia of love for significant others or for the poor and marginalized; and from the perspective of the third person it is the paradox or aporia of love for the poor in the context of short, personal relations or in the context of the long relations mediated by social institutions. Time and again the question is: Who are the "least of mine"?

The First-Person Perspective

The first paradox or aporia that confronts the reader or listener in Jesus' hyperbole of the "least of mine" is the question of whether the care for the other, especially the "least of mine," has priority over the care for myself, or self-care. What is more important: self-care or other-care? What are the implications for one's decision making, acting, and living? The answer as given in the Gospel of Matthew may seem self-evident: why speak of the "least of mine" if they ought not to be given preference! However, a careful analysis of the relation between self-care and other-care will show the aporias that are implied in it.

To begin with, one must think about the consequences of this relationship for the virtuous character. Authors like Adler (1991) maintain that some cardinal virtues, like fortitude and temperance, are primarily connected with self-care; others, like justice, with other-care; and still others, like prudence, with both self-care and other-care. Deciding whether to give priority to self-care or other-care would evidently result in preferring some virtues over others. If the priority is self-care, then one should act primarily on fortitude and temperance; if it is other-concern, then one's choices should be determined primarily by considerations of justice.[19]

But a division between self-related and other-related virtues is not

---

19. Slote (1990, 435) thinks prudence, sagacity, circumspection, equanimity, and fortitude refer primarily to self-concern; justice, kindness, probity, and generosity to other-concern; and self-control, courage, and (perhaps) wisdom in practical affairs to both other-concern and self-concern.

always possible, let alone intelligible. Let us take the virtue of honesty, which implies truthfulness.[20] Part of the problem of honesty is to determine to what degree one ought to open one's heart to another person or keep it locked. To open one's thoughts, ideas, or feelings may benefit oneself, since everyone has a need to discuss with someone else his/her opinions about associates, the government, religion, and so forth, as Kant puts it (Kant 1964, 2:143). At the same time, one may feel oneself restricted in doing so. "He cannot risk it partly because the other person, while prudently keeping back his own opinions, might use this to harm him, and partly because, if he revealed his failings while the other person concealed his own, he would lose something of the other's respect by presenting himself quite candidly to him" (ibid.). Kant, then, is in favor of selective disclosure for one's own benefit.

But see now how Hume interprets and evaluates moderate, tempered honesty. He does not say that people do not dare to express to each other everything they think and feel, but that they cannot, because it would require that they share their entire lives. "We cannot 'let it all hang out'; there just is far too much of it." Time constraints, if nothing else, preclude this. "Whereas Kant sees reticence as primarily a self-protected necessity, a protection against public shame and mockery, on the Humean alternative I am suggesting, it should rather be seen as a form of consideration for others, a protection of them from undue embarrassment, boredom, or occasion for pity" (Baier 1990, 270). In other words, the same virtue, in this case honesty, can be interpreted from the point of view of both self-concern and other-concern. Thus, whether self-care or other-concern is given priority does not affect how honesty is acted on, since this virtue may be understood in such a sophisticated way that the distinction between self-care and other-care blurs.

The picture becomes still more confusing if one takes into account that on the surface, people appear to act from the virtues of other-concern, but on a deeper level they strive to amass self-benefit. A splendid example of the difference between these levels can be found in De Swaan's analysis of medieval society (1988). De Swaan shows how in that society the virtue of charity, which forms the ideological foundations of the social welfare system, was used to legitimate the mechanisms of rational egoism of the propertied class. Gangs of criminals who made the countryside unsafe were kept quiet through a system of daily meals at the doors of convents and farmhouses, but this was done in such a minimal way that it obliged one's

20. Nietzsche notes how hard truthfulness is: "Perhaps nobody yet has been truthful enough about what 'truthfulness' is" (Nietzsche, *Beyond Good and Evil* [New York, 1966], 177).

neighbor to do the same, and if he would not, one did not lose a lot of money by it. This system can be explained by game theory, which identifies the strategic ways in which individuals serve their own self-interest by taking into account the probability of certain reactions by the other player and one's own possible reactions to these reactions. The church functioned as a legitimation of this "game system" by preaching and celebrating in liturgy, homily, and catechesis the virtue of charity, which inspired and motivated people to continue the serving of meals. De Swaan shows that strategic-rational egoism, insofar as it is supported by game theory, served as the basis of a whole societal system, and that the virtue of charity functioned as the legitimation of this moral egoism. Here the ambivalence, even aporia, of self-care and other-care is plainly evident.

Having explained how other-care may be debased by the deeper motivation of self-interest, let me deal with other-care in more depth, especially friendship, which may be seen as the very core of other-care. It is important to remember that friendship can be either an extrinsic or an intrinsic external good. The first is friendship between people who are connected with each other for reasons of utility or pleasure, the second friendship between people who participate in one another's striving for moral virtues, the good life, and happiness. The friends in the first group are means to an end; those in the second are not treated as means only but are loved for their own sake, as ends in themselves. This friendship *(philia)* extends from civic to intimate friends as well as to family, including husband and wife, parents and children, and siblings. These relations contribute to my own happiness to the extent that I take care of the goods of my friends for their own sake. Here the distinction between "means" and "ends" in intimate friendship creates an aporia, because to the extent that I treat my friends as ends in themselves, they also are means to my own happiness.

Yet another aspect must be mentioned here, which goes still deeper. As other-concerned as intimate friendship may be, it is unthinkable to extend the ultimate goal of one's own life, which is happiness, to one's friends. The pursuit of happiness is something that each person must take care of in his or her own life. Happiness is not something that can be divided or transferred. It is comprised of one's own desires, goods, reasons, and actions, and it is not something that somebody else can bring about: "Trying to make someone else happy is as futile as trying to live someone else's life" (Annas 1992, 135). In this sense friendship is contingent and limited; it is intrinsically shaped by human finitude.[21]

21. Plato sees human finitude in relation to friendship from a different point of view, as Sherman (1989, 129) explains: "Friendships, in so far as they depend upon

The question may be whether selfless other-care, which strives exclusively for the other's good life, is really possible. Ultimately, however, the question is irrelevant. As a hyperbole, Jesus' parable about "the least of mine" brings the paradox or aporia between self-care and other-care to a climax. This fictional text does not ask its listeners to do the impossible, but merely turns their conventional thinking upside down. The text surprises, challenges, and opens up one's feeling and thinking as a way of keeping this unsolvable paradox or aporia alive. If the paradox or aporia were "resolved," people would either devote themselves to a self-confident life of happiness and pleasure or to a rigid and fanatic life of self-negation and self-starvation. The middle way between the two extremes would seem to be the royal way, but nobody can know its origin, course, and end with certainty. And precisely this not-knowing is what this eschatological parable aspires to lead us toward. It leads us into the cloud of unknowing about what "good life," "living well," and "loving the other as yourself" really mean. Jesus' eschatological speech implies not foreshadowing or backshadowing but sideshadowing, confronting the listener or reader with responsibility, choice, and initiative.

The Second-Person Perspective

Jesus' hyperbole contains a second paradox or aporia, which also can be formulated in terms of priority: In our other-care, should we give priority to the socially marginalized "least of mine" or to the people we live with — our spouse, children, parents, cohabitants, and friends who are near and dear to us? Who are the "others" whom we should prefer, who are the "you" with whom we should concern ourselves: the beggars and strangers in the streets or the members of our family or primary group at home?

This question also is difficult to answer, because it implies another

---

mutual interests and affections, easily dissolve as these interests and affections shift. To form a friendship is in part to expose oneself to this risk. Even if we try to counteract this vulnerability by making constancy a condition of the best sort of friendship (as Aristotle seems to do in the case of virtue friendship, where the constancy of the friendship derives from the stable interest and disposition of each party towards virtue), still constancy does little to prevent the permanent dissolution of a friendship through death. If anything, the stability of the friendship leaves us least protected against that contingency. For it is when we have lost a lifelong friend or loved one that we truly feel we have lost a part of ourselves and a substantial part of our happiness. Friendship thus makes us vulnerable, and even if constancy is a feature of that friendship, our self-sufficiency remains at best fragile."

paradox or aporia. In the essay "Existentialisme est un humanisme," which I mentioned earlier, Sartre tells the story of one of his pupils during the Second World War who did not know whether he should fight in England with the Free French Forces, or stay in France to support his mother, whose elder son had been killed by the Germans. Were the "you" he felt obligated to support his fellow soldiers, risking their lives and suffering terrible physical hardship, or his mother, who suffered from loss and despair? Sartre admitted that he was not able to solve this problem, but he told his pupil that he was free to make a choice: "You are free, so choose!" Sartre was mistaken, however, in the first place because absolute freedom does not exist. Thoughts and actions are always embedded in thoughts and actions that have gone before, so that we may say we think the thought we are confronted with and we do the actions we are affected by, as Ricoeur (1975) might say. Life is a paradox of activity and passivity, doing and suffering, liberty and tragedy, freedom and fate. Second, Sartre challenged his pupil to make a choice, when this was precisely the pupil's problem: which choice?

This problem illustrates the paradox or aporia one may confront in such situations. If one chooses the first possibility, which is to engage oneself with the collectivity of others who need support, it means letting down one's "significant others." If one chooses for those who are nearest and dearest, one neglects those who may be more needy and destitute than the people in one's own private circle.

Perhaps Kant's proposal offers a solution. This proposal suggests that concentric circles can be drawn, metaphorically speaking, around each individual, and that the narrowest circles be given more attention and the widest ones less. The narrowest circle consists of one's family, followed by the circles of intimate friends, of acquaintances and colleagues, and then of our fellow citizens and compatriots in the wider city-state, the Aristotelian polis (Slote 1990, 445; Kant 1964, 2:118ff.).

The difficulty with this proposal, however, is that it says nothing at all about those outside the polis, outside the circle of fellow citizens and compatriots, for example, people from other countries, foreigners, who mostly live at the margins of society. Aristotle pays no attention to them. He is not morally indifferent to them; rather, he ignores them altogether. To move beyond this one-sidedness, one might look at another concept found in the ethics of the ancients, especially the Stoics: that of familiarization (oikeiosis). The Stoics do not look on friendship (philia) as an almost natural stopping place because, they point out, from a moral point of view we must take care of every human being as a human being for his/her own sake. Here the subjective view of friendship takes second place to the impartial view of care for all. Personal attachments and bonds are transcended, and are extended to every human being so that every human being becomes familiar (Annas 1992, 141; cf. MacIntyre 1988, 146ff.).[22]

Is this Stoic concept of familiarization satisfying? Does it not suppose that we treat every person, including the foreigner, the significant other, and ourselves as well, in a neutral, impartial, detached way? Is it good to treat people exclusively in such an objective, distantiated manner? Cicero asked this question: "'If there is only one plank and two shipwrecked men, both of them [Stoic] virtuous men, would each try to seize it for himself, or would one cede it to the other?' 'One would cede it, and it would go to the one whose life is of more value to himself or his country.' 'What if there is nothing to choose between them on this point?' 'There will be no struggle; one will cede to the other as though the loser by lot or in game of chance'" (*De Officiis* 3.90). This is truly an impartial answer, in which no personal attachments, bonds, or interests play a role. The self is ultimately treated as another, as everyone. This solution is not restricted to Stoic philosophy; it can be found in Kantian moral philosophy as well, like Rawls's theory of justice: "Neither concern for others nor for self has priority, for all are equal" (Rawls 1971, 485). But is this satisfying? Is it possible? Would not everyone in a shipwreck fight to have the plank for himself/herself or for his/her significant other? Even if one did not, should such impartiality be valued as good?

In asking how the foreigner, who is perhaps the real representative of the "least of mine" in our society, should be treated, we confront the paradoxical and even aporetic relationship among care for oneself, for the significant other, and for the foreign other. Evidently, we cannot absolutely transcend ourselves, and treating the foreign other as a human being with neutrality and detachment would imply treating oneself and the significant other in the same objective, detached way. Does this tripartite relationship contain a way out of the paradox or aporia?

One might say that the solution lies in eliminating the care for oneself and one's own interests from the moral scene. Following Plato, Philippa Foot (1978, 125ff.) appears to reject this solution, arguing that practicing moral virtue must benefit the possessor of the virtue himself/herself. Later, though, she retracts this argument, saying that it does not matter whether the person himself/herself benefits from the moral virtue practiced (Foot 1978, 159, 168). In the process, she appears to move in the direction of Kant's moral theory, which holds that we have an obligation to contribute

22. See Cicero *De Finibus* 3.63; Hierocles, *Ethische Elementarlehre*, ed. H. von Arnim and W. Schubart, Berliner Klassikertexte, vol. 4 (Berlin, 1906); Annas 1992, part 3, chap. 3, section 3.

to the well-being of others but no corresponding obligation to advance our own happiness. This is not to deny that we have a duty not to harm ourselves and a duty of self-preservation—such minimal or basic rules evidently apply—but we do not have a duty to pursue our happiness (Slote 1990).

It is legitimate to ask whether eliminating the pursuit of happiness for oneself from moral consideration does not damage the conception of the good life, or at least a fundamental dimension of it, which is at the basis of all moral theory, as I explained in this and previous chapters. The good life is surely not only the good life for me, nor even only the good life for my significant others, but also the good life for every member of human society, including especially those who live at the margins of it, as foreigners often do. In other words, the pursuit of happiness encompasses the happiness of all. Neither the dimension of the self nor that of the significant other nor that of the foreign other must be left out of the conception of the good life. The good life fundamentally is living together, living in solidarity, living in common. The good essentially is the common good.

What this means concretely for decisions, choices, and actions can only be estimated, analyzed, and evaluated in these concrete situations themselves, and is part of the irremovable responsibility of the concrete human actor, his/her unrepeatability, and uniqueness. In sum, there is no way out of the paradox or even aporia that is implicit in this all-encompassing striving for the good life. It is not a conflict between good and evil, but between goods and other goods, as Dewey (1994, 154) rightly says.

This weighing of goods in concrete situations is not a mathematical calculation, in which the advantages and disadvantages, benefits and burdens, or joy and suffering are computed. Real life is confusing, and we can take this side or that side, this direction or that direction, this way or that way. Life does not lend itself to clear, one-dimensional, or precisely formulated conclusions. It often calls for wise estimation, careful weighing, and honest compromises. Life is not a mathematical theorem that we arrive at from an impersonal, detached attitude, but a series of wise decisions, which we make from a personal attitude of participation. Conclusions are the object of constatation, decisions the object of attestation, as Ricoeur puts it. Constatation relates to autonomous scientific knowledge, which is (seemingly) independent of sideshadowing history and contingency, whereas attestation has its base in the singularity and fragility of the concrete situation, by which the idea of autonomy is relativized in the direction of "dependence without heteronomy," as Ricoeur, following in the footsteps of Jean Nabert, might call it (Mongin 1994, 70). Attestation means we are not a hundred percent sure whether we have made the right decision, but after carefully weighing all aspects and especially taking into account the singularity and fragility of the situation, we commit to it and are prepared to express our conviction. It is an "act which completes the negation of the limits which affect individual destiny. It is stripping off into nakedness *(dépouillement),*" as Ricoeur says (Mongin 1994, 70). This stripping off is both paradoxical and radical. The knowledge it implies is not the result of reasoning processes like those that take place within the deductive or empirical sciences, but of understanding within a hermeneutical approach to concrete situations (Mongin 1994, 197). Ricoeur calls it a conviction emerging from practical wisdom in situation.

The Third-Person Perspective

Jesus' speech on the Last Judgment contains a third category of people: the anonymous members of the community to which "I" and "you" belong: they are "he," "she," "they." They are members of one's neighborhood, association, congregation, or organization, but one does not know them by name. Perhaps we recognize some of their faces, but we cannot put names to the faces. They are not an "I" or a "you" for us, we cannot address them in a personal way, because we know neither their first name, which represents their personal uniqueness, nor their surname, which represents their being inscribed in history and tradition (Ricoeur 1992, 52-55). We address them neutrally as "sir" or "ma'am." Although we recognize their faces, they do not have a truly human face for us, because we know nothing about their personal and family stories, their joys and disappointments, their hopes and despairs, their doubts and anxieties, their loves and hates. They are "everyone" for us.

Again, the paradox or aporia implied in Jesus' speech on the Last Judgment can be formulated in terms of priorities. Should we give priority to direct caring for individual poor people or to indirect caring for the poor as a collectivity in and through societal institutions? Ought we to give money to individual beggars and panhandlers we see on the streets or in our neighborhood, or should we rather contribute to economic, political, and social institutions that help all the marginalized members of our society and establish a social safety net? In other words: ought we to favor personal charity or collective justice? Ricoeur calls direct caring, giving alms, and charity the short way of love, and indirect caring in and through institutions, establishing a safety net, and social justice he calls the long way of love (Ricoeur 1968).

On this point, Ricoeur criticizes both Lévinas and Heidegger. Lévinas restricts morality to the interpersonal confrontation in which the other's face, your face, looks at me and reveals its claim to be looked after and taken care of, whereas Ricoeur widens the moral horizon by putting the anonymous he, she, or they into perspective as everyone whom we come across in our daily institutional life. Heidegger diminishes and rejects this third person singular and plural by calling it *das Man*, whereas Ricoeur explicitly takes this neuter being into consideration and accords him/her a moral status, particularly in the context of our associations and organizations, in his moral theory of societal institutions. Ricoeur accepts Rawls's concept of distributive justice, which refers explicitly and primarily to the third person, but also broadens and deepens Rawls's idea of justice by including the perspective of the good life and the common good (Mongin 1994, 100-101).

This does not remove the paradox or aporia, which has to do with whether priority ought to be given to the individual or to the institutional, anonymous other. This dilemma becomes even more acute when we learn from empirical research that church members are generally less inclined than nonchurch members to favor social criticism aimed at institutionally ameliorating the economic, political, social, and cultural situation of the underprivileged (Ester and Halman 1994, 227). Church people appear to favor charity, while nonchurch members dislike charity because they believe it has a dehumanizing effect on the poor, who are expected to show gratitude. Nonchurch members appear to prefer replacing charity by building up just institutions in which people do not have to depend on occasional benevolence but have the right to a dignified existence, protected not only by the primary, individual human rights, but also especially by the secondary, economic, social, and cultural human rights and the tertiary, collective, or solidarity human rights (Andrews 1987; Van Genugten 1992).

The paradox or aporia becomes still more acute to the degree we are aware of the structural ambivalence that underlies the institutions, especially political institutions. On the one hand institutions are the channels through which a just distribution between advantages and burdens, freedom and responsibilities, and rights and obligations is brought about. They contribute to the good life for all. On the other hand they are marked by structures of domination, hierarchization, and bureaucracy, which are as hard as steel. To varying degrees, they are corrupt, violent, and exploitative. They are characterized by a gap between the democratic power-in-common and domination, which should be under the control of the power-in-common but never totally is. In short, the political paradox is that the institutions are a mixture of good and evil (Ricoeur 1992, 258-60). What, then, should one do: support the poor directly via the short way or take the long way, which is even longer than most people think, that is, helping to transform the political institutions in order to bring about justice and the common good for all? Should one turn one's back on the political scene or participate in it in order to purify and transform it?

In his eschatological speech, Jesus says nothing about this paradox or aporia, but his unconventional words make the listener or reader critically think over his/her own attitudes, decisions, and behavior. It also warns him/her not to judge too hastily, either himself/herself or others. Because the Last Judgment is fictionally cast at the end of time, any judging in the here and now must be done from an attitude of what Ernst Käsemann called "eschatological reservation" *(der eschatologische Vorbehalt),* which requires us to suspend excesses of human judgment: "Do not judge, so that you may not be judged" (Matt 7:1). In the letter to the Romans, Paul upbraids the members of the Christian community: "Why do you pass judgment on your brother or sister? Or you, why do you despise your brother or sister? For we will all stand before the judgment seat of God" (Rom 14:10). This "eschatological reservation" is to be understood as "the attempt to use belief in the ultimate judgment by God in order to relativize or to restrain judgments made by individual believers or factions" (Meeks 1993, 188).

Two aspects, two "hidings," in Jesus' speech strike us. The first concerns the Jewish belief that works of mercy ought to be performed without being perceived, observed, or experienced by other people. "Do not sound a trumpet before you," Jesus says (Matt 6:2). The left hand should not know — as the hyperbole goes — what the right hand is doing (Matt 6:3). Giving alms, doing mercy, and promoting justice must be done inconspicuously, unobtrusively, and discretely. One does not deserve the first place in the temple, the synagogue, or the theater because one helps the poor, widows, orphans, or strangers. Mercy and benevolence performed for reasons of social reputation and prestige are unhesitatingly called sin by Rabbi Eleazar. And Jesus adds that people who do so are hypocrites (Matt 6:2). Why should you advertise yourself when "your Father sees in secret" (Matt 6:4)?

The second hiding refers to the religious dimension of helping and supporting the poor. "Truly, I tell you," Jesus explains in the hyperbole, "just as you did it to one of the least of these who are members of my family, you did it to me" (Matt 25:40). Jesus' identification with the poor, whom he calls the "least of mine, members of my family," is not a mystical kind of bond, as if his relationship with the poor surpasses understanding, thought, and imagination. Jesus' identification with the poor is simply a result of the life he lived, the acts and works he performed, the words he spoke, the table he sat at, the streets he walked through: always, time and again with the poor, among the poor, for the poor, in short, as one of the poor. The poor are not only his brothers and sisters; more importantly he is their brother. Or, to put it in the words of the parable of the compassionate

Samaritan: the poor are not Jesus' neighbor, but Jesus proved neighbor to them (Luke 10:36).

Let me reflect on both hidings a bit further. What criterion shall be used at the Last Judgment to separate the sheep from the goats? The criterion is evidently what we have done for individual poor people, even when we did not know it. The awareness with which we assist people and help the poor is of no account at all. What tips the scales is that we have reached individual people. Does this mean that the short way of love, that of giving alms, is preferable? Not necessarily. Perhaps we can reach individual people better by the long way that goes through abstract institutions than we can in the short relations of face-to-face contact. It is not important whether we feel satisfied at helping the poor, but whether what we do is effective. The metaphor of the Last Judgment means that we are judged on something that may have been hidden to us, because we do not necessarily know whether or when we have reached individual people. In the short relations we may have made mistakes and misled ourselves, not really seeing what we were up to, not looking beyond our own neediness, the egocentricity in our helping. The meaning and effects of the long relations are hidden for us, because we are not able to survey them and see the big picture. Often we think that we have reached nobody within the abstract systems of economy, politics, and our own profession, but we may be mistaken. It will be detected, unveiled, revealed whether we fed the hungry, gave drink to the thirsty and clothing to the naked, visited the sick and the prisoners. This judging is not our work; it does not belong to our task; it is not within our authority. We have neither the right nor the power, and the standard is beyond what we can imagine (Ricoeur 1968).

In sum, the hyperbolic character of Jesus' eschatological speech confronts us with three paradoxes or aporias: first, the paradox of self-love or other-love, then the paradox of love for the significant others or for the poor and marginalized, and lastly the paradox of love for the poor in the short relations or in the long relations. What this speech teaches us is to leave the yawning abyss of these paradoxes open and to act out of the clashes of opposing tendencies that emerge from them. It is the only way not to be caught in the pitfalls of cultural and religious conventionalism on the one hand or principled fanaticism and rigid idealism on the other. It is the only way not to fall into the traps of easy self-satisfaction on the one hand or suffer from a guilty superego on the other. It is the only way to avoid foreshadowing and backshadowing, and realize sideshadowing. And perhaps, when the Last Judgment detects, uncovers, and reveals who we really are, according to what we really did for the "least of mine," the aporias will appear to have been paradoxes only.

8.3 Character Formation

From the preceding, the reader may have gathered that character formation within education, as I understand it, should go beyond, transcend, and even reject the attributes of the traditional approach in this area. The virtues that determine the virtuous character, as I have explained them, run counter to the four aspects of this traditional approach, which I referred to at the beginning of this chapter: fixedness, deductiveness, abstractness, and confusing plurality. First, because of the concept of open time, they are not "fixed virtues" within a "fixed character," but "open virtues" within an "open character." Second, there is no "bag of virtues" that should be deductively applied to the situation, but rather each situation must be considered in its contingency and fragility, meaning that the virtues are applied in the situation under the guidance of the virtue of practical wisdom, wisdom in situation. They are virtues under the authority of the wise. Third, when they are applied in the situation, based on the weighing of all relevant aspects, these virtues are not too abstract to function as guidelines. In a sense, virtues do not exist independently from concrete acting, because, as Aristotle says frequently, they are dispositions, which enable their possessor to realize them in and through acting (*EN* 3.5). Virtues are virtues in situation or they are not virtues at all. They embody the contingency of making a choice here and now, the singularity of responsibility in this concrete situation, and the presence of initiative. Lastly, their plurality is not something to be decried but positively evaluated, because it mirrors the plurality of aspects that have to be taken into account in concrete situations, the dynamism that marks the flow and sequence of these situations, and the rich sideshadowing of courses of actions to be taken.

So far I have said what character formation should reject (the traditional approach of fixed virtues and so on), but the far more interesting question is what character formation entails in a positive sense. Let me summarize the insights of the previous sections. Character formation should be based on the three-way interrelatedness of passions, goods, and reasons, as we learn from the ancients, especially Plato and Aristotle. Then this interrelatedness must be interpreted from the perspective of interactionism between person and situation, as we learn from Dewey (at least in my free interpretation of him). Further, this interactionism, being linguistic in nature, has to be understood in terms of its narrative structure. Character is realized in the dialectic relationship between the stories we tell one another and are told. This narrative framework is exemplified in the classic tragedies, which present in a most exemplary manner the paradoxes and aporias that virtuous character is subject to, the pitfalls of one-sidedness to which it is vulnerable, and the importance of tolerating, sustaining, and enduring the ambivalence, ambiguity, and tension inherent in it. Lastly, character formation should narrate, clarify, and initiate the tensions surrounding three fundamental kinds of choices that must be made time and again: the paradoxes and aporias of self-concern versus other-concern, care for the significant other versus care for the foreign other, and the short way of love versus the long way. These paradoxes and aporias are to be endured from the eschatological perspective of the Last Judgment, which will uncover, detect, and reveal who we are according to what we did.

To delineate the conditions moral education must meet in order to satisfy these criteria of character formation, let me clarify the following four aspects: perceiving moral salience; seeing in terms of passions, reasons, and goods; practicing virtues; and lastly narrating, which includes storytelling and participating in the paradoxes and aporias of tragedy.

Moral Salience

Perceiving moral salience refers to the important role the contingency and singularity of the concrete situation play in the developing character. That is, it is important to be aware that the situation one is in requires action or refraining from action, and the nature of that action or nonaction must be decided by reading all relevant aspects of the situation. This reading can happen from a variety of perspectives, resulting in multiple descriptions and definitions of the situation. These descriptions and definitions are informed by the different moral histories and biographies of different characters, that is, by different virtues and interpretations of virtues. In the end, "disagreements may result as to what is most pressing or relevant in a case" (Sherman 1989, 29). In other words, perceiving moral salience leads to the conflict of moral interpretations.

It is important to confront children with the complexity of reading situations in terms of the plurality of virtues and their interpretations and not to press them into only one definition of the situation, the one that is preferred by the educator(s). The child should learn different ways of reading through various moral language games and be encouraged to pose questions in order to acquire a more differentiated and enriched picture. One might call this the requirement of developing discernment. As Aristotle says with regard to the question of how to act in morally salient situations, "the decision lies with our perception" (*EN* 2.9; 4.5).

However, this perception can be distorted by inadequate habits, prejudices, fear, anxiety, or just incomplete or wrong seeing, and for that reason

380

correcting this perception for biases and pleasures toward which one is inclined is of crucial importance. This correction can happen by bringing the child as agent into direct communication with other persons, children, and adults, by which the child can learn to take the perspective of the other, evaluate his/her own perception, and find out what perception is most adequate in terms of the interaction between the child himself/herself and the situation (cf. Sherman 1989, 36).

Moral Passions, Reasons, and Goods

The second condition for character formation is seeing in terms of passions, reasons, and goods, the tripartite structure of which stems from Plato and Aristotle, as I noted earlier. This structure can be seen on the one hand as a kind of specification, and on the other as a kind of extension and intensification of what I said about perceiving moral salience.

The passions must be given their proper place in character formation. What is their proper place then? In Chapter 7 I asked what role passions or emotions may, can, or even must play in the field of morality. Then I concluded that three approaches to managing emotions, that is, suppressing, controlling, and neutralizing, are to be rejected. The other two approaches, ordering and processing, are of utmost moral relevance. Processing implies that one lets the emotions go and allows them to lead, while ordering discerns their authentic and inauthentic aspects and balances the former over the latter. Based on the classic analysis of the structure of character, which I owe to Dent (1984), this emphasis on the proper role of emotions or passions cannot be overestimated.

Character formation is not a matter of will alone, as moral educationists in Victorian times believed. The emotions ought not to be resisted, fought, and killed, because in the process an at least potentially rich, differentiated, and finely tuned instrument for seeing into the moral aspects of life would be lost. Seeing takes place through the emotions, not only through the senses, because the working of the senses and the working of the emotions are interrelated, as modern neurophysiology has learned. This seeing through the emotions provides us with our own awareness of the situation we are in, but equally of how others see it and respond to it. Here I hold up the importance of what I have referred to as the contrast experience as the starting point for the sense of justice, which counts as one of the cardinal virtues, as I indicated earlier in this chapter: "the idea of justice is better named 'sense' of justice on the fundamental level where we remain here. Sense of justice and of injustice, it would be better to say here, for what we are first aware of is injustice: 'Unjust!

381

What injustice!' we cry. And indeed it is in the mode of complaint that we penetrate the field of the just and the unjust" (Ricoeur 1992, 198). This complaint arises from our emotions in the concrete situation we are engaged in: "So, for example, a sense of indignation makes us sensitive to those who suffer unwarranted insult or injury, just as a sense of pity and compassion opens our eyes to the pains of sudden and cruel misfortune. . . . We notice through feeling what might otherwise go unheeded by a cool and detached intellect. . . . The cognitions are essential concomitants for experiencing the emotion. As such, Aristotelian emotions are not blind feelings like itches or throbs, but intentional states directed at articulated features of an agent's environment" (Sherman 1989, 45).

In order to perceive the salience of the concrete situation and act well in it, emotions are not enough. They have to be processed through and through in light of their authentic as well as inauthentic sources, their pure as well as impure inclinations, as I said, but afterward they must be ordered by the reasons in the perspective of the conception of the good life. The rational capacity of human beings must be invested in regulating the sense-desires in light of the virtue of temperance and directing the passional desires in light of the virtue of wisdom toward the perspective of the good life, because, in this area, the task of rationality is to connect these sense-desires and passional desires with the conception of the good life, as Dent (1984) puts it. The child should learn to use this capacity to connect passions and goods by developing his/her rationality. He/she should learn to process explicitly his/her emotions, to discern their pure and impure aspects, to connect them with the goods he/she has in mind, and to do this through practical-rational weighing, estimating, and evaluating. Aristotle uses the metaphor "father" and "friend" to indicate the role of reason in relation to passions (*EN* 1.13): the child should learn to take into account what "father reason" or "friend reason" says of the role passions ought to play in the concrete situation he/she is in.

Living according to passions and living according to reason ought not to be considered as contradictions, not even as contrasts, because their relationship is complementary, in the sense that the one implies the other. Without passion, reason is deaf; passion without rationality is blind. As Aristotle says: "And the irrational feelings are considered to be no less part of human nature than our considered judgments" (*EN* 3.1). This complementarity between passions and reasons should play a key role in character formation, because together they form an anthropologically sound infrastructure for the good life.

What idea of the good life should the child learn to develop? What conception of the good life is worthy to serve as a basis for estimations, decisions, and actions? What goods make the child truly happy? This is the crucial question of eudaemonism that permeates all character formation, because, ultimately, good character is happy character.

From the Aristotelian perspective, some things are in fact considered as good and as worthy to be strived for as goods, but are essentially neither real goods nor means to goods, for instance, fame and power. Other things are strived for as well, but essentially are only means to goods, like money. If one strives for it wrongly, that is, if one seeks it as an end itself and not purely as a means, it destroys happiness. Money should not be strived for, but if it is desired as a means, this desiring is permissible. Still other things are means to goods that are worthy to be strived for, though not as if they were the totality of goods *(totum bonum),* but only as part of that totality. This applies, for instance, to enjoying the pleasure of sense-desires like the taste of a fine wine, the feeling of swimming in pure, sparkling water, or the touch of a lover's skin. Still other things are worthy of striving after for their own sake, because they function as means to goods and are at the same time intrinsic goods in themselves, like friendship and the moral virtues.[23] Of the three kinds of friendship — friendship based on utility, on pleasure, and on goodness — only the last is truly worthy of being strived after for its own sake. Of the moral virtues, the cardinal virtues — courage, temperance, justice, and wisdom — in particular fit this description, although this list should not be considered exhaustive, since so-called new virtues like solidarity are also very important (Mieth 1984), as are "natural" virtues like attention and gratitude (Miller 1995), or "strange virtues," which refer to the openness to cross-cultural experience and communication (Adeney 1995). The highest good *(summum bonum)* is leisure *(theoria),* which should be strived for as an end itself, albeit not as the totality of ends *(totum bonum),* as I explained already.

Virtues

The third condition for character formation is the practice of virtue. Aristotle saw goodness as constituted in practices and virtues as being formed out of the habitual actions of actual people in actual situations. Virtues are the product of the lived-out motivations of virtuous persons, who do the right thing at the right time in the right way. Virtues concretize in virtuous

---

23. Here I take friendship and the moral virtues together, because they are intrinsic goods, even though friendship belongs to the external intrinsic goods and the moral virtues to the internal goods, as I explained in the first section of this chapter.

actions. Good character does not rest only in the motivations and intentions of a virtuous person. Good motivations and intentions must be embodied in right practices. Essentially, the question is not "what is good in this particular situation," but "what is best," which implies taking into account all circumstances relevant to the situation. The virtue that is in question here is practical wisdom, for which Aristotle uses his favorite metaphors of medical skill or navigation: "the individual must know how to exercise judgment and arrive at appropriate choice in relation to particular situations" (Crittenden 1993, 109).

What does this mean for character formation? How can practicing virtue in the situation be learned? The answer is simple: one learns to practice virtue only by practicing virtue, just as one learns to play the piano only by playing the piano or to swim only by swimming. In the words of Aristotle: "But the virtues we do acquire by first exercising them, just as happens in the arts. Anything that we have to learn to do we learn by the actual doing of it: people become builders by building and instrumentalists by playing instruments. Similarly, we become just by performing just acts, temperate by performing temperate ones, brave by performing brave ones" (*EN* 2.1). This evidently does not exclude instruction and communication about virtues and their practice, but rather includes them (Crittenden 1993, 116). From the modern conception of learning by experience, which has been developed by cognitive-social learning researchers, practice on the one hand and instruction and communication on the other are complementary, because they imply, need, and require each other (Bandura 1986).

Narration

The last condition for character formation is narration. Storytelling is important because it offers the possibility of participating in the life, words, and deeds of the great characters whom the story embodies. Storytelling functions as a kind of modeling, as described by cognitive-social learning theory, by offering an example with which the listeners or readers can identify (Bandura 1986). This modeling is not static but dynamic, in that it presents complex situations that characters move through. It carries the audience through the contingencies of time by inviting them into its side-shadowing of possible futures, showing them the responsibilities each of these futures entails for them, and confronting them with the choices to be made in the here and now. It makes them see how chance can be taken as challenge, probability understood as opportunity, and fate transformed into destiny.

384

Tragedy must be given a special place in storytelling, because tragedy is the culmination of greatness and weakness of character. Of all the narrative forms, tragedy most intensely invites the audience to participate in the paradoxes and aporias of individual and social life. It confronts them with the son's desire to kill his father and marry his mother, albeit unknowingly and unconsciously, as in the case of Sophocles' Oedipus. It brings them face to face with the daughter's powerful love for her father, as in the case of Oedipus in Colonos. It shows the fanatic blindness of both Creon and Antigone in their conflict over law and piety, and in the end what it means to find life by losing it. In so doing, it carries the audience beyond optimism and pessimism.

Why did the Greeks go to the theater over and over again to see these tragedies? The answer has to do with the very essence of tragedy. "These people did not go to the theater to learn what happens (they already knew what happened); they came to learn something new about themselves" (Ruprecht 1994, 186). They were not interested in the end because they were already familiar with the domino effect of death at the end of *Antigone,* but to come in contact with their own passions, goods, and reasons, the conflicts among which determined their own individual and social lives. Quite simply, participating in tragedy mirrors, informs, and shapes character.

Religious tragedies also have a role to play in character formation, at least to the degree in which biblical and other religious stories can be interpreted that way. Interestingly, Mark's story of Jesus in Gethsemane can be read as a tragedy from both a horizontal and a vertical perspective. Hegel used the terms *horizontal* and *vertical* to distinguish between two tragic axes or trajectories. The horizontal axis concerns the collision between religious and political power and even institutional-religious and charismatic-religious authority. The vertical perspective consists of Jesus' inner conflict about the relation between fate and destiny, life and death, his own will and God's will. In Gethsemane Jesus is more acted upon than acting, when he cries: "Abba, Father, for you all things are possible; remove this cup from me; yet, not what I want, but what you want" (Mark 14:36). Ruprecht comments: "The agony of this prayer cannot be missed. The extraordinary communion that Jesus enjoys with God, while seldom explicitly mentioned by Mark, has been graphically apparent in word and deed. . . . Jesus' father, while a God of few words, has been a God of decisive deeds. Quite suddenly, his silence speaks louder than his word or deeds have ever done" (Ruprecht 1994, 217). The full agony culminates at Golgotha, where Jesus cries: "My God, my God, why have you forsaken me?" (Mark 15:34). Ruprecht adds: "It would not be too much to say that this prayer is really the only question that Jesus ever asks, the answer to which even he does not know" (Ruprecht 1994, 222n.99). Why do Christian communities enact this tragedy over and over again, in the passion liturgy and passion plays during Holy Week? The answer is that these communities perform this tragedy year after year not to find out what happens and how the story ends, for this they already know, but to learn something about their own Gethsemane and Golgotha, the tragedy that determines and permeates their own lives.[24] Without religious tragedies like this one, character formation would not achieve its full scope and potential.

24. For some readers, the word *perform* may seem to be too theatrical to be applied to Jesus' passion story in Mark, but in a sense it refers to the dramatic and tragic nature of this story, told and retold over the ages (Ruprecht 1994, 186n.17).

Literature

Adeney, B. T. (1995). *Strange Virtues: Ethics in a Multicultural World.* Downers Grove, Ill.

Adler, M. J. (1991). *Desires Right and Wrong: The Ethics of Enough.* New York.

Andrews, J. A., and Hines, W. D. (1987). *International Protection of Human Rights.* London.

Andriessen, H., Nolet, M., and Derksen, N. (1995). *Bibliodrama: Stem en tegenstem. Ontwikkeling van een model.* Werkgroep voor opleiding en spiritualiteit. Warnsveld.

Annas, J. (1992). "The Good Life and the Good Lives of Others." In E. F. Paul et al., eds. *The Good Life and the Human Good,* 133-48. Cambridge.

Aristotle. *Ethica Nichomacheia.* English translation: *The Ethics of Aristotle: The Nicomachean Ethics,* by J. A. K. Thomson. New York, 1976.

Aristotle. *Politeia.* English translation: *The Politics,* by T. A. Sinclair. New York, 1992.

Arnason, J. P. (1994). "Reason, Imagination, Interpretation." In G. Robinson and J. Rundell, eds. *Rethinking Imagination, Culture and Creativity,* 155-70. London/New York.

Assagioli, R. (1973). *The Act of Will.* New York.

Auer, A. (1971; 1984^2). *Autonome Moral und christlicher Glaube.* Düsseldorf.

Auer, A. (1975). "Ein Modell theologischer-ethischer Argumentation: 'Autonome Moral.'" In A. Auer, ed. *Moralerziehung im Religionsunterricht,* 27-57. Freiburg.

Auer, A. (1977a). "Die Bedeutung des Christlichen bei der Normfindung." In *Normen im Konflikt,* 29-55. Freiburg.

Auer, A. (1977b). "Die Autonomie des Sittlichen nach Thomas von Aquin." In *Christlich Glauben und Handeln,* 31-54. Düsseldorf.

Baier, A. (1990). "Why Honesty Is a Hard Virtue." In O. Flanagan and A. Oksenberg Rorty, eds. *Identity, Character, and Morality: Essays in Moral Psychology,* 259-82. Cambridge, Mass.

Baier, K. (1994). "Egoism." In P. Singer, ed. *A Companion to Ethics,* 197-204. Oxford.

Bandura, A. (1973). *Aggression: A Social Learning Analysis.* Englewood Cliffs.

Bandura, A. (1977). *Social Learning Theory.* Englewood Cliffs.

Bandura, A. (1986). *Social Foundations of Thought and Action: A Social Cognitive Theory.* Englewood Cliffs.

Barnes, J. (1976). "Introduction." In Aristotle, *Ethics,* 9-43. London.

Barot, R., ed. (1993). *Religion and Ethnicity: Minorities and Social Change in the Metropolis.* Kampen.

Bauman, Z. (1994). *Postmodern Ethics.* Cambridge, Mass.

Bauman, Z. (1995). *Life in Fragments: Essays in Postmodern Morality.* Cambridge, Mass.

Beauchamp, T. L., and Childress, J. F. (1994). *Principles of Biomedical Ethics.* 4th ed. New York.

Becker, J. W., and Vink, R. (1994). *Secularisatie in Nederland.* Sociale en culturele studies 19. Rijswijk.

Beemer, Th. (1970). "Abortus provocatus en de waarde van het menselijk leven." *Tijdschrift voor Theologie* 10/3:274-90.

Beemer, Th. (1973). "De organisatie van de liefde." In *Politiek of mystiek,* 36-42. Brugge.

Beemer, Th. (1983). "De fundering van de seksuele moraal in een door God ingestelde morele orde." In *Het kerkelijk spreken over seksualiteit en huwelijk,* 15-52. Nijmegen/Baarn.

Bekke, H., and Kuypers, P. (1990). *Afzien van macht: Adviseren aan een andere overheid.* The Hague.

Bell, D. (1993). *Communitarianism and Its Critics.* Oxford.

Bellah, R., and Hammond, Ph. E. (1980). *Varieties of Civil Religion.* San Francisco.

Bellah, R., et al. (1985). *Habits of the Heart.* Berkeley.

Bellah, R., et al. (1991). *The Good Society.* New York.

Bellah, R. (1992). The Quest for the Self: Individualism, Morality Politics. In D. Capps and R. Kenn, eds. *Individualism Reconsidered: Readings Bearing on the Endangered Self in Modern Society,* 115-24. Princeton.

Berger, P. L. (1974). "Some Second Thoughts on Substantive versus Functional Definitions of Religion." *Journal for the Scientific Study of Religion* 13/2:125-33.

Berger, P. L. (1979). *The Heretical Imperative: Contemporary Possibilities of Religious Affirmation.* New York.

Berger, P. L., and Berger, B. (1972). *Sociologie: Een biografische opzet.* Baarn.

Berger, P. L., and Luckmann, Th. (1967). *The Social Construction of Reality: A Treatise in the Sociology of Knowledge.* New York.

Berger, W. (1972). Doodgezwegen geloof en geestelijke volksgezondheid. In W. Berger, F. Haarsma, and P. Prouser. *Wat doen we met ons geloof?* Bilthoven.

Bernfeld, S. (1973). *Sisyphos oder die Grenzen der Erziehung.* Reprint. Frankfurt.

Bertram, H. (1986). "Einleitung." In Bertram H., ed. *Gesellschaftlicher Zwang und moralische Autonomie,* 9-32. Frankfurt.

Beyer, P. (1994a). *Religion and Globalization.* Thousand Oaks.

Beyer, P. (1994b). "Religious Traditions and the Global Religious System: Theoretical Prolegomena to an Empirical Investigation." Paper presented at the 1994 meeting of the Association for the Sociology of Religion, Los Angeles, August 3-6, 1994.

Bien, J. (1995). "Ricoeur as Social Philosopher." In L. E. Hahn, ed. *The Philosophy of Paul Ricoeur,* 287-305. Chicago.

Billig, M. (1982). *Ideology and Social Psychology.* Oxford.

Blankertz, H. (1972). *Theorien und Modelle der Didaktik.* Munich.

Blake, R., and Mouton, J. (1984). *Solving Costly Organizational Conflicts.* San Francisco.

Blasi, A. (1988). *Moral Conflict and Christian Religion.* New York.

Block, J. (1971). *Lives through Time.* Berkeley.

Bloom, B. S., Engelhart, M. D., Furst, E. J., Hill, W. H., and Krathwohl, D. R. (1956). *Taxonomy of Educational Objectives: The Classification of Educational Goals. Handbook 1. Cognitive Domain.* New York.

Bochenski, J. M. (1965). *The Logic of Religion.* New York.

Boff, Cl. (1983). *Theologie und Praxis.* Munich.

Boff, L. (1985). *Kirche, Charisma und Macht: Studien zur einer streitbaren Ekklesiologie.* Düsseldorf.

Boff, L. (1987a). *Und die Kirche ist Volk geworden.* Düsseldorf.

Boff, L. (1987b). *Passion of Christ, Passion of the World.* New York.

Borgman, E. (1986). "Theologie tussen universiteit en emancipatie: De weg van Edward Schillbeeckx." *Tijdschrift voor Theologie* 26/3:240-58.

Borowitz, E. B. (1990). "De Tora, geschreven en mondeling, en de mensenrechten: Oorsprong en tekorten." In *Concilium* 26/2:29-36.

Bowlby, J. (1987). *Attachment and Loss.* Vol. 1. *Attachment.* New York.

Bowles, S., and Gintis, H. (1977). *Schooling in Capitalist America: Educational Reform and the Contradictions of Economic Life.* New York.

Boyd, D. (1980). "The Rawls Connection." In B. Munsey, ed. *Moral Development, Moral Education, and Kohlberg: Basic Issues in Philosophy, Psychology, Religion, and Education,* 185-213. Birmingham, Ala.

Brennenstuhl, W. (1980). "Ziele der Handlungslogik." In H. Lenk, ed. *Handlungstheorien — Interdisziplinär,* 1:35-66. Munich.

Bruner, J. S. (1986) *Actual Minds, Possible Worlds.* Cambridge, Mass.

Bruner, J. S. (1990). *Acts of Meaning.* Cambridge, Mass.

Browning, D. S. (1989). *Religious Thought and the Modern Psychologies: A Critical Conversation in the Theology of Culture.* Philadelphia.

Browning, D. S. (1991). *A Fundamental Practical Theology.* Minneapolis.

Browning, D. S. (1995). "Christian Ethics and the Family Debate: An Overview." In *The Annual of the Society of Christian Ethics,* 251-62. Washington.

Brugger, W., and Hoering, W. (1976). "Kontingenz." In *Historisches Wörterbuch der Philosophie,* 4:1027-38.

Bulckens, J. (1994). *Zoals eens op weg naar Emmaüs: Handboek voor catechetiek.* Leuven.

Bulhof, I. (1989). "Over deugdenethiek en regelethiek." In I. Bulhof, ed. *Deugden in onze tijd,* 7-12. Baarn.

Burggraeve, R. (1987). "'Vrede, vrede voor hen die nabij zijn èn voor hen die veraf zijn' (Jes. 57,19)." In *Om de ander: Elementen voor een ethiek en spiritualiteit van de vrede,* 17-42. Baarn.

Burke, K. (1966). *Language as Symbolic Action.* Berkeley.

Campos, J. J., and Barret, K. C. (1986). "A New Understanding of Emotions and Their Development." In C. E. Izard, J. Kagan, and R. B. Zajonc, eds. *Emotions, Cognition, and Behavior,* 229-63. Cambridge.

Casey, W. M., and Burton, R. V. (1986). "The Social-Learning Theory Approach." In G. L. Sapp, ed. *Handbook of Moral Development,* 74-91. Birmingham, Ala.

Catechism of the Catholic Church (1993). Vatican City.

Clarke, H. D. (1991). "Measuring Value Change in Western Industrialized Societies: The Impact of Unemployment." *American Political Science Review* 85/3:905-20.

Clarke-Steward, A. (1991). "A Home Is Not a School: The Effects of Environments on Development." In M. Lewis and S. Feinman, eds. *Social Influences and Socialization in Infancy,* 41-62. New York.

Clouse, B. (1993). *Teaching for Moral Growth: A Guide for the Christian Community, Teachers, Parents, and Pastors.* Wheaton.

Cohen, A. M. (1980). "Stages and Stability: The Moral Development Approach to Political Order." In R. W. Wilson, and G. J. Schochet, eds. *Moral Development and Politics,* 69-84. New York.

Coser, L. (1984). "Introduction." In E. Durkheim. *The Division of Labour in Society.* New York.

Cox, W. M. (1994). "De motivatie van adolescenten voor het gebruik van alcohol." In G. Schippers and J. A. van der Ven, eds. *Niet bij gebruik alleen: Voorlichting over alcohol en drugs in het perspectief van zingeving,* 59-70. Kampen.

Crittenden, P. (1993). *Learning to Be Moral: Philosophical Thoughts about Moral Development.* New York.

Cronin, K. (1992). *Rights and Christian Ethics.* Cambridge.

Crossan, J. D. (1992). *The Historical Jesus: The Life of a Mediterranean Jewish Peasant.* San Francisco.

Damasio, Antonio R. (1994). *Descartes' Error: Emotion, Reason, and the Human Brain.* New York.

Davis, N. (1994). "Contemporary Deontology." In P. Singer, ed. *A Companion to Ethics,* 205-18. Oxford.

Dean, W. (1986). *American Religious Empiricism.* New York.

De Boer, T. (1994). "The God of the Philosophers and the God of Pascal." In H.-E. Mertens and L. Boeve, eds. *Naming God Today,* 63-78. Leuven.

Declaratio de Educatione Christiana (1965). Vaticanum II. Vatican City.

De Corte, E. (1973). *Onderwijsdoelstellingen.* Leuven.

De Corte, E., and Van Bouwel, J. (1978). "De hiërarchisch-cumulatieve structuur van Blooms taxonomie." *Pedagogische Studiën* 55:228-39.

De Koning, P. (1974). "Interne differentiatie." In *Pedagogische Studiën* 51:105-23.

Dekovic, M. (1991). "The Role of Parents in the Development of Child's Peer Acceptance." Diss. Nijmegen.

De Moor, R. (1983). "Nederland binnen de Europese cultuur: Een studie naar waarden." In J. Becker et al., eds. *Normen en waarden: Verandering of verschuiving?* 117-54. The Hague.

Dent, N. J. H. (1984). *The Moral Psychology of the Virtues.* Cambridge.

Derksen, N., and Andriessen, H. (1985). *Bibliodrama en pastoraat: De Schrift doen als Weg tot dieper geloven.* The Hague.

De Swaan, A. (1983). *De mens is de mens een zorg.* Amsterdam.

De Swaan, A. (1988). *In Care of the State: Health Care, Education, and Welfare in Europe and the USA in the Modern Era.* Dutch translation: *Zorg en de staat: Welzijn, onderwijs en gezondheidszorg in Europa en de Verenigde Staten in de nieuwe tijd* (Amsterdam, 1990).

De Tavernier, J. (1994). "Vraagt ethiek om geloof? Ethische verkenningen in het spoor van E. Schillebeeckx." *Tijdschrift voor Theologie* 34/1:24-48.

Dewey, J. (1986). *Logic: The Theory of Inquiry.* Later Works 12. Carbondale, Ill.

Dewey, J. (1994). *The Moral Writings of John Dewey.* Ed. James Gouinlock. Rev. ed. New York.

Dillmann, R. (1984). *Das Eigentliche der Ethik Jesu: Ein exegetischer Beitrag zur moraltheologischen Diskussion um das Proprium einer christlichen Ethik.* Mainz.

Dunn, J. (1991). "Sibling Influences." In M. Lewis and S. Feinman, eds. *Social Influences and Socialization in Infancy,* 97-109. New York/London.

Durkheim, E. (1951). *Suicide.* London. French original: *Le suicide.* Paris, 1897.

Durkheim, E. (1957). *Professional Ethics and Civic Morals.* London. French original: *Leçons de sociologie physique des moeurs et du droit.* Paris, 1950.

Durkheim, E. (1965). *The Elementary Forms of the Religious Life.* London. French original: *Les formes élémentaires de la vie réligieuse.* Paris, 1912.

Durkheim, E. (1973). *Moral Education.* New York. French original: *L'Éducation morale.* Paris, 1925.

Durkheim, E. (1982). *The Rules of Sociological Method and Selected Texts on Sociology and Its Method.* New York. French original: *Les règles de la méthode sociologique.* Paris, 1937.

Durkheim, E. (1984). *The Division of Labor in Society.* New York. *De la division du travail social.* Paris, 1893.

Dykstra, C. (1980). *Vision and Character: A Christian Educator's Alternative to Kohlberg.* New York.

Eco, U. (1979). *A Theory of Semiotics.* Bloomington.

Eisinga, R., Felling, A., Peters, J., and Scheepers, P. (1992) *Social and Cultural Trends in the Netherlands 1979–1990.* Steinmetz Archive.

Eisinga, R., and Scheepers, P. (1989). "Etnocentrisme in Nederland." Diss. Nijmegen.

Elias, N. (1977). *Über den Prozess der Zivilisation.* Frankfurt.

Elias, N. (1982). *Über die Einsamkeit der Sterbenden.* Frankfurt.

Ellrod, F. E. (1986). "Introduction." In G. F. McLean et al., eds. *Act and Agent: Philosophical Foundations for Moral Education and Character Development,* 1-6. Lanham.

Ellrod, F. E. (1986). "Contemporary Philosophies of Moral Education." In G. F. McLean et al., eds. *Act and Agent: Philosophical Foundations for Moral Education and Character Development,* 9-49. Lanham.

Erikson, E. H. (1965). *Childhood and Society.* New York.

Erikson, E. H. (1968). *Identity, Youth, and Crisis.* London.

Ester, P., Halman, L., and Moor, R. de (1993). *The Individualizing Society.* Tilburg.

Ester, P., and Halman, L. (1994). *De cultuur van de verzorgingsstaat. Een sociologisch onderzoek naar waardenoriëntaties in Nederland.* Tilburg.

Etzioni, A. (1988). *The Moral Dimension: Towards a New Economics.* New York.

Etzioni, A. (1994). *The Spirit of Community: The Reinvention of American Society.* New York.

Everret, W. J. (1988). *God's Federal Republic.* New York.

Felling, A., Lammers, J., and Spruit, L. (1992). "Church-Membership, Religion and Attitude Towards Abortion in the Netherlands." *Journal of Empirical Theology* 5/1:53-69.

Felling, A., Peters, J., and Schreuder, O. (1983). *Burgerlijk en onburgerlijk Nederland.* Deventer.

Felling, A., Peters, J., and Schreuder, O. (1986). *Geloven en leven.* Zeist.

Felling, A., Peters, J., and Schreuder, O. (1987). *Religion im Vergleich: Bundesrepublik Deutschland und Niederlande.* Frankfurt.

Felling, A., Peters, J., and Schreuder, O. (1988). "Religion and Politics in the Netherlands: A Causal Analysis." *Journal of Empirical Theology* 1/1:55-72.

Flanagan, O. (1990). "Identity and Strong and Weak Evaluation." In O. Flanagan and A. Oksenberg Rorty, eds. *Identity, Character, and Morality: Essays in Moral Psychology,* 37-66. Cambridge, Mass.

Flanagan, O. (1991). *Varieties of Moral Personality: Ethics and Psychological Realism.* Cambridge, Mass.

Fleischacker, S. (1994). *The Ethics of Culture.* London.

Fletcher, G. P. (1993). *Loyalty: An Essay on the Morality of Relationships.* New York.

Foot, Ph. (1978). *Virtues and Vices.* Berkeley.

Fortmann, H. M. M. (1968). *Als ziende de onzienlijke: Een cultuurpsychologische studie over de religieuze waarneming en de zogenaamde religieuze projectie.* Part 3b. Hilversum.

Fotion, N. (1968). *Moral Situations.* Yellow Springs.

Fowler, J. (1980). "Moral Stages and the Development of Faith." In B. Munsey, ed. *Moral Development, Moral Education, and Kohlberg: Basic Issues in Philosophy, Psychology, Religion, and Education,* 130-60. Birmingham, Ala.

Fowler, J. (1981). *Stages of Faith: The Psychology of Human Development and the Quest for Meaning.* San Francisco.

Frankena, K. (1978). *Fundamentele ethiek.* Amsterdam. English original: *Ethics.* Englewood Cliffs, 1973.

Freud, S. (1961). *Civilization and Its Discontents.* New York.

Freud, S. (1984). *On Metapsychology: The Theory of Psychoanalysis.* London.

Freud, S. (1985). *Art and Literature: Jensen's Gravida, Leonardo da Vinci and Other Works.* London.

Freud, S. (1986). *Historical and Expository Works on Psychoanalysis.* London.

Frijda, N. (1983). "De structuur van de emoties." In *Pychologie in Nederland,* 219-32. Lisse.

Frijda, N. (1984). "Emoties." *Intermediair* 20/8:17-21.

Frijda, N. (1986). *The Emotions.* Cambridge.

Frijda, N. (1993). *De psychologie heeft zin.* Amsterdam.

Gadamer, H.-G. (1960). *Wahrheit und Methode: Grundzüge einer philosophischen Hermeneutik.* Tübingen.

Galilea, S. (1979). "De kerk in Latijns Amerika en de strijd voor de rechten van de mens." In *Concilium* 15/4:102-9.

Gallup, G., and Castelli, J. (1989). *The People's Religion: American Faith in the 90's.* New York.

Gamm, H.-J. (1979). *Allgemeine Pädagogik: Die Grundlagen von Erziehung und Bildung in der bürgerlichen Gesellschaft.* Reinbek bei Hamburg.

Geertz, C. (1969). "Religion as a Cultural System." In *The World Yearbook of Religion: The Religious Situation.* 1:639-88. London.

Gerris, J. R. M., Janssens, J., and Janssen, A. (1988). "Niveaus van pedagogisch perspectief nemen van ouder en kind in disciplineringssituaties: Een empirisch verklaringsmodel." In J. Van Acker and J. Gerris. *Gezinsrelaties onderzocht,* 7-26. Amsterdam/Lisse.

Gerris, J. R. M., Dekovic, M., and Janssens, J. (1991). "Cultuuroverdracht in de opvoeding." In A. Felling and J. Peters, eds. *Cultuur en sociale wetenschappen: Beschouwingen en empirische studies,* 199-226. Nijmegen.

Giddens, A. (1978). *Durkheim*. Harvester/Hassocks.

Gilligan, C. (1982). *In a Different Voice: Psychological Theory and Women's Development*. Cambridge, Mass.

Glock, Ch., and Stark, R. (1965). *Religion and Society in Tension*. Chicago.

Goffmann, E. (1961). *Encounters*. Indianapolis.

Golding, M. P. (1979). "The Nature of Compromise: A Preliminary Inquiry." In J. R. Pennock and J. W. Chapman, eds. *Compromise in Ethics, Law, and Politics*, 3-25. New York.

Golser, K., and Heeger, R., eds. (1996). *Moralerziehung im neuen Europa*, 131-64. Brixen.

Goodin, R. E. (1994). "Utility and the Good." In P. Singer, ed. *A Companion to Ethics*, 241-48. Oxford.

Groethuysen, B. (1979). *Die Entstehung der bürgerlichen Welt- und Lebensanschauung in Frankreich*. 2 vols. Frankfurt.

Guidon, A. (1986). *The Sexual Creators: An Ethical Proposal for Concerned Christians*. Lanham/New York/London.

Gutman, A., ed. (1994). *Multiculturalism: Examining the Politics of Recognition*. Princeton.

Haarsma, F. (1981). *Morren tegen Mozes: Pastoraaltheologische beschouwingen over het kerkelijk leven*. Kampen.

Haarsma, F. (1991). *Kandelaar en korenmaat: Pastoraaltheologische studies over kerk en pastoraat*. Kampen.

Habermas, J. (1982). *Theorie des kommunikativen Handelns*. 2 vols. Frankfurt.

Habermas, J. (1983) *Moralbewusstsein und kommunikatives Handeln*. Frankfurt.

Habermas, J. (1986). "Gerechtigkeit und Solidarität: Eine Stellungnahme zur Diskussion über 'Stufe 6.'" In W. Edelstein and G. Nunner-Winkler, eds. *Zur Bestimmung der Moral*, 291-320. Frankfurt.

Habermas, J. (1992). *Faktizität und Geltung: Beiträge zur Diskurs-Theorie des Rechts und des demokratischen Rechtsstaats*. Frankfurt.

Habermas, J. (1993). *Justification and Application: Remarks on Discourse Ethics*. Cambridge, Mass.

Habermas, J. (1994). "Struggles for Recognition in the Democratic Constitutional State." In A. Gutman, ed. *Multiculturalism: Examining the Politics of Recognition*, 107-46. Princeton.

Halman, L., Heunks, F., De Moor, R., and Zanders, H. (1987). *Traditie, secularisatie en individualisering: Een studie naar de waarden van de Nederlanders in een Europese context*. Tilburg.

Hare, R. M. (1967). *The Language of Morals*. Oxford.

Hare, R. M. (1973). *Freiheit und Vernunft*. Düsseldorf. English original: *Freedom and Reason*. Oxford, 1963.

Hare, R. M. (1981). *Moral Thinking: Its Levels, Methods and Point*. Oxford.

Häring, B. (1960). *De wet van Christus: Een katholieke moraaltheologie voor priesters en leken*. Parts 1-2. German original: *Das Gesetz Christi*. Freiburg, 1954.

Heckhausen, H. (1980). *Motivation und Handeln*. Berlin.

Heeger, R. (1985). "Utilisme en aanvaardbaarheid." In H. G. Hubbeling and R. Veldhuis, eds. *Ethiek in meervoud*, 18-47. Assen.

Henau, E., and Schreiter, R., eds. (1995). *Religious Socialisation*. Serie Theologie en Empirie 21. Kampen/Weinheim.

Hermans, C. (1986). *Morele vorming.* Kampen.

Hermans, C. (1994). *Professionaliteit en identiteit: Over professionele ethische verantwoordelijkheid van leraren in relatie tot de identiteit van katholieke scholen.* The Hague.

Hermans, C., and van der Ven, J. A. (1996). "Das moralische Selbst: Diskurs und Kommunikation in einer pluralistischen Gesellschaft." In K. Golser and R. Heeger, eds. *Moralerziehung im neuen Europa,* 131-64. Brixen.

Hermans, H. (1987a). "The Dream in the Process of Valuation: A Method of Interpretation." *Journal of Personality and Social Psychology* 53/1:163-75.

Hermans, H. (1987b). "Self as an Organized System of Valuations: Toward a Dialogue with the Person." *Journal of Counseling Psychology* 34/1:10-19.

Hermans, H. (1993). "Het zelf als verhaal: Plaatsbepaling van de waarderingstheorie en de zelfconfrontatiemethode." *De Psycholoog* 28/3:93-100.

Hermans, H., ed. (1995). *De echo van ego: Over het meerstemmige zelf.* Baarn.

Hermans, H. (1996). "Voicing the Self: From Information Processing to Dialogical Interchange." *Psychological Bulletin* 119/1:31-50.

Hermans, H., and Kempen, H. (1993). *The Dialogical Self: Meaning as Movement.* San Diego.

Hermans, H., and Hermans-Jansen E. (1995). *Self-Narratives: The Construction of Meaning in Psychotherapy.* New York.

Hester, R. K., and Miller, W. R., eds. (1989). *Handbook of Alcoholism Treatment Approaches: Effective Alternatives.* New York.

Hirst, P. H. (1993). "Education, Knowledge and Practices." In R. Barrow and P. White, eds. *Beyond Liberal Education: Essays in Honour of Paul H. Hirst,* 184-99. London.

Hoffman, M. L. (1993). "Empathy, Social Cognition, and Moral Education." In A. Garrod, ed. *Approaches to Moral Development: New Research and Emerging Themes,* 157-79. New York.

Hofstede, G. (1991). *Cultures and Organizations: Software of the Mind.* London. Dutch translation: *Allemaal andersdenkenden: Omgaan met cultuurverschillen.* Amsterdam, 1995.

Hoose, B. (1994). "Circumstances, Intentions, and Intrinsically Evil Acts." In J. Selling and J. Jans, eds. *The Splendor of Accuracy: An Examination of the Assertions Made by Veritatis Splendor,* 136-52. Kampen.

Houtepen, A. W. J. (1992). "Gerechtigheid in honderd jaar sociale encyclieken. In W. Arts, P. Blauw, C. Rijnvos, and G. Van der Wal, eds. *Tempora mutantur: Over maatschappelijke verandering en ontwikkelingen in het sociale denken,* 28-50. Baarn.

Huber, G. L., and Mandl, H. (1991). "Kognitive Sozialisation." In K. Hurrelmann and D. Ulich, eds. *Neues Handbuch der Sozialisationsforschung,* 511-30. 4th ed. Weinheim.

Hurrelmann, K., and Ulich, D. (1991). *Neues Handbuch der Sozialisationsforschung.* 4th ed. Weinheim.

Inglehart, R. (1977). *The Silent Revolution.* Princeton.

Inglehart, R. (1990). *Culture Shift in Advanced Industrial Society.* Princeton.

Izard, C. E., Kagan, J., and Zajonc, R. B. (1986). "Introduction." In C. E. Izard, J. Kagan, and R. B. Zajonc, eds. *Emotions, Cognition, and Behavior,* 1-16. Cambridge.

Jackers, J. (1983). "Zelfactualisatie volgens A. H. Maslow: Een nieuwe ideologie?" In *Waardenopvoeding in gelovig perspectief: Van zelfontplooiing naar solidariteit,* 77-96. Nikè-reeks 7. Leuven.

Jackson, Ph., Boostrom, R., and Hansen, D. (1993). *The Moral Life of Schools.* San Francisco.

Jacoby, M. (1985). *Individuation und Narzissmus: Psychologie des Selbst bei C. G. Jung und H. Kohut.* München. English translation: *Individuation and Narcissism: The Psychology of Self in Jung and Kohut.* London/New York, 1990.

James, W. (1975). *Pragmatism.* Cambridge, Mass.

James, W. (1981). *Principles of Psychology.* Vol. 1. Cambridge, Mass.

Jans, J. (1994). "Moraaltheologisch crisismanagement: Achtergronden en implicaties van de encycliek 'Veritatis Splendor.'" *Tijdschrift voor Theologie* 34/1:49-66.

Janssen, J. (1994). *Jeugdcultuur: Een actuele geschiedenis.* Utrecht.

Janssens, L. (1994). "Teleology and Proportionality: Thoughts about the Encyclical *Veritatis Splendor.*" In J. Selling and J. Jans, eds. *The Splendor of Accuracy: An Examination of the Assertions Made by Veritatis Splendor,* 99-113. Kampen.

Jaschke, H. (1974). *Das Böse in der Erziehung: Ein Beitrag zur pädagogische Anthropologie.* Düsseldorf.

Jeurissen, R. (1993). *Peace and Religion.* Serie Theologie en Empirie 16. Kampen.

Johnson, M. (1987). *The Body in the Mind.* Chicago.

Johnson, M. (1993). *Moral Imagination: Implications of Cognitive Science for Ethics.* Chicago.

Joubert, D. (1992). *Reflections on Social Values.* Pretoria.

Jüngel, E. (1982). *Gott als Geheimnis der Welt.* Tübingen.

Kant, I. (1964). *Groundwork of the Metaphysics of Morals.* New York.

Katz, D., and Kahn, R. (1978). *The Social Psychology of Organizations.* 2nd ed. New York.

Kay, W. (1975). *Moral Education: A Sociological Study of the Influence of Society, Home, and School.* London.

Kavathatzopoulos, I. (1988). *Instruction and the Development of Moral Judgment.* Acta Universitatis Upsaliensis. Uppsala.

Kemp, P. (1995). "Ethics and Narrativity." In L. E. Hahn, ed. *The Philosophy of Paul Ricoeur,* 371-94. Chicago.

Kirschenbaum, H. (1977). *Advanced Value Clarification.* La Jolla.

Klafki, W. (1968). "Didaktik." In I. Dahmer and W. Klafki, eds. *Geisteswissenschaftliche Pädagogik am Ausgang ihrer Epoche,* 137-73. Weinheim/Berlin.

Knoers, A. M. P. (1973). *Leren en ontwikkeling: Leerpsychologie ten behoeve van het onderwijs.* Assen.

Kluckhohn, C. (1962). "Universal Categories of Culture." In S. Tax, ed. *Anthroplogy Today.* Chicago.

Kohlberg, L. (1981). *Essays on Moral Development.* Vol. 1. *The Philosophy of Moral Development.* San Francisco.

Kohlberg, L. (1984). *Essays on Moral Development.* Vol. 2. *The Psychology of Moral Development.* San Francisco.

Kohlberg, L. (1994). "The Development of Modes of Moral Thinking and Choice in the Years 10 to 16." Diss. Chicago 1958. Reprint in B. Puka, ed. *Kohlberg's Original Study of Moral Development.* Moral Development: A Compendium. 3:1-499. New York/London.

Kohut, H. (1988). *The Restoration of the Self.* Madison.

Kok, G. J. (1985). "Een model van gedragsverandering via voorlichting." *Nederlands Tijdschrift voor de Psychologie* 40:71-76.

Kok, G. J. (1987). "Gezondheidsmotivering." In D. Mossel et al., eds. *Gezondheid: wiens verantwoordelijkheid? Ethiek en voorkoombare ziekten,* 29-51. Baarn.

Krämer, H. (1992). *Integrative Ethik*. Frankfurt.

Krappmann, L. (1991). "Sozialisation in der Gruppe der Gleich-altrigen." In K. Hurrelmann and D. Ulich, eds. *Neues Handbuch der Sozialisationsforschung*, 355-76. 4th ed. Weinheim.

Krappmann, L. (1993). "Threats to the Self in the Peer World." In G. Noam and Th. Wren, eds. *The Moral Self*, 359-82. Cambridge.

Krathwohl, D. R., Bloom, B. S., and Masia, B. B. (1964). *Taxonomy of Educational Objectives: The Classification of Educational Goals. Handbook 2. Affective Domain*. New York.

Kreppner, K. (1991). "Sozialisation in der Familie." In K. Hurrelmann and D. Ulich, eds. *Neues Handbuch der Sozialisationsforschung*, 321-34. 4th ed. Weinheim.

Kuitert, H. M. (1988). "Secularisatie en moraal." In G. Dekker and K. U. Gäbler, eds. *Secularisatie in theologisch perspectief*, 131-48. Kampen.

Lamb, S. (1993). "The Beginnings of Morality." In A. Garrod, ed. *Approaches to Moral Development: New Research and Emerging Themes*, 9-29. New York.

Lammers, C. J. (1984). *Organisaties vergelijkenderwijs*. Utrecht/Antwerpen.

Landesman, S., Jaccard, J., and Gunderson, V. (1991). "The Family Environment: The Combined Influence of Family Behavior. Goals, Strategies, Resources, and Individual Experiences." In M. Lewis and S. Feinman, eds. *Social Influences and Socialization in Infancy*, 63-96. New York/London.

Langdale, C. (1986). "A Re-Vision of Structural-Developmental Theory." In G. L. Sapp, ed. *Handbook of Moral Development*, 15-54. Birmingham, Ala.

Larmore, Ch. (1987). *Patterns of Moral Complexity*. Cambridge.

Lasch, C. (1979). *The Culture of Narcissism*. New York.

Laumann, E. O., Gagnon, J. H., Michael, R. T., and Michaels, S. (1994). *The Social Organization of Sexuality: Sexual Practices in the United States*. Chicago.

Laurent, A. (1985). *De l'individualisme: Enquête sur le retour de l'individu*. Paris.

Laurent, A. (1987). *L'individu et ses ennemies*. Paris.

Lazari-Pawlowska, I. (1979). "Das deduktive Modell der ethischen Handlungsanweisungen." In H. Lenk, ed. *Handlungstheorien — Interdiziplinär*, 2:581-96. Munich.

Lazarus, R. S. (1991). *Emotion and Adaptation*. New York.

L'Ecuyer, R. (1992). "An Experiential-developmental Framework and Methodology to Study the Transformations of the Self-concept from Infancy to Old Age." In Th. Brinthaupt and R. Lipka, eds. *The Self: Definitional and Methodological Issues*, 96-134. New York.

Lersch, Ph. (1974). *Algemene psychologie*. Utrecht. German: *Aufbau der Person*. Antwerp.

Lewin, K. (1936). *Principles of Topological Psychology*. New York.

Lewis, M., and Michalson, L. (1983). *Children's Emotions and Moods*. New York.

Lewis, M., Sullivan, M. W., and Michalson, L. (1986). "The Cognitive-Emotional Fugue." In C. E. Izard, J. Kagan, and R. B. Zajonc, eds. *Emotions, Cognition, and Behavior*, 264-88. Cambridge.

Lindbeck, G. A. (1984). *The Nature of Doctrine*. Philadelphia.

Liegle, L. (1991). "Kulturvergleichende Ansätze in der Sozialisationsforschung." In K. Hurrelmann and D. Ulich, eds. *Neues Handbuch der Sozialisationsforschung*, 215-30. 4th ed. Weinheim.

Lob-Hüdepohl, A. (1993). *Kommunikative Vernunft und theologische Ethik*. Freiburg.

Lockona, Th. (1991). *Educating for Character*. New York.

Lukes, S. (1989). "Making Sense of Moral Conflict." In N. Rosenblum, ed. *Liberalism and the Moral Life*, 127-42. Cambridge, Mass.

Lukes, S. (1993). "Five Fables about Human Rights." In S. Shute and S. Hurley, eds. *On Human Rights*. Oxford Amnesty Lectures, 19-40. New York.

Maccoby, E., and Martin, J. A. (1983). "Socialization in the Context of the Family: Parent-Child Interaction." In P. H. Mussen, ed. *Handbook of Child Psychology*. Vol. 4. *Socialization, Personality, and Social Development*. New York.

MacIntyre, A. (1981/1984²). *After Virtue: A Study in Moral Theory*. Notre Dame.

MacIntyre, A. (1988). *Whose Justice? Which Rationality?* Notre Dame.

Manenschijn, G. (1985). "Contracttheorieën van morele verplichting." In H. G. Hubbeling and R. Veldhuis, eds. *Ethiek in meervoud*, 48-80. Assen.

Mann, J. A. (1986). "North American Philosophical Background for Moral Education Theory." In G. F. McLean et al., eds. *Act and Agent: Philosophical Foundations for Moral Education and Character Development*, 49-69. Lanham.

Marcus Aurelius. *Meditations*.

Marsh, H., Byrne, B., and Shavelson, R. (1992). "A Multidimensional, Hierarchical Self-concept." In Th. Brinthaupt and R. Lipka, eds. *The Self: Definitional and Methodological Issues*, 44-95. New York.

Maslow, A. (1954). *Motivation and Personality*. New York.

Maslow, A. (1962). *Towards a Psychology of Being*. Princeton.

Maslow, A. (1964). *Religions, Values, and Peak-Experiences*. West Lafayette. Dutch translation, *Religie en topervaring*. Rotterdam, 1972, 1974², 1977³.

Mathys, H.-P. (1986). *Liebe deinen Nächsten wie dich selbst: Untersuchungen zum alttestamentlichen Gebot der Nächstenliebe (Lev 19,18)*. Göttingen.

May, R. (1986). *Liefde en wil*. Katwijk aan Zee. English original: *Love and Will*. New York, 1969.

McLean, G. F., et al., eds. (1986). *Act and Agent: Philosophical Foundations for Moral Education and Character Development*. Lanham.

Mead, G. H. (1934). *Mind, Self, and Society*. Chicago.

Meeks, W. A. (1993). *The Origins of Christian Morality*. New Haven/London.

Mertens, W. (1991). "Psychoanalytische Theorien und Forschungsbefunde." In K. Hurrelmann and D. Ulich, eds. *Neues Handbuch der Sozialisationsforschung*, 77-98. 4th ed. Weinheim.

Merton, R., et al. (1957). *The Student Physician: Introductory Studies in the Sociology of Medical Education*. Cambridge, Mass.

Mialaret, G., ed. (1979). *The Child's Right to Education*. Paris.

Michael, R. T., Gagnon, J. H., Laumann, E. O., and Kolata, G. (1994). *Sex in America: A Definite Survey*. Boston.

Mieth, D. (1984). *Die neue Tugenden*. Düsseldorf.

Mieth, D. (1987). "Waardenoriëntaties." In *Concilium* 23/3:47-56.

Mill, J. S. (1977). *On Liberty*. Collected Works. Toronto.

Miller, D. (1994). "Virtues, Practices and Justice." In J. Horton and S. Mendus, eds. *After MacIntyre: Critical Perspectives on the Work of Alasdair MacIntyre*, 245-64. Notre Dame.

Miller, T. (1995). *How to Want What You Have: Discovering the Magic and Grandeur of Ordinary Existence*. New York.

Mintzberg, H. (1979). *The Structuring of Organizations.* Englewood Cliffs.

Moltmann, J. (1990). "Mensenrechten, rechten van de mensheid en rechten van de natuur." In *Concilium* 1990/2:103-14.

Mongin, O. (1994). *Paul Ricoeur.* Paris.

Mönks, F. J., and Knoers, A. M. P. (1982). *Ontwikkelingspsychologie: Inleiding tot de verschillende deelgebieden.* Nijmegen.

Morson, G. S. (1994). *Narrative and Freedom: The Shadows of Time.* New Haven.

Munsey, B. (1986). "Cognitive-Developmental Psychology and Pragmatic Philosophy of Science." In G. L. Sapp, ed. *Handbook of Moral Development: Models, Processes, Techniques, and Research,* 92-106. Birmingham, Ala.

Murphy, N. (1989). "Truth, Relativism, and Crossword Puzzles." *Zygon, Journal of Religion and Science* 24/3:299-314.

Nagel, T. (1986). *The View from Nowhere.* New York.

Nicgorski, W., and Ellrod, F. E., III (1986). "Moral Character." In G. F. McLean et al., eds. *Act and Agent: Philosophical Foundations for Moral Education and Character Development,* 141-64. Lanham.

Noam, G. G., and Wren, Th. E., eds. *The Moral Self.* Cambridge, Mass.

Nussbaum, Martha C. (1986). *The Fragility of Goodness: Luck and Ethics in Greek Tragedy and Philosophy.* Cambridge.

Nuttin, J. (1981). *De menselijke motivatie: Van behoefte tot gedragsproject.* Deventer. French original: *Théorie de la motivation humaine.* Paris, 1980.

Oksenberg Rorty, A. (1992). "The Advantage of Moral Diversity." In E. F. Paul et al., eds. *The Good Life and the Human Good,* 38-62. Cambridge.

Opdebeeck, H. (1995). "De institutionele vermiddeling van de vrijheid bij Paul Ricoeur." In P. Ricoeur. *Het probleem van de grondslagen van de moraal.* Ingeleid en geannoteerd door J. de Visscher, vertaald door H. Opdebeeck en van afsluitende essays voorzien door H. Opdebeeck en J. Van Gerwen, 67-93. Kampen.

Parsons, T. (1965). "Differentiation and Variation in Social Structures. Introduction." In T. Parsons, E. Shils, K. Naegele, and J. Pitts, eds. *Theories of Society: Foundations of Modern Sociological Theory,* 239-64. New York.

Passmore, J. (1980). *The Philosophy of Teaching.* Liverpool.

Patterson, H. (1927). *Ethics of Achievement: An Introduction to Character Education.* Boston.

Paul, E. F., et al., eds. *The Good Life and the Human Good.* Cambridge.

Pedersen, P. (1988). *A Handbook for Developing Multicultural Awareness.* Alexandria, Va.

Pennock, J. R., and Chapman, J. W., eds. *Compromises in Ethics, Law, and Politics.* New York.

Peters, J. (1957). *Metaphysica: Een systematisch overzicht.* Utrecht/Antwerpen.

Peters, J. (1977). "Kerkelijke betrokkenheid en levensbeschouwing. Een onderzoek naar de verbreiding en de sociale relevantie van kerkelijke betrokkenheid in een nieuwe stadswijk." Diss. Nijmegen.

Peters, R. S. (1974). *Psychology and Ethical Development.* London.

Peters, V. (1985). "Docenten en hun probleemsituaties." Diss. Nijmegen.

Pettit, Ph. (1994). "Consequentialism." In P. Singer, ed. *A Companion to Ethics,* 230-40. Cambridge, Mass.

Peukert, H. (1978). *Wissenschaftstheorie — Handlungstheorie — Fundamentale Theologie: Analysen zu Ansatz und Status theologischer Theoriebildung.* Frankfurt.

Peukert, H. (1988). "Praxus universeller Solidarität: Grenzprobleme im Verhältnis von Erziehungswissenschaft und Theologie." In E. Schillebeeckx, ed. *Mystik und Politik: Theologie im Ringen um Geschichte und Gesellschaft.* Fs. J. B. Metz, 172-84. Mainz.

Pfürtner, S. (1979). "De rechten van de mens in de Christelijke ethiek." In *Concilium* 15/4:60-69.

Philipse, H. (1995). *Atheïstisch manifest: Drie wijsgerige opstellen over godsdienst en moraal.* Amsterdam.

Piaget, J. (1932). *Le Jugement moral chez l'enfant.* Paris.

Piaget, J. (1975). *Die Entwicklung des Erkennens.* Vol. 3. Stuttgart. French original: *Introduction à l'Epistémologie génétique.* Vol. 3. Paris, 1950.

Piaget, J. (1986). "Die moralische Entwicklung von Jugendlich en in primitiven und 'modernen' Gesellschaften." In H. Bertram, ed. *Gesellschaftlicher Zwang und moralische Autonomie,* 118-24. Frankfurt.

Piaget, J., and Inhelder, B. (1978). *De psychologie van het kind.* Rotterdam. French: *La psychologie de l'enfant.* Paris, 1966.

Pieper, J. (1960). "Gerechtigkeit." *Lexikon für Theologie und Kirche,* 4:713-15. Freiburg.

Pieper, J. (1970). *Auskunft über die Tugenden.* Zurich.

Pieterse, H. (1995). *Desmond Tutu's Message: A Qualitative Analysis.* Serie Theologie en Empirie 24. Kampen.

Prein, H. C. M. (1976). "Stijlen van conflicthantering." *Nederlands Tijdschrift voor de Psychologie* 31:321-46.

Rahner, K. (1965). "Über die Einheit von Nächsten- und Gottesliebe." In *Schriften zur Theologie,* 6:277-300. Einsiedeln.

Rang, A. (1994). "Pedagogiek en pluralisme." In F. Heyting and H. Elmar Tenorth, eds. *Pedagogiek en pluralisme: Duitse en Nederlandse visies op pluraliteit in de theorie en de praktijk van de opvoeding,* 18-45. Amsterdam.

Raths, L., M. Harmin, and S. B. Simon (1966). *Values and Teaching: Working with Values in the Classroom.* Columbus. 2nd ed. 1978.

Rawls, J. (1971). *A Theory of Justice.* Cambridge, Mass.

Rawls, J. (1994). "Rechtvaardigheid als schoonheid: politiek, niet metafysisch." In B. Van de Brink and W. Van Reijen, eds. *Het recht van de moraal,* 40-66. Bussum. English original: "Justice as Fairness: Political not Metaphysical." *Philosophy and Public Affairs* 14 (1985): 223-51.

Rest, J. (1980). "Developmental Psychology and Value Education." In B. Munsey, ed. *Moral Development, Moral Education, and Kohlberg: Basic Issues in Philosophy, Psychology, Religion, and Education,* 101-29. Birmingham, Ala.

Ricoeur, P. (1968). *Politiek en geloof.* Utrecht.

Ricoeur, P. (1970). *Symbolen van het kwaad.* Parts 1-2. Rotterdam. French original: *La symbolique du Mal.* Paris, 1960.

Ricoeur, P. (1971). *Kwaad en bevrijding: Filosofie en Theologie van de hoop. Hermeneutische artikelen ingeleid door Ad Peperzak.* Rotterdam. French original: *Le Conflit des interprétations.* Paris, 1969.

Ricoeur, P. (1973). "Ethics and Culture: Habermas and Gadamer in Dialogue." *Philosophy Today* 17:153-65.

Ricoeur, P. (1975). "Le problème du fondement de la morale." In *Sapienza, Rivista internazionale di Filosofia e di Teologia* 28/3:313-37.

Ricoeur, P. (1987). *Hermeneutics and the Human Sciences.* Cambridge/Paris.

Ricoeur, P. (1990). *Liebe und Gerechtigkeit. Amour et Justice.* Tübingen. English translation: "Love and Justice." *Philosophy and Social Criticism* 21 (1995) 5/6:23-39.

Ricoeur, P. (1991). *From Text to Action.* Essays in Hermeneutics 2. Evanston.

Ricoeur, P. (1992). *Oneself as Another.* Chicago/London.

Ricoeur, P. (1995). "Intellectual Autobiography of Paul Ricoeur." In L. E. Hahn, ed. *The Philosophy of Paul Ricoeur*, 1-53. Chicago.

Ricoeur, P. (1995a). "Reflections on a New Ethos for Europe." *Philosophy and Social Criticism* 21/5-6:3-13.

Roebben, B. (1995). *Een tijd van opvoeden: Moraalpedagogiek in christelijk perspectief.* Amersfoort.

Roemer, J., Schippers, G., and van der Ven, J. A. (1994). "Kun je evenwichtigheid leren?" In G. Schippers and J. A. van der Ven, eds. *Niet bij gebruik alleen: Voorlichting over alcohol en drugs in het perspectief van zingevig*, 92-112. Kampen.

Rogers, C. (1969). *Freedom to Learn.* Columbus.

Rondeau, A. (1990). "La gestion des conflits dans les organisations." In J. F. Charlat, ed. *L'Individu dans l'organisation*, 507-27. Quebec.

Roof, W. C., and McKinney, W. (1987). *American Mainline Religion: Its Changing Shape and Future.* New Brunswick.

Rorty, R. (1991). *Contingency, Irony, and Solidarity.* Cambridge.

Rorty, R. (1993). "Human Rights, Rationality, and Sentimentality." In S. Shute and S. Hurley, eds. *On Human Rights.* Oxford Amnesty Lectures, 111-34. New York.

Rosenthal, D. M., ed. (1991). *The Nature of Mind.* Oxford.

Rotländer, P. (1988). "Option für die Armen: Erneuering der Weltkirche und Umbruch der Theologie." In E. Schillebeeckx, ed. *Mystik und Politik: Theologie im Ringen um Geschichte und Gesellschaft.* Fs. J. B. Metz, 72-88. Mainz.

Rousseau, J.-J. (1974). *Emile.* London.

Ruprecht, L. A., Jr. (1994). *Tragic Posture and Tragic Vision: Against Modern Failure of Nerve.* New York.

Sampson, E. (1993). *Celebrating the Other: A Dialogic Account of Human Nature.* New York.

Sandel, M. (1992). *Liberalism and the Limits of Justice.* Cambridge.

Sartre, J. P. (1967). *Over het existentialisme.* Utrecht/Antwerpen. French original: *L'existentialisme est un humanisme.* Paris, 1965.

Schachtel, E. G. (1959). *Metamorphosis: On the Development of Affect, Perception, Attention and Memory.* New York.

Schaffer, H. R. (1991). "The Mutuality of Parental Control in Early Childhood." In M. Lewis and S. Feinman, eds. *Social Influences and Socialization in Infancy*, 165-84. New York/London.

Scheler, M. (1966). *Der Formalismus in der Ethik und die materiale Wertethik.* Bern/Munich.

Schillebeeckx, E. (1972). *Geloofsverstaan: Interpretatie en kritiek.* Bloemendaal.

Schillebeeckx, E. (1974). *Jezus, het verhaal van een levende.* Bloemendaal.

Schillebeeckx, E. (1977). *Gerechtigheid en liefde, genade en bevrijding.* Bloemendaal.

Schillebeeckx, E. (1983). *Theologisch geloofsverstaan anno 1983.* Baarn.

Schillebeeckx, E. (1988). "Befreiende Theologie." In E. Schillebeeckx, ed. *Mystik und Politik: Theologie im Ringen um Geschichte und Gesellschaft.* Fs. J. B. Metz, 56-71. Mainz.

Schillebeeckx, E. (1989). *Mensen als verhaal van God.* Baarn.

Schippers, G. (1994). "De zin van alcohol en drugs." In G. Schippers and J. A. van der Ven, eds. *Niet bij gebruik alleen: Voorlichting over alcohol en drugs in het perspectief van zingeving*, 9-19. Kampen.

Schockenhoff, E. (1987). *Bonum hominis: Die anthropologischen und theologischen Grundlagen der Tugendethik des Thomas von Aquin.* Mainz.

Schorb, B., Mohn, E., and Theunert, H. (1991). "Sozialisation durch (Massen-)Medien." In K. Hurrelmann and D. Ulich, eds. *Neues Handbuch der Sozialisationsforschung*, 493-508. 4th ed. Weinheim.

Schotsmans, P. (1982). "Waardeleer als teken van een geseculariseerde samenleving? Een hermeneutische studie met M. Rokeach's waardeleer als test-case." Diss. Leuven.

Schotsmans, P. (1983). "Waardenopvoeding volgens L. E. Raths: Uitweg uit een beschavingscrisis?" In *Waardenopvoeding in gelovig perspectief: Van zelfontplooiing naar solidariteit*, 97-120. Leuven.

Schreuder, O. (1994). "Culturele individualisering." In J. A. van der Ven, ed. *Individualisering en religie*, 60-97. Baarn.

Schulenberg, W. (1968). "Pädagogische Theorie und Gesellschaftsbegriff." In I. Dahmer and W. Klafki, eds. *Geisteswissenschaftliche Pädagogik am Ausgang ihrer Epoche*, 209-21. Weinheim.

Schüller, B. (1980). *Die Begründung sittlecher Urteile: Typen ethischer Argumentation.* Düsseldorf.

Schulze, G. (1992). *Die Erlebnisgesellschaft: Kultursoziologie der Gegenwart.* Frankfurt/New York.

Schulze, H.-J., and Künzler, J. (1991). "Funktionalistische und Systemtheoretische Ansätze in der Sozialisationsforschung." In K. Hurrelmann and D. Ulich, eds. *Neues handbuch der Sozialisationsforschung*, 21-54. 4th ed. Weinheim.

Schütz, A. (1967). *The Phenomenology of the Social World.* Chicago. German original: *Der sinnhafte Aufbau der sozialen Welt.* Vienna, 1960.

Selman, R. (1980). *The Growth of Interpersonal Understanding.* New York.

Selznick, Ph. (1992). *The Moral Commonwealth: Social Theory and the Promise of Community.* Berkeley.

Sherman, N. (1989). *The Fabric of Character: Aristotle's Theory of Virtue.* Oxford.

Sherman, N. (1990). "The Place of Emotions in Kantian Morality." In O. Flanagan and A. Oksenberg Rorty, eds. *Identity, Character, and Morality*, 149-70. Cambridge, Mass.

Siebenheller, E. (1990). "Problematische opvoedingssituaties: Percepties, emoties and disciplineringsreacties van ouders." Diss. Nijmegen.

Slote, M. (1990). "Some Advantages of Virtue Ethics." In O. Flanagan and A. Oksenberg Rorty, eds. *Identity, Character, and Morality*, 429-48. Cambridge, Mass.

Snik, G. (1990). "Persoonswording en opvoeding." Diss. Nijmegen.

Sobrino, J. (1989). *The True Church and the Poor.* New York.

Solomon, M. (1989). *Narcissism and Intimacy.* New York.

Spiecker, B. (1991). *Emoties en morele opvoeding: Wijsgerig-pedagogische studies.* Meppel.

Spiegelberg, H. (1960). *The Phenomenological Movement.* 2 vols. The Hague.

Spiegelberg, H. (1964). "Phenomenology through Vicarious Experience." In E. Strauss, ed. *Phenomenology: Pure and Applied*, 105-26. Pittsburgh.

Spruit, L. (1991). "Religie en abortus." Diss. Nijmegen.

Stachel, G., and Mieth, D. (1978). *Ethisch handeln lernen: Zu Konzeption und Inhalt ethischer Erziehung.* Zurich.

Steel, C. (1995). "De kardinale deugden." In R. A. Te Velde, ed. *De deugden van de mens. Thomas van Aquino: De virtutibus in communi,* 113-26. Baarn.

Steinkamp, G. (1991). "Sozialstruktur und Sozialisation." In K. Hurrelmann and D. Ulich, eds. *Neues Handbuch der Sozialisationsforschung,* 251-78. 4th ed. Weinheim.

Steutel, J. W. (1992). *Deugden en morele opvoeding: Een wijsgerig-pegagogische studie.* Meppel.

Stevens, B. (1995). "On Ricoeur's Analysis of Time and Narration." In Hahn, L. E., ed. *The Philosophy of Paul Ricoeur,* 499-506. Chicago.

Stiles, W. B. (1978). "Verbal Response Modes and Dimensions of Interpersonal Roles: A Method of Discourse Analysis." *Journal of Personality and Social Psychology* 36/7:693-703.

Stocker, M. (1990). "Friendship and Duty: Some Difficult Relationships." In O. Flanagan and A. Oksenberg Rorty, eds. *Identity, Character, and Morality,* 219-34. Cambridge, Mass.

Stocker, M. (1990a). *Plural and Conflicting Values.* Oxford.

Stoetzel, J. (1983). *Les Valeurs du temps présent: Une enquête européenne.* Paris.

Strasser, St. (1956). *Das Gemüt.* Utrecht/Antwerpen/Freiburg.

Striker, G. (1985). "Notwendigkeit mit Lücken: Aristoteles über die Kontingenz der Naturvorgänge." *Neue hefte für Philosophie* 24/25:146-64.

Suchodolski, B. (1979). "Ethical Aspects of the Child's Right to Education." In G. Mialaret, ed. *The Child's Right to Education,* 35-46. Paris.

Sunner, L. W. (1992). "Two Theories of the Good." In E. F. Paul et al., eds. *The Good Life and the Human Good,* 1-14. Cambridge.

Tafferner, A. (1992). *Gottes- und Nächstenliebe in der deutschsprachigen Theologie des 20. Jahrhundert.* Innsbruck/Wien.

Taylor, Ch. (1988). "Ancient Wisdom and Modern Folly." In P. A. French et al., eds. *Ethical Theory: Character and Virtue.* Midwest Studies in Philosophy 13. Notre Dame.

Taylor, Ch. (1989). *Sources of the Self: The Making of the Modern Identity.* Cambridge, Mass.

Taylor, Ch. (1989a). "Cross-Purposes: The Liberal-Communitarian Debate." In N. L. Rosenblum, ed. *Liberalism and the Moral Life,* 159-82. Cambridge, Mass.

Taylor, Ch. (1991). *The Malaise of Modernity.* Don Mills. American edition: *The Ethics of Authenticity.* Cambridge, Mass., 1992.

Taylor, Ch. (1994). "The Politics of Recognition." In A. Gutman, ed. *Multiculturalism: Examining the Politics of Recognition,* 107-46. Princeton.

Taylor, Ch. (1994a). "Justice after Virtue." In J. Horton and S. Mendus, eds. *After MacIntyre: Critical Perspectives on the Work of Alasdair MacIntyre,* 16-43. Notre Dame.

Ten Haaf, N. (1993). "Opvoedingsdimensies: Convergente en discriminante validiteit." Diss. Nijmegen.

Terpstra, M. (1991). "Zo spreken de schuldigen: Over schuldbetrekkingen en schuldhuishoudingen." In *Schuld en gemeenschap: Hoofdstukken uit de genealogie van de schuld,* 98-135. Baarn.

Ter Voert, M. (1994). "Religie en het burgerlijk-kapitalistisch ethos." Diss. Nijmegen.

Ter Voert, M., Felling, A., and Peters, J. (1994). "Protestants and Catholics in the Netherlands." *Journal of Empirical Theology* 7/2:21-47.

Thomas Aquinas. *Summa Theologica.*

Thurlings, J. (1977). *De wetenschap der samenleving: Een drieluik van de sociologie.* Alphen aan de Rijn.

Thurlings, J. (1980). "Instituties in bewegin: Bouwstenen voor de theorie der institutionalisering." In J. Thurlings, O. Schreuder, J. Van Hoof, N. Nelissen, and J. Janssen. *Institutie en beweging,* 9-57. Deventer.

Tuchman, G. (1988). "Mass Media Institutions." In N. Smelser, ed. *Handbook of Sociology,* 601-26. Newbury Park.

Turiel, E., and Smetana, J. G. (1986). "Soziales Wissen und Handeln: Die Koordination von Bereichen." In F. Oser, W. Althof, and D. Garz, eds. *Moralische Zugänge zum Menschen, Zugänge zum moralischen Menschen,* 108-35. Munich.

Turner, J. H. (1984). *Societal Stratification: A Theoretical Analysis.* New York.

Uleyn, A. (1969). *The Recognition of Guilt: A Study in Pastoral Psychology.* Dublin.

Ultee, W., Arts, W., and Flap, H. (1992). *Sociologie: Vragen, uitspraken, bevindingen.* Groningen.

Uzgiris, I. (1991). "The Social Context of Infant Imitation." In M. Lewis and S. Feinman, eds. *Social Influences and Socialization in Infancy,* 215-52. New York/London.

Van Asperen, G. M. (1985). "Het onbewuste in de moraal." In H. G. Hubbeling and R. Veldhuis, eds. *Ethiek in meervoud,* 116-44. Assen/Maastricht.

Van Bolhuis, M. J. (1987). "Religieuze socialisatie: Een literatuuroverzicht." In T. Andree and P. Steegman, eds. *Religieuze socialisatie: Een uitdaging voor onderzoek.* Utrecht.

Van Braam, A. (1986). *Leerboek bestuurskunde.* Muiderberg.

Van den Beld, A. (1985). "De Plaats van de deugd in de hedendaagse ethiek." In H. G. Hubbeling and R. Veldhuis, eds. *Ethiek in meervoud,* 145-76. Assen/Maastricht.

Van den Berg, J. H. (1958; 1974[8]). *Dubieuze liefde in de omgang met het kind: Over late gevolgen van te veel of te weinig moederlijke toewijding tijdens de jeugd.* Nijkerk.

Van der Lans, J. (1991). "Culturele ambivalentie en het onderzoek naar wereldbeelden." In A. Felling and J. Peters, eds. *Cultuur en sociale wetenschappen: Beschouwingen en empirische studies,* 91-106. Nijmegen.

Van der Lans, J. (1996). "Culturele diversiteit en sociale cohesie." In J. A. van der Ven, ed. *Botsende culturen in Nederland?* 44-57. Kampen.

Vandermeersch, P. (1992). "Moraliseren met de 'natuur' als dekmantel." In K.-W. Merks, ed. *De moeilijke waarheid,* 45-62. Baarn.

Van der Plas, P. (1981). *Waardenontwikkeling in het onderwijs: Theorie, praktijk onderzoek.* The Hague.

Van der Ven, J. A. (1980). "Naar een nieuwe moraalpedagogiek." In *Waarden en normen in het onderwijs, Vrijheid en onderwijs,* 26-45. Baarn.

Van der Ven, J. A. (1982). *Kritische godsdienstdidactiek.* Kampen.

Van der Ven, J. A. (1985). *Vorming in waarden en normen.* Kampen.

Van der Ven, J. A. (1987a). "Diagnose und Therapie in der Werterziehung." In E. Paul and A. Stock, eds. *Glauben Ermöglichen,* 277-85. Mainz.

Van der Ven, J. A. (1987b). "Moral Formation in the Church." In *Concilium* 191/3:117-27.

Van der Ven, J. A. (1992). "Matigheid in de morele vorming." *Philosophica* 49/1:29-54.

Van der Ven, J. A. (1993). *Practical Theology: An Empirical Approach.* Kampen.

Van der Ven, J. A. (1993a). "Religion and the Quality of Life." In U. Nembach, ed. *Informationes Theologiae Europae,* 319-40. Frankfurt.

Van der Ven, J. A. (1993b). "Die Qualitative Inhaltsanalyse." In J. A. van der Ven and H.-G. Ziebertz, eds. *Paradigmenentwicklung in der Praktischen Theologie.* Serie Theologie en Empirie 13, 113-64. Kampen/Weinheim.

Van der Ven, J. A., ed. (1994). *Individualisering en religie.* Baarn.

Van der Ven, J. A. (1994a). "Kontingenz und Religion in einer säkularisierten und multikulturellen Gesellschaft." In J. A. van der Ven and H.-G. Ziebertz, eds. *Religiöser Pluralismus und interreligiöses Lernen.* Serie Theologie en Empirie 22, 15-38. Kampen/Weinheim.

Van der Ven, J. A. (1995). "The Religious and Moral Self as a Process." In H. Pieterse, ed. *Desmond Tutu's Message: A Qualitative Analysis.* Serie Theologie en Empirie 24, 74-95. Kampen.

Van der Ven, J. A. (1996). *Ecclesiology in Context.* Grand Rapids. Dutch original: *Ecclesiologie in context.* Kampen, 1993.

Van der Ven, J. A. (1996a). *Botsende culturen in Nederland?* Kampen.

Van der Ven, J. A., and Van Gerwen, G. (1990). "Ecclesiological Explorations from Volunteer Ministry." *Journal of Empirical Theology* 3/1:27-46.

Van der Ven, J. A., and Vossen, E. (1995). *Suffering: Why for God's Sake? Pastoral Research in Theodicy.* Serie Theologie en Empirie 23. Kampen/Weinheim.

Van der Ven, J. A., and Ziebertz, H.-G. (1990). "Moralpädagogische Überwegungen zur Tradierung von Werten über Sexualität." *Religionspädagogische Beiträge* 26:15-36.

Van der Ven, J. A., and Ziebertz, H.-G. (1991). "Ziele sexualethischer Arbeit im Wertpluralismus." In H.-G. Ziebertz. *Sexualität im Wertpluralismus,* 44-62. Mainz.

Van Eupen, Th. (1962). "De praktijk van de boete in de Middeleeuwen, dl. 1." *Tijdschrift voor Theologie* 2/4:351-74.

Van Eupen, Th. (1963). "De praktijk van de boete in de Middeleeuwen, dl 2." *Tijdschrift voor Theologie* 3/1:12-44.

Van Genugten, W. J. M. (1992). *Mensenrechten in ontwikkeling: Het "goede doel" voorbij.* Inaugerele rede. Nijmegen.

Van Gerwen, J. (1995). "Evangelie en ethiek." In *Paul Ricoeur: Het probleem van de grondslagen van de moraal. Ingeleid en geannoteerd door J. De Visscher,* 95-123. Kampen.

Van Ijzendoorn, M. (1980). *Moralität und politisches Bewusstsein.* Weinheim/Basel.

Van Loon, R. (1996). "Symbolen van het zelfverhaal." Diss. Nijmegen.

Van Nieuwenhove, J., and Klein Goldewijk, B. (1994). "Mensenrechten als rechten van God: Een profiel van kardinaal Paulo Evaristo Arns." *Tijdschrift voor Theologie* 34/1:3-23.

Van Ouwerkerk, C. (1965). "Evangelisch ethos en menselijk compromis." In *Concilium* 1/5:8-21.

Van Tongeren, P. (1991). *Moraal, recht, ervaring.* Inaugurele rede. Nijmegen.

Van Tongeren, P. (1992). "Morality, Transcendence, Conception of Life." In A. W. Musschenga, B. Voorzanger, and A. Soeteman, eds. *Morality, Worldview, and Law,* 39-51. Assen/Maastricht.

Van Ussel, J. (1968). *Geschiedenis van het seksuele probleem.* Meppel.

Van Ussel, J. (1977). *Intimiteit.* Deventer.

Van Wolde, E. (1989). "Trendy Intertextuality?" In S. Draisma, ed. *Intertextuality in Biblical Writings: Essays in Honour of Bas van Iersel,* 43-50. Kampen.

Veldhuis, R. (1985). "Rechten — de moraal van de toekomst?" In H. G. Hubbeling and R. Veldhuis, eds. *Ethiek in meervoud,* 81-115. Assen/Maastricht.

Verbiest, E. (1984). "Andragogie: dialoog en verhaal." Diss. Nijmegen. Lisse.

Veritatis Splendor (1993). Vatican City.

Verschuur, H. (1996). "Ethische grondslagen van de morele opvoeding: Een utilistisch perspectief." Diss. Nijmegen.

Voigt, B. (1973). *Bildungspolitik und politische Erziehung in den Klassenkämpfen.* Frankfurt.

Von Campenhausen, H. (1965). *Lateinische Kirchenväter.* Stuttgart.

Von den Driesch, J., and Esterhues, J. (1964). *Geschichte der Erziehung und Bildung.* Vol. 1. *Von den Griechen bis zum Ausgang des Zeitalters der Aufklärung.* Vol. 2. *Von der Humanität bis zum Gegenwart.* Paderborn.

Vosman, F. (1994). "Het rooms-katholieke geloof en zijn implicaties voor het goede handelen: Moraaltheologische reflecties op de encycliek Veritatis Splendor." In H. Rikhof and F. Vosman, eds. *De schittering van de waarheid: Theologische reflecties bij de encycliek Veritatis Splendor,* 30-61. Kampen.

Vossen, A. J. M. (1967). *Zichzelf worden in menselijke relatie: Een ontwikkelingspsychologische studie van de Rogeriaanse grondhouding en haar verwerkelijking in psychotherapie, onderwijs en bedrijfsleiding.* Haarlem.

Vossen, H. J. M. (1985). *Vrijwilligerseducatie en pastoraat aan rouwenden.* Serie Theologie and Empirie 2. Kampen.

Walker, L. J. (1986). "Cognitive Processes in Moral Development." In G. L. Sapp, ed. *Handbook of Moral Development,* 109-45. Birmingham, Ala.

Wallace, R. A., and Wolf, A. (1991). *Contemporary Sociological Theory: Continuing the Classical Tradition.* 3d ed. Englewood Cliffs.

Walzer, M. (1994). *Thick and Thin: Moral Argument at Home and Abroad.* Notre Dame.

Watson, G. (1990). "On the Primacy of Character." In O. Flanagan and A. Oksenberg Rorty, eds. *Identity, Character, and Morality,* 449-70. Cambridge, Mass.

Weber, M. (1978). *Gesammelte Aufsätze zur Religionssoziologie.* Vol. 1. Tübingen.

Weber, M. (1982). *Politik als Beruf.* Berlin.

Wegman, C. (1985). *Psychoanalysis and Cognitive Psychology.* London.

Weniger, E. (1952). *Die Eigenständigkeit der Erziehung in Theorie und Praxis.* Weinheim.

Weniger, E. (1965). *Didaktik als Bildungslehre.* Part 1. *Theorie der Bildungsinhalte und des Lehrplans.* Weinheim.

Williams, B. (1993). *Shame and Necessity.* Berkeley.

Wils, J.-P. (1996). "Von Verstummen Gottes in der Moral." In P. Hünermann, ed. *Gott, ein Fremder in unserem Haus?* Freiburg.

Wils, J.-P., and Mieth, D. (1992). *Grundbegriffe der christlichen Ethik.* Paderborn.

Wren, Th. (1993). "The Open-textured Concepts of Morality and the Self." In G. Noam and Th. Wren, eds. *The Moral Self.* Cambridge, Mass.

Zajonc, R. B., and Markus, H. (1986). "Affect and Cognition: The Hard Interface." In C. E. Izard, J. Kagan, and R. B. Zajonc, eds. *Emotions, Cognition, and Behavior,* 73-102. Cambridge.

Ziebertz, H.-G. (1990). *Moralerziehung im Wertpluralismus: Eine empirisch-theologische Untersuchung nach moralpädagogischen Handlungskonzepten im Religionsunterricht und in der kirchlichen Jugendarbeit zur Fragen der Sexualität.* Serie Theologie en Empirie 3. Kampen/Weinheim.

Ziehe, Th. (1975). *Pubertät und Narzismus: Sind Jugendliche entpolitisiert?* Frankfurt.

Zwart, H. (1993). "Ethische consensus in een pluralistische samenleving: De gezond-heidsethiek als casus." Diss. Nijmegen. Amsterdam.

Index

activity and passivity, 73, 79, 308
Antigone, Sophocles', 171, 212, 362-65
appraisal processes, 295-301, 331
appropriateness, principle of moral, 120
attestation, 172-73, 349, 374
authority, 262-66
autonomy, 161-63

basic trust, 310-13

cardinal virtues, 150, 352, 365, 383
care, 213-15
categorical imperative, Kant's, 75, 115,
 144-45, 162, 164; Kant's first (universal
 law), 75, 115, 144-45, 162; Kant's second (the end in itself), 115, 145, 164
character, 40-41, 339-86; education for,
 40-41; formation of, 379-86; and narrativity, 358-60; structure of, 346-54; and
 tragedy, 360-65
choices, moral, 119-20
clarification of values, 240-57; as a communicative process, 266-82; as a hermeneutical process, 257-66
cognitive psychology, second generation,
 151-54
communication: models of, 266-77; moral,
 30-35

compromises: moral, 121-24
conflicts, moral, 114-18
convention-critical reflection, 226-34
contrast experience, 73, 161, 381

deontology of the right, Kant's, 155
development: moral, 223-34; Piaget's
 cognitive theory of, 186-99; stages of,
 186-98
developmental stage theory of moral education, Kohlberg's, 115, 183-234
discipline, 48-52, 62-79; authoritarian pattern of, 49; authoritative pattern of, 49,
 50-52; communitarian approach of, 65-
 67; control dimension of, 49; and criterion of universality, 70, 74-76; and the
 good life, 74-76; and human rights, 68-
 76; indifferent pattern of, 50; indulgent
 pattern of, 50; moral aspects of religion
 for, 71-74; multiculturalism approach
 of, 67-76; and self-regulation, 56-62;
 support dimension of, 49; utilitarian approach of, 63-65; wisdom in, 76-79

economism, 93
education: for character, 40-41; modes, 35-
 41; and morality, 21-41; plurality of
 practices, 47-48; paradigms of, 21-30